I0817512

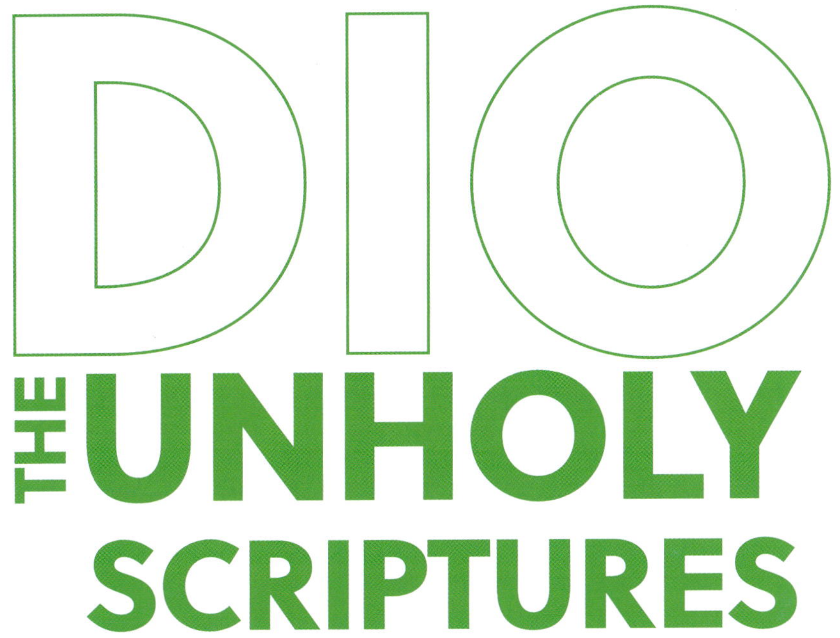
DIO
THE UNHOLY
SCRIPTURES

MARTIN POPOFF

DIO
THE UNHOLY SCRIPTURES

The Complete Unofficial Chronicle of Ronnie James Dio's Solo Canon

SCHIFFER PUBLISHING
4880 Lower Valley Road • Atglen, PA 19310

CHILDREN OF THE NIGHT

Ronnie and Wendy Dio for years were big supporters of Children of the Night. Here is their mission statement:

Children of the Night is a privately funded non-profit organization established in 1979 with the specific purpose to provide intervention in the lives of children who are sexually exploited and vulnerable to or involved in prostitution and pornography.

2025 marks Children of the Night's 46th Anniversary of rescuing America's children from prostitution right here in the United States. Since 1979, we have rescued over 12,000 American children from sex trafficking/prostitution—that is more children than all other sex trafficking programs combined. And in most years, we spend 87 percent or more of our funds on the direct care and education of children and young people who have been victimized by prostitution.

Children of the Night is the only place in America where a child can call from a seedy motel or truck stop anywhere in the United States, reach a skilled caseworker 24/7 who knows how to rescue and relocate a child or young person from a dangerous condition without being arrested by the police. Our 24/7 nationwide toll-free case management services are comprehensive and able to help anyone trapped on the streets of our nation.

See www.childrenofthenight.org for more.

Library of Congress Control Number: 2024942479

Designed by Danielle D. Farmer
Cover design by Danielle D. Farmer
Type set in Soleil/Georgia Pro

ISBN: 978-0-7643-6940-7
ePub: 978-1-5073-0534-8

Printed in India
10 9 8 7 6 5 4 3 2 1

Published by Schiffer Publishing, Ltd.
4880 Lower Valley Road
Atglen, PA 19310
Phone: (610) 593-1777; Fax: (610) 593-2002
Email: Info@schifferbooks.com
Web: www.schifferbooks.com

DEDICATION

For the fallen, Ronnie, Jimmy, and my brother, Bradley,
as well as Wendy, keeper of the flame.

CONTENTS

INTRODUCTION

It's hard to believe that it's been fifteen years since we lost Ronnie James Dio to stomach cancer, on May 16, 2010. The now-silenced voice that roared is of course the stuff of legend, and as I've often said, a man with one of the most remarkable achievements in all of heavy metal, and that's being part of not one but three absolute heavy metal classic albums with each of fully three different bands; namely, *Rising*, *Heaven and Hell*, and *Holy Diver*.

So, it's my pleasure once again to celebrate the accomplishments of this beloved heavy metal icon, and, most pertinently, through the examination of the catalog that was most personal to him, the band with his namesake. Of course, I'm not the most significant force keeping Ronnie's memory alive. That would be Wendy Dio, who has since gotten Ronnie's long-gestating own autobiography out, has regularly and competently reissued product, has mounted a hologram tour (still the only one ever in our beloved heavy metal genre), and has now seen a Ronnie James Dio film documentary through to the finish line. This book is a tribute to her life and her efforts as well, and I'm glad to have her voice as part of this book, most pertinently refuting Viv Campbell's complaints about his tenure in the band—as she says, Ronnie's not here to defend himself anymore.

I suppose I'm going to use this introduction as more of an explanation of process, of what this book is and what it isn't, although I'm pretty sure that many of you who are about to read it know all this stuff. First off, this is a book about the Dio band. I've never written a book on Elf, but there's a big, thick book I did on Rainbow called *Sensitive to Light: The Rainbow Story*. There's also now a big, thick book covering Ronnie's two eras in Black Sabbath called *Born Again: Black Sabbath in the Eighties and Nineties*. And if you think the man's triumphant return to the fold as part of Heaven & Hell has been slighted, look no further than my *Black Sabbath FAQ* book, where that whole album and tour cycle is extensively covered, using quite a bit of interview footage of my own with all four members of the band.

Now, second point of process: as many of you know, I've taken a handful of my very earliest books and greatly expanded and updated them. This is another one of those situations, because I did a book back in 2006 called *Dio: Light Beyond the Black*, which looked at the whole career of the band, and then, in 2022, that book was updated and busted in two. So yes, what you are now holding in your hands is the definitive all-in-one Popoff version of the Dio band story, analyzing how and why the band formed and then quickly getting into *Holy Diver*, followed by chapters on *The Last in Line*, *Sacred Heart*, *Intermission*, and so on, closing out with *Master of the Moon* and *Holy Diver Live*.

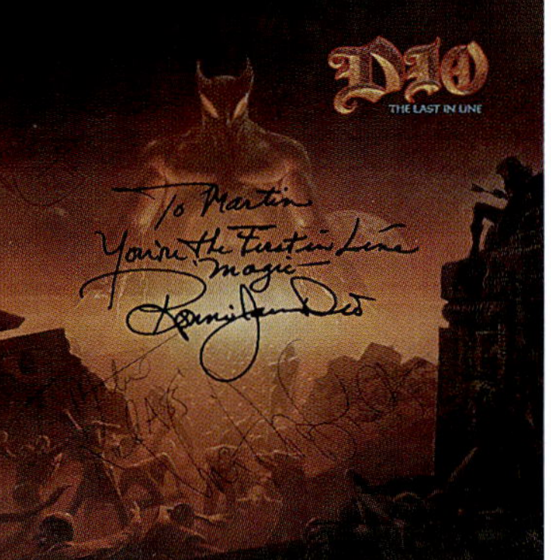

Martin Popoff archive

By the way, if you are following the YouTube show that my buddies Marco, Grant, and I produce, called *The Contrarians*, well, I've done an episode on my favorite Dio album, and it's about *Dream Evil*, dammit! I know, strange choice. But that shows you right there how much I love the clutch of record in the 1980s, extending that far forward. I rank *Sacred Heart* last of the '80s, although by no means do I think it's a bad album. In fact, if you want to talk a little Ozzy Osbourne for competitive fire and ire, I like that record more than *The Ultimate Sin*, *No More Tears*, and *Ozzmosis*, and I just might even rank it worthier than *No Rest for the Wicked*. So there!

But let's not forget that the later Dio years bear heavy metal fruit as well. From the *Lock Up the Wolves* album cycle through to 2004's *Master of the Moon*, Ronnie kept appreciably busy with the band through those fifteen years. We got six studio albums and three live records when Ronnie was alive, and we had three more live records since. And let's not forget that the man went back to Black Sabbath twice, first for 1992's *Dehumanizer* and then later to front the band called Heaven & Hell.

Pin and patch

To be sure, the Dio band lineups were in constant flux, albeit usually with a revolving cast of players, and usually one guy at a time. But throughout it all, a period also that would prove to be a difficult one for heavy metal in general, Ronnie kept up the quality, always working hard, working his players hard, keeping the band tight and on their marks. In the end, he always turned in records that sounded more expensive than waning budgets would afford, with powerful performances and writing, even though the later years would be marked by a predilection from the legend to write slower, doomier songs, which, in the end, made these records less immediate than the '80s canon.

Martin Popoff archive

As for a personal memory of Ronnie, allow me to recount the tale of meeting the legend for the first time. In 1994 I had partnered with Tim Henderson in his bold *Brave Words & Bloody Knuckles* heavy metal magazine project, and we were soon off to the races regularly getting to meet our rock heroes, with Ronnie always being one of the most amenable. One of the fond memories I always talk about is how early on, when Tim was still running the finest heavy metal CD department in Canada at the flagship HMV store, he had set up an in-store performance session with My Dying Bride, who would be supporting Dio later that night.

Of course, Ronnie and the band all came into the store and met with us and signed CDs and records and whatnot, and then later that night we had full backstage access. At one point we were hanging around chatting with Aaron Stainthorpe and his brooding army in black, and Ronnie rolls by and asks us if we're doing okay and if he could get us a beer. For the life of me, I can't remember if we actually had Ronnie grab us a couple beers or not, but I do remember Tim and I just looking at each other and saying, "Did Ronnie James Dio just offer to go get us refreshments?!" That's the kind of guy Ronnie was with everybody. The stories are well and often told about how he would hang out by the bus and sign stuff and talk to fans until the last one was gone, no matter what the weather was like, and he was always quick to remember names. In interviews, he'd make sure he provided substance, explaining himself eloquently, and then in the end, he'd always leave you with a few good messages for life.

Anyway, back on topic, I'm pleased to be able to report that this project encompasses much interview footage of my very own, with pretty much everybody, certainly Craig, Jimmy, Vivian, Vinny, and Wendy, but also from multiple chats all the way up to 2009 with our dear, dear Ronnie. Let's not forget, however, that in addition to losing Ronnie in 2010, we'd lose Jimmy as well, with Bain succumbing to undiagnosed lung cancer on January 23, 2016, actually on tour playing a cruise ship with his Dio tribute band, Last in Line, which also featured within its ranks Vivian and Vinny.

But yes, to reiterate, I've taken pride in making sure that I stuck to the topic and not overlapped by retelling any of the Ronnie James Dio story as it pertains to Rainbow or Black Sabbath, other than perhaps a few quick anecdotes and factoids stuck in the foundational first chapter to set the scene.

As with all my books, in this case it's my hope that the reader listens along with the records as they are discussed and gains a new appreciation for the musicianship across them, as well as Ronnie's superlative lyrics, lyrics that mine a terrain of his very own, espousing a complex, multifaceted life philosophy that no one else could or would ever approximate, because, of course, there was only one Ronnie.

And yes, dammit, the argumentative bastard in me has one overriding goal with this book above all others, and that's to get as many people as possible over to my side in thinking or realizing that *Dream Evil* is every bit the equal of *Holy Diver* and *The Last in Line*. Can you do that for a buddy, do you think?

Gold record award sent by Wendy Dio to the author, who wrote the liner notes to *The Very Beast of Dio*. *Martin Popoff archive*

So, there you have it. Those who have read my books before will recognize the format. It's basically a chapter per album, touching down on every song, with, I hope, enough on production, the album covers, and the subsequent tour cycle. It's an analysis of the albums, in the main, some good stories about some of the lyrics, and a few objective things pointed out by me, topped with the odd subjective opinion. As I say, the hope is that you'll head back to these fine records and appreciate them anew. By the way, another Dio-related episode of *The Contrarians* presents a panel discussion with our Patreon supporters all about *Strange Highways*. If the combination of what you read in this book along with four of us deconstructing the album for fifty-five minutes can't pique your interest in this heavy and doomy dark horse of a Dio home-wrecker, nothing will!

In any event, given the interview-heavy nature of this fat book, here's where you can get a lot less of me and a lot more of Ronnie and all the guys talking about what makes them tick and what makes these records tick. And really, there's no shortage of insights. Unfortunately, the leader of the gang is no longer with us and won't be reflecting any further on these records, but yes, I am pleased to report he does lots of that across the following pages. Given I've just promised less of me, I'll bow out now so that we can get to celebrating just what went on with his darn Dio band across three decades of triumphant, dragon-breathing, heavy metal wizardry.

MARTIN POPOFF
martinpopoff.com
martinp@inforamp.net

CHAPTER 1

"Obviously he was his own person then, and I don't think he would put up with anything anymore."

OF PROPHETS AND ELVES

Players in Dio, as their many faces reveal themselves over the years, shall be introduced as they arrive. But the history of the Dio band as it would emerge (and quickly fire up on all cylinders) is one of four players, the building blocks, the ABCs as it were; namely, Vinny Appice, Jimmy Bain, Vivian Campbell, and Ronnie James Dio.

Yet, naturally, the focus is on Ronald Padovana, born July 10, 1942, in Portsmouth, New Hampshire. Ronnie's musical heritage, and more so his extensive recording history, is shocking, beginning in the 1950s. First playing the trumpet, Ronnie switched to bass, eventually arriving at the supreme stand-alone lead singer role he commanded since 1974 until his death from cancer in 2010. Along the way, he picked up a bit of keyboards and enough guitar to allow him to write songs. His early days were spent in a succession of bands, mostly in upstate New York.

"I'm from a small town up there called Cortland," begins Ronnie, speaking with Kevin Julie back in '96. "I moved to L.A. about twenty years ago; I wanted to get out of the cold weather, as everybody does, I'm sure! My wife is my manager. We don't have any children. I've spent my whole life doing this, I think. Maybe that's why it's not so interesting. I started playing the trumpet when I was five years old, which was great training for me as a singer. It taught me the correct way to do it because I've not taken singing lessons from anyone. I went to the University of Buffalo; I was a pharmacy major. After I finished my university education, I did what I always wanted to do, which was to become a musician. From the time I decided to be a musician, it was a matter of traveling all the time and loving every minute of it. And then to be lucky enough to form

Yearbook entry and early fame

a band with Ritchie Blackmore, and then to be in Sabbath after that, and to have the great success with Dio that we did after that. Most of it's been working; it's been a pretty normal life other than the musical part of it."

Despite going through high school as "the little guy," Ronnie was, in fact, quite popular. "Yes, I was. I was president of my senior class and was in the National Honor Society," Dio told Doug Roemer. "I was always a very good student, and it was always very easy for me. I was very popular. People gravitated towards me. I remember one time the principal called me into his office. I thought, 'Uh-oh, what have I done now?' Because I did a lot of things that people didn't know about. I was a real rebellious kid. But he called me in one time and said, 'You know, you have a great responsibility here. When you walk up the street, you have choices. You can go left and you can go right. When you go left, everyone goes left. When you go right, everyone goes right. That's a great responsibility you have there, so make sure you always take really good care of it.' And I always remembered that. He wrote a letter to my folks, telling them how he thought I was going to be really successful in my life. I guess he saw something that perhaps I didn't. But that responsibility is something that's always stuck with me. Popularity was something that was foisted on me. I was lucky."

As life progressed quite positively, and as he moved toward a career in music, Padovana would transform himself into Ronnie Dio. Adopting a pseudonym has always been a popular solution to names that were tongue twisters, and this practice was even more prevalent in the 1950s and 1960s, sometimes adopted on a whim as much as for any substantial reason. As it turns out, Dio or Deo—or in Spanish, *Dios*, or in French, *Dieu*—are variations on the name God. However, Ronnie's godlike status, along with the irony of the name, given Ronnie's "evil" music (and the attendant sniping accusations of egoism), were far, far in the future. In reality, Ronnie picked the name because of a Florida mobster named Johnny Dio, with Ronnie never apologizing for the fact that Italians didn't have many role models outside of the glamorous male-dominated world of the Mafia. Indeed, cinematic mob classic *Scarface* also includes, albeit quite peripheral to the story, a character by the name of Johnny Dio.

Incredibly, Ronnie's first recording was released in 1958. The 7-inch single, recorded as Ronnie and the Red Caps (the band was based in Cortland, New York, and was originally named the Vegas Kings, then Ronnie and the Ramblers), featured "Conquest" on the A-side, backed with "Lover." Adding a member and switching one, Ronnie at this point adds vocals to his bass duties, for a second single, released in 1960 on Seneca Records, featuring "An Angel Is Missing" backed with "What'd I Say?" The band name is now Ronnie Dio in big letters, with "and the Red Caps" in a smaller point size.

In 1961, the band became Ronnie Dio & the Prophets, releasing eight singles through a variety of labels and territories through 1967, beginning with Jesse Hill's "Ooh-Poo-Pah-Doo" in early 1962, issued separately in both Canada and the US. About half of these releases, those from the midyears, were credited simply to Ronnie Dio. A 1963 single for the Padovana-penned "Mr. Misery" was also issued with an Italian lyric, retitled as "Che Tristezza Senza Te (Mr. Misery)," with the B-side, "Our Year," left in English. There are also two LPs of questionable pedigree, one being *Dio at Domino's*, which captured the band live in early 1963, plus a very independent self-titled release on Jove Records, also from 1963. It should be noted that none of the band's singles appeared on Jove Records. The band also showed up on a number of music samplers, most significantly a series called *The History of Syracuse Music*.

"I'd rather forget about it, yeah," commented Ronnie, on his early pre-Elf ramblings and rumblings. "And it's only because you become something so much different. You understand why you are doing it and what you're doing. I guess erasing it is only because I've become so different. If I listen to that I think to myself, 'Wow, what a wimp, what a jerk-off!' But you have to remember, if only everyone could know that when that was happening, it was pretty hard and heavy stuff. But unfortunately, you can't go around to everyone and say, 'Don't listen to it that way.' There's just been such a drastic change for me. I don't mean to keep going on and on about it, but I think you'd know what I meant if you had written an article when you were five years old critiquing something and when you are twenty-five years old writing for *Newsweek* and someone says, 'Oh, we just wanted to bring up this article that you

Promo shot, plus the covers of the first and third Elf albums.

wrote; here it is.' I don't know if that equates, but you know what I mean." When asked about a possible box set of all that material, Ronnie quipped, "Well, I can only say that I think that they should . . . if they find them all, they should bundle them in a box and blow them all up! That's what I think [laughs]."

Ronnie and his mate Nick Pantas then broke up that band to become the Electric Elves (an appropriate name due to their collective heights), releasing one promo-only single pairing "Hey, Look Me Over" with "It Pays to Advertise." Shortening their name to the Elves, the band released, in 1969, "Walking in Different Circles" and "She's Not the Same," and in 1970, "Amber Velvet"/"West Virginia." After a band car crash killed founding member Pantas, and acquiring a new pianist in Mickey Lee Soule, the band became Elf. Also in this version of the band were David Feinstein, later of The Rods, and drummer Gary Driscoll, both now having been in every incarnation of the Elves.

This is where fortuitous connections with Deep Purple take place, with Ian Paice and Roger Glover having caught the band live at a New York City club. Known for a powerful yet honky-tonk sound, Elf at this stage were also adept at personalizing fresh, very recent covers, with preferences falling toward the Who and Jethro Tull. The debut album, produced by Paice and (mainly) Glover, was recorded in Atlanta in the spring of 1972. Simply deemed *Elf*, the self-titled record was a tough, funky, boogie-woogie, bluesy, and sometimes balladic platter, the highlight being the hard-rocking "Gambler"; that, and of course the fact that the singing on the record was uncommonly good.

Elf then proceeded to tour with Deep Purple throughout the latter part of 1972. "It was great—two of our heroes were producing the album," recalls Ronnie. "It was just great to be around them. It was real quick. I played bass on that album, and we did almost everything live. We went in and I played and sang at the same time. We just did it and away it went! It wasn't like where each instrument was done separately in a different studio, you know, with that craziness. We were very well prepared; it was a good band. We played together for a long time, grew up together. So, we just went in and, bang, did it! It was so much fun to do and it was a really good album as well.

"I wanted to be either the best bass player on Earth or the best singer on Earth," says Ronnie, on putting aside the fat strings, "and I knew I was never going to achieve either one of those. But like I always said, you've got to have goals. So, I thought I was probably a better singer than I was a bass player. So, I decided to hire someone else to play bass, someone who had more expertise than I did. And it gave me a chance to not have to do both, because it was a tough job.

"Deep Purple, Led Zeppelin, Pink Floyd, King Crimson," listed Ronnie, when asked about early influences, "and the Beatles, of course," adding that "at that time, I was just learning how to make music, how to do things right. I had got my stuff together. It was the most important thing in my life then. That led me to what happened in the '70s, when we got our deal with Purple Records. Actually, our first deal was with Epic. Clive Davis signed us. So, I was learning my craft all the way up to that time, learning what was best for me. What were we going to be? What would I become? It was the best time of my life. I saw everything for the first time. I saw Europe for the first time with my new eyes. I saw it with my friends and with my cousin. I'd love to be able to recapture that. Just seeing everything for the first time, wide-eyed and wonderful, without any taint or any of the crap I've had to go through since then."

A second record, also produced by Glover, found Elf at Manor Studios in England. Dave "Rock" Feinstein was gone by this time, with the record coming out overseas as *Carolina Country Ball*, on Deep Purple's own Purple Records, and in America as *L.A. '59*, on MGM, with different cover art. The album actually included a track called "Rainbow."

Around this time, Ronnie worked with Roger on his *Butterfly Ball* concept project, singing three songs, most notably the semihit "Love Is All," while, in December '74, Ronnie also teamed up with an increasingly disgruntled Ritchie Blackmore for the first time for a rough run-through of Quatermass's "Black Sheep of the Family," a song that Deep Purple refused to cover, when approached with the suggestion by Ritchie.

"Elf was opening for Deep Purple in Ithaca," explains Pete Restey, from the Black Sabbath crew (now deceased). "Well, Ritchie was just playing with Deep Purple, and you know, they're just doing their thing. And all of a sudden, they've got a band called Elf to open up for them for a show. And Ritchie's girlfriend at the time goes out and watches Elf do one song, comes running into the dressing room, and says, 'You gotta come hear this guy sing!' Talking about Ronnie. And Ritchie walks out there, hears him sing, sits on the stage for the whole set, follows them into the dressing room, and he looks at Ronnie and he goes, 'Would you like a job with me?' He goes, 'Yes.' He goes, 'How about a couple of your bandmates?' You know, he told everybody except Ronnie's cousin, David Feinstein, the guitar player; he goes, to him, 'You're fired,' and then he goes, 'You're hired, you're hired, you're hired' [laughs]. And they took off and they did Rainbow."

Blackmore and Dio, along with Gary Driscoll and Electric Light Orchestra cellist Hugh McDowell, also cooked up and recorded "Sixteenth Century Greensleeves," with Ritchie enthused by the collaboration process as well as by the final results, given his increasing dissatisfaction for the "shoeshine music" coming out of Deep Purple Mk. III across much of the *Stormbringer* album.

"I didn't do the live show," notes Ronnie, asked about the *Butterfly Ball* live production, a Roger Glover project, of which his role would have been central. "At that time, we'd just put Rainbow together, Ritchie and I, and he felt it was not something that I should do, that we should be concentrating on the Rainbow thing and not be sidetracked by that. It was his band, and he was another one of my heroes, so I figured he knew what he was doing. In retrospect I'm quite glad I didn't do the show."

Interestingly, Ronnie, of course, would end up in Rainbow, but Roger Glover had also wanted the singer for his new southern-rock-flavored band at the time, provisionally titled "Footloose," Roger having parted ways with Deep Purple after 1973's *Who Do We Think We Are*.

Yet, there was still one more Elf album to come, the band's best, titled *Trying to Burn the Sun*, recorded at Kingsway Studios in London before the lion's share of the band would be hauled off to record the debut Rainbow album. *Trying to Burn the Sun* stayed true to the band's complex yet earthy influences, while coming out a tad heavier and proggier; it was the first record on which Ronnie would be credited with the tripartite Ronnie James Dio moniker, actually at the suggestion of Ritchie. In fact, the band was to split up between the time of recording and the actual release of the record. The album did not see issue in the UK, so as not to conflict with the unveiling of the debut Rainbow album, titled *Ritchie Blackmore's Rainbow*.

"They were happy albums, happy honky-tonk albums, featuring a piano," muses Ronnie with respect to the Elf legacy. "Happy subjects for the most part; girl-boy relationships at times. There were a couple of very slanted songs which I think were purveyors of what I would become. They were albums by people who really enjoyed what they were doing, really enjoyed just going out and playing rock 'n' roll and being loud and being a bar band, kind of thing. I mean, we took the bar band attitude and stuck it into big places. It was just fun to do. It was the best time in my life because of all those things . . . being first experiences, doing it with people I grew up with.

"The first album, I think, is the best of the lot from top to bottom, because it's the first album we did, and the magic was there. We were just a four-piece. That's when I was the bass player and singer in the band. That was more fun for me because I always loved to play more than singing anyway. It was just the happiest of the lot. Then we changed guitar players, which always seems to make a difference [laughs]. The whole attitude started to change a little bit, and I think that's where I started to take control of where I wanted it to be. Then the albums became progressively darker. I mean, as dark as you can get with a honky tonk piano. But it became that way. It became more musical, and that probably would've ended up being the downfall of it anyway. Because it survived because of the good time we had playing the music, and the good time that the music was. On the one hand, I probably ended up destroying what that band could have been, and, on the other hand, it gave me a springboard to become what I've become."

UK weekly music newspaper ads for *Rising* and *Long Live Rock 'n' Roll*.
Martin Popoff archive

Ronnie, of course, set in stone his legacy through the first three albums with hard-charging, second-generation metal purveyors Rainbow. The man's lyrical palette, consisting of fantasy themes revolving around rainbows, dragons, wizards, and various other magical characters, would be put immediately in play, continuing through those first three seminal Rainbow albums—namely, *Ritchie Blackmore's Rainbow*, *Rising*, and *Long Live Rock 'n' Roll*—with the *On Stage* live album coming swift and hard between *Rising* and *Long Live*. The double-gatefold live album is most noted for the explosive "Kill the King," offered tantalizingly in live format before the studio version one record and nine months later.

Ronnie, years down the line, summed up in this way the rift with Ritchie that would lead to his next prodigious posting. "It's nothing like it's been blown up to be in the press, you know, 'Ritchie's the most difficult man on Earth to work with!' He probably is for everybody else, but he never was for me. I have nothing but the best to say about Ritchie. He's the one who gave me my first great opportunity, and I learned a hell of a lot from him."

Dio's next posting is one that would previously be thought unfathomable, with Ronnie arriving in 1979 to replace Ozzy Osbourne at the microphone position of a fading Black Sabbath, for two master-blasted classics, 1980's *Heaven and Hell* and 1981's *Mob Rules*.

"It's Heaven and Hell!" Maple Leaf Gardens, Toronto, Canada, November 19, 1981. © *Martin Popoff*

Wendy Dio, Ronnie's amor since 1975 and eventual manager till the end, explains the fortuitous timing of the Sabbath suggestion. "We didn't have any money then. When Ronnie was in Rainbow, Ronnie had a big house to live in, but we didn't get more than 150 bucks a week, so we didn't really have any money. So luckily, or unluckily, my grandmother had died and left me $50,000, so we had some money now. We came from Connecticut to L.A., and we rented a very small house in Encino. And we had, I think, ten people living there. Ronnie was trying to form another band with about three different people, and actually Skunk Baxter was one of them he was writing with.

"And this just fell about; that's how it came to happen. Ronnie was forming another band together with Mickey Lee Soule, who was in Elf originally, and some other musicians. And then he was writing with Skunk Baxter; that

was another thing he was doing. And he was just, you know, floundering around because we didn't know what to do. Of course, Ronnie had gotten fired from Rainbow because he wouldn't write more-commercial songs, so we figured we had to go back to L.A., because in Connecticut there was nothing happening.

"So, we came back here and were just trying to find some work. I believe Ronnie bumped into Tony Iommi at the Rainbow, and they were having some problems with Ozzy, and I think he just went up to have a jam with them and they ended up writing 'Children of the Sea.' I was actually good friends with Sharon Arden at the time, and she actually was one of the people that was saying to Ronnie, 'You should do this; you should go and do this.' So, she was very for it."

As for Tony, Geezer, and Bill, Wendy says, "They were really nice people, and I got on really well with Geezer's wife, Gloria, who actually, we've been friends for forty years now; we talk to each other all the time. She lives just down the road; we live down the same street. And our friendship started there. But I was not the manager at the time, just the wife. I didn't become manager right until I started Ronnie with his own career. And then of course when Ronnie was back with Sabbath the second time, for *Dehumanizer*, there were three managers. There was Gloria Butler, Geezer's wife, myself. and. for Tony, Ralph Baker."

Ronnie's last stand before forming Dio would be a Black Sabbath live album in 1982 called *Live Evil*, where Ronnie is put in his place, his credit truncated for the first time in years to read as simply Ronnie Dio, the significance of which revolves around the bitter acrimony conjured over the mixing of the album.

"Ronnie was very much of a control person," reflects Wendy, "and I think that they resented that. Even though Ronnie was kind of controlling them in the right way. Not in his own way, but he wanted it to be a band effort. I think he was a bit more professional in the way that he went about his business. I don't think Tony is really a control freak at all. They're two different people. It used to annoy them that Ronnie would stand outside forever and ever and ever signing autographs, and they just wanted to get back to the hotel. No, they were different people, but musically, together, they were amazing. When he went into Rainbow, of course, he was a young boy, very naive with everything. But obviously he was his own person then, and I don't think he would put up with anything anymore.

Vinny Appice, *Mob Rules* tour, Toronto, Ontario. © *Martin Popoff*

"It wasn't a happy time at all," continues Wendy, about Sabbath during *Live Evil*. "Ronnie was like trying to be professional. There was a lot of drugs going around and stuff, and Ronnie, he didn't do anything except smoke pot. And he was just very, very upset all the time, and very down all the time, and just not enjoying what he was doing anymore."

Chuckles Black Sabbath drummer Vinny Appice, "If you notice, on the *Mob Rules* album, who's in the band, it's Vinny Appice and then everybody else. I come first. And then when *Live Evil* happens and the band is breaking up and there's bad vibes going on, there's three or four pictures of everybody else, one less of Ronnie, and I only have one little postage stamp picture on the album because I guess somebody was trying to send a message. That's all I know. That happened twice, because I was in Derringer with Rick Derringer, and the first album is pictures of us; the second album, we're on the cover, everybody; and the third album was a live album, and that's when me and Danny Johnson, the guitar player, were leaving, and Rick Derringer wasn't happy about it and blamed me. And so on that album there's a picture of the band live, and it just so happens that it's taken from below the drums, and all you see of me is the tom-toms. I'm not even in the picture. It's like, welcome to the music business, kid."

The final nail in the coffin had to do with accusations of Ronnie and Vinny apparently turning up their own parts in the mix. "Yeah, I think the engineer liked to party at that time. I mean I just remember that me and Ronnie would show up at two o'clock—that was the call—and the rest of the band didn't show up until later on, let's say. It was that kind of vibe going on. And I didn't understand why. I love the band; I love everybody in the band. So that's what happened, and then that came out in the press that Ronnie and I went early into the studio so we could turn up the vocals and the drums [laughs]. Why would we do that? That's kind of defeating the purpose and the theme of the band. But I do remember we started mixing. Because it's like, the studio has been paid for, okay, two o'clock, three o'clock; nobody is here. And Ronnie wanted to get some work done. So, we proceeded to start setting up the mixes and start mixing. So that's what happened. And it got blown up to that."

To reiterate, if I seem perfunctory in summarizing Ronnie's (and Vinny's) crucially important work with Black Sabbath—Ronnie swore to his dying day that his favorite Dio-led record of all time was *Heaven and Hell*—it is because all of this is discussed in my book *Born Again: Black Sabbath in the Eighties and Nineties*. And if you think I've swept past Ronnie's Rainbow years crudely and rudely, well, look no further than my *Sensitive to Light: The Rainbow Story*, in which the first 150 pages cover Ronnie's time in that great medieval metal band. Let's not forget as well that by no means is this a biography of the man, Ronnie James Dio, but rather, specifically it's a book about the band Dio. Therefore, on that tack, it is promised that the originating players of the great Dio band will be introduced across the opening pages of the first chapter more than amply and, I hope, to your satisfaction.

CHAPTER 2

"Jimmy Bain was a full-on 100 percent paid-up, card-carrying member of the L.A. party scene."

HOLY DIVER

Always a leader but never quite allowed to lead (excepting Elf, where Ronnie was clearly the star going places), Ronnie James Dio, in 1983 double famous through Rainbow and Sabbath, found himself the buzz of the town, with folks genuinely excited about what might come next out of this diminutive metal roarer.

"I got the solo deal for him during the time he was in Sabbath," explains Wendy, "but it was not for him to leave. It was just something down the line. And I think it was just, you know, we got a very small advance. And it was just something that Warner Bros. offered, so we said okay, good, yeah. It was just something for down the road. I don't think the Sabbath guys even knew about it; I don't think we ever talked about it."

After the debacle surrounding Black Sabbath's *Live Evil* album, it was no surprise that Ronnie would take the other Italian New Yorker from that band, Vinny Appice, off to forge fire with Ronnie. But with who the heck else?

"Once I was able to do what I wanted on my own," recalls Ronnie, in conversation with Jeb Wright, "which was to have my own band that I had some control over, then all the revolving-door stuff that went on in the past stopped. When you know that if it were done a different way and that it could be better—and it never does get done a different way—then it becomes frustrating for you. It is hard not being in control when you think that you know what you are doing. In the case of Rainbow, it was Ritchie's band, and that's the way it should have been. In Sabbath, it was all of us, and it was pretty democratic. Sometimes it's hard to be democratic. You don't always make the right decisions when three people want to do it and one person doesn't want to do it. I'm not saying that is what happened in Sabbath. We were always very democratic, but it was hard to be that way.

"Dio was a great, great adventure for me. It's easy to look back at it now and go, 'Wow, everything worked out perfectly, didn't it?' But it wasn't easy. When you do something on your own, it's hard. You have a lot of misgivings about it. In the beginning it was only Vinny and I. We didn't even have a guitar player or a bass player. I wrote 'Holy Diver' and 'Don't Talk to Strangers.' Other than that, it was just me and Vinny. I was busy banging on the guitar, and Vinny was playing drums. After a while we said, 'I think we better get a guitar player!' So, we went to England and we met Viv [guitarist Vivian Campbell]. We played with Viv and Jimmy [Bain, bassist] for two nights in London, and it was unbelievable. After that, I knew there was not going to be a problem. Not with guys that play that well. Again, the first album, *Holy Diver*, the songs just came flowing out. Even *The Last in Line* was not too bad. *Sacred Heart* became more difficult, and the next album was a lot more difficult. That is why I say the first things that you do just flow a lot more."

Vinny Appice, from Brooklyn, New York, had come up in the ranks well within the shadow of his more famous brother, Carmine Appice, known mostly for his work with Vanilla Fudge, Jeff Beck, Beck, Bogert & Appice, Cactus, and Rod Stewart. Vinny's main claim to fame by the time he joined Dio would be, of course, his stint in Black Sabbath. But as well as that, he had been with unsuccessful one-record acts Axis (*It's a Circus World*, 1978) and Bruzer (*Round 1*, 1982), along with a more esteemed stretch with Rick Derringer for *Derringer* (1976), plus *Sweet Evil* and *Live* (both 1977).

Vinny says of Bruzer, "That was just Ricky Ramirez, a guitar player who was a good friend; he put that together and said, 'Yeah, I'd love you to play on it,' and I said, 'Yeah, let me hear it.'

"The blue album was my first album," continues Appice, on the underrated *Derringer* record, the truncated name supposed to signify that this was now the offering of a band, a heavy band, and not just another Rick Derringer solo album. "But it was

An ad for 1977's *Sweet Evil*, plus a period promo photo signed to the author at the band's thirty-five-year reunion gig in Buffalo, New York. *Martin Popoff archive*

really dry, really small sounding, very tight sounding," complains Appice. *Derringer* was followed by the aforementioned *Sweet Evil*, a bit of a hard-rock classic, even if it's been somewhat forgotten now.

"Yeah, that was a good album," agrees Vin. "For the first record, I was just a naive young kid. It was my first record, and we put all those songs together as a band. Well, Rick had a lot of stuff written, but we filled it in, put it that way [laughs]. Some stuff we wrote together, but we didn't get credit. Then we went on the road, and we became a heavier kind of band, you know? From playing together. We got really tight, but it was heavier. So, on the next album, we started writing a little darker. The songs were darker, a little heavier, and we got a different producer. Jack Douglas produced that, so the drums were lower, the bass was lower; there's more bottom end to it, and it was bigger sounding. There are some good songs on there. I know 'Sittin' by the Pool' was written about Los Angeles when we came out here. We were a New York band, so to come out here, it was like, 'Oh man,' that L.A. vibe. Everyone was so laid back, but I liked it. I thought, man, this place is cool. So did Danny Johnson, who played guitar. I just remember that Danny came up with 'Driving Sideways,' which is a really cool song [laughs]; he wrote some crazy shit. But Rick was more into pop and writing poppy songs. That's why the first album is poppy and happy, and the second album got darker. But we were a good band. I don't know . . . we got a little heavier there, and maybe he didn't like where it was going. And then after Derringer broke up, we came out here and formed Axis and did one record. We formed out here because it was a lot easier to do business in L.A."

However, through all that recording and touring, one of Vinny's fondest experiences reaches way back to the beginning in New York, with his band being called in by John Lennon from the studio next door, on a whim (Vinny was sixteen at the time), to provide handclaps for 'Whatever Gets You through the Night,' the first of a few minor jobs Vinny did for the now-martyred legend.

"Why isn't Vinny still in the band?" queried Ronnie, back to the formation of Dio, speaking with *Record Review* back in 1983, referring to the recently cleavered Black Sabbath. "That's because he's with me and he's treated with respect for what he is, a great person and a fantastic drummer. Anyone who could do what he did in three days has to be incredible. I don't want this to sound like a British and American split because it isn't. Or else why would I have Jimmy, who's Scotch, and Viv, who's Irish, in the band?"

Vinny says that Tony and Geezer had asked him to stay in Black Sabbath, but that the decision had been made to throw his lot in with Ronnie. Previous to Dio becoming a band, he was under the impression that Ronnie's quietly contracted solo album would be an all-star affair. He'd been asked to play on it, but he also thought that Cozy Powell would drum the hell out of some part of it as well.

On leaving Sabbath, Vinny explained to *The Metal Voice*'s Jimmy Kay that "we played good together, we got along together, Tony, Geezer, and I, and it was a really good relationship. So, when it came down to it, yeah, it was a decision to be made. They wanted me to play with them. And then I thought, well, Ronnie and I get along really well, and we both live in California. Tony and Geezer are in England. It was a little easier to work in California because we're both there. And then it was exciting to start a new band with this amazing singer. Originally Ronnie was going to do an album because he had a deal at Warner Bros., and he was going to do an album that was his solo album with all his friends playing on it, like Kerry Livgren from Kansas, who is a good friend, and back then maybe Cozy Powell. Who knows? Maybe even Ritchie Blackmore. I don't know. But that was the plan originally, to do a solo record, and then this came down. But he was going to do a solo record while he was in Sabbath. Put the solo record out and continue with Sabbath. But things weren't going good with Sabbath, so that's where he decided, okay, I'm gonna leave the band, put a new band together, and use that record deal as the launchpad."

Offers Wendy, "Well, Vinny, he's a Brooklyn guy, Italian descent, American New Yorker. Got on really well with Ronnie, because Ronnie was another New Yorker, even though Ronnie was from upstate. They're both Italian heritage. So, they were both like instant companions, instant friends. They just loved each other and played jokes on each other. And they were very much a unit."

As for the Irishman in the newly formed band, Vivian Campbell's pre-Dio history is brief and will be discussed shortly. But Jimmy Bain's background bears more telling. Jimmy really was known more as a session guy leading up to his work with Dio. Rattling around Scotland, London, and even British Columbia, Jimmy began his career with knockabout bands such as Harlot and Street Noise before winning the Rainbow gig. Jimmy then recorded *Rising*, *On Stage*, and parts of *Long Live Rock 'n' Roll* for the mercurial man in black. This of course put him in Rainbow with Ronnie. Sessions with Kate Bush ensued, for her groundbreaking album *The Dreaming*, along with work for John Cale and Phil Lynott, both for Phil's carousing, semiserious act Greedy Bastards and for his infinitely more elegant and plusher couple of solo records.

But Jimmy's main pride and joy at that time was his minor supergroup formed at the height of the NWOBHM (New Wave of British Heavy Metal), Wild Horses. That band also featured Thin Lizzy's Brian Robertson, and through an alcoholic haze, the geezers issued two albums, *The First Album* in 1980 and *Stand Your Ground* in 1981. As we'll hear, concurrent with his work on the monumental first Dio record, Jimmy also guested on Scorpions' *Love at First Sting*.

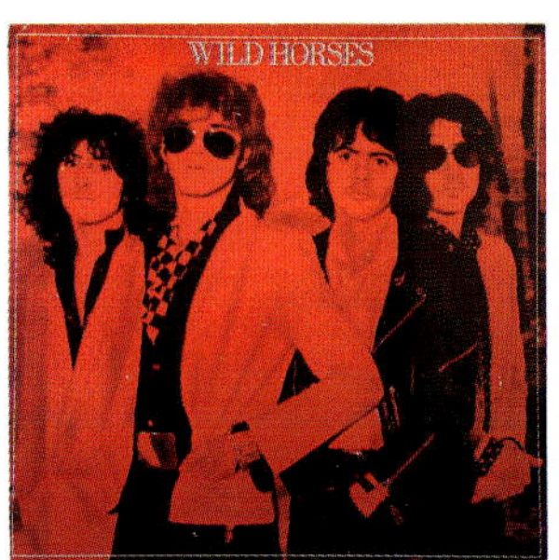

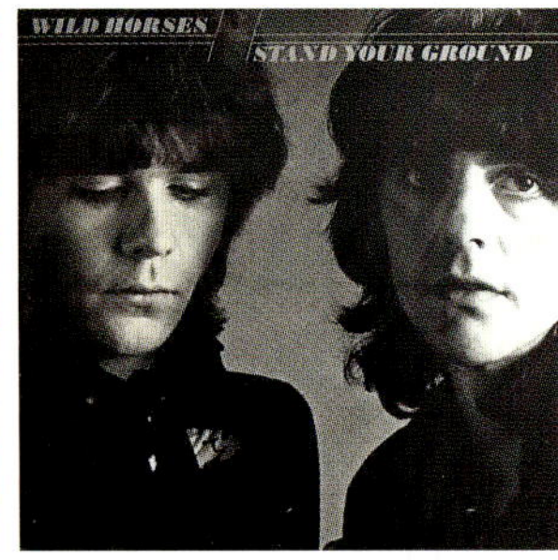

The entire Wild Horses discography.
© Martin Popoff archive

Jimmy confirms the wild times had by all in Wild Horses, his band just prior to landing the Dio gig. "Oh yeah! And Brian's from Scotland as well. I met him when I was in my band Harlot, before Rainbow, and I stayed pretty close to him. After I got the boot from Rainbow, I went straight back to England the next day. And he had been in some kind of skirmish, and he couldn't play with Lizzy for a while, and they were using Gary Moore. So, him and I got together and we kind of clicked and wrote some songs and went in and demoed them. He was with Thin Lizzy's management, and my best friend was Phil Lynott as well, the late lead singer for Thin Lizzy. So I kind of had this idea that Phil and Robbo had had this head-to-head thing that was never ever going to be sorted out. It worked kind of good for me because Phil was basically telling me, 'If you're going to work with that creep, good luck to you!' But I kind of liked it. It was craziness, but we managed to get a record deal and put out a couple of records, one of which was produced by Trevor Rabin. I liked it because I got to sing, and we wrote all the stuff. It was a lot of fun and it was a little crazy too. And you know, earlier when we were in London, you couldn't get arrested if you were playing anything heavy. It was kind of punky and rebellious, and we were playing the wrong kind of music at the time. But it was a lot of fun.

"Phil Lynott was just unbelievable," recalls Jimmy fondly, adding commentary about these other great '80s sessions just prior to his joining Dio. "I was on tour with Dio, and I came back that Christmas that he got sick. He's my daughter's godfather; we were really tight. I was born the same day as his eldest daughter, Sarah, and our wives were really tight, close together. We lived, I don't know, 3 or 4 miles away from each other in London. Actually, I worked and wrote on a couple of his albums, *Solo in Solo*, and his second one. I wrote 'Girls' with him; I wrote 'Dear Miss Lonely Hearts' with him. And then on the second one, *The Philip Lynott Album*, I wrote 'Old Town' with him and the one that Mark Knopfler played on, 'Ode to Liberty,' and I played on all that stuff, keyboards, bass, everything. That was a real buzz because he was a real talent and a really nice guy. Like I say, I was on tour with Dio, and I came back and saw him at Christmas, actually stayed at his house, and I had to leave on Boxing Day. I took his two kids over to see my daughter for Christmas Day, and I never saw him again, because he was taken to hospital that day. And I had to leave the day after Christmas and actually fly to Vancouver to pick up the tour again, and I didn't get to go to his funeral. And I was really kind of destroyed by that. But these things happen, and you never know when you're going to get taken. Pretty amazing."

Just as both Black Sabbath and later Dio would benefit from the bustle of activity that was NWOBHM, so would Wild Horses, pretty much at the exact same time as Sabbath; namely, within that '80 to '81 period.

"Absolutely, yeah!" agrees Jimmy. "I mean Iron Maiden got signed around the same time we did. Previously, there weren't a lot of deals going around with the punk thing happening. But I think Maiden were one of the first ones; it looked like they could just go and take on the world. They had great management and great players and had a great attitude to it, and they've proven over the years that they've done exactly that. Back then it was just playing down the Greyhound or the Marquee and stuff like that, and any other little bits and bobs of gigs you could get anywhere else. It was few and far between at the beginning, but the thing grew pretty quick when it got started, and you could tell there was a lot of talent in England. There's always been a lot of talent. And kids just wanted to get a chance to get away from the grind and stuff. There were a lot of great bands who came out of that time. I was happy for everybody that got a chance to get in the studio and record."

Asked about the extent to which the band got to tour, Jimmy says that "we actually played in Ireland, and we had Sweet Savage support us, Vivian Campbell's band. And we toured with Ted Nugent in England and Scotland, supporting him, and we played a couple shows with Rush at Bingley Hall in Stafford. Who else? The other shows we would do, we were just playing on our own with some local bands. Oh yeah, we had Def Leppard supporting us in Sheffield, a couple weeks before they got signed. Ted Nugent was wild. He had the loin cloth on at that time. The guy came onstage swinging on a vine [laughs]; it was pretty amazing."

Although Jimmy says he was absolutely up for getting called NWOBHM, "we weren't very heavy metal, Wild Horses, but we were happy to get tagged with whatever was happening just to get a bit of recognition. So, I was happy about it. Brian Robertson was a phenomenal guitar player. I loved working with Brian, just one of a kind, and I think he was one of the biggest influences people like Steve Clark from Def Leppard had. He just adored Robbo and the style and everything like that and definitely rooted in the blues. Brian was just a super guy.

Jimmy doing Jimmy, at the Beacon Theatre, New York, New York, October 25, 1983. © *Rudy Childs*

"Maybe I think him and I drank a little too much. Without exaggerating on it, still, we did get drunk a lot. Scottish people do when they get together. But we were friends too. We shared an apartment for a long time. We were never that far away from each other, and it was a perfect partnership for a while. But after a while it just got to be a bit much with the drinking. We got fed up with it and tried a couple other things, but it never worked out as good as the original. As for our sound, we were kind of trying to get something that would get us over to America. Almost like the Faces. Not metal, but more like good-time rock 'n' roll."

Jimmy further underscores the fertile atmosphere for heavy metal at the time, which, again, served as a solid platform onto which the Dio band could and would bound purposefully.

"Oh yeah, like I say, Wild Horses got signed to EMI at the same time, I think, as Maiden got signed to EMI—'80, '81, around that time—and there was a big buzz about all these bands that were coming up. We got to play a lot. We played a lot of festivals together and in England; I was living there at the time, and it was a good time. You could see that there was a real buzz amongst the musicians themselves, that they were onto something. They didn't quite know where it was going to go or how far it would go, but there was a kind of optimism, in London especially, like you see with Saxon and Iron Maiden, especially. Bruce Dickinson was playing in Samson, got the gig in Maiden, and I knew him from Samson because we'd done some shows together, and followed him through into the Maiden days. He was a guy who just had so much enthusiasm for what he was doing. Super guy. Generally speaking, everybody felt that something good was about to happen, and sure enough it did.

"Everybody had a good run at it, from what we could gather, anyway. Maiden, certainly, are still going at it really well. I kind of pat them on the back for planning it the way they did. They never lost touch with their audience, and the records have come far enough apart that they get enough time to go and tour all the places they want to tour. Everything's kind of worked out really well for them. They've been well managed and well directed, and that's very important for a band. I've seen a lot of bands where their timing gets a little off or they get too busy or have too much product out there, and they kind of end up running out of steam. Maiden have always kind of managed to have it right on the money, and their fans are everywhere.

"But again, with the original New Wave of British Heavy Metal, for one thing, the bands got record deals. I got a record deal, Maiden got a record deal, and we were happy just to be able to go into the studio and record some songs and get some kind of product out there so we could move on to something new. It felt good that the labels were interested in that kind of music for a change, because normally, in Britain, they would only be interested if you were Top 10, Top 40 kind of stuff. They weren't interested in heavy rock music, per se."

Before we move on, it appears that Bob Daisley, who had played with Ronnie on Rainbow's *Long Live Rock 'n' Roll* and conducted the extensive touring around that record, had also been asked to join as the bassist in the Dio band. And not for the first time—Ronnie and Bob almost got together before Ronnie joined Sabbath for *Heaven and Hell.*

Says Daisley, "Well, I remember, when I started the thing with Ozzy and Randy and Lee Kerslake, Blizzard of Ozz, I remember Ronnie and Vinny Appice phoning me up, and then they came around to my flat in London, and we went out for an Indian meal together and a few drinks and what have you, and asked me to join the band, the Dio band. But I had already gotten this thing together with Ozzy and it was doing well, so I didn't really consider it."

Replying to the comment that, as history had it, he couldn't lose either way, Bob remarks that "well, I don't know. I think there was more of an opportunity for writing with the Ozzy thing. Because Ozzy himself isn't really much of a writer. And Ozzy's stuff has done so much better than Dio's stuff. Dio has been successful, and he's done well, but not even close to what the Ozzy records did."

True on both counts, but more intriguing on the creative: Daisley, the bassist, wrote all those iconic lyrics on the early Ozzy Osbourne albums, and it would be unlikely he'd have gotten a word in edgewise if he had been part of Dio. Still, he might have collaborated with Viv on the music. Although, of course, that means we wouldn't have gotten the great "secret weapon" music writing provided by Jimmy Bain, who contributed to Dio in much the same way that Pete Way contributed to UFO, as bassist, as a character, a wild man, but also as bench strength in the songsmithing department.

But back in the real world, the original sessions of which Ronnie spoke earlier (just with himself and Vinny) were held at the Californian rehearsal studio where much of *Mob Rules* had been written.

"Vinny and I just played in a rehearsal studio because I wanted to hear what it was going to be like live for me to sing it, so we just played. We had the two songs, 'Don't Talk to Strangers' and 'Holy Diver,' just Vinny and myself. And yes, that is the place where we wrote most of the *Mob Rules* album, that same place. So, after the fact, after not being in Sabbath anymore, we went back to that studio, because we knew the guy who owned it, and he was a good friend of ours. Plus, it was private. I didn't want to go from not being in Sabbath anymore to a place where all ears would be listening to what we were going to do, just for the sake of being one of those paranoid people. I didn't want anybody to hear what we were doing at that time. I mean, we didn't have a guitar player, we didn't have a bass player. It was just Vinny and I at the time, and then we had to go and populate the band. So, to clarify, I've never written anything that wasn't for either a project that was going to be a band, or the band itself. I'm sure there have been rumors at times that said, 'Oh, I heard that you wrote all of *Holy Diver* when you were still in Sabbath. Why didn't you give them those songs?' Well, that's actually crap. I've never done that, and I never would have, and I never will do in my life. So that's just one of those left-handed rumors, I guess."

On the subject of locating Vivian Campbell, the young Irishman who would become Dio's first guitarist—and to this day the most celebrated—Ronnie offers the following: "Vinny and I had gone to a lot of the clubs, but we couldn't find anybody. I called Jimmy Bain and asked him if he knew any guitar players, and he said that he knew two great guitar players. He said he would bring a tape of them over to our hotel room. One was Viv and one was John Sykes. John was brilliant, but I really liked the way Viv played. It was rougher and rawer. Viv was in Ireland at the time, and Jimmy called and asked him to come down, so I got him a plane ticket for the next day. I got him a room, at a place called John Henry's, and we rehearsed for two nights on 'Holy Diver' and 'Don't Talk to Strangers.' It was great. I said, 'Do you want to be in a band, Viv?,' and he said, 'Yeah!' Jimmy assumed he was the bass player anyway, so I didn't bother to ask him, and he didn't bother to ask us—it was a band! I flew them over two weeks later to L.A., and we started to rehearse. And then we recorded it and away we went."

Of note, apparently Ronnie had worked with future Ozzy star Jake E. Lee as well but decided that what he needed was a more European-sounding axman. Also, in the area of guitarists, Viv had been up for the Thin Lizzy job. In fact, the departing Snowy White had flippantly offered him the job. Viv's archrival John Sykes (at the time, John Sucks, according to Viv) got the gig instead, and Thin Lizzy made *Thunder and Lighting*, their final album before Phil Lynott's death.

"That probably came from the little mind that said it," laughed Ronnie in the summer of '83, responding to Viv's "John Sucks" pronouncement. "Viv was pissed that he didn't get the Lizzy gig. I think he assumed it would be his gig because he's Irish and had toured with Lizzy. He thinks Lynott has something against him. After all, he's twenty years old. He'll learn someday, won't he? It's wonderful to have a big ego. We'll see how he handles this situation. I chose him because I like him and he's a great player. He has great potential as a person, which is every bit as important as being a great guitar player. There are a lot of good players out there, and I turned down a couple because I didn't like them. I don't want to get too much into that. Viv's a totally different player. He's very notey and very wild. Tony Iommi is a very unique guitar player, a great rhythm player. He can play full chords with vibrato as opposed to taking the easy way out. As a soloist, he left a lot to be desired. Tony would speed up at the end of a solo because he didn't know how to finish it off. After working with Ritchie Blackmore, someone who really knows how to finish a solo, Tony's solos seemed a little mundane."

Continues Ronnie, settling a few scores, "One thing I won't lay down about any longer is the Black Sabbath situation. I'll answer any questions you have. You should hear my side of the story, and you can believe whatever you want. I've been asked many times, why did I leave Rainbow? I chose not to say anything at the time because Ritchie is a friend of mine. And no matter what was written in the press, I never said anything bad. However, in the Sabbath situation I have read too many things that I must reply to. If you look at *Heaven and Hell*, you'll notice that the songwriting credits are listed in alphabetical order. It's Butler, Dio, Iommi, and Ward. On *Mob Rules*, after Bill left, it's Butler, Dio, and Iommi. On the live album, now, it's Iommi—obviously he's the most important—Butler next, and then it's 'Ronnie Dio,' not even 'Ronnie James Dio,' which is the name that I use. It's easy to see the political references that are going on.

"I went my way. I'm in the studio; they're not. Their success or failure makes no difference to my success or failure. I didn't reply to Ozzy about all the things he said to me. Why should I care? He's of no concern to me. Now with the live Sabbath album out and all of the snubs trying to make me look like a fool, it's time I had my say. Why did Vinny Appice get credits after Geoff Nicholls, who is an average keyboard player? My dog is a better keyboard player than Geoff Nicholls. He didn't do anything, and he overdubbed everything on the live album anyways. And the monster Vinny Appice gets that kind of credit? Come on. Damn right I'm pissed. I'm pissed for Vinny too. I'm mad about what's been said about me, but what they did to Vinny is unforgivable. I was disappointed in the treatment they are giving good musicians. I think they want to cover their tracks and make the press line up in their favor because they are still Black Sabbath.

"Why did they go back to Don Arden, who was their manager? He wanted Ozzy back in the band, and they wanted no part of Ozzy. So, when they get into trouble, who's the first person they run to? Don Arden. Who was the first person they called to replace me? Ozzy. They're still living in the late '60s. Black Sabbath's an identity they refuse to surrender. They're afraid of taking a step out of the late '60s, early '70s. They'll want to go back to the old Black Sabbath sound, which is basically guitar and bass. Since they are the two remaining members, you'll find the vocals mixed way back, and the drums are pretty well nonexistent.

"Unfortunately, after the breakup came, I had nothing to do with the album," continues Ronnie, addressing his last slab with the Sabs, *Live Evil*. "They have said they would go into the studio early in the day and that I wouldn't get there until 11:00 in the evening, and while they were gone, I would turn up the vocals in the mix. Maybe you should get an interview with Lee DeCarlo, who was the engineer, but he would probably be afraid to tell you anything. He actually produced the album anyways, but he could attest to the fact that I was there at two o'clock in the afternoon and they would show up at 11:00 and stay for fifteen minutes."

Further on all this, as Ronnie told Geoff Barton the following year, "With Sabbath, well, they're very self-destructive anyway. They never really took the time to care about the people they were playing for. With them it was just a day-to-day thing and 'How much money are we making?' And that was the big mistake, I think. Whereas with this band, I've tried to take the mistakes that they made in the past—that I made in the past—and correct them by doing it properly. And yes, as I say, I think it's worked.

"I must say that sometimes, *sometimes*, when I'm relaxing, in an evening, I reflect on the situation. I'll think about the bad things that happened in the past, about people I was involved with, about the people who, as you have suggested so kindly, are not quite as big as we are at the moment. And I'll admit that, yes, the corners of my mouth might just begin to turn up a little bit. But mostly I like to think about the good times, about how much fun it was to work with Rainbow and especially with Black Sabbath. You see, I like Tony, Geezer, and Bill; I really do. I don't think they'll ever know exactly how much.

"When I first joined Sabbath, Tony and Geezer were always moaning, always going, 'Oh dear, have we done the right thing? Is it going to work? Maybe we should have called ourselves something else.' But I remember saying to them, 'You fools! This band is Black Sabbath. We can kill anybody. We're the best; we're part of a legend!' That's what Purple should be thinking and that's what Sabbath should be thinking now. That's what I thought when I was putting this band together. It's the right attitude to have, because for me it's worked, worked like a dream!

"It's been a very strange career so far, hasn't it? But most of the things I've done have worked very, very well, and luckily, I haven't made too many people angry along the way. I haven't stepped on too many toes. I tried to be a human being most of the time, especially to the fans, because they, after all, are the ones who buy my records and come to see me live, with the banners and all. So, I never shirk my duty. I always try to sign autographs, to stay as long as I can after a show, because that's very important to me. I know that probably sounds like the kind of bullshit that Iron Maiden or Saxon would say, but I've got proof that I do it. I'm always there doing my job.

"I like to think that because my attitude has been correct all these years. I've taken time to worry about what the kids want to hear, and I've always tried to maintain a young outlook. And yes, I think we have taken that step above Sabbath, that step above Rainbow. Rainbow were never the same band after I left. Okay, admittedly when they had Graham Bonnet, they were still playing strong music. But then they got in a singer who would have been happier doing MOR. I think that at the time, Ritchie was desperately searching for some level of success in the States, and he thought that total commerciality was the way to achieve it. It was a shame, but he was wrong; Rainbow should've gone harder, heavier. I'll just carry on until nobody wants to hear about Ronnie Dio ever again. I'll always feel I've got a statement to make. I've got a big ego like everybody else who's been in this business for a long time. I'll continue to do what I'm doing until nobody likes it anymore.

"It's a different album for the times," warned Ronnie, back in the day, setting the expectations for his debut Dio record *Holy Diver*. "I've tried to vary the album and not get stuck in anything. I have come from Rainbow and Sabbath. This is the logical extension of my career without focusing all of the attention on the vocals. I want this to be a band, an important band. The sounds are right. I paid more attention to the drums than anything else. It should be that way, as good as Vinny is. I don't know if anybody is better. I'm the singer. I try as hard as I can to do it right, make it sound right, but I want to make this a band I always want to be in. I think Vinny, Jimmy, and Viv is a damn good combination."

More on arriving at that combination, at the time of his signing on with Dio, Jimmy Bain had actually still been trying to make Wild Horses move up to a level beyond stumbling drunk. "We had flown back and forth," recalls Jimmy. "We were doing Wild Horses in a recording studio in Dublin, and Sweet Savage was doing stuff in the morning. So, I introduced Ronnie to Viv. Viv was interested despite doing the demos with Sweet Savage. Viv and I shared an apartment together."

Asked by Steve Hammonds from *Metal Forces* back in late '83 about his early inspirations, Viv explains that "Marc Bolan was my first idol, and also Gary Moore. It's not just because he's Irish. I think he's the ultimate guitarist. I don't think I've got my playing together within the band. When I come back, it'll be more together!"

As for an update on his old band, Viv told Steve that "they're still going strong with even more lineup changes. They have now got David Gaynor, from Girl, on drums, but I honestly don't think they're going to do anything because they sound too much like Lizzy. That's the problem. It isn't lack of talent; it's lack of enthusiasm. We did a lot of tours with Lizzy and other bands, but it was a lack of management, and Ireland's a very barren country for bands. You have to move over to Britain. I really don't think you're going to hear much more of them in the future.

"I met Jimmy Bain years ago," continues Viv, "and I have known him for quite a while. Ronnie and Vinny came over to the UK to look for a guitar player, and I had given Jimmy a cassette of my playing, and he got me together with Ronnie, and I was the only guitar player they auditioned, so I got the gig. I was very lucky."

Comparing his old gig with his new one, Viv figures, "It gives me more exposure; it's much better. I'm playing with better musicians. It's strange because in Sweet Savage I was in charge. I formed the band after I left school; myself and the bass player were the only two men who made the decisions. Whereas in Dio, because I'm the most unknown, I don't generally say a lot. Ronnie makes most of the decisions. I don't resent it either. He has the experience. It's strange coming from a band that is virtually unknown. It's a hell of a leap, like cold to hot. It takes a lot of getting used to. The band works really well, unlike a lot of bands I've seen where there has been a lot of tension. Maybe in five years it'll be a lot different. So far it works, even though I'm the new guy and I'm shown a lot of respect. There are in fact four songs on the *Holy Diver* LP that are Sweet Savage songs. They are songs that have been changed with different vocals. Some just use parts of songs. 'Lady Marion' is 'Rainbow in the Dark' practically note for note."

Ah yes, Sweet Savage, a band that along with Trespass was considered one of the most promising of the NWOBHM bands never to release a full album. Back to modern times now, I asked Vivian if that band might have become the reigning kings of the NWOBHM (Viv was from Belfast, so I guess Sweet Savage are technically NWOBHM) had they gotten that eagerly awaited record out on the shelves.

"Yes [laughs], well, actually the irony about the thing is that, you know, Metallica covered a Sweet Savage song, and it was so strange because we sounded so much like Metallica. I mean the singer . . . we were a four-piece, two guitars, bass, and drums, and our bass player, Raymond Hailer, was the singer and he sounded just like James Hetfield. I mean, he really, really sang in that way. And we actually were very much a speed metal band, although we didn't mean to be. We had a very nervous drummer, and if we rehearsed or wrote a song at a hundred beats per minute, by the time we played it, it was closer to 140. So, we tended to do everything a lot faster than we really should have. And having a singer that sounded just like Hetfield. So, in a weird sort of way, we could've been Metallica, and it became very, very ironic that Metallica started covering one of our songs.

"Then it became even more ironic when I saw a Metallica set list, and I noticed that they started with a song called 'Breadfan' by Budgie. And that's how we used to open our show, with Sweet Savage, way back when—we opened with 'Breadfan'; it was so weird! I'm going, hang on, they cover one of our songs, they open with 'Breadfan,' the same cover we opened with. . . . In fact, there was a second cover they did by a band called Earthquake, that we used to play as well. And that's totally bizarre because it's a really, really obscure cover. It's the only track I ever heard of this band. I had never actually heard the original until Raymond . . . he was the big music fan, and he would listen to all this obscure music, and he brought an album or single to rehearsal or whatever and said, 'Listen to this song, it's very obscure; no one is going to know it; we should cover it, it's great.' And then to find out that Metallica did that as a cover as well! It makes me think that somewhere along the line, someone in Metallica heard a lot of bootlegs of Sweet Savage [laughs]. Which is good; in a way it's very flattering, but it's strange too.

Vivian Campbell, Beacon Theatre, New York, New York, October 25, 1983. © *Rudy Childs*

"Almost all of the songs I contributed on the first album had originally started off as songs with Sweet Savage, back in Ireland. I mean, a lot of them were either half-baked songs from Sweet Savage or songs we had written in Sweet Savage but hadn't recorded. Because I mean, Sweet Savage . . . we were an aspiring band. We didn't have a record deal; we released a couple of independent singles, but we never actually recorded an album. We just did a bunch of live gigs, and a lot of them were just songs I had written with Sweet Savage that I just took the chords of them and changed them very slightly. But they hadn't been recorded yet, and they were songs that I had written, so I felt somewhat entitled to do that. 'Straight Through the Heart,' however, was actually generated from a Jimmy Bain riff. That was mostly a Jimmy song. 'Stand Up and Shout' was another Jimmy song. But 'Rainbow in the Dark' was an old Sweet Savage tune. 'Caught in the Middle' was a Sweet Savage tune; 'Invisible' was a Sweet Savage tune.

"Jimmy and I were very productive," continues Vivian, on writing and assembling *Holy Diver*. Indeed, if you think about it, the rich creative arc of the record was propelled by the fact that three enthusiastic songwriters aided in its birthing. "Jimmy and I could write easily together. It was Jimmy who introduced me to Dio. He was the one who got me an audition with the band, and he and I were roommates for all three albums actually, when we were in L.A.; Jimmy and I shared an apartment. Yeah, we wrote a lot of music together because we could. That was one thing about Dio—writing the *Holy Diver* record was very, very easy, because a lot of the music came together just by Jimmy having an idea for a riff or me having an idea and just going in there and having the three of us play it—you know, Jimmy, Vinny, and myself—just kicking it out.

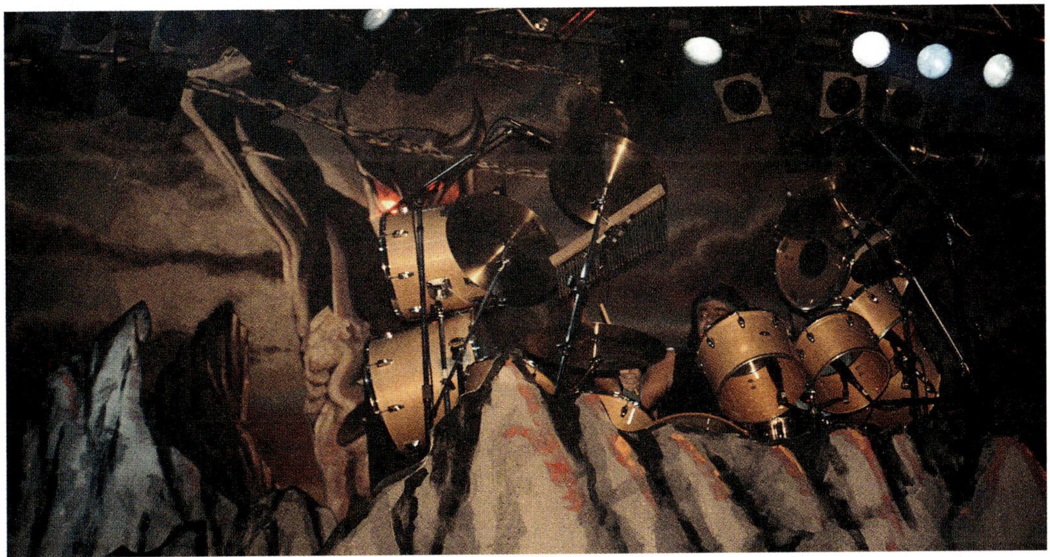

Vinny's back there somewhere. Beacon Theatre, New York, New York, October 25, 1983. © *Rudy Childs*

"And Ronnie would come in and just starts scatting some melody over the top and writing the lyrics as he went. So, it all happened actually very, very naturally. And that process continued with Jimmy and I. We could always sit down and kick out a bit of a tune. I would say that Jimmy and I contributed an awful lot to the music of those albums; perhaps more so than a lot of people would realize. And I would also think it's fair to say that Vinny, even though he wasn't a writer, he certainly did bring a flavor to it, just the way he would turn things around. His signature sound was an important part of it. But who knows, you know? It's like with Def Leppard. When you start, somebody comes in with an idea, and by the time it makes the record, it oftentimes bears little resemblance to what it started as. It's always a collaborative effort. Any time a band is in the studio making a record, things change, and things morph, and ultimately everyone contributes."

"Well, he had riffs and I had riffs," recalls Jimmy, on the bounty within the band. "Sometimes we didn't, and we just went in and came up with something together. You know, Viv and I could write really easy. I'd get an idea, he'd get an idea, and we would just feed off each other. We had chemistry; it was just something we didn't have to work on, something that was just there when we got together."

"Vinny is totally unique as a drummer," comments Viv, when asked about the large, cinematic, mercurial rhythmic backbone the band had. "I mean, Vinny, just his whole style, the way he plays, the way he puts the emphasis, is just totally different from any other drummer I've ever played with or ever heard. He's an exceptional drummer. But it's a question of style. I mean, if you don't like that style, he'd be totally wrong. It's perhaps more important as a musician, whether you're a guitar player or a singer, bass player, keyboard player, drummer . . . the most important thing is that you sound unique, and Vinny certainly has got that in spades. It was a little strange at first because when I would have an idea for a song and would come in and play it to him and Jimmy, where I would hear the two and the four, where I would hear the kick and the snare, was the total opposite of where Vinny would put it. And that's what made him so good and so unique. He just had this whole way of turning things around. At first it was a little disconcerting, but after a while you get used to knowing how Vinny thinks. He would come in and you would say, okay, I see where he's getting that now. That was just part of his whole style, and it made the music a lot more interesting because Vinny didn't play like a lot of other drummers."

And how did Viv get along with him as a person? Were there the cultural differences he felt with Ronnie there as well, given that both Vinny and Ronnie were American?

"No, Vinny wasn't as old as Ronnie. I think when I joined the band, I was twenty and Vinny was probably in his late twenties (actually, twenty-five), so we were probably a little closer in age. But more importantly, Vinny had a real sense of humor; he's very affable, very easy to get along with. So, I never had a problem with him.

"I didn't know a lot of the people who dropped by," says Viv, recalling the *Holy Diver* recording sessions themselves, which took place at the famed Sound City Studios, in Van Nuys, California. "I wasn't aware of who they were. Vinny had a lot of connections and Ronnie had a lot of connections with musicians in L.A. Obviously they lived there for a long time, made a bunch of records. There were a bunch of guys coming in and out of the studio, and I remember when I went to L.A. to make that record, I only had one guitar and one amp. I had a Marshall JCM800 amp head, and I had a Les Paul Deluxe.

And L.A. is guitar city and gear city, so all these different guys were coming down and lending me guitars and amps, and we'd be trying out all this stuff. And ultimately, basically, I ended up using my own stuff. You know, you play with what you're comfortable with. But I can't even remember their names. I know that a lot of the guys from Rod Stewart's band would be stopping by. Rick Derringer as well, yes, because of the Vinny connection. But I can't even recall. There were two studios at Sound City, and there were also three or four rehearsal rooms across the courtyard, and it was a constant stream of L.A. musos coming in and out—a typical L.A. studio vibe. People would come in and smoke a joint and talk bullshit and leave [laughs].

"Jimmy Bain was a full-on 100 percent paid-up, card-carrying member of the L.A. party scene," continues an amused Viv, when asked about extracurricular substance taking. "I must admit I wasn't. I came from Ireland, and the only thing people ever do there is drink. And in fact, I didn't even drink; I was always the designated driver in Sweet Savage. So, it was kind of strange for me being a roommate with Jimmy because there'd be all these people coming by doing all sorts of exotic drugs, and I was absolutely stone-cold sober sitting there watching them, and actually being quite frightened by all of it, just being twenty and coming from Ireland, where nobody does any of that shit. People do now, but it was very weird for me. Ronnie was reasonably straight as well. At the studio we would do some long, long days, and people would be drinking for a while. I remember that a lot of the time I would be staying at Ronnie's house in the spare bedroom, and a lot of the time I'd be driving him home [laughs]. Vinny didn't drink too much; Vinny was pretty straight and narrow. I mean, those guys smoked a lot of pot, but . . . it's L.A."

"We had Vinny in kind of a log cabin," recalls Jimmy, on getting the sounds for the album. "The drums sound really amazing on that album. We put him up on sort of a 6-inch platform or riser, and we built this plywood and particle board box around him, and we had the microphones all built up. And he had his back to the control room, which was glass. And we had a little peek hole to see him, for cues and stuff like that. It was kind of strange, the drummer being in this enclosed area where you couldn't see him at all when you're recording. It was kind of hilarious. You hear these little noises and voices coming out of there.

"Vinny had just phenomenal technique, sound, and attitude," adds Jimmy. "Man, just every department. I think that Vinny has a few, I would say, discrepancies in his situation, but it's not his playing; it's never been his playing. It's maybe some of his personal decisions or stuff like that. But I could never criticize his playing. He's always been spot on."

Indeed, the drums and the drumming did sound good on *Holy Diver*, both fat and dry at once, a bit of an oxymoron, but there you go. The production credit on the album goes to one Ronnie James Dio, but behind a good producer is usually an even better engineer.

"Yeah, Angelo Arcuri was there," recalls Jimmy. "But I think more than that, I think it was just the freshness of us coming in all G'ed up with all sorts of musical ideas and songs, kind of all ready to go. Just that fire you have when you get involved with people, not necessarily for the first time, but in a combination that just seems electric. The first time we played, when Vivian and Vinny and I and Ronnie got together in London and just played . . . after we played for about two minutes, you could tell that there was definitely some kind of chemistry that was just electric. I've never experienced that quite that early on in a situation, in a liaison. It was just incredible.

"So, when we got together and started writing songs, and playing with Vinny and Vivian, who were still fresh and refreshing compared to everything I heard before . . . and man, Ronnie was just the pipes from hell. It was just great, a great time. And that energy went on the album; that power went on there, and the enthusiasm went on there. And the writing was really good too. But the sound was good because you could kind of hear everything. It wasn't a wash of other kinds of textures. It was just the bass, the drums, the guitar, and the voice, with a few little bits of keyboards, but not really a lot of texture. You know, I think the bass sound I had on the album was likely the best I've ever had. And that helped a lot because it was right in your face. The guitar was great, the sound was so big, and it wasn't overproduced."

Jimmy Bain, Dio's own Ace Frehley. Beacon Theatre, New York City, October 25, 1983. © Rudy Childs

As for Vinny's memories of making the record, Appice told Jimmy Kay that "*Holy Diver* was recorded at Sound City. Everybody knows Sound City now, thanks to the Dave Grohl movie. *Holy Diver* was a great time in everybody's life in the band. Vivian was new. He was like a young kid, and Jimmy was Jimmy [laughs]. We were just having a great time. Every night we would go to Sound City at seven o'clock, get in the rehearsal room and write, and smoke a lot of pot. They would drink; I didn't really drink. But we smoked loads of pot, and we'd record stuff. And our soundman, Angelo Arcuri, who recorded *Holy Diver*, was there every night.

"We even got to the point of . . . we'd get really stoned and put down riffs and stuff, and the next night we would come in and we'd ask Angelo to play the riff on the cassette we made. It's a four-track cassette, so you could put everything upside down and it goes backwards. And that's what he did by mistake. And we were laughing at him, 'Ah, you jerk, you put it in upside down.' We're laughing, and then we go, 'Wait a minute; that sounds pretty good.' So, we're listening to some backwards stuff now. And we said that sounds good—let's learn the riff backwards. So, we learned the riff backward, and we used it in the song 'Invisible.' The song 'Invisible' is the riff forward and the riff backwards, too, in the song.

"So, we did crazy stuff. There was nothing we said we can't do. And then we destroyed the place. We'd open up the pinball machines and put little ramps there so we couldn't move the balls, and we'd be playing video games and having a ball. It was like a boys' club every night. That's why it came out so good. We were all having such a great time. And when we were ready, when we had four songs, we just dragged all the stuff across the parking lot into the studio part of Sound City. You had the rehearsal part and then you had the parking lot and then you had the recording part. We set up there and we recorded four songs, and then we brought everything back across the parking lot, put it back in the room. At one time the Vanilla Fudge, with my brother, Carmine, came to rehearse at one of the rooms. So, we're in there, they're in there; let's lock them in. So, we took all the road cases and piled them up so they couldn't get out. We just put them in front of their door, and we left them there for a couple hours. They were pissed off, but hey, what the hell, it was fun."

Holy Diver imagery across various media and merchandise

The very first Dio album—and to this day, arguably the most beloved of the bunch—arrived on May 25, 1983. *Holy Diver* was presented to the public sporting a nasty sacrilegious sleeve illustration by Randy Berrett depicting a priest wrapped in chains and drowning. He's the titular "holy diver" as it were, although one could easily surmise from the graphic action that this leap into the brine was anything but a voluntary dive.

Aragon Ballroom, Chicago, Illinois, October 21, 1983. Supporting was Y&T. © *Greg Olma*

Directing the action was a devil figure affectionately known in the Dio camp as . . . Murray. Er, why Murray? "Because it's silly," answers the man at the mic. "You've got this devil figure with horns, and he's supposed to scare everybody, and you could call him Beelzebub, but I thought it was funnier than hell to call him Murray. I had come from Sabbath, and there was that dark presence there. I was supposed to be the Prince of Darkness at some point, not that I was, but that's the perspective people see you from, especially when you're with a band called Black Sabbath. So, it made sense to carry on with that image. It wasn't meant to paint me or the band as evil people, any more than the name Black Sabbath was designed to paint them as evil people, which they weren't, and which we aren't. But it made sense to carry on with that theme. It was a popular theme at that time; it was an acceptable theme; you know, 'They're pretty evil, aren't they?!' [laughs]. And we thought it was kind of sensible to carry on with our monster, our guy we call Murray, who on the first album was drowning the priest, and of course he's the central figure on *The Last in Line* as well."

It's amusing that Ronnie references the Prince of Darkness, because this is exactly what Ozzy was saying repeatedly at the time, that everybody thought *he* was the Prince of Darkness and that people were reading him wrong. There's another comparison to be made with Oz that we haven't pointed out yet, even though it may be obvious: as with Ozzy's new solo band, Ronnie had with him both a drummer and (writing) bassist who had histories, contrasted against a hotshot young guitarist whom no one had heard of.

Back to *Holy Diver*: "I'm very involved in the cover art process," adds Ronnie. "I think that what is on the cover is going to be representative of how I think. If it's going to be silly and stupid, then I don't want it. I don't want people to think that of me. I have a lot of control in that department. We tried to reflect what the albums were about. That made it seem like the normal progression, as it should have been. It was easy."

Ronnie protects his Chicago fans, October 21, 1983. © *Greg Olma*

"Like everything else that I do, it should represent what the listener and the viewer feels," said Ronnie, addressing the thorny issue back in 1983. "I try not to force anyone to believe what I'm saying, other than what I'm saying is only one tunnel-vision thing. The drowning priest . . . the first thing it did was it made people say, 'You've got a devil drowning a priest on your album cover, and I'm really disgusted.' Which gives me the chance to say, 'Well, that's not really what it is. You don't know whether the person dressed in the priest outfit isn't the devil, or the one you think is the devil isn't God. You don't know what he looks like, or what the devil looks like.' What I'm trying to do is make people ask questions about what's really real in life. Is the devil God or is God the devil? Instead of saying this is what you must believe in, again, shoving it down their throats."

It was soon pointed out that if you turned the Dio logo upside down, it read "Devil" or "Evil" or "Die," all of which are difficult to discern. Ronnie says that this was not planned and is therefore purely coincidental, which underscores why it's a bit of a dodgy story.

The devil figure on the cover, Murray, with his left hand, is making the devil horns sign made famous by Ronnie and living on forevermore as a universal gesture of support for heaviness. Ronnie explained to Sam Dunn how his use of the "Maloik" came about.

"I've been asked many times about 'Did I invent that?' And I said of course not. If I were that brilliant, I wouldn't be doing this anymore, would I? Maybe I'd be president of the United States, and I'd go, 'My fellow Americans . . .' or 'My fellow Canadians' too, for that matter. I'm of Italian extraction, and my grandmother and grandfather on both sides, both my mother's and father's sides, came to America from Italy, and they had superstitions. And I would always see my grandmother, when I was a little kid, with her holding my hand and us walking down the street. She would see someone and go [holds up the devil horns]. 'Oh, what's that?'

"And I eventually learned that it was called the Maloik, and the Maloik was because someone was giving us the evil eye; she'd be giving us protection against the evil eye. Or you can give someone the evil eye too. So, all those years later, especially when I got into Black Sabbath and Ozzy was gone and Ozzy was always doing the peace sign, I of course did not want to do that—that was what Ozzy did. And for some strange reason, even though I had done it earlier than that in Rainbow, it suddenly came out, and there it was.

"So, did I invent it? No. But perfect it and make it important? Yes, because I did it so much, especially within the confines of that great band, Sabbath, which had this incredible name already, and you put that together with what people think it is, it became more mine than anyone else's. And I think the problem is that now we see it in Britney Spears concerts, and we see it in Backstreet Boys concerts and NSYNC concerts, so it's really lost its meaning there. But for me, because I'm lucky enough to have just done it so much, it's been more equated with me more than anyone else. Though Gene Simmons will tell you that he invented it, but then again Gene invented breathing and shoes and everything. Everybody will say that, and no one invented it; it was just superstition from years and years ago. I just decided to use it a lot, so it became that."

Into the very first Dio band record, opening *Holy Diver* is a song that would permanently sear itself into the minds of Dio fans the world over. "Stand Up and Shout" would live on to become a staple of any given Dio concert for years to come. It is of a tempo that is fast but not too fast, just fast enough so that Ronnie sounds on the edge of panic, just fast enough so that Vivian's riffing sounds shred-ready but still regal and in no hurry to please. Lyrically the song is Ronnie's personal call to the metal legions, his "Long Live Rock 'n' Roll" for the more metallically intense—not to mention more metallically demanding—early 1980s.

In essence the song (and indeed the album and the Dio band itself) is the result of all the goodly heavy metal work that had taken place within the now-concluding New Wave of British Heavy Metal, albeit subconsciously, because really, Ronnie was on a different path, synthesizing more so what he had done with Rainbow and Sabbath. And through this nexus in 1983 as something post-NWOBHM as well as rooted in the traditional, what we were getting with Dio was something akin to the first substantial American(ish) proto-power metal band.

"That was an interesting story," notes Ronnie, back to the explosive album opener at hand. "Jimmy Bain and Vivian Campbell went back to England after we had completed the album. But 'Stand Up and Shout' was only a backing track. So, after they left, I had to write a melody and lyrics for it. So, they had never heard the song before, and we sent them over a copy of it. It turned out to be that album's real anthem."

"Yes, 'Stand Up and Shout' is an interesting one," agrees Jimmy. "I had written that song, the music for it anyway; I had written it about a year or two before I got into the band. So, I recorded it with the band, the backing track, and we went and did all the other backing tracks. Ronnie had some vocals done, but he didn't have anything for

'Stand Up and Shout.' He didn't have any lyrics and he didn't really have the melody per se; it wasn't done. And I got all the backing tracks done, and I knew he had done everything but 'Stand Up and Shout.' He hadn't recorded them yet, but he had written them. And I knew what they sounded like.

Jimmy and Viv, Beacon Theatre, New York City, October 25, 1983. © *Rudy Childs*

"And I went off to do the Scorpions, *Love at First Sting*, in Europe. And I had no idea that 'Stand Up and Shout' was going to be 'Stand Up and Shout.' We didn't even have a title, in fact. So, I have tapes of that, as a backing track, without a vocal. So, I went off to Germany, then to Sweden. And then about a month and a half later, when I was over there, thinking when is this going to be wound up, thinking about coming back, while I was still there, I got tapes sent over from Ronnie, with the vocal on it. Which was just totally mind blowing, to have a song that sort of opens your first album with a band that was just so powerful like that; it was just so powerful what he had done. And I had no idea at all it was going to be like that. When you've written something that you think is pretty good, and it's going to go on the album, but you don't know it's going to be going first . . . and then he sent the rough mix of it with the vocal on it. I hadn't heard the words, I hadn't heard the melodies, what he had done with it. And I couldn't wait to get down to rehearsals and play it to Rudolf and the guys. 'Hey, check this out!' So that was funny.

"I've got another one," says Jimmy, of his days spent surreptitiously with Germany's hottest band, as a sort of "threatened" stand-in for Francis Buchholz, as it were. "The Scorpions, every day we'd go to the studio in Stockholm, they would play the rough mixes of *Holy Diver* before they started recording. We had to listen to it from beginning to end, which was really, really cool, that they would get a lot of inspiration from that. They were really into the album. And I came back, and the next thing I did was the video for 'Rainbow in the Dark,' in Europe, after that. Because the Dio album was finished after that."

Lyrically, "Stand Up and Shout" reads like a signature beacon-of-hope song from Ronnie. Artfully abstract and spare, for the opening verses Ronnie uses a quartet of metaphors that point to frustration and inertia. But then late in the sequence, after encouragement from Ronnie to his growing army of acolytes—essentially, you can picture an English NWOBHM fan in the summer of 1980 (but in the rain)—things turn around and all of a sudden, he's "the strongest chain" and "the driver" who "own(s) the road."

The titanic title track.
Martin Popoff archive

Second on the record is the title track, which in retrospect serves as a brilliant spot of sequencing. First you had this screeching fist pump of an anthem, something that was a bit on the rock 'n' rollsy side lyrically, and then . . . boom! You have the album's epic, not at side's end like its comparative sister blister 'Heaven and Hell,' but immediately there, immediately imposing, viscerally present, lending gravitas to the record. And as with many a successful epic, "Holy Diver" achieves that status without the cheap ploy of having to go to epic lengths. At 5:54, it still manages to feel imposing and grand, but it doesn't overstay its welcome.

"'Holy Diver' is, I guess, some form of religious song," explains Ronnie. "It's about a savior figure, like Christ, who is on another planet and has done the same as we know: God supposedly sacrificing his son for the sins of others. At this particular point, this Christ figure had done all that on this other world and now is going to another world to do the same thing, which could have been Earth; it could have been anything. But the point was, the people in this first world were saying, 'Don't go down there. There are evil animals. There are tigers with stripes that are mean, and there are all kinds of bad things. You're going to go down there and you're never going to come back again.' Its whole point was, Gee, aren't people selfish? They just got through being saved by someone who died for their sins, and now everything is okay in their world. But you won't let him go, because you're afraid that he won't always be there for you. What about other people in the universe? So again, it's a 'People are really weird' song [laughs]. I don't think most people know what that song is really about. They have their own interpretation, which is cool to me, because I like to write songs that allow people to have their own judgments and make it their own song in their own special way. But that really is what the song is about."

"Holy Diver" carries forward Ronnie's legacy of sort of medieval fantasy-type tales, which were already plenty marbled throughout his days with Rainbow and Sabbath. Bottom line, the throughput is strong, with *Holy Diver* being the purposeful fifth album in a vision evolving at sober and sensible pace and not by leaps and bounds—after all, if it morphed too fast, if it changed convulsively, gone would be the sense of tradition. Furthermore, our clue that Ronnie is a force of nature unto himself comes with the fact that in the bands with which he'd made the previous five records, he'd been the new guy and, to boot, squarely subservient in the pecking order to massive rock 'n' roll legends in Ritchie Blackmore and Tony Iommi.

With respect to where his oddball life philosophy came from, Ronnie told Sam Dunn, "I think I realized really early in my life, when I decided that I would be a lyricist for some of this music, that to be successful you must be unique. As a child I read constantly, starting four, five years old, starting to read and read things that were a lot of science fiction. Certainly a lot of things by Walter Scott and about knights and dragons, and these were all things I had to create images of in my own mind, and I felt to be unique that I would like to say the same humdrum things everybody else says, but in a very different manner, and that manner became taking people into a world that made them use their imagination.

"I'm not a love-song writer, but were I to be that, then I wrote the song within the perspective of the damsel in distress being saved from the dragon by the knight. And suddenly it's not a love story anymore; it's a little more intricate, a little more interwoven than that. And I think that's what's held me in such good stead all this time and allowed me to write things that allow people to make their own judgment as to what is being said.

"And I think that perhaps my influence on other metal writers has been a little bit important because it's shown them that you can do it. So lyrically, for me, I try to not go right to the point of the argument, or right to the issue. I tend to write around it and use a lot of metaphors, a lot of similes, so that people can make their own judgment. I've been told by many people that one song I've written, for example—and I won't even tell you the name of a song, any song—what did you think this song means? And I'll get ten different answers. So that means that it worked. Now it's *their* song. And in some of those instances, those ten things were nothing about what I was going to write it about, so I felt that I did it correctly. That's what always inspired me. Other . . . I was going to say other great writers—and I don't consider myself to be a great writer—but other great writers have inspired me to be better. Ray Bradbury, Arthur C. Clarke . . . just all the great writers that I've read over the course of my life have inspired me to be better than I ever could be."

As for rainbows, Ronnie told Dmitry Epstein that "a rainbow is a natural phenomenon that is so awesome and so seldom seen, that it never fails to draw a response from us all. Rainbows have always made me realize how insignificant we can be in the grand scheme of things."

Ronnie, ever the sports fan as well as sportsman (he was a pretty good long-distance runner), has remarked in the past, even back to the Rainbow days, that he does his best writing while watching sports on TV. "Holy Diver" was no exception, with Dio recalling the adrenalin high of writing it after watching his Philadelphia 76ers beat the Los Angeles Lakers.

"Yeah, I guess I'm probably the only person who does it that way," mused Ronnie, back in '84. "I could never write songs while listening to music, because I couldn't help be influenced by it and have it take me away from what I want to do. Whenever I hear music, my mind instantly goes right to the music, what it sounds like, how it's produced, what the melody line is like. So, if I listened to music, I wouldn't be able to think for myself. The sporting events on TV give me noise, but there's no music to distract me. The noise is from the announcers and from the crowd, and I can shut it out when I need to. At the same time, I'm watching something that I find interesting, something that's part of my fantasy. I always wanted to be an athlete, so I'm speaking from a fantasy world with my music, while watching my fantasy on the screen. When I'm preparing for an album, before I do any writing, I'll do a lot of reading. Some science fiction, a lot of historical things, anything that isn't quite real—history obviously was real but is no more, and science fiction is something that will be but is not yet. I surround myself with that kind of attitude. It makes it easier to spark me into a futuristic or completely ancient frame of mind."

Asked by Steve Newton in 1985 if he ever gets to play any actual sports on the road, Ronnie replied, "We toss the football around. We kick the soccer ball around. Throw a baseball around here and there. But there's just so little time. The entire day is either taken up with traveling or with sound check, doing the show, or speaking to people before and after. This is just a full-time occupation out there. There's not a lot of time left for fun things. But yeah, all the albums that I've done I think I've been watching some kind of sporting event. And only because it really relaxes me. There's no music in the background, and I love athletics anyway. My favorite sport to write by is basketball. But I would say my favorite sport is football. I like anything."

"He would write something and ask opinions," recalls Wendy. "He loved to write watching sports—always watching sports. I don't know much about sports, but he always said . . . he figured this one was the bass player and this one was the vocalist, in sports; that's how he would do that. He would write mostly with guitar. Because Ronnie . . . people think Ronnie is only a lyricist, but he's not. He writes music also. All the melodies. But he would write with his guitar, watching TV. I think he had a very different way of writing. He didn't want to write love songs. He wanted to write about people's experiences, dreams, hopes, their hopes for the future. And in terms of heavy metal, he loved the power—the power and the strength."

Notes Vinny, "Actually 'Holy Diver' was a riff that Ronnie had from before the band was put together. He and I would go to a rehearsal place, and we would just jam different things, and that became 'Holy Diver.' And then I suggested doing the accents, and he had the galloping part. So, we always had that one; that was one of the audition songs he played when we auditioned guitar players. Different story from the others; 'Straight Through the Heart' was a Jimmy riff he played on bass, and 'Stand Up and Shout' came from a Sweet Savage song."

The somewhat on-the-cheap video for "Holy Diver" would see, through bad cinematography, Ronnie brandishing a sword as he wanders castle ruins, providing more fodder for detractors who would deride his revisitations of such themes in his lyrics. "It should've been a story within itself," sighs Ronnie. "It wasn't what I conceived; the videos are not my ideas. Had either of the songs, 'Rainbow in the Dark' or 'Holy Diver,' been my ideas, they would've been completely different. I shall never let anyone do that among themselves again." The clip was filmed in a church in Silverton, East London, called St. Mark's, which is now a music venue. Again, the imagery throughout

Aragon Ballroom, Chicago, Illinois, October 21, 1983. © *Greg Olma*

provides additional fuel to those who dismiss Ronnie's preoccupation with sword and sorcery themes—in other words, moving pictures carry outsized weight.

After the terrorist attacks of September 11, 2001, "Holy Diver" was included on Clear Channel's memorandum pointing out songs that were "lyrically questionable" in light of what happened that terrible day.

As Ronnie explained to Sam Dunn, "During the aftermath of 9/11, I spoke to a friend of mine, a guy named Eddie Trunk who is a DJ in New York, probably one of the few left who is such a great metal guy. He's supported all metal people in bands for such a long time. I mean he's just the best. And I spoke to Eddie, and he said, 'I just want to let you know that Clear Channel has banned a few songs by a few bands, and one is 'Holy Diver.' 'Really?' I think Iron Maiden, an Iron Maiden track, a Priest track. So, I guess at least I was in good company.

"And my feeling, my first reaction, was why? And they said it was inappropriate now to play these kinds of songs that have a violent image to them. And I never could really understand that, because the song 'Holy Diver' is not a violent song. It's actually about a Christ figure in a positive way. I guess maybe a lot of people don't know that it's that. But the whole point of it all—and I digress slightly but I think this will apply—on the album *Holy Diver* there is what appears to be a monster, and a priest drowning in the water, with chains around him [the priest] and the monster with a broken piece of chain, which meant he must have chained him up and he's going to kill him. So, the question was always why do you have a monster killing a priest on your album cover? And my answer always was because I planned it this way. How do you know that's not a priest killing a monster? All these years later, with what has happened in the Catholic Church, I think I might have had a little foresight into that one, but that was the purpose of it. Ask first what is in the package before you say that it's bad or that's wrong.

"So it really upset me when I heard that we had been placed within the banned territory after 9/11. After all, I consider myself to be a good, caring American, and suddenly I had been put in the position of being an outcast in my own country for no good reason. My reaction? I was pissed off. Really, really pissed off. Pissed off then, pissed off today. And what other reaction could I have?"

When Sam asks Ronnie to reflect on the meaning of that particular act or example of censorship, Ronnie says, "I think it has to happen. I think they feel, they—by they, meaning that section of the media—feels they must make a token gesture. And who are they going to make the token gesture to? I don't hear any rap artists getting too many . . . well, because theirs is all about sex, and that's cool, I guess. But ours is about something evil because we're talking about heavy metal musicians, and that's always been a great part of what metal is supposed to be . . . what is bad about it? 'It's evil.' Well, that's all crap. Sure, there are evil images, but that doesn't necessarily mean that we're all evil. So, I think that we were the perfect scapegoat for it all, just as Judas Priest got sued for the kids who committed suicide, just as Ozzy has been castigated for 'Suicide Solution,' which are . . . they just need to be looked into, and you'll find it's not true."

As for the reference to tigers in "Holy Diver," Ronnie explained to Dmitry Epstein that "the tiger symbolizes strength, while its stripes suggest impurity. The lines 'Ride the tiger. You can see his stripes, but you know he's clean' mean that you must take advantage of the strength you have and not judge the heart of others by what seem to be impurities—these stripes—in the package it comes in."

Back to the sequence, "Gypsy" comes next—third song, side 1 of the original vinyl—striking a balance between commerciality and true heavy metal. It stomps into view, Viv wailing away with a well-positioned introductory ax solo before Ronnie comes in with a theme he knew so well, that of the evil woman, a "Tarot Woman" or "Lady Evil," as it were, with Ronnie injecting a slight bit of humor into his phrases, lending the song a layer of parody. Jimmy offers that "'Gypsy' was one of Viv's riffs that is pretty straightforward. Some of them were just really straight-ahead songs."

"Caught in the Middle" is even more commercial, moving to a standard hard-rock chord structure but hilariously shoved full of some extra notes. "I thought that one should've been a single!" recalls Jimmy. "That was a great song, but it was hard for Ronnie to do live, so we didn't do it. Some of them are pretty high, the keys and stuff. Although we try to do as many as we can as a cross section, that one was never an option." Come verse time, the song is almost languid, Ronnie offering some choice Dio poetry that eventually (nearly halfway through!) gives way to what is arguably the record's most passionate, melodic, urgent, and successful chorus. Viv's solo is gorgeously melodic and not without a hint of Tony Iommi to it.

The title of this one sums up Ronnie's stance in the song, for just like on the opener, failure is mixed with triumph, landing the subject of the song on the razor's edge, caught in the middle. Indeed, most of Ronnie's lines lean toward doom, but among the trauma, "there's some kind of spark," which might be found through some type of courageous self-examination.

Closing side 1 of the original vinyl is another timeless Dio classic, the aforementioned "Don't Talk to Strangers," sounding Sabbatherian and psychologically doom laden. As with "Holy Diver," it manages many moods and movements at a reasonable time count, in this instance under five minutes.

"That was the second of the songs I wrote before we had a band," recalls Ronnie. "I wrote 'Holy Diver' first and 'Don't Talk to Strangers' second. Those two songs are the ones we presented to Vivian when we auditioned Viv; we showed him those songs, and that was the beginning of the whole shebang, really. At the time I was writing it, it was a difficult time. I wasn't in a band yet, and I hadn't put this band together yet. I just went out and wrote those things, really for future reference. When there was a band, there would be some songs to start with. So, it was a difficult time in terms of [wondering] what's going to happen next. It was about how people promise you the world and then just . . . bend over, here it comes. So that's what it was about, the idea that strangers can be devilish if you let them—beware of what's going on. I kind of put myself in that place a little bit, being one of the strangers as well, just for a turn in the lyric, and not because I felt I was one of those evil guys."

Indeed, this one is pessimism personified, but intensely, into the realm of the paranormal. In other words, it's almost as if the dark view of trying anything—flowers, women, dancing in darkness, hiding, strangers—is so bleak that it must be the result of demonic influence. Asked if he really saw the world so relentlessly dark, Ronnie figures, "Not always, but writing allows me to focus on a subject, and the horrible things we do to each other keep appearing without end. I'm therefore very influenced by what's around me, and thus many dark images are aroused. Let's change the world, and I'll change the song images."

"Straight Through the Heart" is yet another proud, regal, and buoyant rocker made of pure traditional metal, propelled along at slow-to-mid-paced velocities by a prominent Vinny Appice beat. "That was something I just had, a riff, something that hadn't become a song yet," notes Jimmy. "All these things were pretty current at the time. They were not more than a year old when I got together with Ronnie. I had riffs and riffs, but I was in a band at the time, and none of the riffs I did with the band ended up being Dio songs. They were all pretty new things. I don't know about Viv's, but mine certainly weren't that old."

Ronnie is again expressing pessimism and bitterness, this time the theme being betrayal, with no hope at the end of the rainbow. There's literally a single line of advice: "Don't stand still; they'll get you," meaning that if you don't want your faith in humanity shattered, keep moving so your enemies miss their marks.

"Invisible" comes next, adding to the brooding, medieval, almost old-school Rainbow feel of the album. "I never liked Ronnie's lyrics," reveals Vivian, looking back twenty years down the line, with an eventual comment on this classy track. "I loved his voice. Well, no, that's not true. There were some lyrics, yeah. I think when he put his mind to it, he could do it. But like a lot of people, regardless, as a guitar player, I fall back on certain licks, and I know when I'm doing it [laughs]. You know when I'm not challenging myself. We're all guilty of some of these indiscretions. But with Ronnie, I mean, I remember with 'Invisible,' I thought the lyrics on that were really good, really clever. But he fell back a lot on his old staples—dragons and rainbows. That gets a little tiring after a while. But he was capable of it if he wanted to."

"At the end of the intro, the slow part, we needed a sound," recalls Vinny, dredging a memory of "Invisible." "We were trying to get a sound like a whoosh, and we couldn't get anything that would suffice. And then somebody said, 'It sounds like you want the sound of air coming out of a tire or something like that.' So, one of our techs at the time, Tom, he went out to his truck and brought his spare wheel into the studio, and we put a microphone on it and recorded the air coming out, this hissing sound. And that's what's on the record [laughs]."

At the lyric end, Ronnie paints two sad, third-person vignettes with an additional one in the first person. A dark reading of Ronnie's message points to a suicide solution, although if indeed Ronnie is playing his trickster games, making us exercise our latent contrarianism, he might just be saying that a person has the option of leaving and starting a new life somewhere else, becoming invisible to one's past and blossoming in a new temporal and geographical future.

Next up, innocently placed second to last on the record, is the track that would forever become Dio's biggest hit. "Rainbow in the Dark" is a fairly commercial track, ebbing and flowing behind a standard, accessible, universal rock chord structure. But it's sent controversial in concentric metal circles by way of its mewling keyboard line—a tsk-tsking no-no to the NWOBHM-trained faithful. And with "rainbow" in the title, the song serves as a constant reminder of those recurring themes of which Viv speaks.

"I don't know why it touched so many hearts, but it did," says a bemused Ronnie on this signature track, one that by its very title sums up Ronnie's central theme of good versus evil. "I wanted to get rid of that song. I hated that song; I absolutely hated that song. In fact, I came real close to taking a razor blade to the tape! Everyone said, 'Please don't do that! That's a good one!' Luckily, they talked me out of it!"

Said Ronnie of the lyric, "I try to take a simple idea and put it in a different way. An example of that might be 'Rainbow in the Dark.' What I tried to do was put together a combination of words that said 'lonely.' I couldn't think of anything that makes me think of the majesty of the world better than a rainbow—it's a magnificent thing, and it needs sunlight, moisture, and refraction to survive. And if you take something that beautiful and stick it away in a dark closet . . . well, I can't think of anything more lonely than that.

A cherished but water-damaged tour program. *Martin Popoff archive*

"I'll generally write a song on guitar," continued Ronnie, in the same 1984 interview. "I'm not the greatest guitar player in the world, but I play good rhythm, and that's how I write most of my material. I write it with the feel first, as opposed to the melody first. I'll just write a simple, basic riff, because as a guitar player, I'm sort of like everyman, so my riffs are like everyman's riffs. It would be easy for just about anybody to pick up a guitar and play the changes that I write, because they're very natural. I'll tell Vinny how I want the drums to sound and what kind of feel I want, and I'll let him create everything around that. And once I've shown Viv and Jimmy the changes, I'll let them expand on that. I like to wait until it's kind of close to the moment, because I like to be put under pressure. I think that the natural method is the best way for this band and this kind of music. I generally tend to come up with exactly as many songs as I'll need. I usually throw away five or six songs per album, but I find that I'll usually retain part of what song I've thrown away, and it will usually fit into another song."

"Basically, 'Rainbow in the Dark' was written in about ten minutes, the whole thing," adds Campbell. "I basically had the chord ideas and I started playing it, Vinny started putting in those backing things, and Jimmy started goofing around on the keyboard and did that little keyboard lick. And Ronnie just, you know, he didn't have the lyrics for it, obviously, right away, but he basically nailed the melody right from the first time. So, stuff came together pretty easy. Most of the songs on *Holy Diver* and *Last in Line*, they just came together rather effortlessly. And the quicker and easier they came together, the better the songs tended to be."

Viv at the Tower Theater in Upper Darby, Pennsylvania, checking out the shooter's shots from an earlier show at the Beacon Theater in New York. Supporting on the night was Twisted Sister. © *Rudy Childs*

"You know, I'm the one who's always coming up with the idea that we should be more commercial," says an exasperated Jimmy Bain, having fought this battle many times over the years. "You know what I mean? It's just like, 'What's so bad about being commercial? What's so bad about success [laughs]?' So, I've had songs rejected because they were too commercial, or they lean towards it. And I respect his opinion, but at the same time you're kind of telling people that you don't want to be successful. And I don't think the theory behind having a band is to be unsuccessful; I think it's to become successful. At the same time, Ronnie always seems to get together with me when he needs to write something, kind of for a film or something like that [laughs]. Because I lean towards more of the melodic things, things that would be more appealing to a wider market. And I think that's what happened with 'Rainbow in the Dark.' It's Viv's riff, but I came up with the keyboard thing, and that was the little hooky thing that went with the good riff, and it made it successful, I think. And God, it's been hard to come up with another one [laughs]. But I've always been sort of . . . and I'll stick to my guns too. If it's too commercial, well, I'm sure you're really unhappy with all the money it's made for you [laughs]."

Jimmy credits some of the success of the song to its promotion on MTV, which at this point was two years runnin' and at the height of its almost mythical hold on

Massey Hall, Toronto, Canada, December 12, 1983. © *Martin Popoff*

American rock fans. "Yes, well, luckily so many bands got onto MTV. We were lucky that Dio got right on there with 'Rainbow in the Dark,' which got heavy rotation at that point because it was new. I came over to L.A. and I just watched it for days on end without sleeping. I couldn't believe it; it was so great, to watch videos constantly, in music. It was phenomenal. But at that time, the strength of the New Wave of British Heavy Metal . . . maybe it did stop, somewhat, that invasion that was supposed to happen. But MTV invariably helped the bands that lasted; it actually helped them. But for a lot of those British bands that didn't get videos out at the time, it didn't help them very much at all."

Indeed, "Rainbow in the Dark," released on October 21, 1983, as the second single from the record (backed with "Gypsy"), would be the track that propelled the band to its first fame, with the song reaching #12 on Billboard's secondary Album Rock Tracks chart. The UK got a live (from Donington) version of "Stand Up and Shout" for a B-side, as well as a picture sleeve. A 12-inch issue added "Straight Through the Heart," also from Castle Donington. Earlier in the year, on July 11, 1984, Japan went with a five-track 12-inch maxi single, consisting of "Rainbow in the Dark," "Holy Diver," the two aforementioned live tracks, plus "Evil Eyes," which wouldn't show up on an album until *The Last in Line*, and at that point rerecorded. Notes Viv, "Phonogram came and asked us for a B-side, and we went into the studio with no idea what to do and it just came about, and we recorded and mixed it in thirty-six hours."

"Evil Eyes" was also used as the B-side for the record's first single, "Holy Diver," although that one didn't see issue in the US. Among this tangle of ancillary releases are the most-famed songs of the band's career—"Holy Diver," "Rainbow in the Dark," and "Stand Up and Shout" were played at virtually every Dio show. But it's "Rainbow in the Dark" that crossed over the most, with the song even getting turned into a Budweiser commercial with new beery lyrics.

"Exactly," laughs Jimmy. "And they're still making a nice little situation from that song; it goes on every compilation and whatnot. He should say, 'Okay, I didn't really want it on the album, but when you see what it's done, and we do it every night, it's always kind of our key song at the end of the set.' I think he's a little overcritical in that department. But he just likely has to stay with the same thing he said back then. He may lean a little more towards the commercial or he might not, I don't know."

Viv's solo on "Rainbow in the Dark," like pretty much all of them on the album, is a soaring, triumphant combination of the rhythmic, the melodic, the technical, and the versatile. He proves himself as not only a damn good heavy metal guitarist, but a composer, a musician. Yet on the subject of heavy metal, it seems more than a bit ironic that Viv, quickly after his departure from Dio, became quite negative on the subject of the genre inside of which Dio squarely sits, positioning himself comfortably within Def Leppard (after brief stints with Whitesnake, Riverdogs, and Shadow King) as a pop guitarist—that is, when we heard him at all. But then again, the early 1980s was an altogether different climate.

Vivian Campbell, Aragon Ballroom, Chicago, Illinois, October 21, 1983. © *Greg Olma*

Viv gives us a bit of insight into his mind space with respect to his guitar work. "You know, I've got to say, I'm not the kind of guitar player that really puts a lot of thought into what I'm going to do when it comes to cutting a track, cutting a solo. And that's not necessarily a good thing, and I certainly wouldn't recommend it for other guitar players. But there's a certain amount of excitement. Sometimes it can work, and most of the time it doesn't [laughs]. Either you're going to get it right away, you're just going to be inspired with the moment and come up with something brilliant, or it's going to be a couple of hours and you're eventually going to have to concede defeat and sit down and actually think about where you want to go with the guitar solo.

"Now, the very, very first solo I did for Dio, for the *Holy Diver* record, was indeed 'Rainbow in the Dark.' And I didn't have any preconceptions of what it was I was going to play. But as it was my first cut, and here I am in L.A., in a studio making a major record, I went into the studio in the afternoon and went into a little room with a practice amp and my Les Paul, and the only thing I knew is that we were going to cut the solo for 'Rainbow in the Dark' and it was going to be in A minor. So, all I did was play guitar in A minor all day, just mindless riffing, and noodling. And I went in and they rolled the tape, and the first solo I did was the one that's on the record. Ronnie went, 'Wow, that's great, that's brilliant. Keep that; let's go to another track and do another one.' So, I did another one and it wasn't quite as good. 'Okay, let's try another one.' I did a third one and it was even less good. So, you know, that was a totally spontaneous solo. The problem with doing stuff like that—and me as a guitar player in general—is that if I do something great like that, I can never repeat it. And I never, ever played the solo the same way again, in all the times we'd played it live. So that one stands out as being a strong one.

"When I was with Dio cutting those early albums, it was all about the guitar to me," continues Viv. "Plus, it was the '80s and it was the era of the guitar shredder. That's a lot less important now than it was then, both in terms of the whole musical scene and in terms of where I am personally. I mean, to me it's much more important to write a good song than it is to cut the guitar solo. It's also important to me that I sing well. Back in the Dio days, I barely even sang, so it wasn't anything that was on my radar. So, my priorities have changed a lot. And I'm a lot more comfortable now as a guitar player with my own style. I don't feel that it has to always be something that's technical anymore. In the Dio days there was certainly a sort of push/pull battle going on; I wanted to demonstrate a certain amount of dexterity. Ronnie was always telling me, 'That's not always going to be appropriate for this particular song.' So that's the one thing I did learn from that. He and Jimmy and Vinny would sort of hold the reins and pull me back a little bit when I was just whacking off and playing notes for the sake of it.

"But I agree with Jimmy," adds Viv on the whole "Rainbow in the Dark" discussion. "Ronnie had a great sense of pop melody, but he would never, ever, ever let himself use it. Any time we would start heading down that road toward something really, really poppy, he would kill it. He was just very, very mired in the whole slow, slow style of Black Sabbath, of classic heavy metal, the dark side of heavy metal. And he never wanted to explore the pop elements, which he had a great talent for. It's a shame he didn't let that out."

"You'll have to ask the director about 'Rainbow in the Dark,'" sniped Ronnie about the second video from the album. "I write songs so that everyone had his interpretation, and that was his interpretation. His was that someone came from a working town in the north of England to London, to look for a romantic involvement. I sang on the roof the first part of the song, then it shot to a guy, and he saw a girl walking down the street and he was attracted to her and he followed her, and she went to the erotic section of Soho. He thought this must be it. She must be really easy. So, he followed her. And then she came down the stairs again and Vivian was playing. She was on his arm, and all his dreams were shattered—she became his rainbow in the dark. So, the whole idea behind

Viv, Ronnie, and Ronnie's nose, October 25, 1983, Beacon Theater, New York. © *Rudy Childs*

'Rainbow in the Dark' is lonely. But I never would have done that. Nor would I have done 'Holy Diver' the way he did. They are both good, but not what I would've done. 'Holy Diver' is good; I like that a hundred times better than I like 'Rainbow in the Dark.' I don't like that at all."

Closing out the album is the slowest song of the lot, "Shame on the Night" sounding very much like something Sabbath would do, black 'n' blue shade of the blues included. Ronnie's not only casting shame on the night, but also the day, the sun, and shame on you and shame on my dreams. The result is an odd message, yet another echo of Ronnie's enigmatic life philosophy of sorts, with lots of resentment and again pessimism built up through the relentless "shaming," but an interesting spot of doomy poetry all the same.

"That was another riff I had with the band Wild Horses, the intro piece," notes Jimmy. "It had the doom riff—that's what we called that one at the end of the song. It's funny, but all of the other sound effects while that's going on, I got on chorus pedals and stuff like that." Perhaps to rib the anti-"backmasking" zealots, the track closes, in its fade-out, with a backward recording of the word "crucify" followed by "the diver" recorded properly, resulting in "Crucify the diver."

And that was it; *Holy Diver* drew to a doomy close behind the graceful thud of a plush and purple theatrical curtain, offering in its wake all sorts of great songs at a multitude of speeds and moods, with the guitar work of Vivian Campbell setting in stone a legacy for the man that has yet to be exceeded. "Well, yeah," laughs Viv, on this idea of *Holy Diver* being the public's idea of his chief career accomplishment thus far. "I'm glad. When I listen to those solos, I kind of hear the faults. I can see what maybe I was trying to do, but sometimes it's really hard to be objective. There's a certain something to it. I've made a few records and played in a few bands, but most people tend to get excited over that stuff, the early Dio records."

Comparing Ronnie's lot in life with Ozzy's, it's interesting that both experienced renewed career excitement at the same time, Ronnie with the two Black Sabbath albums against Ozzy with his first two solo albums. At this point, Ozzy had lost his guitarist and got a new one in Jake E. Lee, and the records, pointedly a third one in *Bark at the Moon*, kept selling by the truckload. Ronnie, who oddly almost had Jake in his own band, had also lost his guitarist, Tony Iommi. Now his "third" record was doing brisk business, essentially matching the pace of *Mob Rules*. But lots of '70s rockers were pretty happy at the time, putting out records such as *Screaming for Vengeance*, *Blackout*, and *Lick It Up*. Less happy was Ronnie's old guitarist, whose subsequent run of albums—*Born Again*, *Seventh Star*, and *The Eternal Idol*—failed to make much of a dent upside the heads of metal fans in the 1980s.

"God, it wasn't much of a tour, to begin with," recalls Jimmy, with respect to the roadwork for Ronnie's notably high-quality and commercially accepted album. "We did seven shows with Aerosmith, supported them. And then they had a big fight onstage in Ventura, and that was the end of that tour. It was supposed to be a lot more shows. And then we just went out ourselves and did sort of two-thousand-seat theaters and stuff like that. But the last thing we did with Aerosmith is that we went with William Morris, and the agent there said, 'Well, if you sign with me, you'll be in the Long Beach Arena by the end the year.' And this was in August, I think. And sure enough, the thirtieth of December, we were playing Long Beach Arena. So, we went from the Santa Monica Civic to Long Beach Arena in four months. It became big very quick [laughs]."

In fact, the stint with the Toxic Twins lasted ten gigs, Aerosmith apparently lasting four more dates after the Ventura County Fairgrounds dustup in front of seven thousand bemused fans, at which Aerosmith's set lurched to a stop after about forty-five minutes. Touring for Dio began in Antioch, California, in July '83 and continued through until August 20, when Dio played the famed Monsters of Rock festival at Donington, alongside Twisted Sister, ZZ Top, Diamond Head, Meat Loaf, and Whitesnake.

"It was awful," Viv told Steve Hammonds. "It could've been so good. I don't like festivals anyway because I don't think they're worth the money because many people can't see or hear. Whitesnake will be okay, because it will be at night, and they'll have effects. But all the bands before have no chance because everything's hired. Vinny's drum kit was rubbish. You've got to go on there and organize everything while you're still playing. It's chaotic! I like playing live, but I hate doing it in half measures like Donington was. The idea of festivals is like communism. They don't work in practice. The wind blows the sound, too many bands; it just doesn't work. I prefer playing indoors. I get annoyed because you can't do your best. I would prefer them to see Dio headlining."

Things went better with Aerosmith. "We've been opening for them in the States. We did eight shows with them. It was all our crowd, definitely; about 70 percent of the audience were wearing Dio shirts. They come to see Ronnie, not Aerosmith. The crowd wanted heavy metal, and Aerosmith are certainly not that."

Recalls Jimmy on Donington, "When we played Monsters of Rock the first time in '83, when we came over there the album had been out a month and a half or something, and boy, 85,000 people stood up when we came on at 2:30 in the afternoon, and they stayed stood-up until we finished. And then Twisted Sister came on and got completely bottled by the crowd [laughs]. It was funny. I think they were ready for a heavy band that was competent, that had the youth of Vivian, a little bit of the experience of ourselves and Ronnie's voice, and a big, heavy drummer. I mean, Dio was fuckin' ready-made for what Brits love. You know, the heaviest guitar, bass, and drums with the most incredible voice on top of it. It's perfect for metal, you know? And we carried on to the next stage of metal, kind of thing. But metal never goes away for very long. It's always going to come back in some aspect, and you just try to continue doing the same thing.

"But Monsters of Rock in '83; God, it was instant—we sold out the entire tour. For forty minutes of music, we just played Monsters of Rock, one day, one show, and the promoter told us that you just sold out your entire tour, because there were people coming there from Russia, Poland, Israel. I asked some of them backstage, 'ZZ Top are on; how come you're not watching them?' 'We came here to see Dio,' you know? Our album had only been out two months, three months, something like that, and there were already phenomenal, fanatical fans of the band who just weren't interested in anybody else—they just came to see us.

Tools of the live trade.
Martin Popoff archive

"It was amazing, because Diamond Head played first and didn't get a very good reaction. Like I say, we played, everybody stood up, and then when we finished and Twisted Sister unfortunately had to go on; it wasn't such a good scene for them either. They got pounded with mud, bottles, rocks, whatever they could find to throw at them. Because they just . . . I don't think they had . . . they didn't respect them. They didn't like them too much. But metal was doing great. At Monsters of Rock, the patches were everywhere. It was just a sea of Saxon and Maiden and Priest patches, and then when we quickly became successful, the Dio ones in red were put on those jean jackets as well. It was a sea of denim, and it looked great—it was cool."

Joining the band in time for the *Holy Diver* tour was keyboardist Claude Schnell, filling out the sound but relegated to the wings in what is a time-honored heavy metal tradition dating back to both Rainbow and Sabbath.

"I was born in Brooklyn and then I quickly went to France," explains Schnell, in conversation with Jimmy Kay from *The Metal Voice*, "because my grandmother wanted my first grandson to be raised in a family, and there was no family to speak of in New York. My dad had a few scattered cousins, but in France there was my uncle, there was my aunt, there is a family house, basically. So soon after I was born, we moved back to France and I lived in a suburb of Paris in my family home, until I was five or six. The important detail was that I was back in New York by age six to start school in

Tower Theater, Upper Darby, Pennsylvania, December 10, 1983. © *Rudy Childs*

America. In the first post–World War II generation, that was a big plus, to be able to raise a child in America. Because as you probably know from your history, the valor with the Allies emancipating France, that is something that has been looked on fondly for decades.

"I got into the Dio family via kind of a detour through the Hughes Thrall band," continues Schnell. "I was acquainted with Ronnie and Wendy because when Wendy first decided that she was going to try her hand at band management, Rough Cutt was the first band that she considered taking under her wing. So Rough Cutt had arranged to do a showcase, to present ourselves to her, and we were moderately nervous. I mean, not terribly. It was not a big deal. So, we rented a big soundstage at S.I.R. in Los Angeles, one of the bigger rehearsal studios, and we were a pretty seasoned band. Jake E. Lee was on guitar, there was myself, Joey Cristofanilli, who went out with Ratt, there was a drummer by the name of David Alford who disappeared into the woodwork, and then there was Paul Shortino, who seemed to turn up everywhere.

"In any case, we knew what we were doing. Paul and I worked on the songwriting for a long time, so we had our stuff down pretty well. We were just going through the set, and the door to the studio opens and in walks Wendy, with her unmistakable snow-white hair, and behind her was her business partner, a lovely woman by the name of Patty Stein. If you don't recognize the name, she was the wife of Mark Stein, who was perhaps one of the world's best organ players—his claim to fame was being the keyboard player and one of the singers in Vanilla Fudge, Carmine Appice's band. So, Wendy and Patty and Mark walk in—okay, here they are—and Mark slid behind Patty and in comes Ronnie. So now the nervous factor went up a little bit. Mark Stein is a fellow keyboard player, and he's also from Brooklyn. I was a big fan of the Fudge when I was a kid, so I knew who he was. He kinda knew who I was. But having Ronnie there was a kind of pressure we hadn't anticipated. Because as far as we knew, it was only going to be Wendy coming to listen to us.

"In any event, we finish the song we were playing, and just as we finished the last note, they broke into applause, which completely broke the tension. And Ronnie just jumped off the couch and came up to the stage and shook my hand and said, 'Hello, Claude; I'm Ronnie Dio.' 'Yeah, no kidding, dude.' That's basically how we met. But Ronnie was always a very magnanimous, friendly, and openhearted guy. So, the tension was pretty much over instantly. And I daresay, long before we were bandmates, we were well on the way to becoming rather good friends. So that's how it started. And of course, he went on to produce some songs for Rough Cutt, which our more astute listeners may have heard on YouTube. Particularly not for any other reason, unfortunately, other than the fact that Jake was on those demos, and a guitar solo he played in a song called 'A Little Kindness,' for my money, is as good as pretty much any solo he's ever played. If you've not heard the guitar solo in Rough Cutt's 'A Little Kindness,' you owe it to yourself to go crawling through the internet to find it and give it a good listen. Because you will not be disappointed.

"So anyway, Ronnie and I established a relationship based on our mutual interests. We had gone to the same university. We had both been involved in animal rescue and

Aragon Ballroom, Chicago, Illinois, October 21, 1983.
© *Greg Olma*

a bunch of other details. We were both from New York. But beyond that, we just got to be friends. And when he left Black Sabbath to begin the *Holy Diver* record, there were some conversations about me being the keyboard player in the band. But there was some tension whenever that discussion came up, and it became apparent that Jimmy Bain, you know, the legendary bass player from Rainbow and eventually Dio, he had his intention set on being a kind of Geddy Lee, where he would be the bass player as well as the keyboard player. And frankly, if the Dio set had been limited to the *Holy Diver* record with 'Rainbow in the Dark,' he probably could've pulled it off.

"But the truth was that, honestly, I wasn't very excited at the prospect of being known for the nine notes in 'Rainbow in the Dark.' I had been playing keyboards for a very long time. Regardless of how good I was or wasn't, I was ambitious in terms of what I wanted to be able to do. My tastes ran more to . . . well, if you listen to the Hughes Thrall record, that would give you a pretty good idea. So it was clear that Dio was basically going to be a three-piece band with just the occasional keyboard flourish. That didn't really speak to me. Plus it was an afterthought. That person wasn't going to be a member of the band. He was just going to be somebody that was there to do the parts that nobody else could do.

"So that was fine," figures Claude. "I was perfectly happy to continue playing with Hughes Thrall, which was very challenging. Of course, Glenn Hughes is one of the great musical geniuses of our time, and what I learned from him was just invaluable. And Pat Thrall, of course, an equally important musician and guitarist. Unfortunately, Glenn was in a place in his life where he was still wrestling with his demons. And as a result, Pat and Glenn decided that they would part ways. Which meant that Hughes Thrall had kind of come to an end. So that gave me pause, because I didn't really know where the next step was going to be. But Glenn was very anxious to have me continue on with him in what was going to be the Glenn Hughes Band.

"Unfortunately, in the course of doing our demos, it became obvious to me that if it was going to become a successful project, it was going to be a very, very difficult environment to exist in. For my taste, being the young New Yorker that I was, there was just too much distraction. It was more about Glenn as the legend than it was about Glenn as the musician. There were many, many distractions when we were in the studio. I mean, the music was brilliant. Glenn's singing was without parallel. But unfortunately, there were so many other things that intruded into the process that the amount of time we actually spent playing or writing was unacceptably low for me.

"And then this reached its crescendo. Max Norman, who was producing the demos, very famous producer from the Pat Travers days, he and I had to sneak out of the Record Plant without Glenn knowing it because we just had to escape what that evening had turned into. But because of the way we left, I ended up having to walk home from the studio. Which was just fine. The sun was coming up; it was late summer; I think it was a September morning. And it was really good to cleanse the soul and to think about the crossroads that I was finding myself at.

"You know, I left Rough Cutt for the opportunity to play with Glenn," reflects Claude. "I kind of passed on the Dio option, even though it wasn't actually offered to me at that point. But because of my loyalty to Glenn, here I was really with no idea what I was going to do with the rest of my life after that night. The one thing I knew was that I couldn't carry on with Glenn the way we were going. So, it took me about an hour and a half to walk home from where the studio was. And I get home, my wife is just about to leave—'Hi, baby; bye-bye, see you'—and all I wanted to do was find the bed and become horizontal for a while.

"Just at that point the phone rings, and I answered it and it's Ronnie. As if there was any doubt when you hear his voice, you knew who it was. I go, 'Hey, Ronnie, what's going on?' 'Did I get you at a bad time?' 'Well, no, actually; it's good to hear your voice.' I didn't want to bore him with the details of the previous night. Because Ronnie, having known Glenn for a decade, he certainly knew and shared his stories about him. He said, 'Listen, the reason I'm calling is that I want you to join the band.' 'Excuse me?' He says, 'Well, so as it turns out, we're going to start touring pretty soon. We don't have enough newer material with the *Holy Diver* album to cover the amount of time we're going to have to play in our set, and we're going to have to supplement the Dio tunes with some Rainbow and possibly some Sabbath as well, and there's no way that Jimmy can cover the keyboard parts in that. So, if you'd be interested in doing it, I would look no further. You will be the guy.'

"I'm like, 'Wow, well, I can't tell you how fortuitous this timing is.' And then I proceeded to give him a little bit of a taste of what had happened the night before, to which Ronnie said, 'Well, you know, that's Glenn. If you play with Glenn, you have to assume that you're going to have to be dealing with those consequences. So let me tell you a few things about it. You're actually just going to be a sideman. The band is really just going to be Jimmy, Viv, and Vinny and myself. But if things go well, I can't see any reason that keyboards can't be a part of the band. But at least in the initial touring cycle, we're going to want you to be offstage.'

"And of course that didn't really sit well with me. But after the night I just had, as far as I was concerned, the stage was the last place I was going to be again anyway. And I was armed with the knowledge that if I said no, there would undoubtedly be a parade of a hundred guys behind me just chomping at the bit to have that opportunity. Plus which, I'd already grown very, very fond of Ronnie. Vinny was on his way to being my best friend. So yeah, I don't care, sure, let's do it. So that was it. That was how I worked my way into the Dio family in earnest. And that's how I got to be on the *Holy Diver* tour, at the end of which Ronnie approached me and asked me if I wanted to make this kind of a full-time commitment."

Now as a five-piece ready to take on the world, a typical Dio set list of the day might have included, from the new album, "Stand Up and Shout," "Straight Through the Heart," "Shame on the Night," and "Rainbow in the Dark." "Children of the Sea" and "Heaven and Hell" (Ronnie was wont to remark that the version on *Live Evil* was good for helping you sleep) sprung from Ronnie's Sabbath experience, with the show rounded out by a Vinny Appice drum solo as well as "Man on the Silver Mountain" and "Starstruck," both hearkening back to Ronnie's days with Rainbow. "Evil Eyes" surprised the crowd, due to its non-LP status at the time.

Asked by Steve Hammonds if he enjoys seeing a sampling of Rainbow and Black Sabbath songs in the set list, Campbell told him at the time, "I love playing them better than the Dio ones, not because I think they're better than Dio songs, but because we wrote, recorded, and rehearsed the songs time and time again. It's maybe okay if we didn't play them for a year. But to me, it's refreshing to play that Sabbath stuff, as I haven't played it a lot before. Also, there are two reasons we have to play the songs. One is because we're a new band and have to do them; otherwise we would have to do the whole LP, and I don't think some of it's suitable to play live. And the second reason is that I think we have a right to, because we have two guys from both Sabbath and Rainbow, and what's more, they were songs that Vinny, Jimmy, and Ronnie were all involved in, and people want to hear them again. I don't think Ronnie's trying to live on past glories."

Geoff Barton asked Ronnie if he'd always envisioned paying homage to his past. "Yes, with Sabbath numbers as well as Rainbow numbers," answered Dio. "I happen to like 'Heaven and Hell' very much. I think it's probably my favorite out of all the songs I've written. It was something Sabbath had never done before, to play that well and write that well, and that was very important to me. 'Man on the Silver Mountain' has become something of a trademark; I think it would be foolish if I didn't do it live. As for the rest, well, 'Stargazer' and 'Starstruck' I'm beginning not to care too much about anymore. But I always like to keep some connection with the past, and that's not just to please my older fans. Like today, I saw some shiny little fourteen-year-old faces singing along to 'Man on the Silver Mountain,' and it was great."

Speaking with Paul Elliott from *Music Express* the following year, he doubled down on this assertion, saying, "I set myself up as what I am, and I should play 'Heaven and

Hell' just as Ozzy should play 'Paranoid.' Robert Plant has been very wrong not to touch on any Zeppelin songs; it was his mark, his stamp that made those songs, just as it was Jimmy's and Bonzo's and John Paul's. Robert has to do what he has to do. I'm just saying that if it were me, I'd draw on the past. It works. It lifts the set up and takes it to a different place. It's not just 'Oh, we've heard that' or 'Oh, there's the new album.' You can excite them with something else, something that's become maybe legendary. And let's face it, 'Stairway to Heaven' certainly was that."

After taking September off, the band picked up in October with Queensryche in tow, the well-regarded, highly technical debut *Queensryche* EP having just been released the previous month. These were western US dates, ranging from a rare low of 1,200 people upward to 6,000, with some second shows being added in cities that sold out at 5,000. After a handful of dates with Queensryche, the backup slot shifted in mid-October to Rough Cutt (who, as alluded to, Wendy Dio would soon be managing) and then Y&T, with crowds averaging in the three thousand range. Other backup acts through the year included Mountain and, yet again, Queensryche.

Over to the UK at the end of October and into November, Dio was joined by Waysted, the raucous hard-rock band formed by UFO's Pete Way and Paul Chapman, who also wobbled aboard as the good ship Dio took on nine European countries.

"It was great for everybody," laughs Wendy Dio, responding to the assertion that a big part of the Dio band's success had to do with the enormous appetite for metal that arose out of the NWOBHM. "It was a great time, because it comes around in circles, rock, every ten years, a resurgence of heavy metal. But you know, it never goes away. Those fans are the most loyal, wonderful fans. There's nothing like the heavy metal kids. There's a lot of depressed people a lot of times that have to hang on to something. And this is something to remember, that Ronnie really loved his fans so much; he loved the people that were there. He loved them and always remembered that where he was was because of those people."

Dio recommenced touring North America again on December 10, 1983, in Pennsylvania, playing, variously, with Anvil (in Toronto, Anvil's hometown, at the venerable Massey Hall), Humble Pie, Danny Spanos, Dokken, Black 'n Blue, again Rough Cutt and Y&T, but most regularly with Twisted Sister, who supported the first leg of this second go-round. True to Jimmy's version of events, Dio played Long Beach Arena on the thirtieth of December (with Y&T and Dokken in support, both no doubt helping to sell a few ducats), to a crowd estimated to be around eight thousand damned souls strong.

In tandem with these strong show attendance numbers cited, *Holy Diver* would be certified gold in the US quite quickly, reaching that status on September 12, 1984, a couple of months after the release of the next album. On March 21, 1989, the album would reach platinum.

"With the Dio band years, everything was new for us," reflects Wendy, "because of course Ronnie could now do whatever he wanted—although it was quite frightening too, because that was a big responsibility for him. And in the beginning, we had some money, but we didn't have a lot of money. We actually took a big, huge mortgage out, a second mortgage out on our home, to start the tour off with [laughs], and to make sure that we could have the same things that we had, that we enjoyed in Sabbath. It was a new and exciting time. The band was on fire. We didn't expect *Holy Diver* to jump out of the box the way it did, but it did, and it was incredible. It was an incredible ride."

I asked Wendy if she remembered her first business meeting as a manager. "Yes [laughs], I had a meeting with an agent that was representing Ronnie at the time, and I was late, ten minutes late, and he tells me, 'You have twenty minutes left.' And I said, 'Well, I'll tell you what. You've got all the time in the world because you're fired.' And I went on from there and I was told by many people that you don't know what you're doing, you should relinquish it to someone else, and whatever. And many years later, everyone said I had done a good job. I mean, I didn't just come into this business as a wife. I worked for booking agencies in England; I'd worked for attorneys in the contract department; I knew a lot of things, the inner workings of record companies. And the touring aspect, I learned that, and I learned it very fast."

Years later, Ronnie still looked back at the *Holy Diver* experience with something approaching amazement. "The push we had was a push from the fans, not a push from the record company. The record company didn't have a clue what we were doing. They called three weeks into the recording and said, 'What are you doing?,' and I said, 'The album I owe ya.' Because I had a solo deal with Warner Bros. People are stupid. Record company people are really stupid. Especially in those days they were. So, the push was because the kids liked what we did. *Holy Diver* was a great album with great players, and it just sold itself. The same as *Heaven and Hell* did. It was a people's record. And at the end of the day, when an album's successful, the record company always says they did it. And they didn't. We did it ourselves. That was a great time. But I'd been doing it for a long time by then. I wasn't going through a whole lot of new learning experiences at that point, so it was what it was. Who knew that it was going to be that much of a classic album?"

CHAPTER 3

"Being unaccustomed at that elevation, we'd take two steps and we couldn't move anymore."

THE LAST IN LINE

"It's twice the album *Holy Diver* was," pronounced Ronnie James Dio, explaining to the esteemed Geoff Barton what to expect with his second album, just around the corner as they spoke back in the early summer of 1984. "Mind you, I've only just come around to forming this opinion. I thought *Holy Diver* was a very, very nice first effort, so I didn't have to bother to try convincing myself that it was good. With this one, I don't know why, maybe it was because *Holy Diver* had so much impact and we had something to prove, I just felt that it fell down in some areas. But now, after listening to it a few times, I'm really pleased with it. Very pleased.

"If you look inside the songs, I think you'll still find the same old Ronnie Dio trying to come out, the man who doesn't seem to be making a point until you've heard the material a few times and you begin to say to yourself, 'Hey, yeah, I think that's what he means.' I hardly ever make the lyrical messages up front. I think if you start forcing and feeding people with opinions, eventually they'll say, 'Aw, cut it out, we've got imaginations too, you know.' People come up to me and say, 'I know what you wrote that song about; you were talking about so-and-so.' And I say, 'Yeah, you're right.' And then the next minute someone else will offer me a completely different interpretation. And I'll say, 'You're right as well.' The true meaning of the song only exists in the ears of the listener."

Riding a nice wave through two squarely successful Sabbath albums (three, counting the live one) and an instant classic of a debut in 1983's *Holy Diver*, Ronnie could—and would—do no wrong, at least for now. *The Last in Line* stormed out of the gates with

The UK Vertigo record label, plus a "We Rock" single and a "We Rock" ad. *Martin Popoff archive*

the military magic of drummer Vinny Appice, each track thenceforth solidifying Dio as a powerhouse band brimming with chemistry, from the man at the top all the way through to the reverberating bottom end. Jimmy Bain had proven himself a writer extraordinaire, Vivian Campbell as the most musical guitar hero runnin' the fret boards of the day, bar none, and then Appice as a hard hitter with almost ethereal finesse. And then there was Ronnie, an artfully frightening lyricist delivering his sage-like pronouncements with a voice that could cut steel.

So yes, *The Last in Line* regally announces itself with a single-stroke-snare onslaught from Vinny Appice, providing the framework for one heck of a showcase barn-wrecker called "We Rock," a track that Viv Campbell acknowledges was written by Ronnie—lyrics *and* music.

"'We Rock' was the last song written, as a matter of fact," explains Ronnie. "First song on the album, but the last song written. We felt we wanted this one to be like 'Stand Up and Shout' from *Holy Diver*—a type of anthem. So, we wrote the song, and I took it away and wrote that melody and the lyrics for it after the track was written, much the same way 'Stand Up and Shout' was written. I'm jumping to the other album, but that was also an interesting story. Jimmy Bain and Vivian Campbell went back to England after we had completed the album, and 'Stand Up and Shout' was only a backing track. So, after they left once again, I had to write a melody and lyrics for it. So, they had never heard the song before, and we sent them over a copy of it. So, I felt confident with what we were going to be doing with 'We Rock.'"

Curiously, back in '84, Ronnie had bristled somewhat when Geoff Barton used the word "anthem." "The only anthemic part of that song is its punch line. I don't write stupid songs. I don't consider myself to be a stupid writer or a stupid person. It's a song that says, 'We rock.' We had one like it on the last album, 'Stand Up and Shout.' I just happen to like numbers like that, numbers that aren't your traditional dyed-in-the-wool headbangers, but which nevertheless give people a chance to participate. It makes no sense for 'We Rock' not to be on the album; I'm sure if the record had been on release and people had had the chance to hear it prior to today's show, they would've been chanting, 'We rock! We rock!' before we went out onstage. It's that kind of song, only unlike many of its ilk, it's not insulting. It's not condescending."

Definitely not, because Ronnie has a point: the verses, even though they are brief and there are only two, seem to have nothing to do with how Dio rocks. And the opening sequence just might be the most glory-bound dozen seconds of the entire Dio canon, and a large part of its largeness and largesse comes down to the fill that Vinny does just before the guys launch into the song's quick groove, but also his snare-dominated intro, some well-placed bass notes from Jimmy, and of course the song's hard-charging riff.

"My favorite Dio albums are the first and second ones," says Appice, who looks on his years with the band not without some bitterness. "And then least favorite would be all the rest of them [laughs]. It just was because the first and second ones were fun, and everybody got to do what they wanted to do. We would just jam and come up with stuff. It was fun, we were partying, coming up with stuff, recording it—'Yeah, that's cool!'—and it just shows in the music.

"The second one, we weren't in L.A. when we did it, whereas with the first one we were. We went to Caribou Ranch and did it, and it was the same vibe and then Ronnie started taking over control a little bit more. We had about six or seven, six and a half songs written. So, we recorded those first, and then it got down to 'Geez, we need a couple more songs, man.' So, I think 'I Speed at Night' was written up there. And then one we put together up there was 'We Rock,' which I think we did in a couple of days, and then Ronnie wrote some good lyrics. I believe a lot of the chords on the chorus was Ronnie's work. That album didn't have the same exact vibe as the debut, but it was still good.

"And then the third one, he started worrying about, well, we can't do that chord from this chord. A lot of the stuff was getting more bitsy, too many little parts here and there. And more keyboards were added, which kinda smoothed the sound out a bit. With each album, Ronnie took more and more control, and everybody didn't throw their ideas around as easily. It was kind of more walking on eggshells. And that's bad, because then you're inhibiting the creativity of all these guys you've got in the band. So, it shows, and shows in the sales of the album. The first two albums did really, really well, and these other albums didn't do as well; they only sold on the strength of the other ones. And my theory would be, if you've got a winning formula, do the same thing the next time. You've got four people writing some good stuff; let's do the same thing. You don't have to have an ego thing involved with it all the time and have control over it."

Vinny chimes in on the presence and importance of bassist Jimmy Bain within Dio's solid, sparkling, early chemistry. "He's great, a great guy, a great bass player to play with. He's not a technical wizard on the bass but he's got a great sound, and he just lays down a great foundation. So, it's great for me and him, because I kinda overplay sometimes. I played lead drums, and he held it down. Or we would come up with a couple things together. We had a great sound; he would just plug in and boom! And he's a good writer, came up with a lot of ideas, a lot of riffs. He had songs written, and when we were stuck, he always came up a something. So, he was great to work with, Jimmy Bain."

Vinny with lots of things to hit. Tower Theater, Upper Darby, Pennsylvania, December 10, 1983. © *Rudy Childs*

The revealing word there is overplay. But Vinny is being modest: his fills, his style, his sound . . . rarely has a metal band been so defined by the percussive input and creativity of the man pounding the skins (one might include in this camp Saxon's Nigel Glockler, or indeed, both John Bonham and Jason Bonham!). And like Led Zeppelin (and Black Country Communion, come to think of it, who, granted, also had keyboards), Dio was special because they were a band with four weapons. But Vinny is undercutting himself when he says he overplays. Fortunately, and blessedly for the fans of Dio, he plays a lot, and he plays interestingly, but what he does never feels like overplaying.

"I don't know, I guess you can tell it's me when I'm playing, just from the way I tune the drums," reflects Appice, when asked about his sound. "And I always play with the front bass drum head off, so it just fucking blows some wind out there; it kicks a lot of bass drum out. And I play really hard; I like to play as hard as I can, with dynamics and that kind of stuff. I would say I'm more of a . . . not a lead drummer, but I take more chances than a lot of guys would. I like to play for other drummers. Not overplay, but I kinda do it from whatever comes out, from the heart, you know? So, I do think about other drummers when we're recording and making albums. I always think of other drummers because that's the way I grew up. I listened to Bonham and my brother, Carmine, plus Ian Paice, Mitch Mitchell, people like that who played, you know? You listen to it as another drummer and you go, 'Whoa, what's that?!' You know, guitar solos were in every song—well, in those days they were—and guitar players could get off on the solos, so why not drums? Why should drums just plod along on two and four? There should be something interesting behind it."

At the mention of a parallel between the memorableness of his fills and those of Neil Peart, Vinny says, "Well, thank you, that's a nice complement. Neil Peart is very musical and he's a great drummer. Sometimes I would work out stuff in my head and hear it and think, well, I have to play this way until it comes out right. A lot of it is just being inspired by the people I'm playing with or the song itself. If everyone was kicking ass and Ronnie was singing great, it just inspired me to blow one out [laughs]. Kind of like a fart, you know [laughs]. And in terms of my actual sound and tone, a drummer can develop a sound just from years of playing, just the way they hold the sticks and hit the drums. I mean, I can get on somebody's set, and you can tell it's not them playing because they have their own sound and I have my own sound. On my own drums, I do certain things. I take the heads off. I used to play with a lot of the heads off the bottom of the tom-toms. And the head is definitely off on the bass drum. And I use Aquarian heads with the dot on them so they have a lot of punch, and you can smack them really hard. One of my favorite drum sounds would be [on Black Sabbath's] *Dehumanizer*, I would say. But it would sound outdated now. You know, I don't like to keep getting the same exact sound. If I did something now, it would be a little different."

Back to *The Last in Line*, "We Rock" gallops to a fading close, with ever more examples of Vinny's imaginative fills holding attention for us drummers. We're now primed for the title track: a song of pronounced contrast versus the wall-of-sound opener. As befits its title status, "The Last in Line" is an epic that had no problem enduring as a Dio live favorite through to the end of the band in 2008.

Ronnie summarizes the song's inspirational lyric. "Well, once again, I write songs for people, how people feel about being lonely, for being picked on for not being the greatest physical specimens on Earth—things like that just happen. So, this one for me describes people who persevere through all the stones and slings and arrows that are tossed at them. 'The last in line,' that's usually where people like that are placed, the end of the line. But to me, just because you're at the end of the line doesn't mean that you can't succeed. And I usually find that the people who are willing to stay there at the end of the line will succeed, so it was just written about that generally."

Ronnie elaborated on this theme within his music, telling Sam Dunn that "I view the music that I make as being so much about the little man, which is perfect for me. But about everyman. I tend to observe what we have in society where we have people who are castigated because they're too tall, too short, too fat, too thin, too stupid, too intelligent. Hair too black or too brown, whatever. All the little things that you could . . .

this is what drives humanity, because we're basic at the end of the day. If you see Cindy Crawford or if you see Natasha Henstridge, you go, 'Wow, I want to be like them.' But what about the ugly chick or the ugly guy? What about those people? I tend to write about them because I think because metal music has always been looked down upon, then obviously it's going to be something that affects people who have been looked down upon for their, perhaps, physical attributes that don't . . . they just don't conform to what we see on the cover of *Elle* magazine. So, I've written songs about them. That's where it comes from; for me it's about people and their problems day to day."

Asked by Sam if he can personally identify with the sentiment, Ronnie figures, "I always felt that way. As a kid I felt shorter than everybody else. Now what it depends upon is how you accept that or how you don't accept that, and I never accepted that. So, excuse me, I'm shorter than you. Yeah, and? Well, you're shorter than me. Oh, well, good. Well, you're taller than me—fine. Life goes on, doesn't it? Those are stupid things, that people attack physicality. But what that does, unfortunately, is destroy the lives of poor people who accept that. You're too fat. Well, what's a little fat girl in school? Poor soul, she doesn't deserve that. She may have a fat exterior but inside is this wonderful butterfly waiting to get out and fly around and give something to the world. But we as human beings have this tendency to really hurt people, to really kick them. So, I've written songs about that most of the time because it didn't bother me, and I always wanted other people to know that, hey, look at me, look how little I am. Didn't stop me, did it? I'm not afraid of anything or anyone or trying to achieve. I'm not afraid of that. So, look, if I can do it, you can do it. That's always been the thing I've written about more than anything. I've always written songs from the perspective of the average person."

Martin Popoff archive

Conversely, in official press at the time of release, Ronnie had this somewhat, ahem, enigmatic explanation of an extra little diamond hidden in this particular song. "'The Last in Line' is about people who are last in line, the last searchers to find out 'Are we good or are we bad?' and 'What is good and what is bad?' It's the search by the people for the truth, their own truth."

Dio framed it somewhat this way when speaking with Geoff Barton, explaining that "it's basically a song about people who are looking for the answer to a question. I tend to cover the subject a lot; the *Holy Diver* album obvious dealt with this topic: What is good and what is evil? What does evil look like? What does good look like? Everyone said the cover depicted a devil drowning a priest. But how do they know? How did they know that the devil wasn't disguised as the priest and vice versa? That's on the outside. What's on the inside? 'Are we evil or divine? We're the last in line.' I just wanted to write a song about people who have balls enough to go out and search for the truth, for the truth that matters. It's important to find out."

Remarks Claude on the construction of the song, "So on 'The Last in Line,' even though there are those who would take issue with this, but you can believe whoever you choose to, the intro and the chorus part were written on keyboards. Now I'm pretty sure that it was Viv who wrote the rhythm track for that song. But however the intro began, he didn't have the same voicing that became prominent when I played it on keyboards. Same thing with the chorus. Which is why, if you listen to the chorus—I talked to Ronnie about this briefly, and he would give me the satisfaction of confirming it—but if you listen to the chorus on the title track of the *Last in Line* album, you can barely hear the guitar. It's virtually all keyboards. I mean, the joke was 'Yeah, you must've tipped Angelo [Arcuri, engineer] to put the keyboards higher in the mix.' But the truth is, there isn't a speck of sound on any Dio record that didn't pass Ronnie's approval."

Claude is philosophical on the subject of the writing credits across these early Dio records. "I think because Ronnie got the short end of the stick in much of the Rainbow credits, as well as possibly Sabbath . . . I mean, I don't really know Ronnie's business, nor would I presume to have asked him. Because that's something most people don't like to talk about anyway. But I suspect that the fact that there was the omnipresence of 'All lyrics and melodies written by Ronnie James Dio' was just to get it out of the way that this was his project. Every word was his, every note was his, and as such it was the band Dio. It wasn't the collective assortment of everybody chipping in, because that isn't how the songs were written. Ronnie would write the lyrics, Ronnie would write the vocal melodies, and as far as the music went, everyone would contribute. We would do a jam or whoever the guitar player du jour was would have some kind of a riff, and Ronnie would play with it a little bit and Vinny would put down the rhythm. And Jimmy was actually good at fleshing out the simplest ideas for making the more sing-songy things work. But all of that stuff qualified mostly as arrangement."

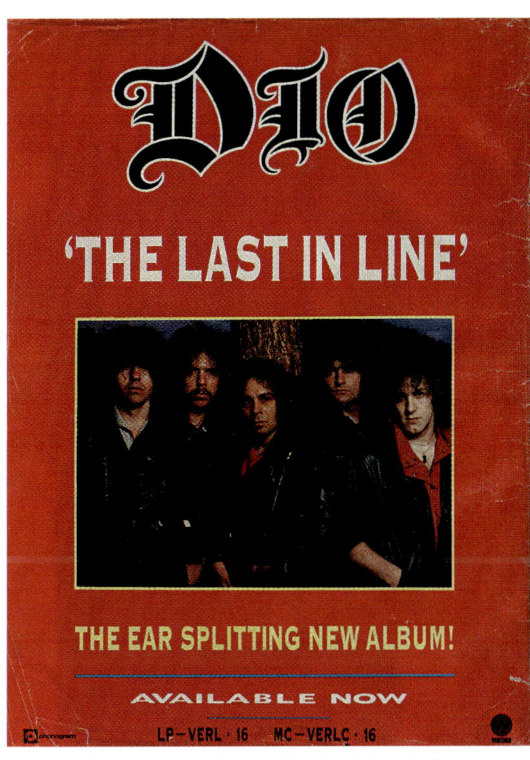

UK ad for the new album. Claude Schnell pictured as a card-carrying member of the band (*second from left*). *Martin Popoff archive*

As for a stickier topic when it comes to Claude, well, that would be this "band member versus sideman" business.

"Well, when you get into the area of semantics, it's usually subject to interpretation," reflects Schnell. "For better or worse, for the first three albums, the first four years of that band, '83 to '86, we were a band. There's no question about it. The band isn't determined by who gets paid what. What makes a band is much more visceral than the business arrangements. It has to do with how you hang out and the mutual respect. It's very hard to describe. Especially for me, because on the first three records, I basically was just a salaried player. But regardless of who says otherwise, I was in the band. I mean, we were in a band. Ronnie would call me in the middle of the night to go hang out—it was a band.

"Now if you want to get strictly semantic about it, a band is, for example, Aerosmith, where the guys are all students together and they started it as a group. No matter what they do, they split everything equally. That's a band. But that's kind of a dated paradigm; I don't think that really exists anymore. Most bands now are just about the songwriter and the guys who come along. Like Bon Jovi, for example: Bon Jovi may give the illusion of being a band, but I can guarantee you that if you got into the accounting books, that isn't the way it is."

"There's a story about that one," says Ronnie, back to *The Last in Line*, concerning one of the lazier, hazier, poppier songs on the record—namely, "Breathless," a track that has fallen by the wayside with the elapsing, collapsing years in terms of stature across this now universally respected album.

"We did the *Last in Line* album in Colorado at a studio called Caribou Ranch; I loved that studio. It was a studio 10,000 feet up in the air (in Nederland, actually 8,000 feet) owned by a guy named James William Guercio. He was the guy who put together Blood Sweat & Tears, and he eventually owned a soccer team in Denver. We hit right at the beginning of the very worst storm they had in about thirty years. It dumped about 8 or 9 feet of snow, and being unaccustomed at that elevation, we'd take two steps, and we couldn't move anymore; we just couldn't get our breath. So, when we did 'Breathless' . . . the song starts with that breathing. So, I did it first, and hell, I couldn't breathe in about ten seconds, because we hadn't been acclimated to that height yet. So, everybody tried it, and almost everybody almost passed out. Finally, we got our engineer to do it, and he did pass out at the end of it [laughs]. He finished it, but then he just went down in the heat. We had oxygen tanks all around the studio, so we did finally get acclimated, and there was no problem after that. But 'Breathless' was exactly what it says, especially for the engineer."

Pretty cool lyric on this one, with Ronnie sort of abstractly addressing a sense of hope and potential in the character portrayed in the song. As with most of his lyrics, he (or she)—there are lots of lost girls in his songs as well, not just angry male metalheads—begins at the usual place, at the end of the line. But there's a sense that the character ultimately triumphs, fueled by a sort of "breathless" pent-up energy and enthusiasm.

Without a doubt, "Breathless"—music by Viv, lyrics by Ronnie—was a commercial rock track, as was "Mystery," a happy, melodic mess, the two marring what is otherwise a dead-perfect record of shiny diamonds. "Yeah, they were," agrees Ronnie. "With the first album, having 'Rainbow in the Dark' the focal point of that record, we had a record company that obviously felt that we needed to stay in that vein. I didn't agree, but they were paying the bill, so I tried to be as understanding as I could, tried to give something back to them, because after all, we were writing 'The Last in Line,' and maybe they didn't want to hear that either, but they were giving us latitude to do that. But 'Breathless' and 'Mystery' were attempts to be somewhat like 'Rainbow in the Dark.' You'll hear some similarities there."

Even as far back as the press junket around the time of the record's release, Ronnie pulled no punches with respect to the inclusion of such "commercial rock tracks," remarking to *Hit Parader*'s Rick Evans, "I don't even like some of the songs on the

Tower Theater, Upper Darby, Pennsylvania, December 10, 1983. © *Rudy Childs*

album. There's one song, 'Mystery,' I actually hate. It's very pop oriented, and that's not where my strengths lie. I feel like I'm selling out my musical principles by including it on this album. But the other guys in the group liked the song, so I relented. I just don't want fans coming up to me saying, 'Hey, Dio, you sold out.' I want them to know 'Mystery' wasn't my idea—I was just being a nice guy." Ronnie added that "the material on *The Last in Line* is not that different from the songs I did with Rainbow or Sabbath. I also don't think it's a much-better album than my first solo LP, *Holy Diver*, which came out last year. *The Last in Line* is a strong record which happens to be the right record at the right time. Its success just proves that persistence is rewarded."

"He hated that song," adds Wendy Dio. "That was the start of the demise of him and Vivian. Because it wasn't all about money. It was about the difference in their writing. Now Vivian wanted to get more commercial, just like Ritchie wanted to do, and that's why that song 'Mystery' was on there. And Ronnie's like, 'You know, this is not what I'm going to do. I didn't do it before, and now that it's my own band I'm not going to do that'—musical differences were a big thing as well as the money. Same thing happened with Rainbow: a lot of that was the record label talking to Ritchie, saying, you know, 'I think you should go more commercial; you need to get a hit,' and Ritchie wanting Ronnie to write more commercial songs, more love songs. And Ronnie just stuck to his guns. He said that's not what he wanted to do, and he was very unhappy. And then in the end, they basically parted ways—he got fired, really."

In another interview also conducted at the time of release, Ronnie brought up his most recent parting of ways, remarking that "the fact that I brought up the subject of Sabbath first is a defensive gesture on my part, because I feel it's better for me to get it out in the open and out of the way before the inevitable questions are asked. I don't know if I'll ever get through an interview without Sabbath coming up. In a sense it's to be expected because I made some good lasting music in that band. I do feel however that this album is a big step forward, away from the Sabbath connection. People no longer consider me that former singer with Sabbath. In the public's eyes, I'm now the singer in Dio."

Further pontificating on Sabbath, who, post-Ronnie, had featured Ian Gillan in the ranks before that also crashed, Ronnie told Geoff Barton, "It was wrong getting Ian Gillan in, for a start. It was also wrong hiring Bev Bevan. It's not Bev's fault. He's a great drummer. But Tony and Geezer should have realized that they were Black Sabbath, not Black Purple or Electric Light Sabbath or whatever. What they should've done in the first place was to find a young singer, taking their time, and discovered someone who wrote in a young way and who could really sing and identify with younger people. With Ian Gillan, Sabbath once again became dinosaurs, and that hurt me a lot, because I thought I provided them with a new lease of life. It was crazy for them to throw that away."

But in 1984, Ian was back with Deep Purple. "Let me take this one step at a time," reflected Ronnie. "Deep Purple were my favorite band. They made me want to do what I'm doing now. Ritchie Blackmore was the greatest influence in my life. I've got incredible respect for the man's musical intelligence and general intelligence. Now that Deep Purple

Ronnie channels his muse at the Tower Theater, Upper Darby, Pennsylvania, December 10, 1983. © *Rudy Childs* have got back together again, I want them to be incredibly successful. I'm sure that they'll make an album and that technically it will be a masterpiece. And then I think they will tour, and I think that tour will probably grind to a halt somewhere in the middle. I hope it doesn't, but it must be very difficult to leave a situation because of personal differences and then try to make it work again after all this time. I think that will be very hard."

Ronnie was partly right, with Purple making more of a dent than he predicted. *Perfect Strangers* would pretty quickly go platinum, with the band lasting through its tour cycle to create *The House of Blue Light*. That record didn't reach RIAA certification, and soon the team would implode once again.

Back to the present day, I asked Ronnie if *The Last in Line* was written and recorded at the height of his interest in the dark side.

"No, I was just cruising along, very happy with writing that kind of subject matter," says Ronnie, with the vagueness I've long since come to expect on the subject. "We carried on after this one with the *Sacred Heart* album, which had its dark moments as well, but no, that wasn't the culmination for me. I look at every project as being a beginning.

"But what it did spell was the end of Vivian's tenure in the band. I think he just started becoming more confident with himself and more opinionated, and unfortunately his opinions were wrong. And I felt his work ethic was falling apart and he had other agendas, other things he wanted to do, and that doesn't fly with me. I don't mind if people do other projects, but if your first concern is not for the band, not for the group, I really don't want you around. So that was the beginning of the end of it all. But making the album up there was absolutely incredible—the location, the facilities, were beautiful. Shortly after we finished making that record, a fire started in the studio. It started on the top floor, where there was a pool table, and it burned on and nobody knew it, because it was the middle of the night. And the fire in the top room undermined the flooring, and the pool table fell to the next floor, landing right on the desk, the console, and destroyed that, and the fire carried on, and then the piano and the desk went down to the next floor and destroyed what was there as well, and the studio was completely gone. And he decided he wasn't going to rebuild it again, and he never did."

But well before the studio was no more, Dio was fortunate to rock it hard and fast with the production of "I Speed at Night," fourth track on *The Last in Line*, the song blessed, cursed, and damned with a scorcher of a riff wrapped around a sparkling, energetic lyric. "Yeah, we wanted to do something as fast as we could," explains Ronnie. "So, we said, 'Pick a tempo, Vinny,' and he did, and we just wrote the song. The title certainly fits the mood of the song. We wanted something really, really quick, something faster than anything we'd ever played before."

The "I Speed at Night" lyric finds Ronnie further building a reputation for writing words that paint great pictures while also containing layers of meaning. In this case, despite the title, there's nothing about driving a car (or doing speed!); rather, the idea is that his brain just works better at night, with favorable outcomes upon any task more likely than those attempted in the daytime.

For the record, none of the riffs on the second album came from Sweet Savage songs. "No, anything he had ever written before was on the first album," says Ronnie, referring to Vivian's well-regarded pre-Dio band back in Ireland. "So, with *The Last in Line,* the slate was clean. We wiped him out of whatever he had.

"Viv is one of the hottest young players around," said Ronnie, out on the press trail at the time. "And in my opinion, he's also the most underpublicized. I see so many guitarists turning up in different magazines, like Yngwie Malmsteen. To me, he's nothing more than a younger Ritchie Blackmore. I think that's what he wants to be, and it's sometimes embarrassing the way he cavorts and does his thing. The guy's a good player, but he gets all this incredible press, which I don't think he deserves in the way Vivian does. Viv is totally undersung, but he's happy within himself because he knows just how well he plays. Most of the people who come to see Dio are real hard-core guitar fanatics, and he's out there playing and they're enjoying a really great guitarist.

"Ritchie is a great lead player, who plays with a lot of emotion and empathy for what's around him and how he feels at the time. He's just got a good rapport with the guitar, and his sound is still very unique. But Ritchie isn't much of a rhythm player; he doesn't like to do it very much and just kind of twangs away on the E string here and there to keep the feel. He allows the keyboards, bass, and drums to carry the rest of it. Tony Iommi, on the other hand, is a great rhythm player, really brilliant. As a soloist he has his moments, but he isn't nearly the player Ritchie is. Viv fits both categories. He's great on rhythm, and that's one of the reasons I wanted him in the beginning. Plus, he has lots of raw energy, which really excites me. Quite often, his solos are just beyond belief. We sat there with our mouths on the floor on several occasions, and that's what it used to be like with Ritchie. With Viv, I've really got the best of both worlds."

Pretty cool point that Ronnie is making here: indeed, you can tell that Viv has the rhythmic sixth sense of a good drummer, and you can hear that in both his rock-solid rhythm guitar playing, despite substantial complexity in his riffs, as well as in his soloing, where he regularly becomes the six-string equivalent of his drummer. In this respect, he's playing with the awareness that he's in a power trio, knowing that if he stays anchored for his solos on the records, that will make the band sound better onstage when it comes time for him to let rip.

"I don't mind responsibility at all," continued Ronnie, in the same interview, with respect to the pressures of fronting his own band. "Someone has to do it, and I found that it comes quite naturally to me. So, I might as well apply my talents in the right direction. There are definitely extra pressures when it's your own project, though. If the band fails, then you're the one that has to take the rap. If you succeed, then you have to share the triumphs with the people around you. But that's fine by me. When I joined Sabbath, everything was great. The band had a lot to offer, and it was fun. In the end, though, it all fell part. There were too many knives being shoved in people's backs. I was a bit disappointed at the way things turned out. But there you go. When I left Rainbow, Ritchie and I didn't part as enemies, contrary to some reports. We were friends and we still are. But I know I will never be a friend of either Geezer Butler or Tony Iommi. I respected Ritchie Blackmore because he was a gentleman. I wish I could say the same for the Sabbath guys. I can say more, but it isn't worth airing dirty laundry."

Back to the record, "One Night in the City" takes over from "I Speed at Night" with a classic riff and a deeply passionate melody—the song is certainly one of the best "unsung" songs from the Dio catalog and straddles the best of pop worlds, being both somber and heavy yet somehow accessible, like a ballad, albeit a ponderous one. "That's one of my favorites from that album," offers Ronnie enthusiastically. "I think it's a great song. It's nice because it has a little story line to it, which is different from most songs. The subject matter is about a rich person, a rich kid and a poor kid; I guess the story that's been told many, many times from *Pygmalion* onward. But I just wanted to write something a bit more personal. I liked the song from the moment we started doing, fell in love with it right away."

Indeed "One Night in the City" represents another impressive exercise in wordplay, in contrasts, in balanced structure and architecture, and definitely in layered and veiled meaning, for it's hard to spot the rich versus poor dichotomy of which Ronnie speaks. Rather, it seems like a tale of a guy and a gal who separately yearn for the bright lights and then each makes the move. And typical of a Dio tale, things might not have gone so well.

Ronnie reiterates that all of this *Last in Line* material was brand new. "As I say, we write for the moment, the project; you don't bring in things that had been done before. My feeling on that is that if you've done it before and it didn't fly then, why the hell should it fly now? But there have been times that we've taken bits and pieces from things we've written before and did work on it and said, yes, that's a good riff; we'll keep it and apply it to something else."

In later years I asked Ronnie whether he remembered any strange effects or sounds applied to this album. "No, nothing I can remember aside from 'Breathless,' although I think we did some backward effects on this album. It's been so long, I don't remember. But I think we did something backward on one of the songs. Remember, it was so fashionable in those days, until it became illegal, I guess [laughs]. But aside from that, I don't think we did anything like get an elk or a caribou and get them to moo or try to get them to rut in front of us. To me, the instruments are there to be played, and anything extra just always seemed to take away from the heaviness of it all."

A couple of "Mystery" releases. *Martin Popoff archive*

Opening side 2 of the original vinyl is "Evil Eyes," previously a *Holy Diver*–era B-side, now rerecorded with a bit more gravitas, less perky. Smartly, there's a carryover from the themes addressed by "One Night in the City," with evil eyes—"It's the call of the city"—causing temptation. What's more, they can't be escaped by sailing "into the never."

Second is the aforementioned "Mystery," making it sort of two songs in a row on this second side that are a bit poppy. "Mystery" gets a Bain/Dio credit, while "Evil Eyes" is credited to Ronnie alone, as is "We Rock." And then outside of "Breathless (Campbell/Dio), everything else is credited to the whole band. Back to "Mystery," the somewhat happy music of this one works hand in hand with Ronnie's lyric, which seems to address the mystery of positive thinking, perhaps most pertinently as it applies to creativity.

At the personnel end of things, when Ronnie hired Claude Schnell, he had told him, "'We're going to get ready to do the next record, and I would like keyboards to have a more prominent part than they had on the *Holy Diver* record.'" And as Claude relates, "Of course the title track, 'The Last in Line,' kind of speaks for itself in that regard. But funny enough, when it was time to do 'Mystery,' I had a long-standing appointment with an attorney in L.A. that I had postponed twice before. He was doing my wife and me a huge favor, and he was giving us . . . so I really had to go for a day to fly to L.A. to take care of this family business. And the day that I was gone was the day that they did 'Mystery,' and it was Ronnie who actually played the keyboards on that.

"'Mystery,' as jolly as it is, you know, Ronnie was under a lot of pressure from Warner Bros. to come up with a follow-up to 'Rainbow in the Dark.' Understandably. 'Rainbow in the Dark' was just a huge, huge hit for the band. So 'Mystery' was the song that they had come up with, with very little input from me. But Ronnie had wanted a keyboard hook much like the 'Rainbow in the Dark' melody. So, you come up with a melody which was the melody that exists on the record, but in a livelier, more poppy formulation. If you think that keyboard part is cheesy the way it is, you should have heard it before. Ronnie insisted, 'I really hate this fucking keyboard part, but it has to have something. What could we do to kind of darken it up?' So, I simply said, 'Just make it in a minor mode rather than major.' 'Well, how do we do that?' 'We'll change the major third to a minor third.' And the riff changed, and it became the one that is on the record now. Even though I never got to play or got any credit for it or anything else."

Jimmy Bain and Viv Campbell picks, front and back

"It's just about a boy/girl relationship really," explains Ronnie, addressing the song "Eat Your Heart Out." "You know, the girl screws the guy over, and he's so angry about it, he finally leaves her and finds someone else, who he is much more happy with, and leaves the first one in the dust and tells her now you can eat your heart out because I'm gone. So, it's the usual theme. Of course, the things I write, as a lyricist, are very personal. But for some reason, I don't write the song and say, 'That's about you, you bitch.' I don't normally do that. Once I start, I try to put it in somebody else's perspective. I try to think of how the injured party would feel, not me as the injured party, but somebody else as the injured party, so I can speak for them. Because that's my point. I try not to write the songs for me or about me; I try to write them for people, and they turn out to be about other people. So again, I put myself totally in someone else's place, and I don't really find any of them to be autobiographical. But of course, they are, because songwriting is a very good therapeutic tool. You can really release a lot of demons by saying what you need to say. But most of the time I don't consider them to be about me, but of course they are."

"'Eat Your Heart Out'... I think he was directing that one to Wendy," laughs Viv.

Finally, at the end of what many consider Dio's last truly timeless album, a harbinger of sorrow is called upon to close the affair, with "Egypt (the Chains Are On)" closing the door to the record on a somber note, the acquired mass of the album sort of fading away into the sunset. At the lyric end, Ronnie gives us at least two tales here,

Baltimore Civic Center,
Baltimore, Maryland,
August 14, 1984.
© *Rudy Childs*

Baltimore Civic Center, Baltimore, Maryland, August 14, 1984. © *Rudy Childs*

the literal one about Egypt and, second, the use of that tale as a metaphor for not letting one's life slip away unexamined and unexplored.

Ronnie told Dmitry Epstein that he wrote about Egypt "because we don't live in that area of the world, and I think it's a very mysterious place to us. Of course, it has been mysterious through our history, with all the writings from the Middle East, the Bible, all of the biblical stories—from all religions, really. I think that that's one thing that I like to do: I like the idea of having to use your imagination to think for yourself what that area is all about. And that's just from a historical aspect. But I love the Middle Eastern scales and just the attitude of the music as well. So, a lyric is written that's very influenced by the Middle Eastern music, and that I think is the only thing you can write about, for things like 'Egypt' or 'Stargazer.'"

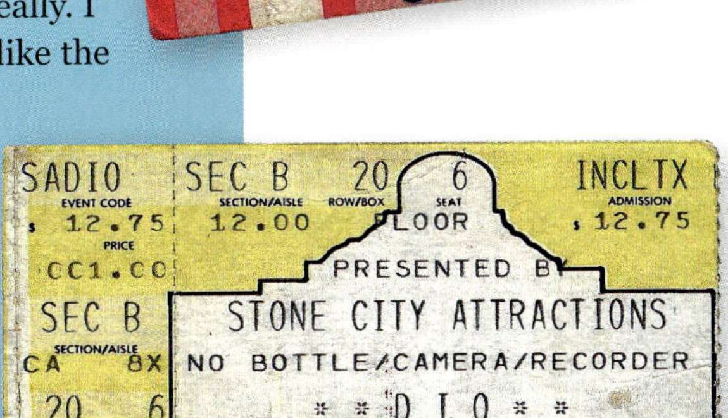

Proof of performance, 1984

Amusingly, when Dmitry asks Ronnie about singing songs like this, and if he misses the "soulful" type of singing he did back with Elf, Ronnie says, "I think that's the matter of the music that you make, especially when it becomes more metal kind of music, when it becomes more blacky, where the songs lead themselves along, and there's not a lot of spaces, not a lot of holes for soul. In Elf, we had a lot of space; we had the piano player that was featured really in the band, and that made for a lot of open holes for me to sing that way. But it was the music itself, really. I mean, the music was a lot more bluesy, perhaps—I think this is the word for it—bluesy and soulful, so I could do it that way. Once you start writing songs like 'Egypt' or 'Man on the Silver Mountain'—a little more blacky songs—there's not that much space to be that soulful. But that was okay with me because I know I can sing soulfully, but I just liked the strength and power of the music that didn't have a lot of spaces."

Asked if he regrets "losing that softness," Ronnie says, "No, I don't. That has never really been my attitude, really, to want to be in a 'ballad' band of any kind, or a soft band; that's not something that ever made me happy. That's why eventually I became what I have become: from Elf and the soulful times to what it is now. It's what I've always wanted to do. I take a chance and sing a few little soft things here and there in some of the songs that we do, but they usually lead to the big heavy sounds. That's kind of to make you think, oh, this is gonna be a soft song, and then bang!—you get hit with it."

"'Egypt,' I thought, always could've been better," recalls Viv. "I thought we were on to something when we started that one. I mean, it came out good, but I thought we lost it a little halfway through. But I like my solo on that a lot. I think that one, as was the case with 'Rainbow in the Dark,' was one of the first ones I did for that album."

It is of no consequence, however, Viv's vague dissatisfaction with the song, not to mention the fact that's it's both slow and depressing. *The Last in Line* could not be stopped, quickly pounding its way to gold status on September 12, 1984 (ten weeks after its release date), and then platinum on February 7, 1987. The album also certified as silver in the UK, for sales of over 60,000 units, achieving that status in January 1986.

More importantly, *The Last in Line* vaulted to an impressive #23 placement on the main Billboard chart, while also reaching #51 in Canada, #23 in Germany, and #4 in the UK, a fitting result for a band that Ronnie always considered "English sounding." Sales and chart success simultaneously took place against what most consider to have been the greatest tour of Dio's long career, featuring the classic lineup at its fiery peak met with headbanged enthusiasm from the metal minions showing up to see Dio perform. Also fueling the fires, "The Last in Line," "We Rock," and "Mystery" all were issued as singles (across various territories), even if none of them did particularly big business. But that's of no consequence either—Dio was an album band.

The *Last in Line* tour began on a bizarre note, with Dio playing the Pinkpop Festival on June 11, 1984, along with the likes of John Hiatt, Jimmy Cliff, Big Country, Marillion, Billy Bragg, the Pretenders, and Wang Chung. With this bit of silliness aside, the band set up at their strong California base in mid-July for five dates supported, in the main, by Whitesnake and Black 'n Blue, both familiar to Dio fans from the *Holy Diver* campaign. As the tour progressed through the States, crowds numbered in the 6,000–12,000 range, with the July 24 date at Spokane Coliseum being recorded by Westwood One in front of 10,000 fans. Twisted Sister, just starting to explode with their third album, *Stay Hungry*, were picked as support for approximately twenty dates in August.

"That was effectively for *You Can't Stop Rock 'n' Roll*," qualifies Twisted Sister's Jay Jay French. "That was the first album for Atlantic, and that was the one we got no tour support for. We had to do it ourselves. Yeah, I think we hung out with Ronnie for a while. He seemed to be a nice enough guy. I mean, we were on a mission from God, you know. We were just hell-bent on breaking our record and finally getting recognition. And I think my biggest memory of that is that we played Nassau Coliseum, and our fans rioted, destroying four thousand seats, and we were banned from Nassau Coliseum after that. He was pretty big. We played Red Rocks, in Denver, and that was about nine thousand. We did spectacular business in Canada with Dio. And Ronnie was fine, but Twisted didn't hang out much with anybody. It was a business."

"Let's see, we had Queensryche on the first tour," notes Bain, when asked about memories of backup bands and the like. "They were good; they were exciting. We had Dokken for a while. I used to watch George Lynch a lot; I was always amazed at how he could play. I mean, we even had Yngwie for a while, talking about players. Twisted Sister, well, they were nice guys, but they weren't the greatest band. I was famous for being lit up and still being able to play. I even fell over a few times. It was like it was part of the show. Ronnie and I got pissed together a few times, but I got carried away and had to be carried to the limo and stuff. But as long as I played live and was creative and wrote the songs, it didn't matter."

Highlights of a typical Dio set on that tour included "Don't Talk to Strangers," "The Last in Line," "The Mob Rules" (as encore), "Egypt (the Chains Are On)," "Mystery," "One Night in the City," "We Rock" (second encore), "Holy Diver," "Rainbow in the Dark," and "Man on the Silver Mountain." Concerning that last selection, Ronnie was known to quip that it had become one of his signature songs, a bit of a history lesson, and besides, Ritchie probably needed the money.

Next up was the Breaking Sound Festival in Paris, France (attendance: 10,000), Dio playing alongside the likes of Tokyo Blade, Virgin Steele, and Blue Öyster Cult—Accept, Queensryche, and Mercyful Fate had canceled. The two-day Monsters of Rock festival in Germany followed on September 1 and 2. Headlined by AC/DC, top billing also went to Van Halen, with secondary billing going to Dio, Ozzy Osbourne, and Mötley Crüe. Also on the ticket were Accept and Gary Moore. Attendance was pegged at around 45,000. An uncommonly intensive UK tour followed with Queensryche in tow. Dio was brought back down to earth, playing to crowds in the 2,000–2,500 range, but upward of 3,500 in London. The rest of Europe followed, with Sweden becoming particularly rich terrain—shows in Gothenburg and Stockholm attracted 6,500 and 7,000 fans, respectively. The rest of the draws varied wildly, with Germany proving to offer up the smallest crowds for Dio.

Back in North America for November 1984, Dio took out Dokken for upward of fifty dates and resumed the golden years of their career, playing arenas and coliseums to thousands of people, occasionally in the five figures, almost always over five thousand, although the Deep South continued to be a soft spot in the attendance figures. Curiously, as with Iron Maiden out with *Powerslave*, the stage set was Egyptian in nature, with the drums set atop a pyramid (30 feet high, with the top 12 feet lopped off for the drums). There were also swivel-headed sphinxes packing both laser and smoke-billowing capabilities, along with Murray and a 10-foot-tall, three-headed cobra filling out the malevolent display from a band well at the height of its powers.

"There was one incident on this tour that was quite memorable," recalls Ronnie. "Our stage was set up to resemble a pyramid, and at the beginning of the show, an intro tape would play the opening chords to the song 'The Last in Line,' and at one point there is an explosion that blows the top off the pyramid, revealing Vinny playing the drums. Vivian started the song out this one night, and I came out from the bottom of the pyramid through a tunnel shooting lasers. We were just playing merrily along on the first song, and Jimmy started motioning to me to look at something. I didn't know what he wanted me to look at until I looked at the pyramid. It had never come off with the explosion, and Vinny was underneath there playing away. The crew finally got it off in time for his drum solo later on in the show. We still laugh pretty hard over that one."

CHAPTER 4

"I refuse to be told what to do, and I won't let idiots lead me around by the nose."

SACRED HEART

With two outstanding albums and tours under their belts, Dio was about to hit a rough patch. But, as these things go, the headbanging public wouldn't really notice, with the band's gripes being kept private. Their third record, although harshly recorded and ever so slightly commercial, still pleased the fan base, more or less.

And I stress that choice of words: "more or less": *Sacred Heart*, issued August 13, 1985, would turn out to be an album that benefited in an abstract, elusive manner from the world-weariness the band was experiencing, those 1,000-mile stares resulting in cynical wisdoms from a perch atop the heavy metal heap. It was an album written by and for pessimists, for despite Ronnie's messages of hope, the darkness is always there. Now it had infected the band. Had they achieved their goals and thus lost the hunger of definable and intense dreams? Fortunately for the resulting art, this sense of quiet desperation and roiling anguish is intensified by the increased amount of melody the band would be proposing across this particular batch of tracks, more to be sure, but almost all of

CNE Grandstand, Toronto, Canada, August 31, 1985. Supporting was Helix. © *Martin Popoff*

it poisoned by a sense of melancholy. "Hungry for Heaven" would be the album's smash hit, and man, is it a seductive, trundling, somehow sad hard rocker for the ages, a microcosm for the wider album's devil dance with accessibility.

"The whole band was falling apart," recalls Viv. "Nobody wanted to be in the studio. Once we got some tracks cut and basics done, I don't think there was ever a time when all of us were in the studio at once. The vibe was just very poor. I know I didn't want to be there, and I did what I had to do and I didn't want to be around Ronnie. I don't think anyone else wanted to either. And you know, I think that reflects on it. It's been many, many years since I've listened to the record. I don't even know what's on it. I remember thinking at the time that it was all a bit strange. Even when we were writing it, I remember being in the rehearsal environment, and, you know, it was more difficult to put together. Even from the creative process, day one, it didn't flow like the other two records did. Even in rehearsal the vibe was bad, even before we got into the studio. It seemed disjointed; it seemed like we were trying very hard to piece together things, like a square peg in a round hole with a big hammer, trying to make it work. You know, a lot of those songs sound like the same song to me [laughs], with slight variations. I have no real fond memories of the record, or that time in my life, to be honest."

"That album was a transitional one for us," figures Claude. "I describe it as . . . if you think of a band as a tight knot where all the ropes are all firmly together, at the time *Sacred Heart* was being recorded, the knot was loosening. For one thing, we had enjoyed being up at Caribou Ranch, where we recorded *The Last in Line*. For whatever reason, it was decided that the *Sacred Heart* record would be recorded here in L.A. Which is fine. I mean, we'll get to spend more time with our loved ones and see our dogs and take care of stuff, not just disappear.

"But that had a consequence. I think in addition to everything else, that added stress in everybody's lives. Because you were living at home and basically going to a day job, it made it a less productive and less conducive environment than what we had on *The Last in Line*. Not to say that we didn't do a good job, but I think we were all looking forward to the same escape that we had when we were in Colorado recording the *Last in Line* album. In doing *Sacred Heart* here in the valley, it just wasn't the same. It was at that time when it became obvious that it had become a bit disenchanted. Ronnie had become, for lack of a better word, a bit cranky. Probably justifiably so. Again, just because, well, I don't want to speak out of school, but instead of being far away from the things that aggravated him, he was very close to them. And you can read into that whatever you want."

"That was an album that was Viv's last shot at it," dismisses Ronnie, looking back at *Sacred Heart* with some pain and regret. "I think he was going to go after that anyway. Either himself, or via me. And again, it was a little bit more difficult of an album to do because there wasn't all that enthusiasm. But hey, that's life. I mean you can't have that enthusiasm all the time. Perhaps Viv had some good gripes. He might have done. But again, it was more of a difficult album to do. But I did like the songs on it."

Schnell's keyboards can be heard prominently, if brashly, on this shockingly midrangy, braying record. "A lot of textures" is the way Campbell describes Schnell's contribution to the band. "There's only so much you can do with an electric guitar, really. So, we had Claude there as a keyboard guy. Ronnie would spend a lot of time after-hours, after we were done. He obviously wasn't a keyboard player himself or a technician, but he would sort of direct. He had very clear ideas of what he wanted texturally, and Claude would do that. Claude also was a classically trained player, so when we wanted a musical dilemma solved [laughs], we'd ask Claude. He was the smart one. But for the most part, Claude was really a fringe player because that's the way Ronnie wanted it to be. He didn't really want keyboards to be a prominent part of the band, so he kept it to a minimum. And a lot of what Claude did, unless we wanted something that was keyboardy or texturally specific, was play on the clavinet, through a sort of distortion device or a preamp to get an edge to it. Basically, it sounded like guitar, so he would be reinforcing what I was doing."

CNE Grandstand, Toronto, Canada, August 31, 1985. © *Martin Popoff*

I wondered if Viv was participating less come the *Sacred Heart* sessions, as Ronnie has said. "I always tried to participate as much as I could, with whatever band I'm in," reflects Viv. "But I'm not a pushy A-type personality. I say my piece and I tend to back off. A lot of being in a band or any sort of group, if you have an idea, you really have to politic for it. I wouldn't say that I wasn't participating in *Sacred Heart*. I mean, certainly when we got to the studio and got into the overdub stage of the record, yeah, I maybe started to withdraw then. But I would say in preproduction and rehearsal and writing, I think I was as involved as I was in the other two records."

It seems that this phase in Campbell's life might have marked the turning point toward pop- and song-based genuflection versus the shredding ax-mad pyrotechnics of, say, George Lynch or Yngwie Malmsteen.

"Well, as a guitar player, I always wanted to play like those guys, but I never could. I'm a blues-style player. I never had that sort of technique. But at the time, I was very insecure about that because I wanted to play like that, and I would try and try and try, to no avail. But certainly, by *Sacred Heart* time, I was definitely starting to be influenced by a lot of different music, not just guitar-driven music. Up until that point . . . well, actually, I remember being on tour, and I'm not sure which tour it was, could've been *Last in Line*, probably not *Holy Diver*, when I really started listening to pop music and singers and soul music and getting out of the headspace of just being a guitar player. Up to that point I had really been influenced by guitar-driven music.

"You know, the style of heavy metal that Dio dealt in was not my first choice of music. I could play it and I proved that I could adapt to it, but it wasn't the sort of stuff I was listening to. I always wanted the band to take more of a pop direction. But the same could be said for Def Leppard. You know, I love Crowded House, but Def Leppard is never going to sound like Crowded House.

"I've got to tell you, all those records were hard to make, for personal reasons," continues Viv, standing back and taking in the scope of his entire, much-loved catalog with the band. "Because I never actually got along too well with Ronnie; we never had much of a relationship beyond the music. It was just cultural and personal differences—and age differences—more than anything else. You've got to understand me: I grew up listening to Ronnie Dio. When I was a little kid, he was a rock star. So, it was very strange to go from that, from being a fan, to actually being the guitar player in his band, writing with him.

"So, there was always a sort of . . . I mean, it was a strange relationship. He was almost like a father that I didn't talk to. I mean, I had a sort of respect for him, but we couldn't find the common ground. We just never really got along too well. But having said that, I enjoyed playing with the band. I really, really thought it was a great, great band, and I have a lot of respect for him as a singer and musician. He's probably got the greatest voice in rock, and he's a good writer. He wasn't a fun guy to work for, but there's no point getting into any mudslinging or anything. It was a fun band while it lasted, and I enjoyed the music and I learned a lot from the experience.

"I like *Holy Diver*; the songwriting part of the record was easy, but when we got into doing the guitar solos and stuff, it was very, very difficult. Ronnie was the producer of the record, and I don't rate him as a producer. As much as I admire his musical talent and his musical instincts . . . I mean, a big part of being a producer is to bring out the best in the people you're working with, and I don't think that's a skill that Ronnie has. He doesn't have the people skills, and that's 50 percent of being a producer, in my opinion. You have to make people feel comfortable to bring out the very best in them. It actually got to the stage, certainly by the *Last in Line* record, but even by the end of the *Holy Diver* record, when it came time to cut guitar solos, I couldn't have Ronnie in the room. I'd have to ask him to leave [laughs], because he wasn't helping, you know? I mean, of the three records, as good as *Holy Diver* is, *Last in Line* is probably the better record. And *Sacred Heart* is just a steamin' pile of poo, as far as I was concerned.

"So that's when things went tragically wrong," reiterates Viv, "not just with me but with Vinny Appice and Jimmy Bain too. There was a lot of tension in the studio; no one wanted to be there when Ronnie was there. We'd come in and do our parts and leave. There was no cohesive vibe in the band at that stage, because of things that really started to go wrong from a business point of view. We were feeling very betrayed and whatnot, so no one had the enthusiasm for it."

Asked if there was a reason that the production on *Sacred Heart* was so harsh, so screechy, while the first two albums sounded powerful but high fidelity too, Viv figures, "Probably because there was no consensus because the rest of us weren't there. Ronnie wanted total control. He's a control freak, but at least on the first two records we were

CNE Grandstand, Toronto, Canada, August 31, 1985. © *Martin Popoff*

A cassette copy and an ad for the *Sacred Heart* album

all standing behind him, giving our opinions. And like I say, for that record, we just weren't there. Our hearts and souls weren't in it, nor were our ears. Ronnie wanted to do it, and we just let him do it."

"In the early days, I had stuff from Wild Horses, Viv had Sweet Savage stuff, we were all writing," reflects Jimmy Bain, on what went wrong. "I wrote a lot on the first two albums, but it just got harder and harder to come up with stuff. The first album was really raw. I don't want to be mean, but at the time, although Ronnie was producing, we had this really great engineer who was a big part of the sound. We all thought *The Last in Line* was a bit smooth, but I liked everything about it, the cover, everything. By the time of *Sacred Heart*, I looked at that monster on the cover and thought, he's laughing at me now. Ronnie was having fights with Viv, and you get to a point where you just think you've got it, and you think you can bring in keyboards and play with the arrangements. I always thought we had such a unique sound, that we could just be Dio. We didn't have to try to write like anybody else."

The record the band came up with, working at Rumbo Recorders in Los Angeles, began with a tired orange, butt-ugly brown, and washed-out blue front cover, upon which Robert Florczak's depiction of band mascot Murray had him looking comically cuddly. At least it incorporated a word puzzle. Inscribed in Latin around the edges (similar to Ozzy's *Speak of the Devil*), according to Professor Thomas Ruggles from Northern Arizona University, is something to the effect of "Comes the end by sleep, I will prepare for you the Sacred Heart which is the magic that opens upon the altar." The phrase was supposed to kick off a contest, never executed, that entailed finding the sacred heart, with the payoff being a brand-new car.

Dave Dickson's review of the album in *Kerrang!* had this to say about the cover message: "Incidentally, for those of you not well-versed in the Latin tongue, the messages stamped around the picture read (loosely translated and working from the bottom left clockwise) 'a boundary/limit through dreams,' 'I will get back to you, Sacred Heart,' 'the sorcerer/poisoner,' 'door,' and 'golden,' and if you can decipher its meaning, you are a better man than I."

Once into the meat of the matter, *Sacred Heart* represented a parallel with another difficult follow-up album in Rainbow's *Long Live Rock 'n' Roll*, both records opening with a rollicking title track all about . . . rock 'n' rolling, a bit of a low-rent idea for a peerless wordsmith such as Ronnie. This time it was "King of Rock and Roll," which, of course, was immediately taken as egotistical self-appointment. Just like "Long Live Rock 'n' Roll," its spiritual heir from 1977, the track (credited to the whole band) gallops along without much purpose and even less medieval levity. An ill-advised throwaway—in the pole position, no less—the song is presented faux live, with Ronnie in fact laying out a cautionary tale to both the flash-in-the-pan rocker and the fan who buys into the narrative, with both parties sure to end up disappointed, used, seduced, even damned.

Two-color ad from UK music weekly *Sounds. Martin Popoff archive*

"Sacred Heart," another full-band collaboration, follows, instantly redeeming the album. An uneasy cross between Dio's two preceding title tracks, the song is nonetheless an ambitious journey with a fine though characteristically cryptic lyric, "an epic sort of track that had some merit," according to Viv, who singles it out as his favorite on the album. As the song moves forward, resolutely, like the hypnotic click of a metronome, Ronnie weaves a tale about the dreams and hopes of youth balanced against wisdom attained through acting ("attacking"), or potential wisdom forfeited through hesitating, thereby, through allegory and imagery, passing on an urgent message concerning time's indifferent march toward the "black."

Said Ronnie of the lyric, in conversation with *Kerrang!*'s Dante Bonutto, "Dreams to me are goals set for you with little hurdles in front of those goals, but overcoming them makes you a better person. Without dreams, I see no sense in the brain being anything but linked to a computer; dreams make things come alive for me. It's about the search for the truth about yourself and what's around you, about why we do the terrible things we do to each other, just all the trials and tribulations you have to go through to find that form of truth. I write about that a lot, and the sacred heart is emblematic of that quest."

"Another Lie," another good-quality but less heralded composition, is next. The track is one of those that points to the band's subtle shift toward accessibility but still with thorns, or, more accurately, a new type of thorn, this idea that the band has now seen it all and are cynical or even dead in the soul over what they've witnessed. Lyrically the song is neither cryptic nor all that poetic, with Ronnie nonetheless combining evil-woman themes with magic and the "lie" implicit in dark powers.

"Another Lie" is the first of two songs credited to Ronnie alone, with "Rock 'n' Roll Children" being the second and last. It feels right that the two are sequenced together to close side 1 of the original vinyl, because the latter represents the same sort of deflated, sorrowful quality as "Another Lie." Like its predecessor, it's in this melodic space half-designed to please the record company, and it moves at a relaxed pace. Yet, there's intense passion from Ronnie, who really digs deep into his soul for a lyric addressing one of his large, commendable themes, that of the misfit.

Ad promoting the single issue of "Rock 'n' Roll Children" in the UK. *Martin Popoff archive*

"'Rock 'n' Roll Children' has always been one of my favorite songs," noted Ronnie, looking back nearly twenty years down the line. "I think lyrically the whole thing is very descriptive of what especially young people have gone through, loving metal music or rock 'n' roll music, whatever it may be, and being told that you're a fool for listening to that crap. You're an outsider and being treated like an outcast. Therefore, 'Rock 'n' Roll Children.' We do that now in our sets, and it's great to do. I love doing that song every night. It always moves me in some way because they were really personal statements to me. I put myself in the place of those people. It's difficult to be hurt a lot, and those people were hurt a lot. And again, it's a song I really like from the album, and a song I really, really enjoy doing live. And I think the others in the band enjoy it as well."

The lyric is much more than that as well, enveloping the concept of runaways, with Ronnie's ad-libbed "children of the night" clarion-calling Ronnie to help with the charity of the same name. As well, there's an almost "(Don't Fear) the Reaper" / *Romeo and Juliet* quality to it, with Ronnie, in a very short but cherishable and charitable space, equating the love of rock 'n' roll to the love of two people, evoking an element of escapism, of a tragic love, of a doomed intertwining, the idea of an eternity shrouded over the paralleled relationships. It's a struggle—ironically for both individualism and desperate connection—to the death.

"I only feel comfortable writing and recording one type of song," mused Dio, speaking with *Hit Parader*'s Andy Secher in 1986. "I don't like ballads and I don't like pop tunes. They don't reflect my personality or what this group is trying to do. On the last album, the group wanted to write songs that could expand our audience. That's where 'Mystery' came in. This time we saw no reason to do that. We knew we had an audience out there that would react favorably to the music we do best, so we saw no reason in playing games with what was essentially inferior material. Songs like 'Rock 'n' Roll Children' are tuneful without sacrificing the intensity that makes Dio special. The songs on the album have a great deal of integrity. Some people may listen to things like 'Fallen Angels' or the title track and say, 'Oh, that's Ronnie James Dio; he's still singing about the same wizards and magic he sang about ten years ago.' That may be true, but I don't think there's anyone who writes that type of music better than I do. It's no secret that there are a lot of bands around today who seem determined to sing about mystical subjects, even if they have no idea what they're doing."

Speaking with Paul Elliott from *Music Express* at the time, Ronnie framed the album this way: "Big drum sounds, big guitar sounds, no ballads. We have a lot of melody inherent in the songs, but keyboards are just for shade and color. If we do anything that smacks of a ballad, like 'The Last in Line,' then it's only to lull the listener into a false sense of security—then the hammer bludgeons down."

Asked by Elliott about the health of his ego in all this, Ronnie tells him, "I don't dismiss the fact that I have an ego. I can only say that if I'm an egomaniac or megalomaniac, then I shouldn't be talking to you about Jimmy, Vinny, and Vivian and saying all these laudatory things about them. Then again, maybe some people will construe that to mean that I'm only furthering my own and by saying, 'Yeah, they're terrific.' So, people have to make their own judgment. I only know this: people who know me know that I've not really changed from the beginning of my career until now. I prided myself upon caring about other people, although that, I know, seems very inconsistent with the image that has been built up around me. I'm sorry that in Black Sabbath we had to start throwing things at each other. I've since spoken to Tony. I decided that it's not worth going through life with vengeance in my heart forever. It's the same with Ozzy. Ozzy happens to be a friend. I'm sorry, but that's the way it is. So, if that's someone with an ego problem, then yes I am, and I'll just have to live with it. But I don't consider myself to be that. I consider myself to be just a run-of-the-mill person who happens to have a little talent in some direction."

Along these same lines, however, Ronnie told Richard Hogan from *Circus*, "Absolutely never could I work for someone else again. I just couldn't give away that kind of control. I've always been a part of the band, and in Dio, if I didn't do my job as well as anyone else did, I'd feel as though I let them down. But I do feel different about the writing, the production, and the degree of control. In this band I've had to take a lot more control. I've had to contribute more, and I've had a hundred times more headaches. I had spare time before. Now there's no time for privacy, no time to be an individual. In Dio, I don't ask the others to be there from beginning to end. It comes down to me because I set myself up that way. But the headaches are worth it.

"I've always wanted to have the same people in the band and care about them, have them care about me. That's the way you build success, and that's the only way I know how to do it. Rainbow was different from that. In Rainbow, my naivety would not allow me to realize that everybody isn't like that, that everybody isn't a caring soul who says, 'Here's your credit for doing a great job!'

"Disenchantment sets in when you keep changing a band's lineup. You always think the ax is over your head when you see people come and go: 'Am I next?' That's not the way to run any organization, by fear. Fear never gets the best out of people. It always paints things in black and white. There's no rainbow in fear. Vinny and Jimmy are both my best friends in this band. It is difficult to have those friendships within a band, and yes, it is a business. But they don't have those egos that I've dealt with in the past. I've seen the mistakes before where there was no honesty among musicians and no honor among thieves. The difference is that I started this situation with total honesty. Here we talk to each other, so we won't be hiding anything in shadows. We've remained the best of friends because we are honest with each other, and they know I care about them."

Back to *Sacred Heart* and over to side 2 of the original vinyl, "Hungry for Heaven" leaps out of the speakers with angelic voices followed by a shamelessly melodic intro. Once the vocal starts, the song becomes gritty and chugging and, yet, still immensely catchy, worthy of its hit status. Viv's solo is one of the most lyrical and elegant of his career.

A couple of ads promoting the single issue of "Hungry for Heaven" in the UK. *Martin Popoff archive*

In actuality, "Rock 'n' Roll Children," backed with "Sacred Heart," was the album's first single, launched in August '85 along with the album (the UK 7-inch was a plush, full-color gatefold with live shot and lyrics to both tracks; oddly, Claude Schnell is not listed as a full member of the band). But "Hungry for Heaven" (backed with "King of Rock and Roll") followed two months later, showing up in multiple versions in the UK, along with front placement on *The Dio EP*, a UK four-tracker that also included "Shame on the Night," "Egypt (the Chains Are On)," and a non-LP Dio/Bain composition called "Hide in the Rainbow," a moody, rumbling, mystical track with a deep, rich verse melody and an eerie synth line come chorus time. The 7-inch version of this item is a double set (two 45s), again with gatefold and dramatic live shot.

"Like the Beat of a Heart" is a thudly, serviceable-enough anthem much like "Sacred Heart" or "The Last in Line" or "Invisible," even if the opening lyrical and vocal salvo seems to dissipate much like the collective enthusiasm of the band. Indeed, the lyric to this one is clipped, disconnected, but still adequately poetic. Ronnie seems to be celebrating the passion that builds toward nighttime, a passion that explodes with a yearning to escape. This one is quite illustrative of the album's unforgiving production values, in particular a drum sound out of Vinny that tends to lean toward the *Dehumanizer* whack of that album's producer Mack.

Next up, "Just Another Day" rocks and chugs hummably like "Hungry for Heaven," but its chorus is a gorgeous and welcome shaft of arcane melody, a little psychedelic rock in tenor, maybe (ironically) even a little punk, certainly a high point of the album. The lyric is an admonishment of a dark, cynical, unspecified character, seemingly counteractive or counterproductive to both the chorus lyric and melody.

"Fallen Angels" serves as a microcosm for all that is wrong with *Sacred Heart*. Although the lyric is quite good, with Ronnie laying out an impassioned paean to the innocent and shunned who are served a bad hand, the music is wishy-washy, sort of melodic, sort of heavy, almost frumpy, and awkward, with Vinny not doing this one any favors.

Sacred Heart closes with "Shoot Shoot," again, like the song immediately before it, not one of Dio's most remembered numbers. Fittingly, with this brownout of a filler track, the album limps to the finish line on a sour and suicidal note, climactic through the violent lyric but anticlimactic through the track's combination of nondescript, almost "hair metal" music and the ear-yanking production of this dour, spent album as a whole.

Turns out, "Shoot Shoot" was the last song written for the album, with the label, as Ronnie explains, leaning on the band to deliver . . . soon! "So, I said, 'Tell you what, why don't you just shoot me? Will you get it done then?' To which they said, 'No, but it has to be done.' So, I said, 'Well, then shoot me, 'cause I'm not gonna do it!' They found a few more days, all the days we needed. So, my message is, next time someone points a gun at you—and this has nothing to do with a real gun; it's only imagery—just say, 'Shoot shoot, I don't care. I have to live my own life, so shoot me if you want me out of the way. But if you don't, then let me do it my way.' I said to the record company, 'If I don't have the time to do it properly, I'm only gonna burn the tapes, so it really doesn't matter to me.' And I would have too; I don't care. I refuse to be told what to do, and I won't let idiots lead me around by the nose.

"I didn't care for 'Shoot Shoot' very much," notes Ronnie, his tone dismissive of the album as a whole, looking back from a 2004 vantage point. "I like 'Sacred Heart,' the song, very much. There was another 'heart' song with that one, wasn't there? 'Like the Beat of a Heart,' great song, I love that song. I really remember more, at that time, when recording that album, that we were doing the *Hear 'n Aid* project. That's what I remember most about that time."

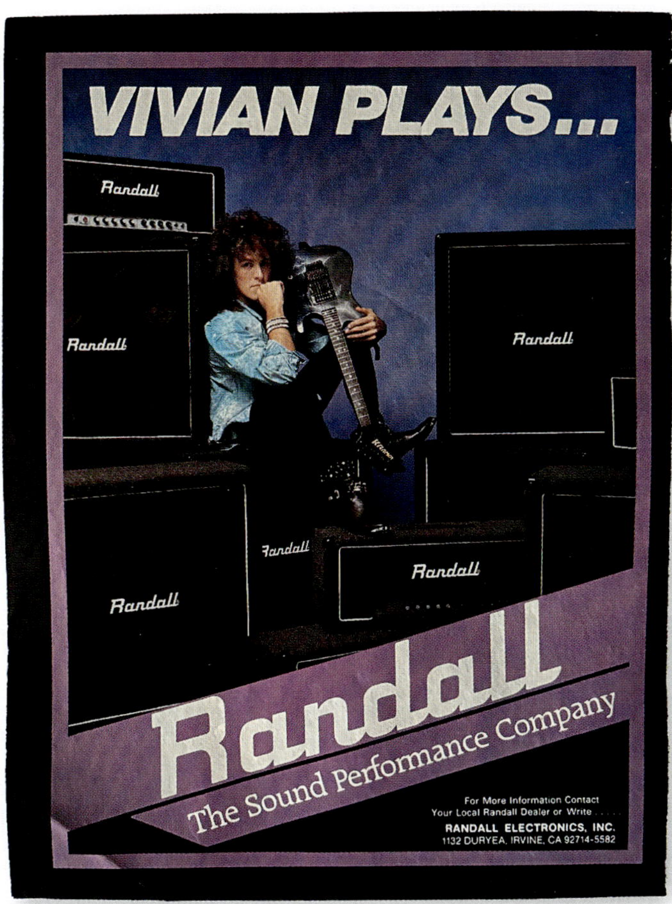

Viv looking fine, endorsing Randall amps.
Martin Popoff archive

Of note, there was another track that was cooked up for the album. "Never Again" made it all the way to mixing but was then nixed. In April 2003, it reared its head again . . . "We have an interesting song we're doing for the Children of the Night charity," noted Jimmy Bain at that time. "We have a song—as we were saying, the commercial aspect—that we had done for *Sacred Heart*, that I put forth, that Ronnie thought was too commercial, and we didn't do it. And now it's raised its head again, because now we're doing this song for Children of the Night, and it's called 'Never Again.' And you'll see what I mean when you hear that one [laughs]. Here's a hit song that we didn't do. It could've been on an album back in 1985, which would've been a big help. It didn't go on, and it might sound a little dated now, but the song was great back then."

Looking back, Vinny is at least happy he picked up on some of the finer business points by the time of his Dio experience; for example, insisting on getting credited for writing—his name is on four *Sacred Heart* songs, although that represents a reduction from the first two albums.

"Yeah, from Dio on, it was like, you know what? Hey, we're writing the songs together, and I'm not going to do it if I'm not going to get any credit now. I'm not a stupid little kid anymore, so here we go. But it still wasn't fair. It wasn't fair for anybody. Ronnie got the bulk of everything.

Ronnie in the spotlight, Toronto.
© *Martin Popoff*

But you know what? When you think that way, and everything is me, me, me, that's short-term thinking. So, what happens is you're successful for three or four years, playing big places, albums selling millions, and then it goes down the toilet because nobody is as happy as they were in the beginning, and you're kind of suppressing all the creativity, so in the long run you're playing clubs. Ozzy's not playing clubs, you know what I mean? So, it's just really short-term thinking from people who are in a position that should know better. Not only him, it's management too. 'Let's take everything.' Okay, then we'll be playing clubs in five years, and that's what happened."

In conjunction with the pained assembly of *Sacred Heart*, as alluded to, Dio found themselves admirably immersed in charity work, something that was near and dear to Ronnie's heart until his death.

"Jimmy Bain and Vivian Campbell came to me when we were making the album *Sacred Heart*. That was in 1985. They said they wanted to get something together like the other artists who were doing the rock relief stuff for Africa. They wanted to do a metal version of it. I said, 'Bless your hearts—go for it. I am doing this album now, but any support you need from me, you just ask. But I want you to go do this as it is your thing.' We carried on doing the album; I think we were mixing. They went out and got some people who said they would love to do it. They began to write the song and then came to me and told me that they needed my help to finish the song. They asked me to talk to some people to get them involved as well. I called a few people, and my management started getting real involved with it and eventually took it over—I wrote the song and became the producer of the project; Wendy became the executive producer. The credit needs to go to Jimmy and Viv; they contacted a lot of people. I just did the grunt work. I produced it and helped write the song. I dealt with the guitar players and vocalists, which was a joy. When you have all the talent around you, then you just can't lose. They did me a favor by getting me involved.

"It was great for us because we really didn't have the time to do it at that point! Everyone said, 'Whenever you want us to be there to do it, we will be there.' Not one person said no. It lasted for two days. The first day was for guitar players and the second day was for singers. It was unbelievable. It was one of the best times I ever had in my life. We had all that wonderful talent there, and they were such wonderful people too. It is just about caring. It's not a big thing to lend your name and talent to something like this. It's really nice to be praised. I'd rather be praised than have no one ever know that I did it! It's not that I don't want people to know that I have a good heart. It's not that at all. It's something that you do for yourself, and you do it as an individual. I think that is the best kind of reward that you can get. I mean, it is nice to be thought of, but I share it with all those other people, but thanks for the praise."

But yes, Ronnie, later speaking with Jeb Wright, indicated that he was right in there heating up the phones, gathering the metalheads . . . "Sure—you have to. Some were contacted by our management, but the ones we knew we just called up and asked them if they wanted to do this. They, of course, said, 'When do you want me to be there?' Especially Rob Halford, who was just the best of the lot. I told Rob we were booking Tuesday and Wednesday for the vocals. He asked me when I wanted him to be there. I told him that if he had other things to do, then I could deal with it because he was very important to the project. He asked me again, 'When do you want me to be there?' I said, 'How about I make it easy on you? Be here at one o'clock in the afternoon.' He was there at 9:00 a.m. He asked me, 'How long do you want me to stay? A week? A month? I am here for whatever you need me to do because this is such a wonderful project.'

Ad for the VHS version of *Hear 'n Aid*.
Martin Popoff archive

"Working with those kinds of people was a real joy for me," continues Ronnie. "It was a joy to get to know them and to be respected by them. It didn't do any of us harm to do something from the heart that helped other people who were struggling. That was the best part. It earned about $3 million, but who knows how much of that actually got to those people? Even the 'We Are the World' project ended up with food on the pier rotting away. There were tribal chiefs who came in and took it away without giving any to the people. Our attitude was that if we could save one person from starving to death today, then we have done something good."

The end result of all of this was, as Ronnie has alluded to, a record issued in which the proceeds went to charity. The album was called *Hear 'n Aid* and featured seemingly all the big metal stars of the day belting or fret-burning their way through a damn good arch-Dio song called "Stars." The track went seven minutes to allow for everybody to participate. To flesh out the record to full length, recent hits from Accept, Motörhead, Rush, Scorpions, Y&T, Kiss, and of course Dio were added, with Jimi Hendrix representing the spirit of the '60s. The cover shot is classic, with everybody gathered in "We Are the World" fashion for a gang photo graphically illustrative of the well-wished vibe of the project.

Speaking with Steve Newton, prerelease back in '85, Ronnie said that schedulingwise, "We wanted to make it kind of after the fact—after a lot of the Live Aid and "We Are the World," etc. We wanted to have it not so much more special, but just to remove it a little bit. The kind of music that we play and the people who are involved with it are always accused of being something other than what they are anyway—something awful—so we thought we may as well just take it all the way, and we'll just separate ourselves from everybody, 'cause I guess that's what they'll do to us anyway."

The years seem to have mellowed the memory for Ronnie, however, because also back on the press trail for *Sacred Heart* the following year, Ronnie publicly stated that not everybody was so quick to help. "I can't understand when Rob Halford flew up to

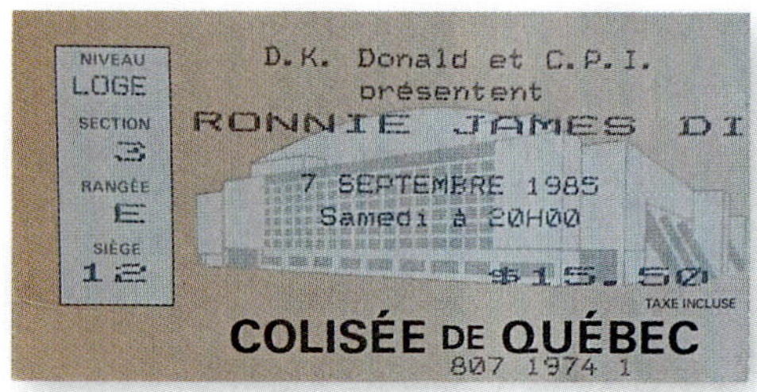

Assorted proofs of purchase

Los Angeles from the Bahamas just to participate, people who live in Los Angeles couldn't find the time. All of a sudden when Nikki Sixx found out that *Hear 'n Aid* was hot, he decided to show up the next day. Too late, I'm sorry. Vince Neil, who's as nice a guy as you'd want to meet, managed to make it there the first night. So did Mick Mars. But I guess Nikki just had more important things to do—like go to a bar."

Queried about his old Rainbow and Sabbath mates, Ronnie said, "I guess Tony Iommi figured he could get more exposure by playing the Live Aid show. There are some people who are only concerned with how famous they can become or how much money they can make. I know Sabbath didn't receive any money for doing Live Aid, and I certainly wouldn't criticize them for playing that event, but it's too bad they didn't have time for *Hear 'n Aid*. One person I would like to single out for criticism, however, is Jimmy Page. He had agreed to participate on the 'Stars' record. We had arranged to meet with him after the Led Zeppelin reunion at Live Aid. I flew in from Los Angeles with my crew, and we rented a studio so he could lay down his guitar solo. To make a long story short, he never showed up and never even offered an explanation. I feel sorry for him."

In the same interview, Ronnie gamely put forth the view that things were more than healthy down at Camp Dio. "Please realize that I'm just the singer in this band. I have people like Vivian Campbell, Jimmy Bain, and Vinny Appice kicking me in the ass every night onstage. There are so many negative things associated with heavy metal these days—blood, guts, and a mentality that often seems nonexistent. We try to elevate that. On an album like *Sacred Heart*, we're trying to capture the spirit of King Arthur, of chivalry and good values. We're not degrading women in our songs—I sing of being a knight and protecting them. Our music is an escape from reality, yet there are many elements that are lessons that can be applied to everyday life. We're a very honest band,

and honesty is the key to happiness. We always discuss our problems and try to find solutions to them, which is something that certainly wasn't true for Rainbow or Sabbath when I was in them. I want this band to become a legend one day. I think we have the talent to do that on musical terms. I don't know if too many other bands—if any—have that talent."

"I don't deny that there are similarities between the two albums," Ronnie told Andy Secher, that same year, comparing *Sacred Heart* to its predecessor. "But I think *Sacred Heart* is a major leap ahead for us. We've never done a song like 'Rock 'n' Roll Children' on any of our albums. It's true that the song 'Sacred Heart' is similar to 'The Last in Line' and 'Holy Diver,' but it's very much in the tradition this band has created. Actually, I think *Holy Diver*, as an album, was far more musically adventurous than either *The Last in Line* or *Sacred Heart*, but that doesn't mean I don't feel this is our strongest album, because it is.

"I may begin investigating new frontiers to explore, like film," offered Ronnie, looking ahead, perhaps knowing something that he wasn't letting on about relations within the band. "It's very important to me to avoid being one-dimensional. There are things I feel I must do in my life. Production is very important to me. I'd love to produce a band like Judas Priest. But that will wait its turn. Right now, my commitment is to the band. Everything else takes a back seat to that. After this tour, I'm going to sit back and reassess my position. I'm not going to go on the road for six months at a stretch anymore. I have a feeling I may die pretty soon. I'm not looking for sympathy when I say that, but I've always had a very intuitive sense about myself, and I can sense that I don't have that long to do everything I want to do. I'm not putting a time limit on myself, but I know I will not achieve all I want to unless I take time away from the band to work on them very hard. We need to take a little time away from each other. I want everyone to take a chance to explore their talents, to work with other people if need be. No, Dio is not breaking up, but we are going to reevaluate our commitments. Hopefully, there will be time for us to take on some little projects on our own, yet still keep Dio going. We've worked too hard to throw anything away. But there is more to life than living out of a suitcase. I'm determined to find out exactly what life has in store for me."

Back to the chat Ronnie had with Steve Newton, Dio said that the new album was doing great guns at the box office, (over)estimating US sales at about 900,000 copies, but also complaining that "the problem at this particular moment is that there's not very much radio play, especially in this country, because of all of the rating situations and again the occult situations, the PMRC, all that, which has really soured a lot of people from playing this music. That's very stupid, by the way, but it really has hurt. If your music can't be heard, nobody's gonna know that it's available, or even know if they like it or dislike it, so then they won't buy it. But in a climate where there's not a lot of sales happening, our product always does well. We always have a very broad base of loyal supporters who are gonna be there, and then our show and word of mouth converts the others. So, I'm very pleased with what has happened with the LP."

Asked specifically about the then hotly discussed PMRC censorship issue, Ronnie indicates that "we've not nearly been attacked as much as some of the others have, but then again, we didn't deserve to get attacked in the first place. I don't write that kind of material. They have preconceived notions as to what someone is going to be because he or she is in heavy metal music, and right away the stamp is on there: 'You're heavy metal; you must be as bad as Blackie Lawless or as bad as Dee Snider' or whoever they think is bad—whom I don't think are bad at all.

"It's not been nearly as vicious for us as it has been for a few, but then again, why should it be? We don't write that kind of music. I have no interest in black magic whatsoever. I've always been a practitioner of white magic, which is for good. I know anything you'd want to know about the occult because I've studied it for a long time. Ignorance leads you down the wrong path. I don't want to be ignorant about it. I learned long ago that you don't meddle with spirits. You don't meddle with good ones, you don't meddle with bad ones, because once you open the door and let them in, they never go away. You can't say, 'Well, your time's up—bye!' You know, you're opening up something horrible there when that happens, so my advice to anyone is just to stay away from any kind of black magic. White magic is fine; it's for the good. And that's the only thing I've ever been interested in."

Ronnie continues, explaining that when Rainbow was recording *Long Live Rock 'n' Roll*, "We had some real weird devil experiences with a real bad spirit that was there posing as Baal, who is the earliest form of devil worship by the primitive people. And we got someone who claimed to be Baal and created a lot of chaos up there at the studio. Tapes would stop, and we'd go into a locked room and machines would suddenly go on. We had a lot of problems with that, but we got over it. It was our own fault because we started dabbling again, and calling up something that we shouldn't have dealt with. But being strong believers in God . . . and by god, I mean, I'm not talking about *the* God that perhaps everyone thinks of. My feelings of religion are a lot different than others. Mine is that God and the devil reside in both of us, in all of us, and you just walk that fine line, teetering on the brink. You can choose either the good way or the bad way. And again, the god I'm talking about, we believe in something good, not something bad. The good side, not the bad side. And because of that strong belief that all of us had in that band, we were able to overcome any problems that might have arisen because of dabbling in the dark side. But yeah, we had some problems with that one."

Sacred Heart managed an impressive #4 placement on the UK charts (no doubt aided and abetted by the ancillary single and EP product) and #12 in Germany but stalled at #29 on Billboard and #35 in Canada. "Rock 'n' Roll Children" got to #26 in the UK and that same number on the Billboard subchart, Mainstream Rock. "Hungry for Heaven" peaked at #56 in the UK and #30 on the Mainstream Rock grid. On October 15, 1985, three months after hitting the shops, the album certified gold in the US but has not to this day managed to find platinum.

As far as important reviews go, *Kerrang!*'s Dave Dickson was up to the task of tackling *Sacred Heart*, writing, "Much as I like Dio as a band, and as much as I admire Ronnie James Dio as a vocalist and a performer, when push comes to shove, it has to be said that this is not a great record. Why is this not a great record? Certainly, *Sacred Heart* is a good album, but then Dio set such high standards for themselves with their debut effort, *Holy Diver*, that they have failed to live up to them since. Well, no, that's not fair; in fact, the problem is that they failed to exceed those standards. Dio's last effort, *The Last in Line*, was not a great album either and here we are, two years and three albums on, and where's the progression? Where's the indication that Ronnie has anything other than variations on a theme to offer us? The truly disappointing aspect of *Sacred Heart* is that any one of its nine tracks could've appeared on *Holy Diver*, and indeed all three albums have a collection of interchangeable tracks that wouldn't upset the balance of the records wherever they were placed.

"A word for Vivian Campbell," continues Dickson, "who seems to have earned himself some space at last. His playing here is quite exceptional and his histrionics on 'Just Another Day' and 'Fallen Angels' are staggering. This man is rapidly turning into a sensational guitarist of major stature! The use of Claude Schnell's keyboards is more imaginative than of old, but then both these instances are more cases of band members having a greater say than their boss pulling his finger out, I suspect.

"Ronnie has stated that this album is based around the power of dreams, but his lyrics and melodies on the record leave me firmly earthbound. Granted, the man has every right to be a romantic, but when he insists on writings lines like, 'You fight to kill the dragon / You bargain with the beast,' I begin to wonder just what it is that Ronnie is trying to tell me. I wanted an album that gave some indication that Dio were going to be forging a path through a rather turgid market and assuming a role at the forefront of the rock field like Zeppelin did in the '70s. Instead, I get an album that displays some technical advances but is essentially the same animal as its two predecessors. Ronnie, I do not detect much in the way of useful movement; your pace seems to have slowed and your punch is no longer as sure, swift, and deadly."

Before Ronnie could indulge in his imagined next career as a film director, there was more-pressing business to address. Dio's *Sacred Heart* tour kicked off with a bang, with Dio and a bunch of other acts, most notably Foreigner and Sting, playing a rock festival in Japan on August 10,

CNE Grandstand, Toronto, Canada, August 31, 1985. © *Martin Popoff*

1985, to a crowd of 25,000. Then it was back to North America for upward of ninety dates, all over Canada and the States, including Hawaii. The Wendy Dio–managed Rough Cutt was the backup band of choice for this extensive trek, with Yngwie Malmsteen logging on for the back ten dates.

Then it was over to mainland Europe and the UK on April 14, 1986, for another couple of dozen shows with Keel in tow. Shockingly, Vivian Campbell would not be in the band starting at this juncture, replaced by Craig Goldy (more on this later).

America saw a second assault (supported by Accept) commence on June 6, 1986, the trek winding up on August 1 before a trip to Japan and Australia for ten shows through mid-September, and an oddball stop in Puerto Rico winding out the exhaustive fourteen months on the road to rock. Crowd sizes varied wildly, with 5,000 being a good average for Europe, 6,000 or 7,000 in the States, although oddly there were a lot of shows pulling 4,500, 5,000, and then another clump up around 9,000 or 10,000.

One milestone was the performance at a nearly sold-out Madison Square Garden on June 20. It was so significant, as Wendy Dio explains, that Ronnie wanted to end his autobiography—or at least his *first* autobiography—with the accounting of this event. "Ronnie wanted the book to end in 1986 at Madison Square Garden, because he had intended to write another book. His life was so long that there was just too much to be in one book. So, he decided that he would . . . well, when he was playing Madison Square Garden, a journalist said to him, 'How did you get started in the business?' And he said, 'I was going to give the usual answer and then I thought, well, how did I get started?' And he figured that was the right time to start and end the book. So that's what his plan was. When he was in bands, before he was in Elf or anything, he would drive down to New York City and pound the pavement and get somebody to listen to his demos and so on and so forth. And looking up and seeing Madison Square Garden, he said, 'One day my name will be up there in lights.' So that's why that was such an important thing for him to start and end the book there."

"Once you had artwork like that on the front of your covers, then there's your show! *Sacred Heart* has a dragon? Let's build a dragon!" said Ronnie, a little tongue in cheek, sensing that the stage show had gotten a little out of hand at this point. Vivian is in full agreement: "I mean, from day one, the whole thing was over the top. We used to call Ronnie, Walt Dio, because he was so into the theatrical aspect of it. We were pretty modest propwise on the *Holy Diver* tour because obviously we were just starting out, but I mean, *The Last in Line* was pretty epic [laughs], pretty *Spinal Tap*–esque. There were a few nights where Vinny and Jimmy and I were in the top of the pyramid that didn't open, like being in the pod in *Spinal Tap*. We had a few of those nights. But yeah, by the time we got to *Sacred Heart*, we had a couple of successful tours, so I guess Ronnie decided he would spend more money on the prop aspect of it. It was never my thing. I guess kids going to the shows, it was part and parcel of what they wanted to see, but it was never big on my criteria list."

The show indeed featured a dragon, an 18-foot-tall mechanical one at that, with a 35-foot wingspan, along with a castle set complete with parapets, all on a 60-by-40-foot stage. The long tail of the dragon blended with a set of stairs. Keyboardist Claude Schnell was perched upon high, and lasers (both krypton and argon; remote scanning was also utilized) shot everywhere, amid smoke and dramatic lighting and sparks, exploding parapets, and a backdrop screen featuring all manner of monsters. Also, part of the stew was a working drawbridge, a 6-foot crystal ball featuring holographic images and two 8-foot battling knights. Also on the equipment list: 468 lights, with 320 above, 70 on the floor, 30 Vari-lites, and 48 aircraft lights—the lighting alone accounted for a half-million watts of power. In all, it cost close to a million dollars, and it took five 48-foot semis to transport. Three buses were also needed to transport the band and its twenty-man crew.

"I doubt anyone will ever see a show like this again," enthused Dio at the time, speaking with Carol Wilshire of the *San Francisco Times*. "Until next year when we do it up even better. I try to write about values of older times, medieval times, when a knight would try to save a damsel in distress, instead of dragging her behind a bush and having his way with her. We live in a world that day after day is so depressing, that I think it's nice once in a while to escape. We spend a fortune to keep the show on the road, but we get it back by the appreciation. I really care about my audience. They've been through all the musical and band changes with me and have remained loyal. They have a lot of choices to go to shows today, and it costs a lot of money to see each one of them. I'd like them to realize that when they come to one of our shows, they will get value for their money.

"People who are going to our show are not the same people who would go see Lionel Ritchie or Chicago," continued Ronnie. "When they come to our show, or an Iron Maiden show or a Ratt show or a Judas Priest show, it's a total experience. In a Kenny Rogers show, you don't see the stage blowing up an awful lot. Ours is a very aggressive form of music, so why not have aggressive effects with it? I think the show does take away from the music in some ways, but I think the project in the end is most important. I'm not worried about the music because I know how good we are as a band. We're the best in the world at what we do."

In conjunction with the start of the second American leg of the tour, the band issued a fairly insignificant EP called *Intermission*, which we will deal with in the following chapter. First, however, we must address the stunning departure of Vivian Campbell from the ranks of Dio.

"The whole thing, the whole situation was sort of unjust," begins Campbell. "Financially we were being screwed; we were being ripped off. And to add insult to injury, we weren't being treated very well, on a personal level. And I know that we all shared those grievances, because Ronnie and Wendy didn't discriminate when it came to dumping on people [laughs], no matter if it was the guitar player or the drummer or the roadies. You got to see the wrath of shit. I don't honestly know if they had any other beefs. I actually thought that Jimmy and Vinny enjoyed better relationships with Ronnie than I did. I didn't have a problem with that, but I was always aware of it, that they could actually have something in common and laugh and talk and have a conversation. I never felt that I had anything in common with Ronnie, other than the fact that we were in the same band.

"It was run like a fucking shambles," replies Viv, asked about the operation of the band as a business. "Not that I know anything about business, but yeah, it was run really

. . . I think any sort of business where you don't respect the people that you work with is not a business that is run well. Any business's most valuable asset is its people. And Ronnie and Wendy did not treat people well, and that's not a good position to run a business from. People don't want to work for you."

And so, Viv leaves. "We did the first leg of the American tour, and then there were two or three weeks before we started in England. That time was for the equipment to ship over. And during that time, I went back to Ireland. We'd been having—or we'd been trying to have—negotiations with Wendy Dio about getting more money. We were salaried. We got none of the tour, none of the records, none of the T-shirts. And we were earning less than the road crew. Literally. Less than the sound engineer, less than the lighting guy. And you know, it was wrong. We had been promised something else, and so I was the one who had the least to lose. The other guys, Vinny and Jimmy, they were homeowners, and they were married, and they had mortgages and stuff. I had none of that. So, I had nothing to lose. So, I was the one who was pushing the issue.

"And I kept trying to call Wendy. You know, 'I'll talk to you next week. I'm busy. Well, when we're on tour, we'll sit down and talk about it.' So, she kept stonewalling me. And then, I went back to my parents' house in Ireland, expecting that we would be starting the UK tour a week or two later. And I got a FedEx package, and it was an employment contract from Niji, from Wendy's company. They were going to give me . . . I don't know what it was, an extra $200, $300, $400 a week—whatever it was—to bring my pay a bit more in line with the road crew [laughs]. And basically, they wanted me to sign this contract. And the cover letter said, you know, if you do not wish to sign this contract, basically don't bother showing up for the first UK gig. By this stage already, I'm sure they knew I wasn't going to sign it, and they already had Craig Goldy waiting in the wings, hovering [laughs]. It was just wrong. The whole situation was just wrong. It wasn't pleasant.

"It was all strictly business," shrugs off Campbell. "I mean, that's what it all came down to. The thing was, I was twenty; I didn't mind working for peanuts, which I did. The problem was, we joined a band. I remember the very first time we all met in London, when I auditioned. We got together and we played, and it all went great, and then went and had a drink, and we were talking about the band, and it was Ronnie's record deal. And he said, 'I'm going to call the band Dio because it's my name, my record deal, blah blah blah.' And you know, that was fair enough, but he said, 'If things go well, by the third album, we'll make it equitable.' And things did go very, very well. And by the third album, it wasn't to be equitable. And I just called him on it and said, 'You know, you promised us this, and it didn't happen.' And he said, 'Well, you can stay, or you can go, but it's not going to change.'

"And to add insult to injury, I mean, like I said, when we were out playing on the *Last in Line* tour and *Sacred Heart* tour, the guys in the band who had written the music, Jimmy and myself, were getting paid less than the guy who was mixing us out front and getting paid less than the guy who was doing the lights. You know, these guys were professionals, and they wouldn't work for less than a certain amount, but we would because we're stupid musicians. And that's okay if you're just a hired musician and it's totally Ronnie's gig. But the fact was, he always presented it as a band, even though it was his name. But he would always harp on about that.

"And you know, it was. It was very, very much a collaborative effort with everyone contributing all the way along the line. And we got none of the record sales, we got no points from the records, and we basically got beat up over our publishing. 'Rainbow in the Dark' was a Sweet Savage song, but I got less than a quarter of it; I got 12.5 percent. And Vinny Appice was delegated as much publishing on that song as I was because he put in those backbeats before the solo, which is good, because they're part of the song. But it was just so wrong in that way.

"So, you're up there onstage playing the L.A. Forum or whatever, sold out; you know that Ronnie's making several hundred thousand dollars that night; you're earning less than the guy mixing the sound and the guy doing the lights, only a hundred bucks more than the guy who is tuning your guitars for you. You get none of the T-shirt sales, none of the ticket sales, none of the points from the record. And you know, that was okay for a while, paying your dues or whatever, but he had promised us something and I called him on it, and he wasn't prepared to keep his word. So, I was the first to get fired, and I don't know what the deal was exactly with Jimmy and Vinny, but they had a couple of comings and goings. But at the time, I was probably the most vocal about it because I had nothing to lose. I wasn't married at the time, I didn't have a home, so I had no mortgage payments. I had no debts hanging around my neck, so I could take the chance and I did. It was unfortunate, you know, because it really, really was a great band and we could've had a future. But it all came down to the dollars and greed, and I don't know how much of that was Ronnie and how much of it was Wendy."

I asked Viv during this interview—this was 2004—if he had kept in touch with Jimmy Bain. "Yeah, but I don't get to talk to him very often," answered Campbell. "Maybe once a year I'll get to talk to him or see him. And Vinny, I barely get to see or talk to. As far as I know, he's not even playing drums at the moment. And Ronnie, I never see or talk to [laughs]. There's not a lot of love lost."

As a bit of an exercise in psychological profiling over time, here's how Viv viewed this painful part of his story fifteen years later, in conversation with Jimmy Kay. To be sure, the lion's share of his views and recollections haven't changed, but there has been a shift in perspective.

"Maybe I was fearless or maybe I was stupid," begins Campbell. "Maybe it was a bit of both. But I was in my early twenties and, you know, it wasn't about the money—it was about the principle. I'm very, very big on principle. When somebody makes me a promise, I expect them to keep it, you know? Because I keep my word. That's just the way I was brought up. When I tell somebody I'm going to do something, I do it; I meet my commitments. And Ronnie had promised us. We worked for very, very little money, like I say, less than people on the road crew. We never got royalty checks. We worked for minimum wage, even though we were writing the music. But we were willing to do it. We'd been promised by the third album it would be an equity situation, and that was the principle that got me fired. And the band was very, very successful. First album went gold pretty much right away. *The Last in Line* went platinum; *Sacred Heart* went gold.

We have the gold records. We were selling a lot of records, and we were all very involved in the creative process. It really, really was a collaborative process, you know?"

In other interviews on the subject, Viv clarifies that this discussion about what would happen on the third album was conducted between the four guys in the band, and that Wendy "was not in the room." This took place at John Henry's rehearsal studio in North London, and Viv has even remarked in the past that Ronnie was "so stoned," he might not even remember making any such agreement. Viv also says that the pay went up fairly substantially from tour to tour, and repeatedly expressed regrets at some of the harsh things he said about Ronnie in the press, which resulted in a sort of "burning of bridges" effect if one is to take into account the ire that Ronnie had toward Viv years and even decades later.

Of note, Jimmy Bain went even further, remembering that it was supposed to turn into an equitable band situation after the *first* album, while repeatedly, again, Viv always mentions the third album. Bain also has put a dollar amount on what the band members were paid in the beginning—$150 per week—and that he was resentful when it didn't go up immediately once the guys were well into the tour cycle for the first album, when it was obvious that things were working out.

"We were getting squeezed on that as well, but we paid our dues," continues Viv. "That's kind of how we look at it. Ronnie was the big name, where it made sense to name the band Dio. But I think Wendy Dio never really saw it as a band. Wendy, Ronnie's estranged wife and manager, she never really saw the value, I think, in the band. And that is something that really upset me with Ronnie. After I was fired, I think Ronnie knew better. He understood the real magic that the original band had and the chemistry we had and how we created it together. So that was really sad that he was willing to capitulate to Wendy. I think he was really fearful of her, and he never stood up to her. And you know, like I say, it was never about money. People said to me, 'Oh, Campbell wanted the same money as Dio' or whatever. No, I just wanted Ronnie to fulfill his promises. It was a contract that was between the four of us, and he just wasn't man enough to follow through on it. I called him on it, and I got fired as a result. So, it was very, very painful for me, for many, many years. I didn't react to the situation very well.

"Such is life, you know? You look back and you say, well, I wish I'd done this a little differently or whatever, but I wouldn't have done anything differently in regard to the principle of that situation. I still would've got myself fired. I would've stood up and said, hey, you promised us by the third album you would make it an equity situation. Like I say, they offered us a few hundred dollars more per week, and I got sent a contract by Wendy that said fill this out and return it by this date, and it will constitute you no longer being in the band. I tried to call Ronnie. I was in Ireland between time, between legs of the *Sacred Heart* tour. I'd been in the UK, and I got back to visit my family and parents. I got this contract in this FedEx envelope, and I was shocked. I tried to call Ronnie, and he wouldn't answer the phone. The next thing is the band was up in the UK with Craig Goldy. I remember watching them on TV, this live TV show, thinking oh my God.

"So that was it. I mean, it was a seamless transition. Obviously, it was well executed and planned. But I wouldn't have changed any of that. I would change maybe how I reacted to it over the years. You know, both Ronnie and I made the mistake of airing our grievances in public, which is never a good idea. But it is what it is. And it was only after Ronnie passed away that I was really able to kind of look at that entire situation in a very different light. For years I didn't really want anything to do with the discography of Dio, and after Ronnie passed away, I've finally been willing to look at it. And over the years I had my own cancer diagnosis, and that really changes a lot of things."

"Also, around that time, I went on tour playing guitars with Thin Lizzy, and that really reignited my youthful passion as a guitar player. Lizzy meant so much to me growing up in my teenage years, and really my formative years prior to Dio. And so, all these things kind of happened and coalesced, and I really wanted to play guitar again like that. To really reconnect with that fire that I had as a teenager. So, I was able to look back on the Dio catalog, and my thinking about it just changed dramatically. I thought, you know what? I created those songs together with Ronnie, and together with Jimmy and Vinny we wrote those songs, we made those records, we toured, we sold those records, we created that magic. So, it's as much our legacy—Jimmy and Vinny and myself—as it is Ronnie's. But I walked away from that, and I just disowned it for many, many years because of the hurt that it caused me. But like I say, after Ronnie passed away, I was able to look at it in a different way and enjoy it. I thoroughly enjoy being up there onstage playing with Vinny in our band Last in Line now. And it was great when Jimmy was alive, the original magic, just to be able to play this music and our new music now with Andrew Freeman and Phil Soussan and myself. It's just a great band, and it really feels cathartic to me. It really makes me feel alive, to get back to that, you know?"

"There were some business problems within the band," explained Vinny, summing up the situation in 2017, so only a couple of years earlier than this Jimmy Kay chat with Viv. "We were promised an equal share in things, and we gave it up for the first album and tour, because okay, it costs a lot of money to launch a thing, and Ronnie is putting in his money and whatever. Then it never happened. We were doing tours in arenas. Back then, one of the tours grossed $8 million, and that was in those dollars. That's probably $80 million now; I don't know. But we got nothing out of it. We were on salaries and stuff. So what was promised never happened. And Vivian really called him and the management on it, and it kind of became bad blood with money. But we all felt the same way, that we were getting a little bit . . . we're not getting what we were promised, and we should be doing better than we were doing. Somebody's making a lot of money there, other than us. So that's what happened with Viv. Ronnie and Viv didn't see eye to eye.

"And then finally Ronnie said to me, 'I'm going to fire Viv.' And I went, 'What?!' I was in shock, and I kind of mentioned that that's not a great idea, because he's part of the sound of the band. And he decided that, you know, we could go on without him, and that's what happened. Now, whenever you've got something that works with a band that is magical with the people in it, you don't do that. He was part of the sound. It's like Led Zeppelin. They didn't even continue with another drummer. They could've made zillions of dollars, but they didn't. And then they got his son Jason for that one reunion show. Magic is within certain people, and it really worked. And when you change the parts around, it's not the same. Nowadays it's different because there's all these bands out

München Basketball
Halle, Munich, Germany,
April 25, 1986.

with one original member or no members. Because somebody owns the name and it's a commercial enterprise and they go out and play. But they're good. But back in the day when you're writing and stuff, classic rock, and it's in the history books, then that's where it's important to not make changes."

Asked by Jimmy Kay if he could comment about Viv's issues with Ronnie, Claude Schnell chuckled, "I could. Here's why I won't. Because it's not my place to talk about what monies other people did or didn't get. I will say this. For as much as I was led to believe what I would get early on and didn't, it's frustrating. I found my solace in the fact that I knew what Vinny was promised when he left Sabbath to be Ronnie's right-hand man, and then he never got it either. So as bad as I felt about not getting whatever it was, I could only imagine being in Vinny's shoes, being promised the world and not getting it."

Generally, however, Claude looks at the situation somewhat philosophically. "Okay, so that goes to more of an anthropological issue than it has to do with the band. I don't know what situations you've found yourself in with other people, but the people that usually speak up the most are the people who have the least to lose. So being in a band in L.A. in that day, no matter how secure you were, it was a very tentative position.

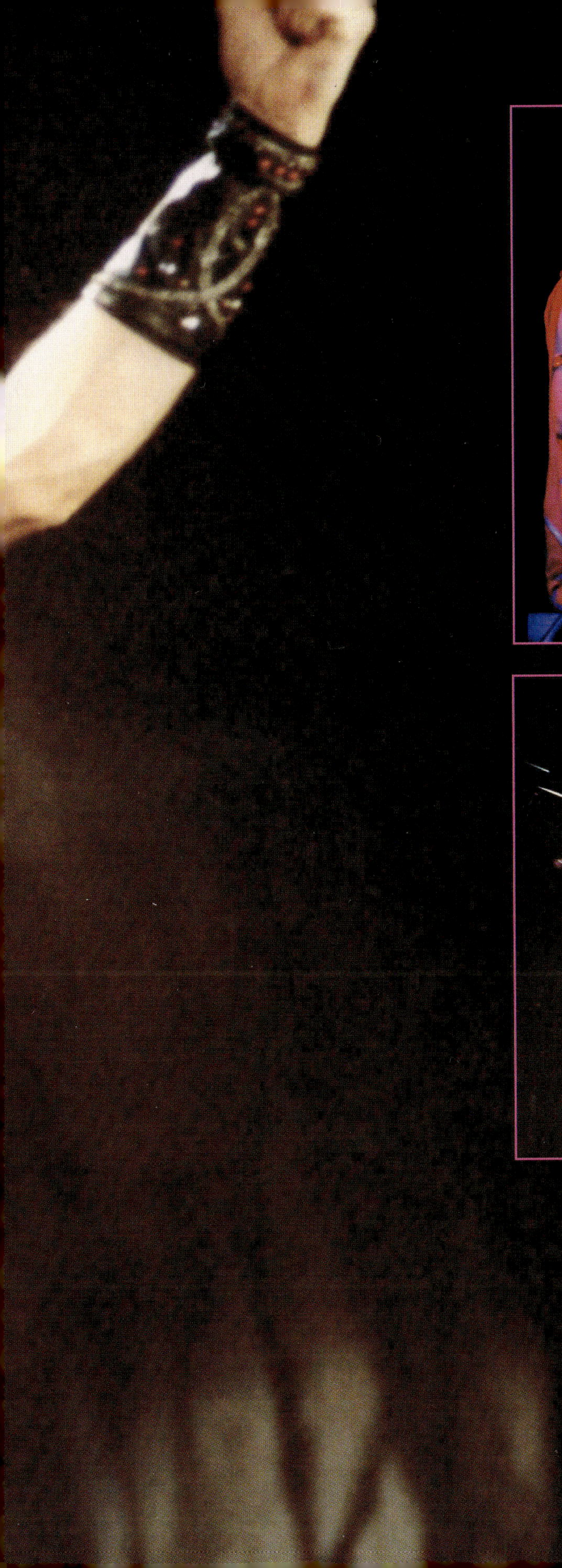

More shots from the band's show at the München Basketball Halle, Munich, Germany, April 25, 1986.
© *Wolfgang Gürster*

Because there was always somebody trying to get your gig. There was always somebody who thought they were better than you. There was always somebody who is newer, who had a better reputation, who had some tricks, who is better looking or younger or who knows what.

"But if you look at the lineage of especially guitar players, their life span in most bands was extremely limited. I mean, Ronnie used to say that musicians in L.A. bands are basically interchangeable parts in a jigsaw puzzle. And look at, for example, Deep Purple, Whitesnake, and what was Mel Galley's band?—Trapeze. They are interchangeable parts. I mean, there are so many different incarnations of the same guys being in different bands, you don't really know. And look what happened to Jake with Ozzy. Or Daisley with Ozzy for that matter. Nobody could really say that they knew that what was true on Monday was going to remain true on Tuesday. So as a result, that keeps people in those positions relatively docile. You don't want to stir the shit; you don't want to make waves when it could mean losing your meal ticket.

"Enter Vivian, who came from a wealthy family, right? Exactly. So as far as Vivian was concerned, the pennies he was getting paid by Ronnie . . . I can tell you this much: in the early days, our salaries were not anywhere near what much less famous bands were making. But you know, we had the distinction of playing with the greatest singer of the day, so okay, fine, whatever. And you know, nobody had a gun to our heads. If we didn't like what we were making, we were more than welcome to go and find a gig somewhere else.

"Which, interestingly, is not very well known, but in . . . I want to say 1985, after the *Sacred Heart* tour, I got invited to go audition for Foreigner. And it was a big-money gig. And Lou Gramm was a friend of mine from my days in Buffalo. Lou Gramm used to play in a band called Black Sheep, before he went into Foreigner, and Black Sheep was a band from Rochester. I was going to school in Buffalo. So, we played a lot of the same circuits, crossed paths a lot. I actually think I met Lou through Billy Sheehan, who is a very, very close friend of mine. So, when I got the call from Foreigner's management, I was in Corpus Christi, Texas, and he said, 'Yeah, look, Foreigner is going on tour.' And this is, by the way, the album that had 'That Was Yesterday,' *Agent Provocateur*.

Pass and poster

"So, they wanted me to fly up like the next weekend to audition, and I'm in the middle of the tour with Dio. 'But yeah, we hear you're not really happy there.' Well, be that as it may, I'm not going to walk out on a fricking tour. That's just not done. 'Oh, well, we might find somebody else by the time you're ready to come audition.' Well, if that's what happens, that's what happens. But I don't want to be the guy who leaves someone like Ronnie in the lurch. That's just not the way I was brought up.

"So, by the time the tour was over, I got a call from Wendy, who called me into the office. 'So what's this I hear about you going to play for Foreigner?' I'm like, 'Well, I don't know. Did I already pass the audition? Because I haven't even auditioned yet.' 'Well, are you going to audition?' And I'm like, 'Well, you're my manager; should I?' 'Well, I guess if you want to you can.'

"I said, 'Look, I need to go to New York to see my mom anyway.' My mom was in quite ill health. They were going to buy me a first-class ticket to go to New York. I love that *4* album. My wife and I, our song was 'Waiting for a Girl Like You' from the Foreigner *4* album, and the opportunity to go out with that band and do that was just too tempting not to do. And honestly, I didn't really think that it was going to be something that would take me away from Dio. That being said, after the unfulfilled promises, I felt that I owed it to myself to at least consider my options.

"So, I'm all set to go to New York. I spend like two days crashing, trying to learn all the songs at the same time; basically, didn't learn any of them because they just turned into one big mush in my head. And the night before I'm about to leave, I get a call from Ronnie, who asked me to come over to his house for dinner. Which is fine; I don't know how many guys you've spoken to, but Ronnie was quite a decent cook. And he was known for inviting people over to his house, just for a meal. He would always do Thanksgiving on his own, and he would always cook and all that kind of stuff. So anyway, I didn't want to say no, because you don't say no to somebody who invites you to dinner, especially if it's Ronnie. Even though my flight was like at seven o'clock the following morning.

"So, I went over and we're having dinner and having a great ol' time, and it was 'Listen, the real reason I called you over is that I really have to apologize. I know that we promised you a bunch of things that for reasons out of our control never really came to pass. I'll give you my word of honor that on the next tour, on the next record, you're going to have everything that you wanted. We may even throw a keyboard solo on the record. You certainly have a keyboard solo in the live show, and I really want to exploit your abilities and let you become the keyboard player that you've worked so hard to become.'

"So, I was like, 'Well, that's nice to hear, but actually, do you really expect me to believe that there's anything that was out of your control?' And he says, 'Well, whether you believe it or not, it was. When the set was designed, it was designed in a way, through nobody's fault, that didn't include the provision for where the keyboards could be. And as a result, we kind of had to stick you wherever you could be. At least you weren't offstage.' I don't know if you saw that tour, but I was like parked next to the Sphinx. It looked like I was taking care of the Sphinx or something.

"But anyway, for Ronnie to open up to me, that meant a lot to me. I mean, I think that might've been one of the first times that we really had a heart-to-heart. And I knew that this was Ronnie, the person, speaking to me. Not Ronnie my boss, not Ronnie the brilliant artist, not Ronnie the producer, not Ronnie the singer—just Ronnie my friend. There was, if I dare say, a bit of humility in the discussion that we had, and that meant a lot to me. Because frankly, I didn't think I deserved to be offstage. But frankly, I agreed to that from day one. You can't disagree to something you want to do with your eyes open."

And the end result of this dinner with the boss? Says Claude, "Assuming that you saw the *Dream Evil* tour, absolutely it came to pass." Schnell's role, as promised, would indeed gain in prominence, while, as we know, Viv would be fired.

Final word goes to Wendy, who vehemently refuted Viv's telling of the tale, which, pertinently, leaves out Wendy's assertion that Viv, before he received his FedEx package in Ireland, had an attorney call her up outlining a series of demands.

"Well, I mean, they were the band, but they were paid employees," begins Dio, explaining all this to Jimmy Kay and Alan Dixon. "We paid for everything when we were out of the road. We paid for the hotels, the crew, the buses, the trucks. We also actually mortgaged our house in able to do that. So therefore, they were a band, but they were still employees. They got paid whether we got money or not. And Ronnie, being the top draw of course, it's his band, so . . .

Ad for a concert video

"I know Vivian Campbell always said he was cheap," continues Wendy. "Ronnie was never cheap with anyone or anything. Never, ever. I don't know how many people believe those things, but that's the way it was. Normally I don't address this, but I wanted to put in the book about exactly how much was earned. Because Ronnie was never cheap, and he didn't pay him $100 a week! How did Vivian buy a Ferrari on $100 a week? How does Vinny Appice buy a house and Jimmy Bain buy a house if they were being paid $100 a week? And that's something where Ronnie can't defend himself. I got really angry about that. Because a lot of people say, 'Oh, Ronnie's cheap.' But Ronnie was never, ever cheap. He never cared about money. He was never cheap."

Asked by Jimmy about Viv's oft-repeated remark about getting paid less than the road crew, Wendy says, "I'll explain that. All right, so they were on a retainer, which means they got paid every week whether they worked or not. We went on a six-week tour, and the soundman probably got $2,000 a week, and he was getting $1,700. So there—yes." The implication there is that for many, many weeks, Viv was getting $1,700 for each of those weeks, when any given rigger or sound or lighting guy was earning nothing.

As she details in an aside in Ronnie's book, Wendy recalls that Viv was asking for his weekly pay to double from the $1,700 he was getting, along with various forms of equity, and that she had five days to respond, or else Viv wasn't going to do the European tour. When the lawyer called back five days later, Wendy informed him that Campbell had already been replaced.

"Rock 'n' Roll Children" in three places, plus a pass to see it performed live. *Martin Popoff archive*

On the subject of misconceptions about band management, Wendy says that "I think people fail to see how much we actually do. Especially when I was managing the band, there was only really Sharon Osbourne and myself as the only two women managers. You had all these men telling us that we didn't know what we were doing, and they could do a much-better job than us. Which I think is wrong, because women are detail oriented. Men might just go, 'Oh, you know . . . ,' but we worked really, really hard. And I think the misconception is that the managers take the money and that's it. There are so many things. Especially with me. I did business management as well as regular management. I was the one who called the bus company, the truck company, the crew, the hotels—everything was done by us. Everything was done from the office. The expenses on tour . . . you've got your buses, your trucks, you've got all that crew to pay, you've got the per diems, the hotels. I mean, it's like never-ending. Never-ending money being taken out. When we started the band, we didn't know what was going to happen with Dio. And like I say, we just mortgaged our house and went all the way for it and did everything. And luckily it was a success. But it could've been a disaster."

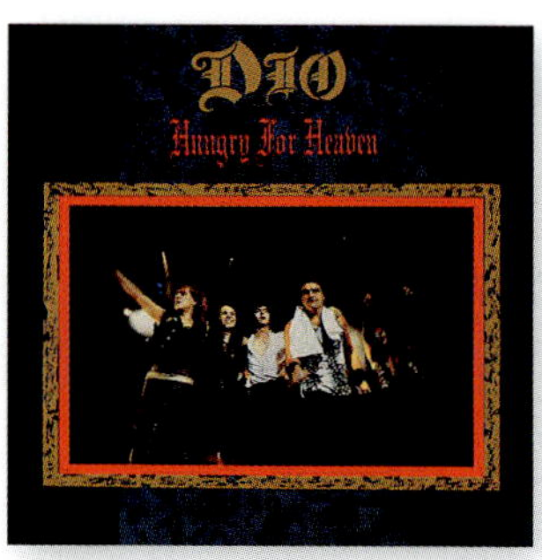

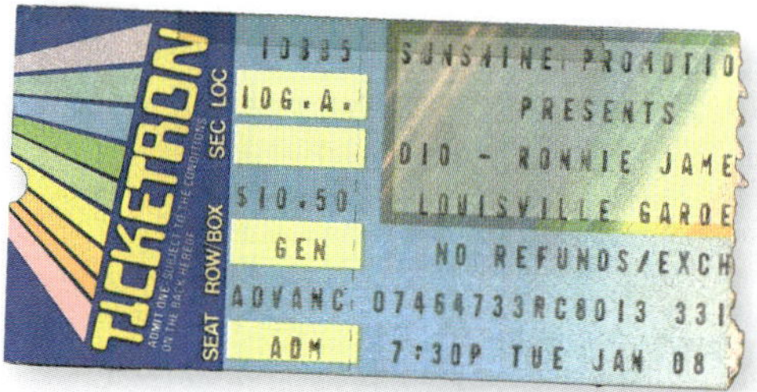

A couple of stubs, plus the "Hungry for Heaven" UK single picture sleeve. *Martin Popoff archive*

CHAPTER 5

"We weren't allowed by the record company to do a full live album."

INTERMISSION

To commemorate the second leg of the *Sacred Heart* tour, and to introduce the band's new guitar player, Craig Goldy, Dio issued *Intermission*, a six-track live EP that also featured a new studio number called "Time to Burn."

"Yes, but it's still not the same," sighed Dio, looking back on a missed opportunity for a live album. "That was a compromise. It was 'Okay, we know you really want to do a live album; well, we'll let you do half of it live, and the other half . . .' That's not representative of the live show. So, I don't consider *Intermission* to be an ultimate live album. The unfortunate thing to me was that we, Dio, never made a live album. I think that was an opportunity well missed—not missed by us but missed by the record company."

At least there was "Time to Burn." "I don't remember which film it was for," says Ronnie, obviously searching. "I'm pretty sure we wrote it for a film. We did 'Hide in the Rainbow' for *Iron Eagle*. 'Time to Burn' was for something else. But I like that song a lot. It was a good place for us anyway, the good times; we really could just write what we wanted. Whether it would be accepted, it wasn't quite so difficult in those days [laughs]. But I remember enjoying the song very much. Like I say, *Intermission* was done because we weren't allowed by the record company to do a full live album. They wanted us to give them another studio album, but I wanted to do something live. So, the compromise was 'We'll let you kind of have half of it live, half the other way.' 'Well, okay.' So, whatever that was worth, that's what was done."

Intermission cassette cover, along with an ad for the EP from *Kerrang! Martin Popoff archive*

Craig tapping his way through a gig at the München Basketball Halle, Munich, Germany, April 25, 1986. © *Wolfgang Gürster*

Craig Goldy (also, aggravatingly, widely spelled Goldie) learned his trade around San Diego and came to the attention of Ronnie through Rough Cutt. As discussed, Claude Schnell also surfaced via Paul Shortino's Rough Cutt—the band had business ties to Dio through shared management. Goldy was soon to find himself dissatisfied with Rough Cutt, who were much older and condescended to the twenty-one-year-old "kid." Next, he joined Giuffria, only to find out the leader of the band, Greg Giuffria of Angel fame, wasn't interested in having Goldy write any of the group's material.

Subsequently, Goldy was to join Dio in March 1986, playing his first shows in April, and so he's not the soloist on these live renditions, which had been recorded back on December 6, 1985, at the San Diego Sports Arena, using the Le Mobile mobile. However, he's been overdubbed playing rhythm guitars, which . . . the point of that can only be seen as a negative, one supposes. That work took place at Amigo Studios and the West Coast location of the Record Plant, in L.A., while the band was concocting "Time to Burn." The EP emerged quickly after Craig's addition to the band, hitting the shops in June 1986. In any event, sleight of hand aside (including no mention of Viv in the album credits, although, granted, no other performers are named either), Ronnie had rationalized the decision to tour with Craig rather than go straight in and make a new record, as an opportunity to break Craig in, as well as to get maximum mileage out of the extensive and expensive *Sacred Heart* stage set.

"We're coming through the second time," Ronnie told K. K. Percy of *Northern Metal* magazine in the summer of '86. "It seems like the tenth time [laughs]. It's a show that, to our minds, needs to be seen again, or can be seen again. It's like a book or film where you see or read it again; you see something you never saw the first time. So, it's a repeat of the *Sacred Heart* tour, but we don't feel as if we're cheating anyone. We're going into some secondary markets that we couldn't get to last tour. Like Flint, Michigan, or Grand Rapids and a lot of places in Florida. We brought two sets with us this time. There's a smaller version of the *Sacred Heart* set in case the venue is too small for the full-sized one. It's virtually the same, but there's different people, and this time we've been able to perfect the show since we've been working on it for a year. We've done Europe, so now we're heading for Mexico, South America, Japan, and Australia."

Asked about *Intermission*, Ronnie begins by pointing out that "this band has been very available since 1983. Not only for tours and albums, but for projects as well, and I think it's time we stopped being so available. It's time we did something for ourselves, take the time to do this next album the way we want to. Let people water at the mouth a little. Not like now, where people say, 'Well, Dio will be here next week; if not next week, the week after or the week after that.' We have another album to make, and I insist it be a stupendous one. And with the new guitarist, we have a new infusion of life and blood. What I really wanted to do was, chronology-wise, at least my history on a live album. Because when you see this band, you get snatches of Rainbow, Black Sabbath, and all of Dio. Now with this new guitar player, you've got this great history to draw from. But we were only allowed to do five songs on the mini-LP, and the studio track. So, we did as much as we could. As far as a double live album, who knows?"

"Well, that goes back to Rough Cutt," Goldy told me, asked about his origin story into the Dio fold. "It stems back to one specific day. Back then, the budgets were much more generous than they are now [laughs]. So, guitar players would work their solos out in the studio. So that meant like anywhere from three to eight hours per solo, and that's a lot of money being spent, working them out. And it worked out for a lot of guitar players that way. But I was the kind of guy who liked to work the solos out first and then tailor . . . to me, the solo was supposed to be the instrumental version of the song topic, and you know, it was almost like a paragraph where it starts with an opening statement, supporting facts, and then closing statement. Opening with hello and ending with goodbye. So, to me, improvisation couldn't do

"I want you . . . to stand up and shout," says Ronnie, in another shot from the München Basketball Halle, Munich, Germany, April 25, 1986. © *Wolfgang Gürster*

that. And I didn't want to sit around and certainly didn't want to spend five to six hours coming up with it right there and then in the studio.

"But at the time we had two guitar players," continues Craig—he's referring to Rough Cutt here, and the recording of the band's early demos with Ronnie producing. "The first one took about three hours to do his solo, and then it was time for me, and once we got the headphones and everything set up, I had worked something out the night before, and said, 'Can we try that first? Is that okay?' Ronnie, who was producing us, said, 'Yeah, go for it.' So, I did it, and then I looked back to the control booth, and they were laughing. And I thought oh no. 'Can I do this one more time?' And so, I did it again, and I look back and they're laughing. And I hear in the headphones, 'Just one more time, with a little more confidence.' And they're laughing, and they say, 'Come in.' And I hear laughing in the background, and I come in there, and he goes, 'Take a listen.' And so, I hear two go by, and I said, 'Can I hear the other one?' And they go, 'No.' And I thought, man, I'm really in for a lecture here. What did I do wrong? It was 'No, that's all three—you're done.' Apparently, it worked it out so well that all three guitars sounded like one. And that sparked something with him and I. And then whenever we worked together in the studio, he would have an idea, and I would just go in and do it right then and there. We had a great working relationship, and we were friends off studio as well.

"And one day in the studio, Ronnie looked at me and said, 'You know, if Vivian doesn't ever work out, you would be my first choice.' And then that was it. That's why there were no auditions, because he's a man of his word. And I was in another band with Rudy Sarzo and Tommy Aldridge at the time, and I got the phone call that Viv was out, and I was in, and that was it. And a lot of it was because of our studio relationship and our friendship prior to all that. This band was called Driver; it was just . . . it was the thing that turned into Tony MacAlpine and Project: Driver.

"But I mean, at the time I was in Giuffria, and searching for something more along my roots, and that's where I had heard that Rudy and Tommy were putting a band together. And luckily, I got that spot, because that was closer to the kind of music I wanted to do in the first place. But at the time, they were doing *Hear 'n Aid*, and I know that it was quite an undertaking for Ronnie and Wendy and Vivian and Jimmy, and they kind of put all that together and used all of their network, because it was . . . I can only imagine with touring schedules and recording schedules, to get all those people in the same place at the same time must've been an absolute nightmare."

But because of Rough Cutt, as well as being part of the L.A. underground or foundation, as it were, Craig goes back within the scene, as revealed by this nugget.

"Yes, well, the only thing I ever remember was one time where Ronnie seemed a little nervous, because he had left Black Sabbath, and it was during the *Holy Diver* recordings, and I was over at his house, and he pulled me aside and played something and asked me what I thought. And he kind of . . . he seemed nervous because he . . . for the first time I saw him as being kind of nervous about what are people going to think—what are they going to say? And to me, it seemed obvious how great it was, because it was. At the time, *Holy Diver* had everything. There were certain songs that . . . to me, it had a song for everybody. You know, people who were musicians had something to glean from it, and people who aren't musicians had something they could glean from it. It was unique, it was one of a kind, and it just was odd to see him almost question himself for the first time that I'd ever known him. That didn't last for long, because he soon said, 'I'm not going to worry about it—it is what it is.' And then it just took off [laughs].

"Claude was great," continues Craig, asked about the keyboardist in the band he was now part of. "Great sense of humor, and very, very talented. In fact, yeah, there was . . . Ronnie thought I was crazy, because I loved Deep Purple so much, I was saying, well, why don't we have a keyboard solo on 'All the Fools Sailed Away?' At first, he thought it was crazy; then we brought the idea to Claude, and Claude took the track back and just came up with this really cool keyboard solo, and to be honest with you, I'm glad that worked out. Because Ronnie's funny. If you do something or say something dumb, you're branded for life. Just, you know, not cruel, but just . . . it'll be inside jokes forever about it [laughs]."

More on *Dream Evil*, the band's first album with Craig, later, but for now, in actuality, *Intermission*, at thirty-two minutes, was longer than most Kiss and Van Halen albums. As well, it's quite "useful." Here, "King of Rock and Roll" is much more youthful, fast, and scientific than the stodgy version on *Sacred Heart*. "Rainbow in the Dark" is also a little quicker than the original, a little more compact and all business. "Sacred Heart" contains a bit of jamming but is otherwise not much altered from the original. "Rock 'n' Roll Children" also carries over this nimble and quick vibe, and it also contains segments of a very fast—too fast—"Long Live Rock 'n' Roll" and a very fast (kind of cool at this speed) "Man on the Silver Mountain," both of those being old Rainbow songs. The last of the live material is "We Rock," again executed at quite a clip. The production, for a live album, is adequate, even if the horrid front cover art is not. Talk about underselling the buffoonery of the *Sacred Heart* stage show—this squeezed picture does that in spades.

The new studio track, "Time to Burn," is quite poppy of construct and melody. Schnell is heard prominently, and Ronnie is singing in a hair metal danger zone. Still, this song could have fit just fine on *Sacred Heart*, and not as any sort of fey attempt at a hit.

"I really like the rhythm sound on that," reflects Craig, who figures his guitars on "Time to Burn" and the *Magica* album are the best sounds he ever got with Dio. "Ronnie told me that we were going to be doing an album track, and he said, 'Do you have any riffs?' So we were in the studio, and I just started playing a couple of things I had, and he goes, 'I like that, don't like that, that sounds good, that sounds like this, that sounds like that, ooh, what's that?' We narrowed it down to that one."

All told, across *Intermission*—EPs could be a thing, or they could fizzle—the band is fired up, even if it's the old band playing and not the one pictured, just like some insipid replay of Ozzy's *Diary of a Madman* debacle, where Rudy Sarzo and Tommy Aldridge are pictured, but it's Bob Daisley and Lee Kerslake playing on the album. Focusing on the new studio song (and the only place where there's truthfulness), Craig's solo there is quite worthy, standing up to Viv's hooky ax musings across the five live tracks. We'd soon get to see Craig's approach to solos (i.e., on the subsequent tour cycle),

Sporthalle Böblingen, Böblingen, Germany, April 29, 1986. © *Wolfgang Gürster*

but indeed, Dio guitarists since Goldy, whether it's from personal preference or direction from Ronnie, have at least sporadically dipped in and out of Viv's lines from the studio albums, as testimony to the musicality of the original solos. Indeed, the lines that Campbell plays across those first three solo albums were usually so singable, so hummable, so memorable, they became integral to the compositional identity of the songs at large. Bottom line: Viv knew the value of not winding up high up the squealing, squalling end of the fret board, and as a result he made solos that continually orbited the idea of fleeting riff.

As introduction to Goldy, Ronnie told *Hit Parader*'s Don Mueller at the time that "having Craig in the band has been a real shot in the arm. He's like a breath of fresh air. He's so full of energy and ideas that he's motivated all of us. Before, it had gotten to the point where some of the musicians—Vivian in particular—didn't see things the same way I did. That's fine, but don't tell me, as Vivian did, that you don't want to play heavy metal anymore. The guy's ego just got too big for his own head. Is he still off playing Irish disco music, or has he come to his senses? It's a shame what happened to him. I think people will be amazed by how well Craig plays. He grew up listening to people like Deep Purple and Rainbow, so obviously his influences and mine are very much the same. I used to say that I never wanted to work with an American guitarist, because they were more into theatrics and soloing than playing strong rhythms. But since Craig was weaned on classic rock, he's able to bring together the solid style of European guitarists with the flash of the Americans. He's got the best of both worlds."

Says Craig on this deep well of influence Ronnie alludes to here, "The first time was probably the most challenging just because people didn't really know that I was a big Deep Purple / Dio fan, because I came from Giuffria, right? They had the wrong impression of me from the beginning; that was the hardest part, to let them know that I wasn't just a wimpy guy coming from a wimpy band, playing with this dark heavy metal icon. This man has actually been a part of my life since I was a little kid. So that was the hardest part, really. Because I spent so many years trying to learn Ritchie Blackmore solos note for note that I kind of developed a way to be able to learn other people's solos note for note. And then throughout the years, Ronnie would say, 'You don't have to do it note for note,' and 'You can kind of do your own thing here, and just play some of the main parts.' And so, we did that for a while. A lot of people say, 'Oh, you can do a lot of things in the studio, but can you do it live?' So, I try to emulate the solos the best I could live, so that way when they're listening to it, it sounds like they're listening to the CD, but at the same time it's live. And in a lot of people's minds, that's kind of rare, to be able to play CD quality live. That's been the most challenging thing."

Meanwhile, rumors of Jimmy Bain's dissatisfaction with the Dio band perpetuated. "After hearing some of those stories, I just picked up the phone and called Jimmy," said Dio, back to that *Hit Parader* chat. "I asked him rather jokingly, 'So, I need to find myself a new bassist?' I think Jimmy was in shock for a minute. He didn't have the slightest idea what I was talking about. Evidently all the stories started one night when Jimmy was drinking at the Rainbow in L.A. He does drink quite a bit, and evidently when he was a little drunk, he was approached by another musician who asked him to appear on his album. Jimmy, in his normal enthusiasm, started shouting, 'That's a great idea! We ought to form a band together.' Some people who aren't familiar with Jimmy's sense of humor must've gotten the wrong idea. Before anyone knew it, those stories about him leaving the band were popping up everywhere."

Added Ronnie on the situation with Viv, "He simply lost sight of where he was headed. I've always said I want the people I work with to feel free to try their hand at other musical projects, but Vivian took his one step too far. He formed his own band and his own organization. I could've even handled that, but it was a little upsetting and unfair to the other members of the group. It made it seem like Vivian's mind was not on the band. He's changed his musical perspectives. He doesn't want to play the kind of music we play anymore. He's ready for the Thompson Twins. The reports I heard was that it was reggae music, and we all know how famous the Irish are for their reggae! There's nothing wrong with reggae, and there's nothing wrong with Vivian wanting to play it, but in subsequent conversations, I found out he really didn't like the music we were making. He didn't want to be a guitar hero anymore. That's when I knew I was being handed a load of bullshit. Right then, he was out of the band, and we brought Craig Goldy in. If he wanted to be in the band, he wouldn't have made as many waves as he did. Obviously, he saw his position in the group as being a lot stronger than it actually was. While I have a great deal of anger for Vivian, if we ever come to blows, it will be no fault of mine. The simple truth is that the band left him in his tracks."

Asked whether problems with Viv's girlfriend added fuel to the fire, Ronnie offered that "unquestionably, personal relationships did come into play a bit, but those were not at the core of the problem. I had heard a lot of rumors going around about what was being said behind my back. I've learned over the years that usually, rumors have a great deal of basis in truth. That didn't make me very happy, to say the least. To my mind, it was up to Vivian to tell the people around him to keep their mouths shut."

Sporthalle Böblingen,
Böblingen, Germany,
April 29, 1986.
© Wolfgang Gürster

US vinyl issue of *Intermission*, signed by Vinny. *Martin Popoff archive*

Getting to the sacred heart of *Intermission* was *Kerrang!*'s dependable Dave Dickson, who wrote, "Complaints? Well, the cover is one of the worst I've ever seen, but at least Dean Dragon appears to be getting the upper hand (or nostril); and nowhere does it tell you that the guitarist on the five live tracks is the now-departed Vivian Campbell. So let me be the one to break the news to you. This may also explain why the guitar has been mixed down so much. Rarely does Campbell get to display any teeth on this record. With replacement Craig Goldy, however, it's a different matter. The most fascinating thing about this release is the Craig Goldy / Ronnie James Dio–penned track, 'Time to Burn.' If this is an indication of the way Dio plan to move forward, then book me a ticket in the same carriage. It's more commercial, sure, but it breaks a too-long-established mould in Dio songwriting, a mould that has already become too rigid, too unimaginative. There's no mention of demons, wizards, or even rainbows! But it's strong stuff, a positive step forward and highly recommended listening."

UK ad for *The Dio E.P.*, featuring, in the inset picture, *left to right*, Craig, Vinny, Ronnie, Claude, and Jimmy.

Featuring

HIDE IN THE RAINBOW (PREVIOUSLY UNRELEASED)
HUNGRY FOR HEAVEN • SHAME ON THE NIGHT
EGYPT (THE CHAINS ARE ON)

The DIO E.P.

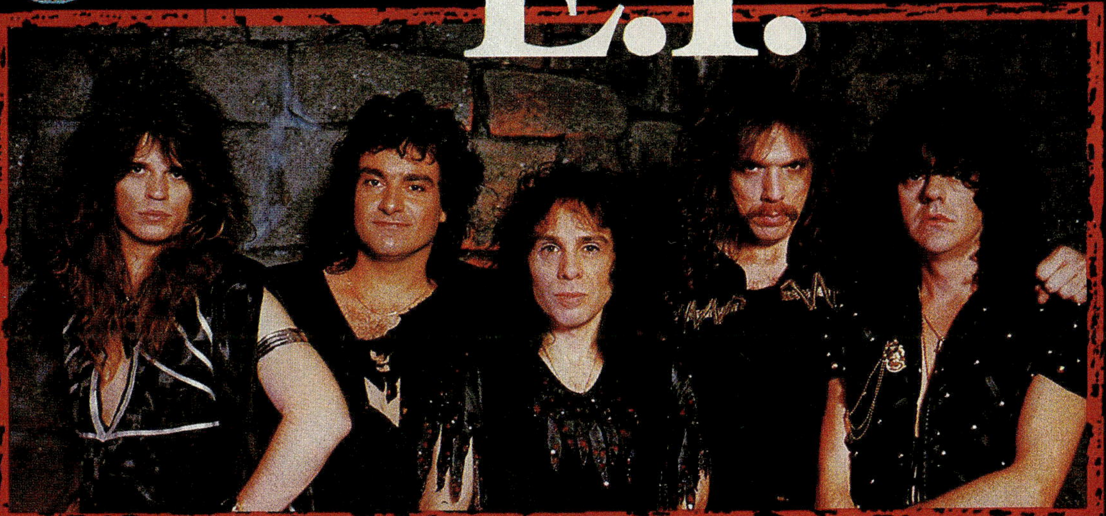

LIMITED EDITION AVAILABLE AS
DOUBLE 7" IN A GATEFOLD SLEEVE
4 TRACK 12" & FREE DIO FAMILY TREE

THE SENSATIONAL SACRED HEART TOUR

MAY 7th – BIRMINGHAM, NEC
MAY 8th – NEWCASTLE, CITY HALL
MAY 9th – EDINBURGH, PLAYHOUSE
MAY 10th – LEEDS, QUEENS HALL
MAY 12th – LONDON, HAMMERSMITH ODEON
MAY 13th – LONDON, HAMMERSMITH ODEON
MAY 14th – LONDON, HAMMERSMITH ODEON

special guests KEEL

CHAPTER 6

"Now, wasn't it wonderful to walk along the rainbow?"

DREAM EVIL

"To tell you the truth, I thought *Dream Evil* was a total pain in the ass to record. So many problems, and it took so long to write. By that time, I should have like left the band, but didn't. And subsequently, it's just not one of my favorite records. *Sacred Heart*, to a lesser extent, as Vivian was in the band and there was still sort of some hope [laughs]. When it went to Craig Goldy . . . I didn't care too much for him—for his playing or anything. Vivian was a much more innovative player. But by the time we did *Dream Evil*, I was like, 'What's happening?!' [laughs]. With Dio, we were best at the beginning and then gradually weren't as good [laughs]. Which is probably the case with most bands."

Record company promo shot of the *Dream Evil* band

So says beating heart of the Dio band, Jimmy Bain, on a record that in fact many fans, including this writer, appreciate far and above such dismissals. And yet, indeed, Ronnie himself demonstrates this nonplussed attitude toward a record that many thought reversed the trajectory of decay found on *Sacred Heart*.

"*Dream Evil* was all right," says Ronnie without enthusiasm. "Again, new guitar player on that one. We didn't have the same writing impetus that we had on *Holy Diver* and *The Last in Line*; we had written those two and *Sacred Heart* with Viv. So, in comes a new guitar player, and who knows how he's going to write with you? Craig's writing style was totally different to what Viv's was. Viv was more like we were, live players, so we'd just go into the studio and play—'Oh, that'll be cool; let's try that,' and just write the songs that way.

"With Craig, he had to more or less take something away with him and come back and go, 'What about this?' And most of the time we would say, 'Well . . . that's all right.' So, I had to do a lot on that one. Jimmy had to do a lot on that one. Because of the difference in the guitar player / bass player / singer writing combination, it was not a happy album. People were starting to get really down on Craig. And now I know why, but certainly I didn't at the time. But it made for an unhappy time; it was tough, like pulling teeth. *Mob Rules* was kind of like that too. You had to really work at writing the thing for some reason. There was just this big, horrible, dark cloud over everything, it seemed like. So, *Dream Evil* was a difficult one. There were some good songs on it, but I don't think it holds up at all next to *Last in Line*; not even close. I think it's a good album, but I don't think it's a great album.

Ad for the new album, also promoting the first single.
Martin Popoff archive

"Vivian was gone, and Craig was going to be with us," continues Dio. "I think there seemed to be, on the end of the other musicians, a little bit less acceptance of Craig than there was going to be of Vivian. Vivian was there in the beginning. And the things you start—and certainly the successful things you start, or the things that you want to keep going—it ended for whatever reason. It ended because of Viv's attitude or because of my attitude toward Viv, whatever that may have been. That really doesn't matter. It really wasn't going to work with him, so what the hell was the sense of carrying on? I may as well try someone else. So, I think there was the resentment that Viv was gone, and I think that Craig just wasn't so readily accepted.

"You know, most people who are good at what they do are rather unique and odd anyway, and he certainly fills that bill as well. So perhaps he just didn't fit into the camaraderie that we had initially. And that was at the time we were having to do another record. And it was difficult, difficult to write that way. It's a lot easier for me to write with Craig and myself on our own, because there isn't any outside influence or interference. Although certainly, outside influence we do look for, and if it's a good one, we'll take it. But in the case of the writing style we had before with Viv, we would go into the studio and we would write all together as a band and play. And that seemed to be more difficult with that lineup than it did with the one before it.

"Although, having said that," continues Ronnie, "I found *Sacred Heart* to be just as difficult because Viv wasn't really contributing anything at that particular point. But I think *Sacred Heart* was a really excellent album. *Dream Evil*, again, in retrospect, I listened to some of those songs, and I thought, wow, that's quite a good album! It's got some good songs on it. We were doing 'Sunset Superman' before on tour. We were doing 'Dream Evil' on the last tour that we did, which always went down a storm. So, listening to those songs, it's a much-better album than I thought it was. But still, that was hard because it was a transition between guitar players."

"That was a bit of a mixed bag," reflects Claude. "On the one hand, Craig is a very accomplished guitar player. But we all felt that Viv was really treated very badly. Not so much by Ronnie, but it was obvious that those decisions were being handled, for lack of a better word, by Wendy. And I mean Viv was basically set up, and he was put in the position where the only thing that he could do was the exact thing that would get him kicked out of the band. And when it came to pass, Wendy was chomping at the bit to walk Craig into the band. And Vivian just got very unceremoniously let go. And in my humble opinion, for no real fault of his own. You can say a lot of shit about Vivian about a lot of different things, but none of it has to do with his guitar playing."

Ronnie looking fine on the cover of *Kerrang! Martin Popoff archive*

On the topic on Ronnie putting down Viv for migrating over to Def Leppard (with a whistle stop at Whitesnake in between), Schnell says, "You see, that's an interesting thing. To go ahead and say that after you've been paying him a pittance far beneath his market value, then you fall to a gig where he's making ten times what he did in Dio . . . that's a little bit disingenuous, when you're bringing home the lion's share of the money. 'I can't believe that guy got a job at GM making fifty bucks an hour when I'm making ten.' But, you know, that's the way life goes. And for whatever Def Leppard is or isn't as far as music is concerned, they're a machine. They will be a legendary band that will never be forgotten. So, for Vivian to become part of that, I think was a very good move for him. Unfortunately, I think the best move for Vivian—I think the best move for all of us—would have been had we stayed together. Had Wendy been able to allow a more equitable split, we could all have had a living wage and allowed the band to develop the way bands used to develop back in the day, before it became all about the money. Not to take anything away from Craig, but I think *Dream Evil* would've been a better record if Vivian was doing it."

Asked about the rumored aggravation with respect to Craig having a hard time putting together the required guitar solos on the record, Claude chuckles, saying, "So here's the thing. There are different schools of thought on what makes a good solo. For my money, the best solo is the one you play when you're not thinking about it, and you stop and go, 'Holy shit, how did I play that?!' Once upon a time, the solo was just an emotive part of the song. It was a chance for you to have your own little signature thing, and it was great, so much the better, but even if it sucks, it was you, it was who you are, it was like a thumbprint on the song.

"And at some point, when the guitar hero thing came into play, people became very analytical about solos: 'Well, if you listen to the thirty-second bar of the solo, he plays.' If you listen to Led Zeppelin, Jimmy Page is really sloppy. Who fucking cares! It's Jimmy Page. It's Zeppelin. It is not about . . . the thing is, people can't create things as magical as some of these people; all they can do is find things to criticize. And if you get analytical, believe me, I'm as anal as they come. I can find shit to criticize about anybody on anything. But that's not what normal life is about. Life is about standing back and allowing the vibe to flow over you and just basking in the genius of the individuality. Sometimes the best thing about a performance is the mistakes. It's not about being a technician, although there are those who swear that it is. I mean if you like that kind of technical perfection, well, then good for you. You're entitled; everybody is entitled to like what they like. But that's not what the art is. The art is the flaws, the character, the depth of feeling that is emoted by the ability of the art, whether it's a painting or a drawing or a poem or a solo. It's not about precision.

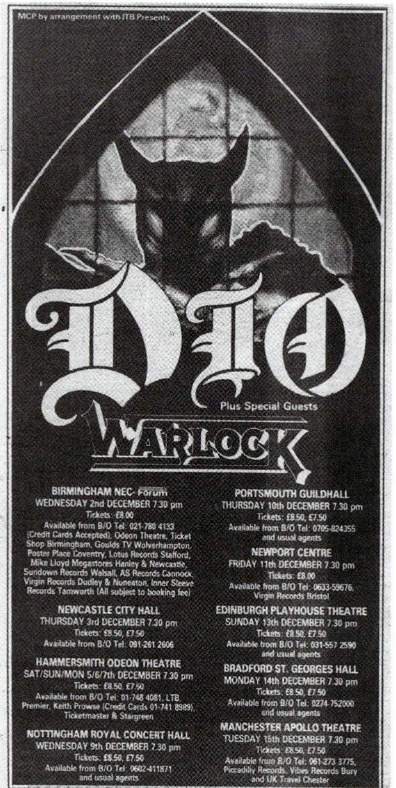

Front cover and inside ad page from the *Dream Evil* tour book. Also shown, a UK newspaper ad similarly promoting the dates with Warlock. *Martin Popoff archive*

"Still, to be honest, there was a lot about the *Dream Evil* record that was memorable," continues Claude. "For one thing, again, we were doing it at home. But this time we were doing it at a really, really fantastic studio, a place called the Village Recorder. I think that's one of the places where Fleetwood Mac did *Tusk*, Pink Floyd had recorded there, Paul McCartney recorded there, Mr. Mister recorded there—I can't even remember all the bands. But it was a very, very well-respected and wonderful studio to work at. So we were in a much-better place by the time that record rolled around.

"Because Craig had already done the tour, he was reluctantly now one of the boys. To me, it was what it was. Everybody seemed to be in a better place mentally. Unfortunately, right around the time when we were doing that, Vinny's mom passed away. So that was a very sad but unifying event. But the thing about that record is, we had a very firm game plan going into the studio. We had done a lot of preproduction at Ronnie's studio in his home. And as result, the recordings were pretty straightforward. We knew what the songs were going to be, we knew how to play them, we listened to a lot of stuff that had been done on the fly, whereas *Sacred Heart* was like pulling teeth, because of all the stress that was there."

From left to right, Craig, Ronnie, Jimmy, and Claude at the Monsters of Rock festival, Pforzheim, Germany, August 30, 1987. © *Wolfgang Gürster*

Dream Evil, the result of this six-month procedure, was issued on July 21, 1987. Featured once again on the front cover was the band's mascot Murray, this time staring malevolently from the depths of some mental nightscape.

"That was Wendy's concept," explained Ronnie back on the press trail for the record, in conversation with Greg Fasolino from *Faces*. "We normally conceive everything from artwork to stage sets. She leaves the music to me! The title and artwork are just a child's

Vinny and Ronnie (a.k.a. half of Black Sabbath), Monsters of Rock festival, Pforzheim, Germany, August 30, 1987. © *Wolfgang Gürster*

nightmare. It's what we all experience when we're kids—even when we're not kids. Something under the bed . . . 'Mom!' Something in the closet . . . 'Dad!' It's just a part of life. It wasn't meant to be devilish or satanic—it's not. When you dream during the day, you dream usually about good things. Then when you go to sleep at night, the subconscious takes over, and a lot of those fears that you pushed away during the day come and go, 'Guess what? Here I am.' It wasn't meant to be horrifying or unsettling, but to ask a few questions."

Ronnie chose to open his fourth record with a little something called "Night People," featuring six laser-like synth stabs at the dark before the band rumbles in with a brisk classic Dio rocker, foreboding, sorrowful, and drenched in heavy metal optics. Ronnie turns in a succinct, not-so-veiled paean to the night and all its unexplainable, seductive charms. Craig's solo is a barnstormer, grinding but musical like the cream of Viv's canon, Goldy allowed to rip for a long sequence over a number of backing beds. Remarks Goldy,

"I would think the first solo in 'Night People' is a highlight for me, the really fast part that I did. That was really cool; it's kind of a hard pattern to play."

Vinny Appice is also key to this track's deft touch. As the song progresses, Goldy is back for more soloing, dueling with Ronnie for the spirited fade. All these *Dream Evil* problems folks have talked about . . . down here at the fan level, I ain't hearing them—"Night People" craps all over anything from *Sacred Heart* from a height of several miles and gives most of *The Last in Line* a run for its money as well. And what a deft use of keyboards, I might add, with Claude massaging in these old-school melody washes, broken up by pregnant pauses, allowing for the glorious dark metal of the song to breathe.

The album's title track is next, "Dream Evil" being a gothic, pomp-and-circus-pants romp on the "Holy Diver" side of the castle, even if the verse construct is one of the least inspired of the entire record at hand, very much a plodder of a chord sequence in the middling miasma of *Sacred Heart* mode. Lyrically, Ronnie is elusive on this one, mixing nightmare imagery with what sounds like advice against following one's dreams, something that emerges as ironic, given that we get a song messaging exactly the opposite later on the album.

Once more, Claude Schnell's keyboard wash provides a nice backdrop during the opening salvo. "Claude wasn't asked to contribute a lot," reflects Ronnie on Schnell's role in the band. "He perhaps could have contributed more, but I'm not really Mr. Keyboards, to tell you the truth. I think keyboards should be used in a very specific way. For me, it's always been drums and bass first, then blasting guitars and a strong vocal. And keyboards have always been there to do wonderful filling parts, slight movement parts here and there, just to be a little orchestra on its own. But I think a lot of times, when you deal with a keyboard player who is as good as Claude or is as good as Scott [Warren] these days, they tend to want to overplay. 'Oh, let's do it this way. I can play this, and I can play this.' Well, that's not the way I hear it. You know, I didn't ask Claude to be a great contributor. But he contributed an arrangement part here and there. But again, I didn't ask him to do that. It's not his fault. You know, Claude, bless his heart, put up with my idiosyncrasies, which is to have the keyboards be a bit of a secondary instrument."

Discussing his lyrical devices with Dmitry Epstein, Ronnie explains that "I consider myself to be more of a storyteller than a songwriter. I have the greatest sources of subjects in the world: that's the people who live on this planet, who are always the best things to write about because they're very predictable and very unpredictable. And if you write about a subject that people know about—and everybody knows about the people because we see each other all the time—that's very important. What I do is I try to write those songs about real subjects, but I put them in a different place. I put them in a fantasy place, perhaps, or I put them back thousands of years because that makes you have to use your imagination. You have to think about what a dragon looks like, because none of us has even seen one. We've only seen pictures that people drew up in their minds. But once again, I think it's very important for people to use their imagination. But again, I'm telling the same story, probably, that everyone else has told; I'm just saying it in a different way, maybe in a way that perhaps is a bit more interesting and imaginative."

Asked if he associates himself with the more negative sides of human emotion—darkness, anger, pain—Ronnie figures, "Yeah, of course I do. I'm all of those things. I am those things. All of us are those things. There's darkness in everyone. There's pain in many people. There's goodness in everyone. We have choices to make, and our choices are 'Am I going to be at that dark side?' or 'Am I going to be at the good side?' That's up to each person to make that determination. I'm worried about things that are inside of me and inside of everybody else, too, because I'm not just writing the songs from the first-person aspect: there's a message inside of every song, it's meant to be said to the people I'm singing a song for. So, there are songs that I have written a little bit more in the first person than others, but mainly I write songs so that people can make judgments as to what I'm saying and perhaps have a better time of it, so to speak.

"I get angry as much as anyone else does," continues Dio. "I get angry when I see injustice. I get angry when I see people suffer. Of course, I am very sad when I see people suffer, but I'm very angry too, because this suffering shouldn't be. We waste so much in this world on pleasure things and don't really seem to care about the people and, especially, children—that's the worst kind of suffering and that makes me very, very angry. Government makes me angry because of the bad choices that it makes, not just this government here in this country, but governments everywhere. I'm angry about those things, just like any other person should be. Of course, I'm angry sometimes about the music if it's not right: I get angry because I need to have it right. So, there are many things that can make me angry, but I'm not an angry person all the time. I'd like life to be good, and I like to share the good things with other people."

Dream Evil, from Japan, twice

Back to the track list, "Sunset Superman" is one of the great unsung Dio anthems (of note, folkie Donovan had a hit in 1966 with a song called "Sunshine Superman"). Dense, malevolent, egregiously heavy, this one seems to carry the weight of the world on its shoulders, with Goldy turning in a slashing riff that sits back and cruises confidently come verse time. The melodies are timeless and hooky but not in any way cute. Commented Ronnie, "'Sunset Superman' tells the story of office workers dressed in drab suits who, when the sun sets, rip those clothes off to reveal a big red "S" on their chests. They live for the energy of the night."

"Some of the riffs were Ronnie's," Craig explained to me, when asked about the writing process. "I was telling somebody about this the other day. People don't really know that because he's a bass player, but he can also play guitar. So, when we would write, before we would get together, there would be a time when he would write some songs on his own and put them together in his home studio. I would do likewise, and then we would get together and he would play me his ideas that he had recorded, and I would play him my ideas that I had recorded.

"And then some of those songs, he would say, 'I can't wait to see what you would do to this song,' and sometimes we would change them, and sometimes we wouldn't, and he would be surprised, because he would be expecting me to change the guitar riff because I was the guitar player. Most people would try to change it so they would get their name on the song credit for the publishing money. But for me, I couldn't do that with him. I just couldn't. I would be like, 'That sounds cool the way it is. I'll just play that.' And he'd go, 'Really? You think so?' And I would go, 'Yeah!' He would come up with some really cool riffs, and we would just keep them as is. If I thought they needed to be changed or twisted, I would tell him that, only because I really thought that, and I wanted to put my stamp on it.

"But the greatest thing about writing with Ronnie was his work ethic," muses Craig. "He really, really worked hard, and he would really search through his mind to see if we had done something like this before. He would never settle for second best. I'm sure people probably thought he did, but he didn't. I remember how much work he put into it. We would start at maybe eleven o'clock in the morning and go until two o'clock in the morning the next day, and go and go and go, and next thing you know, seventeen days have gone by and we haven't had a single day off. But we didn't know it because we just wanted to do it.

"Whereas most people would write songs, and if they needed a second verse, they would write a second verse. If they needed a bridge after the second verse, they would write it right then and there. If they needed a solo section, they would write it right then and there and it was slotted in, in that particular part of the song. But what they would miss, what I had learned, the way Ronnie would do it, is that before he would go into the second verse, before he would go into a second chorus or solo section or bridge, he would start the song from the beginning and see if anything needed to be changed up to that point. And he would stop it and he would go, we need to make that shorter or we need to make that longer, or we need to change that chord there. And then we would do it and play it from the beginning again. Or we need to change that part. Or can that part come up higher, or can we bring that down lower, or we need to add another thing here, and then do it again, do it again, until from the intro to the riff to the first verse and the first chorus is okay, and then we try for the second verse.

"Because sometimes we'd put on the second verse and make it just slightly different, even though it might not be to most musicians, they would probably understand, or we'd put a minor chord there instead of a major chord, or we would change the bass note against the guitar part. Even though the guitar part was the same, the bass part was different, or add a keyboard part."

Next up, "All the Fools Sailed Away" begins with a relentlessly sad and mellow intro before the band enters grand and slow, with Vinny's spare Sabbatherian pattern knocking it home. "That continues the tradition of these ones with epic qualities," reflects Ronnie. "It tells the tale of people who listen to the false promises that people throw at them. They don't realize that the only ones who gained from those promises are the people who make them, and there are just too many people like that in the world."

"I think some people got the wrong impression," answers Craig, when I asked him what he thought of Ronnie's lyrics. "But not everyone. Because I remember, his lyrics meant a lot to me. When I first met him, I told him how much his lyrics meant to me, when I found out what he was actually saying. I would quote from his lyrics, and I would say, 'You're singing this, but it sounds like it means this.' And he would say, 'Exactly!' And he would grab my arm and go, 'Exactly; you understand!'

Ronnie and Craig, all smiles, Monsters of Rock festival, Pforzheim, Germany, August 30, 1987. © Wolfgang Gürster

"So, from that point on, he would call me, and even when he was with Heaven & Hell, he would say, 'Goldy, you're going to love this!' And he would recite me the lyrics to a Heaven & Hell song [laughs]. I think people don't understand that he often presents both sides of the situation. It sounds like he's trying to promote darkness, but that's why he says, 'We're evil and divine.' Or else he'll say things like, even in the song called 'Hungry for Heaven,' when he talks about the person who doesn't deserve it and the person who does deserve it, who's been tread upon, like the underdog. Both of those people can be hungry for heaven. People are hungry for it because they're yearning and they're starved for any kind of light because their life is darkness, and then there are other people who are living spoiled rotten and they're hungry for heaven. They think they can get anything they want, whenever they can get it. And I think that's where people misunderstand him; that's where it would come from. Because he talks about both sides at once—it's very kind of all-inclusive.

"I know that for 'All the Fools Sailed Away,' the theme, the part of the music that comes right after that really kind of mellow intro, Ronnie had written that by himself," continues Goldy. "We knew that that song was going to be special, just because of that alone. The intro hadn't been written yet; the song hadn't been written yet—he just had that piece. And so, we needed to set it aside, and it had to be treated special. That was our first kind of epic song we wrote together, 'All the Fools Sailed Away,' and that sort of started another method. Ronnie and I knew that we were capable of writing an epic-type song, and that carried on with *Magica*. Not to compare to 'Stargazer,' because nothing compares to 'Stargazer,' but that was an epic song, and this was the closest thing to that. So, when we started doing 'All the Fools Sailed Away,' that would've sparked his imagination that 'wow, I can do this with Craig too.' When we were doing *Magica*, Simon would come downstairs and he would listen to it and go, 'Another epic, another epic' [laughs]."

In true epic fashion, with a template established by "Stairway to Heaven" on Led Zeppelin's fourth album, the inner sleeve of *Dream Evil* presented a single set of lyrics, that of "All the Fools Sailed Away." Also in epic fashion, the song features choir augmentation, specifically the services of "the Mitchell Singing Boys," also known as the St. Brendan's Church Boys Choir.

"Great song," added Ronnie, years later, again referring to "All the Fools Sailed Away." "Great video too. It's just something I started on my own. Before we started writing, I'll usually write a lot of riffs and a few bigger, more-completed ideas, and that was one of them. So, I knew where I wanted to go, and all we had to do was flesh it out, put it together. And it worked, but again, more difficult in those times."

Late in the track, Claude Schnell gets to turn in a baroque Rainbowesque keyboard solo, followed by Goldy playing bluesy and melodic. This represents the most salient and satisfying promise that Claude had secured out of Ronnie, and it is indeed Schnell's most triumphant contribution to the catalog.

"Ronnie approached me and said, 'All right, dude, you want your solo, you've got it. This is the song I want it in.' And of course it's in like some fucking C sharp, minor seventh flat stupid Plutonian fuckin' mode. And I'm like, really?! This is the song I

Sporthalle Böblingen,
Böblingen, Germany,
April 29, 1986.

have to do a solo in? All right. That's cool, that's cool. And luckily, Ronnie told me early on enough that I could have a little time to work on it. And in complete contradiction to what I just said about how lovely it is to play a solo by the seat of your pants, I promise you, that solo I could never play by the seat of my pants. That solo represents considerable hours of intense labor of writing it, of calculating how to play it, of making it difficult enough so that I could be confident enough that it would be impressive. And practicing it up so that I would be confident enough so I wouldn't fuck it up playing it live. So, I worked pretty diligently on that.

"But it was all in a void. I knew that I liked what I was doing. I had a roommate at the time, Joey, my best friend from childhood, basically, who I owe my career to. Because he's the guy that turned me on to my first Deep Purple record. And every time I worked on it, 'That's really great, but that one part really sucks.' He goes, 'It just sounds like you're going to the obvious place, man. I mean, come on, you can do better than that.' And I go, 'I'm not sure I can,' and he's going, 'Come on, man!' Another kid from Brooklyn. 'Come on, man!' So, I fucked around with it and went, 'What do you think of that?' 'Yeah, that's better, but come on.' Oh man, he's known me since I was seven or eight years old. So, when he first heard me play, he heard me as some little classical nerd. And I think that's what created his interest in me as a musician. Just because I was very schooled, and he was not at all. But that's a story for another day.

"In any case, I finally get the solo pretty much finished and now I'm just, as a matter of course, practicing it three times a day. When I get up, before I even brush my teeth, I sit at the piano and go at it. I'm working on it before I leave for the day. Before I crash, I'd play it one more time just in case there was anything that bothered me and to get it pretty much ingrained in my head.

"And then the moment of truth comes," chuckles Claude. "We're in the studio, 'Okay, come on, we're doing the solo tomorrow.' 'What, really?' 'Yeah. Not ready?' 'No, it's fine.' But this was the moment of truth. And this was, what, 1987? So, I've been working up to getting a solo on a Dio record for four years. This is the moment of truth. The day comes, we go to the studio, and nobody else is there. So, it's going to be Ronnie and Angelo, our engineer, and myself. Because nobody else needs to do anything. I walk in and my keyboards are set up in the control room. And Ronnie wasn't around, but Angelo was already getting it together. Angelo, also from Brooklyn, Vinny's best friend from childhood, who grew up three blocks from me. 'Cool, you ready to do this or what?' 'Yeah, sure, Angelo; let's have one.'

"So, he puts up the backing track to which I'm going to play the solo. And I try to find the exact right sound. I had the idea of what I was going to do, but I was dialing it in. So, listen, for real, okay, so he's playing it, and I start playing along. Ronnie walks in in the middle of this, and he's sitting down, and he looks, when it's done, he turns to Angelo and he goes, 'So did you get that?' And Angelo goes, 'Well, yeah, sure. Why?' He turns around to me because I didn't know they were recording this. I even looked and I didn't see the red light on the machine. But apparently Angelo had recorded it.

"Then Ronnie turns to me and goes, 'Claude, that was fucking magic! Can you double it?' 'Sure.' So, I doubled it. I played it again virtually the same way. It's like when you double a guitar track. Just put down the same track, and it's the slight difference that makes it sound a little bigger. So, we did it four times, and Angelo bounced the four of them together, panned left and right; they were spread apart across the audio spectrum.

"And that was it. The solo I played when I didn't even know I was being recorded was the one that ended up on the record. But a lot of practice had gone in before, and Ronnie didn't look to me and go, 'What the fuck are you thinking?' The fact that this one was like, 'That was fucking magic' . . . I mean, Ronnie really, really, really liked it. It wasn't like a pretend 'Oh yeah, that's okay. I want to see what else you can do.' No, he dug it. He totally . . . even live, I remember, after we'd been touring for months and months, I would be doing the keyboard solo, and he would be checking it out. It was kind of cool."

"Naked in the Rain" is another fine, underrated *Dream Evil* track, reminiscent of "The Last in Line," hugely gothic, rhythmic, opaque, and inspiring in a damned heavy metal manner that only Dio can deliver. Vinny proves once again that he is the king of making slow songs interesting, this one moving at the lower end of midtempo, with Appice dressing it up with novel snare fills.

"Overlove" picks up the pace, Craig opening the song with an intimate bit of blues, in fact a blues version of the riff. Vinny rolls out an opening fill, and the band is off to the races, framed by Goldy's aggressive, impressive riff. "People like the intro to 'Overlove,'" notes Craig. "That was pretty cool the way it came out. The ending of the solo in 'Overlove' is fun because me and Vinny do the same pattern: he does it on the snare drum and I do it on the guitar. I thought that was pretty cool. Because it's fast; it's almost like a drumroll or several drumrolls in a row, but I'm playing a drumroll on my guitar [laughs]."

Says Ronnie, "'Overlove' I wrote, actually, about Craig's wife, who really, really, loved him a lot. I mean, she really, really loved him a lot, and she showed her affection. And I'm not talking about sexual matters. But she would string balloons up on the street, when we came back from the road, and there were signs up there saying, 'I love you, Craig! So glad you're home!' And I thought, my God, I gotta write something about this. And I just thought, what a great title, 'Overlove.' Just too much love."

Said Ronnie back in '87, with respect to *Dream Evil*'s next track, "'I Could Have Been a Dreamer' is our first single, and it's a real straightforward kind of song, which is a nice change for us. It's about people who are followers, those who have no desire to take hold of their lives. They like to sit and dream about what could have been or what should have been. Those people are to be pitied in my book, because I believe there's always time to change your own life."

Looking back fifteen years later, Ronnie says, "I remember being in the studio, putting a backing track down for some song, and we had a lull in the action and I stopped and said to Craig, 'Oh, Craig, I've got this great little hook' [sings the chorus], and I played it for him and just quickly put together that little chorus and said, 'Let's remember that.' So, after we finished that particular track we were doing, we needed to write another song anyway, and that became 'I Could Have Been a Dreamer." All told, the song is a successful example of Dio in commercial mode in that the melody is nonobvious, none too cliché, quite depressive, in fact, and yet still not unfriendly in a radio sense.

Maple Leaf Gardens, Toronto, Canada, January 9, 1988. Supporting was Megadeth and Savatage. © *Martin Popoff*

This one is credited to Ronnie and Craig alone, as is "Dream Evil" and "All the Fools Sailed Away." There are four full band credits, but that's the only place we see Jimmy.

"Because of the fact that him and Ronnie wrote most of the songs up to that point, Ronnie put off writing with me right away, because he wanted to give Jimmy a shot," explains Goldy. "And so, after him and Jimmy had done their thing, he brought me in, and it worked out good for me, because at the time, while I was waiting to be called in, I came up with 135 ideas and stored them on cassette tapes, back then. So, when we got together for the first time for *Dream Evil*, I had all these ideas. 'Oh, I love that one, like that one, we gotta use this, we can use that.' And then when we were in rehearsals and we needed a part—'Oh, anybody have an idea?,' I would go through my file. But Jimmy, at the time, I can only speak for myself and what I thought was happening, but it seemed as though he wasn't as enthused or as enthusiastic as he had been before. He always had a lot of ideas, but I think this time he was just a little less enthusiastic about that particular era, so it really ended up becoming me and Ronnie.

"It wasn't explained to me," continues Craig on Bain's reduced role. "Ronnie just wanted to see what ideas we had to pick from there. He just wanted to . . . it was new for him too. Because him and I worked in the studio together before, when I joined Rough Cutt, producing. So, we had a good rapport and working relationship in the studio already. But we never sat and wrote a whole entire album together. So that was mainly the thing in his mind. New guitar player and a first-time writer, on a full-length

Ronnie and Jimmy, end of show, Maple Leaf Gardens, Toronto, January 9, 1988. © *Martin Popoff*

record, and so it was mainly me and him instead of him and Jimmy. It used to be him and Jimmy, and now it was him and I. So, I think it was kind of 'Let's just see what happens' [laughs]."

"But yeah, again, I'd say back in the *Dream Evil* days, when I first joined Dio, it was Ronnie and Jimmy. But like I say, Jimmy, for some reason, was a little disenchanted with things, so Ronnie called me up and said, 'Hey, I guess Jimmy isn't really into it right now.' He knew how excited I was. I was into Rainbow and Black Sabbath, as far as his era was. I wasn't really into the Ozzy Black Sabbath. I liked Ozzy's solo stuff, but I didn't like the Ozzy Sabbath stuff. I liked Ronnie's version of Sabbath, and Rainbow, and Deep Purple, so him and I had that click together. So, it kind of created a new . . . what's the word I'm looking for? Kind of like a new method of how Ronnie would write music with a guitarist, whenever I was in the band, be that then or later when I returned. It would be basically him and I, because we knew what we were capable musically of putting together."

Ronnie expands on his fascination with his definition of the word "dream" as addressed in "I Could Have Been a Dreamer"—it's what he calls "goal dreams." "I have fantasies for it. I'm talking about dreams that can come true, or at least dreams that are great because you try and make them come true. I always kind of put it this way: if we could walk along a rainbow, our goal would be to get to the end of that rainbow, to find that dreaded pot of gold. Now, if we forget about the pot of gold—we still have that as our final goal—we never reach it. Now, wasn't it wonderful to walk along the rainbow? Good lord, that's got to be the most wonderful thing in the world.

"And that's what you do when you go for your goals. You walk along a rainbow, and it doesn't really matter about the gold at the end. It's just that it's wonderful trying to get to the point of reaching it. And along the way to the pot of gold, you do obtain some really nice positive things. You make your dreams come true, because in the end, the dreams are what reality is made of. If you can't conceive something and try to make it come true, then there is no reality. Those are the kinds of dreams I mean, and I am fascinated by them, and I'm adamant about the fact that there are too few people in this world who have enough dreams. With more people trying to reach goals and having dreams, we'd have a lot better world here. I mean, isn't it a nice dream to not have homeless and starving people in this world? That's a dream, and lord knows we'll never accomplish it, but at least we're trying."

The Great Goldini. Maple Leaf Gardens, Toronto, January 9, 1988. © *Martin Popoff*

Recalls Craig, "The song 'I Could Have Been a Dreamer,' we had a different ending for that, which was really cool. Ronnie was doing the lyric 'Running with the wolf pack,' and he was going to make a little more of that on the end section, and the record company guy came in and said he thought it was a hit song, so he thought we should've gone out with 'could've been a dreamer' as the chorus. But Ronnie wanted to mess with 'running with the wolf pack' more. It was really cool. I was the one who got upset; Ronnie was the one who wasn't upset. He just said, 'Hey, Goldy, this is just the way it is sometimes. They think it's going to be a hit song.' Chances are, a lot of times if they get involved and they get their ideas on there, chances are they're going to push it even further. For no good reason other than just, you know, of egos. So you're just shooting yourself in the foot. And he had a point—and it did become a hit song. Maybe not just because of that, but still, Warner Bros. thought, 'Hey, wait a minute; this has hit song potential—let's treat it as such.'"

"Faces in the Window" is another stellar forgotten track from this record. Reminiscent of "We Rock," this one gallops along loud and proud, the band's chemistry still obviously intact. I mean, even though Viv is gone, Vinny provides a huge service to Dio's stamp of originality. What's more, Craig is fired up, his riffing smart and malevolent, his soloing forceful, stabbing and very electric of tone like Jake E. Lee in Badlands.

Dream Evil closes with "When a Woman Cries," again the band turning in a funky but pounding rocker every bit as high quality as the best songs from the first two much more famous Dio albums. Goldy's riff on this one is particularly Viv-like, and Vinny throws in many of those boulder-shouldered fills we love to hear. Claude Schnell's keyboard patterns are inventive and add much to the song, and Ronnie's curious lyric, about the power of a woman crying—with a hint of the ruse to it—is yet another strong aspect to this top-notch Dio closer.

And closer to what? As we've seen, *Dream Evil* seems to be a record with subtexts its creators describe only as negative. Personally, I've never doubted the record, seeing it as strong and respective to *The Last in Line* as *Master of Puppets* is to *Ride the Lightning*. And what I mean by that is that *Master* lines up nearly track for track as a bold reprise to *Ride*, so boldly executed, however, that some see it as a slight improvement on the earlier great album, while others see it as slightly lesser due to this whiff of imitation. In any event, both Metallica records are two of the greatest albums ever crafted, as are both the Dios. Again, to reiterate, even if a hugely positive view like that toward *Dream Evil* is in the minority, I swear that a good reassessment applied to this record would have most Dio fans shocked at its quality, followed by a quick leap-frogging of it in value past *Sacred Heart* and, in the end, nipping at the heels of *The Last in Line*—running with the wolf pack, indeed.

Unfortunately, Craig Goldy would return to disappoint on later Dio albums, even if we have Ronnie to blame more than Craig. To be sure, it's a debate we'll have later, but perplexing and distressing to this Dio fan, Ronnie fell in love with soul-crushingly slow tempos, hitting us over the heads with them repeatedly across most of the rest of the catalog whether Craig was the guitarist in the band at the time or not. But in the rockin' case of *Dream Evil*, by design or by happenstance, he seems to have encouraged his new guitarist to demonstrate just enough Viv-acity to lend aggressive and rhythm-mad continuity toward and onto the last Dio album of a golden-era set.

"I think it's underrated too," chuckles Craig. "I think, unfortunately, it's not sonically the greatest-sounding record, but also, I think it's the first Dio record that was kind of like Blackmore-esque. It was a little more Rainbow-slanted than any of the other Dio stuff, because I was a huge Ritchie Blackmore fan. That's where I heard Ronnie's voice in the first place, because I was disappointed when Ritchie first left Deep Purple. But then I heard 'Man on the Silver Mountain' and I was like, 'Who the hell is that?!' [laughs]."

"You know, in some way I miss the old ways," sighs Goldy. "Meaning we wouldn't play to a click. And I think there's something to that. In fact, next time I do an album, where I could have that kind of option . . . with computers now, you can kind of change the tempo of the click at the end of the song, to give it that human feel. Because to me, in my world—I can only speak about myself with this—that when you play perfectly to a click, it doesn't have that human feel. Usually towards the end of the song, the drummer has sped up just a slight bit because of the excitement level, and that excitement level spills out through the speakers into the hearts and souls of the listener. I miss that a lot."

Craig's opinion that the production on *Dream Evil* isn't the greatest is something that's never bothered me or any ardent Dio fans I know or have discussed this with. It's usually *Sacred Heart* that is singled out for scorn, with words like midrangy, noisy, and distorted coming to mind. In fact it's almost like a mid-1980s proto-take on what would be called "the loudness wars" in the CD age, this idea of lack of dynamic range. Up into *Dream Evil*, however, to these ears, there's a return to roundness, with a sense of electric fire surging through as a subnarrative. Bottom line: no complaints.

"Well, I think it's a matter of taste," counters Craig. "It's just, at the time, for whatever reason, Ronnie was real adamant about using Marshalls. And at that time, I didn't really like the way the Marshalls sounded. If people were to hear the guitar tones and the overall tonality, they might not necessarily like the song 'Time to Burn,' but the overall sound quality of 'Time to Burn' was kind of what I was envisioning. Because at the time, I was using Fender London Reverb heads and Yamaha power amps and Marshall cabinets, and I was getting a kind of special guitar tone. And that was the one we used on 'Time to Burn.' But for some reason we scrapped all that, and the overall tonality and sound quality of *Dream Evil* I didn't think was as impressive as 'Time to Burn.' The recordings that we did with Ronnie in Rough Cutt, and the recording we did with 'Time to Burn,' there was really something special that a lot of other people didn't have. I thought he was going to incorporate that same kind of specialness into *Dream Evil*, and it didn't seem to have that. But I love that album, and it will always be a special album for me because that was the very first full-length Dio record I ever did with Ronnie."

Asked about Wendy's level of involvement in the project and the band, Craig says, "Well, that was the one thing about them, is that they were such team, and Wendy knew how great Ronnie was, and so she kind of stayed out of that. We would play it for her, to let her know how things were going, so she in turn could keep the record company abreast of what was happening. But Ronnie was so special that a lot of times people just kind of left him alone, because they knew what he was capable of creating."

Weirdly, it continues. Like everybody else in the band, Vinny also finds fault with *Dream Evil*. "It's a good album, but it just lost the rawness of the band. And that's because of two things. One of them is that more keyboards got into the music. We weren't really a keyboard band. On *Holy Diver*, Jimmy played the 'Rainbow in the Dark' thing, and sometimes Ronnie played some backing chords on a couple of songs and that was it. We were a guitar band. So as the tours went on, we got a keyboard player in Claude Schnell, and Claude is a great keyboard player and a great person, but the keyboards worked their way into the music more, and that kind of smoothed it out. It didn't have that rawness, that meatiness. And second, Craig Goldy played a different style than Viv, so the direction of the band changed. And then also on top of all that, Ronnie started taking more control over everything, like being a producer. Before, we did what we wanted to do, and everybody's ideas counted and that's what made a great band. And it became less of that and more Ronnie running the ship, you know? All those things combined made the band a little less vicious, I would say."

It should be noted that once more, like the times before, the official production credit went to Ronnie, with Angelo Arcuri engineering. Was Ronnie a good producer?

I would go with a resounding yes, and that's in all departments: sounds, performance, work ethic, caring. Logically the only box not ticked is "an extra set of ears," which can often go further, where the producer has a lot of authority to nix things, change the songs, pick the songs, lay down the law in any number of ways. The Dio band didn't ever have that, but again, they didn't really need it. Or at least they didn't need it in the '80s, when the band generated two albums widely considered top-shelf heavy metal classics, and then two that are generally well liked. And then, add to that, I know many folks who think *Sacred Heart* is a very, very fine album. Plus you've heard my view that *Dream Evil* is the equal of the first two and therefore way up the list of greatest heavy metal albums of all time by proxy.

"When Vivian Campbell left Dio," begins a December 1987 review in *Guitar* magazine, "speculation ran that the Dio beast might never be the same, and indeed, *Dream Evil* shows that the Dio band isn't quite the same. But while new guitarist Craig Goldy, late of Rough Cutt and Giuffria, might not have the charisma of Campbell, nor [*sic*] the high-tech flash and '80s electronic élan, his solid riffing and close-to-the-melody soloing seems a better match for Dio's murk and '70s mysticism. Ronnie James Dio, whose throat has never sounded thicker and juicier, has attempted to fill his dreamy, sinister lyrics with a tinge of conscience on *Dream Evil*, a dose of reality that doesn't always match with his serpents and magic spells. Yet, Goldy is able to ground Dio's flights with his spirited chording and clever solos that, while involving and close to each song's heart, are distanced in the album's mix. Nonetheless, on 'Dream Evil' and 'All the Fools Sailed Away,' Goldy's midrange excursions are very much a part of the songs, helping to solidify Dio's dream rather than to fracture off the instrumental sections. Tune in to 'Naked in the Rain' for some great guitar rhythms and Dio's most effective messaging."

Which to my mind amplifies this idea of a reassessment of *Dream Evil*: the lyrics are great, the riffs are great (as Craig enigmatically frames them, "Blackmore-esque"), and his soloing, like Viv's, is smartly anchored in the midrange, down the fret board, on the fatter strings, against the squealing, fast shred technique so prevalent at the time through guitar hero records, hair metal records, and even thrash records.

Which brings up the idea of context. With *Dream Evil*, birthed and essentially headquartered—by the band living there and Warner Bros. being there—in Los Angeles, Ronnie and Wendy had to look on in dismay as less substantive bands such as Mötley Crüe, Quiet Riot, Ratt, Dokken, Great White, Twisted Sister, and Bon Jovi (these last two are anomalies; i.e., not from there) did big business. Scorpions, Priest, and, worse, Ozzy were also in pretty fine shape. Metallica, Megadeth, Slayer, and Anthrax were causing some excitement with a style of music that made Dio (and Accept and Metal Church) sound anachronistic. And then soon we'd see an explosion of interest in Guns N' Roses, Poison, Cinderella, and, to a lesser extent, Skid Row, Warrant, and Slaughter.

It was a crowded field, and Dio were about to be crowded out: although I'm sure the public number is egregiously understated, *Dream Evil* is widely reported as having sold 52,000 copies in the United States, which would peg it at around a tenth to a fifteenth (or, if Ronnie is to be believed, a twentieth) of what *Sacred Heart* sold. Supporting my suspicions that this number is artificially low or underreported, the album reached #43

Maple Leaf Gardens, Toronto, January 9, 1988. © *Martin Popoff*

on Billboard, along with an impressive #8 in the UK and #12 in Germany, although those postings don't affect US sales. "I Could Have Been a Dreamer" was issued as the album's only US single, reaching #33 on Mainstream Rock but failing to chart on the main Billboard grid.

Hitting the road, Dio took a lot of stick for telling the press that the band wouldn't be touring this new record in North America. This did eventually happen, and in the usual big and exhaustive way, but talk in '87 revolved around Europe, with Ronnie explaining that *Sacred Heart* was toured so heavily in the US (two legs, more than a year in total) that a *Dream Evil* tour might be a case of, ahem, "overlove."

Ronnie had said that the idea for the *Dream Evil* stage set was to mesh with the theme behind the album, things that frighten during the night or "things that go bump in the night." Said Graham Wright, head carpenter of the tour, renewing his friendship with Ronnie from the Sabbath days, "I think the design had something to do with a company out of San Francisco called Nomad. But it was this sort of over-the-top Venus flytrap, which had lasers shooting out of it, and this mechanical spider came out of the truss, and they had this battle on the stage. It was all Dio—typical Dio.

"But the Venus flytrap looked like a sort of sad weed [laughs]. It looked quite funny, so we sort of had to strip all the cloth off it and turn it into a kind of mechanical alien [laughs]. It was huge. It worked—to a certain extent. This mechanical spider used to come out of the stage; it was on a chain motor and was to be lowered onto the stage, and it was supposed to walk across the stage and have a laser fight with this Venus flytrap. So yes, we turned the Venus flytrap into a mechanical alien. But it used to leak oil. Jimmy Bain used to get covered in hydraulic oil, and he never noticed [laughs]. It was great. I mean, I really miss those days because it was like pre–*Spinal Tap*. But there were those moments. It was good fun. It didn't have the corporate tension that you have on tours these days.

"Oh, he's a drunk!" laughs Graham, asked for an impression of Jimmy Bain. "He was just out of his head all the time. But he was a nice guy, Jimmy was [laughs]. A great guy. He was one of them sort of 'Hey, I've got a talent, looky me, and I'm going to enjoy it!' [laughs]. I mean, there's a lot of these guys . . . you just think to yourself, God, they seem to fumble through life. But at the same time."

Kicking off the tour on August 1, 1987, with a Children of the Night benefit concert, Dio then went straight to Europe for a huge round of dates, main backups being Helloween and later Warlock, who logged the lion's share of the dates. A tour highlight was Castle Donington's Monsters of Rock festival on August 22, where Dio was billed second to Bon Jovi but ahead of Metallica, who were then positioned above Anthrax, W.A.S.P., and Cinderella. Back in the States on December 28, 1987, Dio was supported by Savatage and a drug-addled Megadeth over what was to be three solid months of touring America and Canada.

"That was my first time ever playing that large of a crowd," recalls Craig, of Donington, asked about highlights across the expanse of his road life. "We had done some touring with Deep Purple, which was really great for me. And even with Giuffria we toured with Deep Purple, *Perfect Strangers*, which was great for me, because I never got the chance to see Deep Purple with that lineup before; it was always on an album that I listened to and learned. Never got a chance to see it live. We also had a chance to tour with the Scorpions and Iron Maiden and with Motörhead. So, it was great memories for me, because these were bands I grew up listening to, and I got a chance to meet but then became friends with, because they'd been friends of Ronnie's. And any friend of Ronnie's becomes a friend of yours because it's just that way [laughs]."

"I think what you learn the most is dealing with people," reflects Ronnie, as our tale of this album draws to a close, on what he's learned throughout this long life as one of heavy metal's biggest legends. "When you start a band, you never think about what problems there are going to be. All you think about is the music that you're making and how much fun it is to play music, to sing, to write, all these things. And then you start to realize that you are dealing with people who have got their own problems, so that means that nothing is going to last forever. I think that's the lesson I've learned from all the bands that I've been in. I always thought that each band that I was in was going to be the beginning and the end, that I would always be in that band, and when I retire, I would retire from that band; that we'd become like the Rolling Stones and go on forever and never change anything. But what I've learned is that never happens, because people have different priorities: they have lives to live, they have problems, and their problems affect what's going on in your band. Then people have problems with each other and sometimes can't stay together forever—I learned that.

"Another thing I've learned is that there are always people out there wanting to take advantage of you, because musicians are usually very childlike people because all we do is play. We say we're going to play a song and we'll play it—it's somewhere in the air for musicians: we don't think about anything but the music, because it's all that gives us the joy. And in the meantime, there's always a manager, or an agent, or someone who wants to take what you've got and what they can't do and make lots of money from that and leave you lying there on the ground.

"Those are the two things that I've learned the most. So, I think what the lesson learned from that is, it's that you should never go into something with your eyes closed. I've always realized that there are not only a few bad people in this world—there are many, many bad people in this world. And it's one thing that you love the music, but as long as you're smart enough to see that someone is out there trying to take advantage of you, you learn a little more about this business, which I did. I've learned more about it, who was going to take advantage of me and who wasn't.

"Musically . . . music is music, and it's either you get better or you don't get better. To me, the greatest lesson I've learned musically is that if you're not different, no one's going to care about you. You can't be a copy of someone else, and if you're good enough to create your own identity, then people will like you. But no one wants to have the same thing over and over and over again. So as a musician, it's one thing to be a good player, but it's another thing to have an identity, to create something that is so different from what all the other people are doing that you will be the best.

"I also think you should take everything that comes your way as it's been happy and enjoy it," continues Ronnie, "while things that would happen that seem to be really terrible and make you angry are better left unsaid. There are two roads to take, the low road and the high road, and I've always felt with people I've worked with, if it ended badly it didn't matter, because all the good things that happened—whether it's musically or the good times we had together as people—are more important than to shout it to the rest of the world. You have to remember that if you're strong enough, you can just carry on on your own anyway. It doesn't matter what anyone else has done to you: just put that away and be poised to be carrying on. So, I have no reason to say anything bad about anybody; they've all been such an important part of my life that it's something I just keep in my heart.

"That's from my parents. They always told me, 'Don't think that you're better than anyone else, that you're so special just because you can do one thing well.' I mean, I can sing well but I can't repair my car, so that doesn't make me better than the man who can repair my car, which doesn't make him better than me because he can't sing. So, my parents told me, 'It's your way to make, and along the way you're going to have problems, but it's always better to smile with the problems and to carry on and just go on with your life.' It all comes from them.

"But sure, I'm a perfectionist who wants everything to be great. I want each person in this band to be recognized for being as good as they are, individually. I'd never considered any of the Dio albums to be solo projects: they've all been by the band who just happened to have the name Dio because it was easy for people to connect with the name when we started because they knew at least who I was. That's what I am. I'm difficult at times, difficult only because I want things to be right, but I think you couldn't find a better friend than me."

Of course, that one thing Ronnie did well was metal. As we've seen throughout this chapter, Ronnie didn't start out metal—there was no such thing in the 1950s!—but once he discovered it, albeit circuitously through the psych of the Electric Elves and the honky-tonk rock of Elf, he grabbed it with both white-knuckled hands and never let go. He was the metal in Rainbow, and you know, he might have even been more metal than Tony Iommi in Black Sabbath.

Once heading up Dio, he was always first to regret any of the instances where he compromised for the sake of the label or for his fellow band members and leaned to commercial for his own tastes. There'd be no ballads and nothing too close to a traditional boy-girl love song. No, Ronnie loved his metal, which you also got to see when he talked so favorably about other metal bands. Still, as the '80s ended and the grunge era began, he was left championing a more traditional definition of the form, one more suited to and rooted in his generation, represented most elegantly by the four records from the 1980s.

"It's become very compartmentalized now," opined Ronnie, speaking with Sam Dunn at the Wacken festival, ground zero for heavy metal. "It used to be metal. Now it's black metal, death metal, speed metal, grass metal, and tree metal and sky metal. At one point it was just metal, and that's what it was. That's the thing that I see the difference in, is that it's just become so pigeon-holed. It used to be one great big family. and it has to be given attention to what its title is now. That's the way I've seen it change.

A couple more from the Toronto show. © *Martin Popoff*

Maple Leaf Gardens, Toronto, January 9, 1988.
© *Martin Popoff*

"Changing it is a hard thing. I think it's really impossible to drastically change it, or it will not be that form anymore. But just from my own personal view, I've always considered it to be music, and I think it has changed a lot and not become the music that I loved. Melody for a long time was gone. Singers just went to some other place; I don't know where it was. It just became guttural to me. I would like to see it remain what it was when I started. And not the music I played but, you know, Zeppelin was always a metal band. In the early days, Deep Purple were a metal band, but the musicianship was just so wonderful. It wasn't just a matter of going up and flailing away somewhere. It was people who cared about music. And that's the place that I came from, was listening to those great bands and wanting to be like them. So, I hope that more of the melodic content can be there at some point, so new bands that come out will say, 'I want to be like them.' So, it's not really a matter of it changing; perhaps it's a matter of it going back a little more to the musicianship part of it, and certainly from a vocalist perspective. I like to hear some more great singers. There are some still out there, but not enough for me."

Asked by Sam if heavy metal was art, Ronnie says, "Yes, of course it is. Absolutely. For those who don't know how to do it, it's difficult to explain to them. But if you talk to any other musician—one of your peers or even someone who isn't your peer—you find out how difficult it is to do that. Boy, it's really hard. And it's only successful people who can tell you how hard it is, because it takes a long time to do it. I've done this all my life, and I know how damn hard it is. It's hard.

"But it's a way of life. It's a way of life for people like us, it's a way of life for the people who are at this concert, and it will always be a way of life. Our job is to maintain it and to be sure we do the best we can to keep it alive, and it'll never die. It'll never, ever, ever die. They said rock 'n' roll would die after Elvis Presley was a big sensation for a year, and guess what? Now we have presidents who grew up with rock 'n' roll music that are older than Elvis Presley. So, it'll always be there, and it'll be our job to do it.

"Only a few other musical forms have the lasting power that most music doesn't. I think one is country music. If you're a country music fan, you're there forever. If you like Dolly Parton in the early days, you'll still love Dolly Parton in this day and age. And I think metal has always been the same way. Once it captured the imagination of the kind of person that liked that kind of music, they're your fan forever. You're talking about music that can have a lot more darker themes, as well. We could get into gothicness and things other music does not touch upon. But I think probably more than anything, it's the fact that it becomes a great big family of people who all share one thing, and that is metal. We just love it, and it's really us and them against the world—it really is."

CHAPTER 7

"No, we're not going to play 'Last in Line.' We're going to write."

LOCK UP THE WOLVES

After a somewhat acrimonious split with Craig Goldy—one could see it coming, given the previous comments over his lack of fit with the guys—Ronnie and his band sifted through a rumored (and likely very exaggerated) five thousand tapes over the course of six months in search of a new guitarist for the Dio band.

"He left the band because he wanted to," said Ronnie to *Metal Hammer*'s Edgar Klusener—at the time, Dio was between axmen. "And that was because of the famous 'musical differences.' We still get on well privately. The split didn't affect our friendship in the slightest. Craig couldn't get on with our musical direction. He always felt more at home with the commercial side of things, as he had played in his earlier band Giuffria. Craig was turning up with ideas that were completely different from anything Dio really wanted to play, and different from the straight heavy rock that was my trademark and the trademark of the band. A reorientation towards commercial rock or even pop was something I really didn't want anything to do with. So, Craig found himself in a dilemma. He was having difficulties living out his ideas and preferences within the band, especially as any and all major musical decisions are down to me. I guess the situation was frustrating for him in the long run, especially as he is a really good guitarist and talented songwriter. On the other hand, Dio is my band, and I think I'm experienced and competent enough to know exactly what sound the band should have, and in what musical direction we're heading.

"Some of the criticism was justified," continued Ronnie, with respect to the last Dio album of the '80s, *Dream Evil*. "I'm completely aware that we have to develop further. That doesn't mean that I have to change myself and the band's style fundamentally. Typical Dio characteristics will be tapped throughout the future. Dio will remain a heavy band, a band so uniquely different as it was in the olden days. It's always the same with the critics. Basically, you can't do anything right for them. If you venture into completely new direction as a musician, the possibility is very high that the critics tear you apart. They talk about selling out for 'He's going completely commercial now,' and 'He's trying to make a fast buck,' or even start claiming, to take it to another extreme, 'That's not the old so and so,' or 'He's gone crazy now.' If the change isn't so obvious, and you can't hear it is easily, they just say, 'Stagnation; he's ripping himself off,' or whatever else they can think of. It's always risky to depend on the critics' judgment; it's much more important to follow the fans' judgment. After all, I make music for the fans and not for the critics. And above all, I want to stay true to myself.

Record label promo shot of the *Lock Up the Wolves* lineup. ***Left to right:*** Rowan, Ronnie, Jens, Simon, and Teddy.

"I write new songs just about every day, so I've got quite a selection," explained Ronnie. "But I'll have to wait and see what happens in the studio, and the kinds of influences and ideas that come from the new guitarist. I play the guitar, so I could play the basic guitar parts by myself. But I can't play anywhere near as well as a real guitarist. Which is the reason I'd rather wait until I can work with one again. The demos came from all over the world. At the same time, I have to stress that most of them came from California. Which says something about where one can find most of the guitarists in the world! There was quite a lot of rubbish amongst the entries. I listened to every single tape really well, sometimes more than once. Only a few were left over in the end, and ten of those were from California. These were the first ten guitarists we invited to audition. We'll be listening to the last of these tomorrow. If we can't find the right man amongst them, we'll invite a handful of guitarists from Europe to fly in for auditions. Whatever happens, I'm slowly running out of time, because I'll have to go into the studio pretty soon if we want to stick to the original timetable and record a new album by autumn."

Ronnie then goes on to address the possibility of Vivian Campbell getting back into the band, given that Viv had just quit Whitesnake, a mess of a band at the time, laden with a revolving door of hotshot guitarists. "That really is an interesting idea, and under the right circumstances it would even have been worth a try. Although, I don't know whether we would have all been so happy in the long run. All musicians go through

particular stages of development. The way my phases happened, I went through my Rainbow phase, then came Black Sabbath and Dio. Viv has basically been through his Dio and his Whitesnake phases. Each phase forms a musician and means an important step in his development. You discover things for yourself, and you mature enough to go for something new. But that shouldn't necessarily have to be a step backwards. And that's what working with Dio would probably mean for Viv. That's just purely speculation anyway, because Viv has started working on his own project again and seems very happy.

"Nothing will change that either," offers Ronnie, when queried on whether his lyrics will stay fantasy based. "I want to offer escape routes. What's the point of describing in your lyrics the whole madness, the dirt, the scandals, wars, and wrongdoing everyone experiences daily? I'd rather lead the kids into a world of fantasy and adventure for a few minutes or hours with my music. Of course these are only dream worlds, and it shouldn't be understood as anything else. But they are worlds where everyday life bears no particular importance. It's enough that everyday life plays such a dramatic role during the rest of your lifetime."

Interestingly (given the credits of the record that would become *Lock Up the Wolves*) that for a large part of the album's thought processing, the old band—Claude Schnell, Vinny Appice, and Jimmy Bain—were still on board, along with the eventual new hire, an English hotshot from Cambridge named Rowan Robertson, all of seventeen years old at the time, a veteran of such rock titans as Indiscretion and Shoot the Moon. I guess that in the end, it turned out that California had no good guitarists.

"I was in England, where I grew up," Robertson told me back in 2004, on landing the gig. "I read that Dio had lost, or fired, their guitar player. I'm not quite sure how it happened, but they needed a guitar player. So, I just went ahead and sent him a tape from England, of me playing, and forgot about it for six months. And then out of the blue I got a call from Wendy Dio, his manager, and they flew me up for an audition and that was it, really. And I got the gig and have stayed here for the last fourteen, fifteen years [laughs]. I think Ronnie specifically said he liked the way English guitar players played, so he had his sights on getting an English guy, so that was a big plus in my favor. But I can't really say. Probably chemistrywise as well. I was easy to get along with for Ronnie, plus he liked the way I played; it just fit the bill. I guess I was what he was looking for."

And this, having never written a song! Amusing how rock 'n' rollers think—or fail to do so completely: "five thousand" tapes and Ronnie hires a guy who's never written a song. "That's right," chuckles Rowan, "because I spent all my years learning how to play the guitar, not learning how to write songs. That is often the thing with musicians. When you learn, you kind of go one way or the other: you become a player or a writer to some degree. Of course, there are some people who can do both, but I definitely had my sights on just becoming a great player and left the writing behind. I didn't ever really develop that. Influencewise, my first big idol was Jimi Hendrix, and then people like Angus Young, Brian May from Queen, Gary Moore from Thin Lizzy, John Sykes, a bit, from Thin Lizzy. And then once I heard Steve Vai, I just went mad for Steve Vai for a couple years. And of course, Eddie Van Halen. Then I got into the Shrapnel guys, at the end, Tony MacAlpine, Vinny Moore. I always did want to play fast [laughs]. When I was fifteen or whatever, I found out that if I worked at it, I could play pretty fast."

Speaking with Jimmy Kay from the *The Metal Voice*, Rowan recalls that "when Wendy called me up, I was pretty surprised and pretty shocked. But I was a bit of a cocky kid. So, when Wendy asked me, she said, 'How would you feel playing in front of 20,000 people?' And I said, 'All right, I guess' [laughs]. And she said, 'You know, Ronnie would like to see you play. How would you feel if we brought you out?' And of course I was thrilled, but I was very nervous; I really got quite nervous about it. And my dad had some good words of wisdom for me. He said, 'Look, you're getting a free vacation to go out and play with your heroes in Los Angeles. It's all a great situation, so just have fun.' When I got there, the first thing that Ronnie said to me in the audition is 'I want this to work; I really want this to work.' We played through a couple of songs, and I remember looking over and seeing Jimmy Bain smiling away and grinning away. I thought, well, I must be doing something right."

Two-color ad, with UK tour dates, promoting *Lock Up the Wolves*. Support for the campaign came from legendary Chicago doomsters Trouble, which made sense, given the Dio band's dark turn circa *Lock Up the Wolves*.

Concerning the age gap, Rowan figures, "Yeah, there was a lot of that, but there was a lot of interest for a young kid being thrust into the limelight. But at the same time, there was 'What's this kid doing?' There was definitely some of that for sure. And I think a couple of the publications liked to say Ronnie was too old. 'What's he doing getting this kid into the band?' But that was just a little sideline to it. It was a very positive experience."

But then came the thorny issue of having to actually create new music. "Right, well, the first thing when we did the audition was play songs like 'Rainbow in the Dark' and 'The Last in Line,' which I just loved so much. I just loved playing them and I was just so full of enthusiasm for it. And then it came time to do the first session to write, and I said to Ronnie, 'Can we play "Last in Line"?,' and he goes, 'No, we're not going to play "Last in Line." We're going to write.' And I said, 'Wow. I don't know if I can do this.' And he says, 'Trust me, you can do it. You're going to be fine.'

"So, to answer your question, the writing process would go . . . usually it would be sparked from a guitar riff, or mostly a guitar riff, and sometimes a keyboard riff or a bass riff. But Ronnie liked to work from a riff first, which he usually came to his guitar player for. So, what I would have to do, what the guitarist would have to do, is come up with loads of different riffs and you'd play them one by one. 'No, no, don't hear anything, don't hear it; oh, what was that?' And then what we would do is, we would jam the riff and sit or stand there and go, 'Well, where can we take it? Anybody got any ideas? What's the chord change?' And this is where Ronnie would lead the ship; he was definitely in control of it. So, we would find, let's say, two parts, and then we would record them—part A and part B—on a boom box, and Ronnie would take them home overnight and come up with, let's say, a vocal melody. Or he may even have a title sitting around. I remember he came in a couple of times with titles. He came in once and said, 'I've got it. Title of the album: *Lock Up the Wolves*!' And in fact, the riff for 'Lock Up the Wolves,' he actually came up with on the guitar.

"But Ronnie worked with the band all the time. He'd say, 'For this kind of music, it comes from a band in a room.' That's where it comes from. And that's not to say that I came up with every riff. I think most of the guitar riffs on there I came up with, but Jimmy Bain came up with riffs too. Jimmy might come up with an idea or Vinny might come up with a certain beat. But Ronnie got most of his initial ideas from the guitar player. Unless he had the riff himself."

Despite Rowan's predilection for playing fast, the album that the newly configured Dio band came up with turned out to be notoriously slow, so much so that *Lock Up the Wolves* is seen as flawed for that reason, showing up quite low with respect to fan preference when the Dio albums are ranked. I asked Rowan if he had a theory as to why it came out so heavy, slow, and sluggish. "Not really. I mean, it was probably to some extent reflecting how he was feeling. But I think more to the point, he always said that medium-tempo songs are easier to write than rockers. Up-tempo songs are really quite difficult. I mean, there are a couple of up-tempo ones on there, but I guess just that sort of ponderous, plodding thing that album has is, I guess, just what came out of us at the time."

But before the album got recorded, original members Vinny Appice and Jimmy Bain were out of the roster. Jimmy's replacement was Teddy Cook. "I'm not sure what he had done previous," recalls Rowan, "but he was from New York City. I know he went on to play with Great White for a long time afterward, but I don't really know much of his story. Really good bass player, knew all the metal stuff. Teddy came in toward the end, so I don't think he had a lot of writing, if I remember. I don't think he has any writing credits on the album [In fact, he has one: 'Evil on Queen Street']. I don't know, maybe Ronnie was just searching for a new sound. Vinny left when the album was about to be recorded—he just left. And that's when Ronnie called up Simon Wright to play drums. I think Ronnie was just looking for another sound, some experimentation."

"All the things that were going wrong with the band were escalating," explained keyboardist Claude Schnell, also in conversation with Jimmy Kay. "Whether Vinny had gotten fired or not, I knew that he was planning to leave to go play with Jeff Pilson in the band called War and Peace [originally called Flesh and Blood]. Jimmy had already been fired. The guitar player we wanted to replace Craig—when I say we, it was Jimmy, Vinny, and I all in unanimous agreement—was a guitar player by the name of Gary Hoey. Little-known fact: Gary had auditioned for us, and he was amazing; I don't think the band ever sounded better. I think the only way Dio would've sounded better was if Tony Iommi was playing guitar. Gary just did a phenomenal job.

"And the three of us—Jimmy, Vinny, and myself—were convinced that Ronnie was going to love this guy. He's going to be the guy we were going to move on with, and it was going to be better than when Vivian was gone. And after Gary left, Ronnie was in the studio and he goes, 'Guys, you'll hate me for this, but he's not the guy.' You could just hear our collective hearts fall. Because he *was* the guy! For whatever reason, Ronnie didn't want him. But Gary should've been the guitar player and got that gig.

"So, given that we were saddled with a guitar player that we didn't want in the first place . . . mind you, not that it isn't Ronnie's decision. Because I'm first to acknowledge that what Ronnie wants, Ronnie gets, and rightly *should* get. It's his band, he writes the checks, he should be allowed to do whatever he wants to do. But his choice in Rowan we all thought was somewhat uninspired. And then as badly as rehearsals were going, Rowan was having a very hard time at the beginning keeping up with the pressure that Ronnie puts everybody through. Because Ronnie is Ronnie, a very demanding producer and basically a boss. Rowan was having problems keeping up with it. The tension was just building and building, and it got to the point where, as I said, Jimmy got fired and then Ronnie seemed terribly upset with Rowan's performance. The songs were lukewarm at best. So honestly, I really didn't want to be in a band that Jimmy and Vinny weren't going to be in."

Adds Rowan on the subject of musical chairs, "Well, not only did I audition with Jimmy and Vinny, but the whole album was written with the original lineup. With the exception of . . . well, the first lineup change was when Jimmy Bain was out and Teddy Cook was in, and that was during the writing process. It was a ten-month writing process, and I'd say halfway through, that change happened. But Vinny stayed right to the end of the writing sessions. He left two weeks before the recording. So, the whole album was written with Vinny. Then Ronnie scrambled to get Simon and Aynsley Dunbar in at the end. But as far as the reasons for it, you'd really have to talk to Wendy. Because Ronnie is not here. I know it was a difficult time for Ronnie because you feel the changes in the industry. I didn't know it at the time, but looking back it was obvious that it was coming to an end, and I think Ronnie felt the pressure of that. I don't know whether he thought he should try to change with it. That's probably talking too much, because I don't want to speak for him. But as far as the lineup changes go, I don't think it had anything to do with the industry. That was something that Ronnie felt he needed to do, with the exception of Vinny, who left to join Mandy Lion in WWIII."

With Claude Schnell now also exiting, Jens Johansson, seasoned Swedish veteran of Silver Mountain and Yngwie Malmsteen fame (currently with Stratovarius), became part of the mix. Jens offers his recollection of his brief Dio tenure. "Well, Ronnie as a person is very, very nice, and also as an employer. I would say he's almost the ideal employer, a very nice situation to be in. It was a very happy time for me because I came from this chaotic Yngwie thing and, briefly, I found a new home. But writingwise, the thing was, they had been writing already about a year and a half when I came into the picture; I came in something like two months before the album was done. I think they were frustrated with the old guys, the old bass player, and the old keyboard player, because they weren't enthusiastic enough or something. So I didn't write so much; I think I only cowrote one or two songs [Jens is credited on "Walk on Water" and "My Eyes"]. It was still a fun thing to do and fun touring; quite nice. We did one tour in Europe and one tour in the States. The one in the States was longer, I think. And they were with that exact lineup. Rowan as well, he was great, a very young guy, open to new things, very easygoing."

Ronnie spilled the beans about the new Dio lineup to *Kerrang!* just before the release of the album, explaining that "Simon's been a good buddy of mine for a long time, and once we realized that AC/DC's schedule allowed him to help us out on this album, he was the inevitable choice. The band is a great one. We recorded twelve tracks, which is three more than Dio have ever worked on in the studio before. The writing partnership between Rowan and myself has gelled so quickly. He's an incredible player too. He can do anything, play fast like Steve Vai and also encompass all of the soul of the great players. Long after I'm dead and gone, people will be talking about this guy!

The author's CD copy of *Lock Up the Wolves*.
Martin Popoff archive

Teddy Cook is a very different player to Jimmy Bain. A much-younger player. He doesn't have Jimmy's incredible feel, but he's a little heavier and he takes a few more chances. Jens Johansson is one of the most brilliant musicians I've ever heard, my absolute first choice as a keyboard player, and he's a hell of a person as well. What we have here is a lot of the *Holy Diver* and the *Last in Line* albums, but with the more modern feel that myself and Rowan have introduced. We have a couple of working titles for the album, so I won't let you in on the secret yet, but some of the tunes that we'll include are 'Hey Angel,' which is a song about suicide, but written from an unusual angle in that the person is already dead! There's also 'Evil on Queen Street,' a real slow, heavy track, and 'Why Are They Watching Me,' which reflects a little of my usual paranoia."

A Ronnie James Dio collector card

The construction of *Lock Up the Wolves* was quite the protracted process, with songs originating from jams and getting pounded into position over long periods of time. The record was written and recorded at a Victorian house in Reno, Nevada, so the band could "live and breathe rock 'n' roll." Tony Platt of AC/DC fame would coproduce and Nigel Green, notable for glossing up Def Leppard's *Hysteria*, would mix. Said Ronnie, in an interview for the album's official bio, "If we wanted to record something at 6:00 a.m., we did. Away from Los Angeles, you don't have to worry about the mundane aspects of your life. You get to focus purely on music. The city of Reno is great. One night we all went down to this club and met up with these Marines who just got back from the invasion of Panama. They told us they listened to Dio music down there and kind of goaded us to perform. So, we went up onstage and used the house band's equipment. It was great; we did three songs and burned the place down!"

The official name of the studio was Granny's House. "Well, what is Granny's House?" begins producer Tony Platt. "It's in Reno, Nevada, and it was called Grammy's House, but then the Grammy organization made them change the name. It was basically a large house in Reno with a studio in it. It wasn't a studio that I'd actually chosen. The studio had been kind of chosen for me, and it wasn't particularly live for making rock recordings. I was having a bit of difficulty getting a drum sound because the studio was so dead. I ended up sending the road crew down to the local lumberyard to buy some really big eight-by-four plywood sheets that we put on the walls to get some extra reflection, much to the annoyance of the guy that owned the studio, because he'd spent a fortune on the acoustics. So, we had to sort out the acoustics of the studio to get things happening a bit, you know, a bit fatter and so on and so forth.

"It was an interesting album to make," continues Platt. "The drum tracks all went down pretty well. I mean, it was a coproduction with Ronnie, who was a lovely man to work with; I really enjoyed working with him. And Rowan, what an amazing guitar player; it was a privilege to work with him too. He was absolutely fantastic. You know, I got on pretty well. We used to go to the gym every morning together and so on.

"I mean it was a strange place to make an album, Reno. I mean, we got there and there was no snow on the ground. And then a couple of days after we got there, it snowed really, really heavily and Reno was then cut off; you couldn't get out of the place. And Reno looks okay when it's snowing, but when it's got no snow on it, it's a real shithole. People don't go there for the scenery; they go there to gamble. And all the hotels of course have got casinos in them. I was staying in a hotel because there was only a limited amount of accommodation actually at the studio. So, I was staying at a hotel just down the road, which is a little bit like living inside a pinball machine, both from the smell and the sound. It was very strange because I'd get up and about, I'd go to the gym and then come back again, set off for the studio about ten in the morning. I'm walking out through the casino because that was right through the reception. And you'd see people on slot machines at ten o'clock in the morning, and then I'd come back at like midnight, and they'd be still on the same spot.

"But I think all these young guys were very stoked to be playing with Ronnie," continues Tony, "because in some ways they were contemporary players. They were the new guys on the block. And I think in some respects, that was one of the things that the diehard Dio fans were a little bit taken aback about, that it wasn't the straightforward pumping sort of stuff that Ronnie had done before. It had a little bit more lightness in it and a melodic touch to it. But no, they were all great. Every single one of them was fantastic. They played great and we had no real problems. I mean, we recorded it very, very quickly. It went very smoothly. And then I went across to London to do the mix. We were all kind of jokey types of people, really. The one who was most nervous was Rowan; he was probably the least experienced out of all of them."

Responding to the description of the album as slower in tempo, Tony says, "I don't think I particularly noticed it. I mean, I've always been a great one for experimentation and so on. I have the greatest affinity for artists who have reinvented themselves time after time. So, I found it quite interesting working with Ronnie at a point where he was trying to expand. One of the problems I've always had with heavy rock music and heavy metal is that quite often, bands paint themselves into a corner. They become so synonymous with their particular sound that they paint themselves into a corner where at first, it's kind of great because they're immediately identifiable, and then I think they start to get frustrated by the whole thing and then try and do something different.

"But I don't know; Ronnie had a pretty clear idea of what he wanted. I wasn't involved in the preproduction for the album, but he did rehearse them quite extensively before we got to the studio. You mention the songs being slower; if I recall correctly, going back to my conversations with Ronnie before we started the album, he very specifically hired each one of those people for the album. And I think he specifically hired me as well. Because he wanted an engineer who had a production head on. So, in a way he didn't really necessarily want me to produce the band. He wanted me to produce *him*. So, you know, he brought everything to the studio fairly, fairly well formed. We muddled around a little bit and then went from there. I think he also was looking for this guitar/drum combination. I mean if I remember rightly, that record probably has got more of a guitar emphasis than a keyboard emphasis."

Cassette, vinyl, and CD of *Lock Up the Wolves*. *Martin Popoff archive*

And back to the subject of preproduction, "Like I said, there were no songs," says Rowan, recalling the early stages. "I had a couple of riffs I had tried to put together. All the album was written over, say, ten months, in rehearsals. I think the way Ronnie writes is mainly with his guitar player, usually. Basically, he'd come to one of the band members, be it the bass player or the guitar player, and we would present him with a riff or a part or something. He might like it, he might not. He will sort of throw something out there: 'Oh, where should we go from here?' Maybe a chord change or a riff or something. And then he'd find something that he liked, and we'd just start hashing it out. Everyone would throw their lot in, and then he would take it home from the first day of sort of birthing the idea, come up with lyrics or a melody idea, and then just come in the next day and keep at it, until we'd hit a brick wall and maybe start on something else for a while. He definitely uses the band as sort of the beginner of parts, and then he picks and chooses to put songs together; he's got a very strong songwriting style. I just learned a lot from him, you know; great to work with. Obviously, he's a perfectionist; he wants things done his way. Well, not really wants things done his way; it's just that he wants things done right and satisfactory, and he runs a pretty tight ship that way. And he's always really fun to hang out with."

"I think only not so bright lights," recalls Jens, when asked whether the band had "vibed up" the studio at all. "I think, like me, Ronnie doesn't ascribe to the 'dressing up the studio' idea. What you need is competent people and that everything works so you can make the takes easily enough. It was actually a very nice studio, tailored to these things. We turned down the lights and had competent people."

"At the time, I suppose I met a few, like David Coverdale [laughs], at magazine parties, or whatever you have to do," answers Robertson, on the subject of meeting his rock idols during the recording of the *Lock Up the Wolves* record and beyond. "Say hello to Steve Vai or whatever. But no, in fact, Ronnie didn't really like having open rehearsals. If there was anybody dropping by, it would be a close friend of his. And never any friction. It was always a really professional working environment. Just having fun, really. Jens, just great, a wonderful guy, always joking, funny, tricks, just a madman, booby-trapping people's houses, all sorts of pranks. And Ronnie loved it. The only problem having Jens in the band is you'd be killing yourself too much laughing, so it was a good thing. Simon is great. Just a solid guy, very friendly, easy to get along with. And he loves playing the hard rock, and he's still doing it."

Simon of course was none other than Simon Wright, drummer on AC/DC's *Fly on the Wall*, *Blow Up Your Video*, and the new tracks on *Who Made Who*. Previous to that, Wright had done his time with NWOBHM B-levelers AIIZ and Tytan.

"A drummer like Simon tends to play with a great deal of power yet keeps things rather simple," noted Ronnie, on Wright's fit for the newly pounding Dio sound. "Vinny had gotten to the point where he was playing a lot of fills to make up for the places the bass player should have been. But a busy drummer doesn't provide the proper foundation for a band like Dio. It takes the music in a different direction. We're back on course with Simon on drums and Teddy on bass. It's very important that the fans hear the spaces that are designed to be in the songs. Some of those had disappeared on the last few albums. You have to hear the music and relate to it, not be hit over the head with it like some of the thrash bands do. That's not my style at all."

Added Ronnie, on Simon's hiring, "I had always been a fan of his from his AC/DC days, and we had talked in the past about working together if the situation ever arose. When Vinny decided to leave the band, some people I knew put me touch with Simon. He wasn't doing anything at the moment because AC/DC was on vacation. I needed a drummer for the album, and he was looking for something to do, so I asked him if he had any interest in playing on *Lock Up the Wolves*. That was really as far as it was to go. I had no intention of stealing him from another band. I know I've already been accused of that, but perhaps it's better to let Simon tell you what really happened."

"It's really just as Ronnie said," confirms Simon. "He never asked me to leave AC/DC. But I'd been in the band for eight years, and I felt it was time for a little change. The breaks between recording and touring in AC/DC were getting longer and longer, and I like to keep busy. I always admired Dio, and when Ronnie offered me the chance to work on the new album, I jumped on it. It just sort of developed from there."

"I didn't kind of audition," Simon explained to me years later. "It's surprising, because there have been a lot of people in Dio. But he didn't really like change. I'm not sure exactly why. But no, it was through a friend of a friend. My ex-wife was friends with Wendy and mentioned that I was kind of knocking around. I'd left AC/DC, and I was lucky enough to get on the phone with Ronnie and the next thing we're rehearsing. It all happened very, very quickly. That's what they were doing at the time—getting ready to do an album—and it happened very quickly. We got straight in there and did it, and during the making of the album, I just thought this was great; this is very, very cool. And I mentioned that, and Ronnie said, 'That would be fantastic, Simon. Yeah, let's do it.' I was in the band, and we were planning tours, and it was great."

Simon emphasizes that Ronnie never asked him to play dead-simple, like he did with AC/DC. "No, no, he didn't. He was always for drums. He always encouraged me to try more. Not too much to get completely silly, but he always loved drums. He had some great ideas of what worked well together. When we were creating the songs and stuff for playing live as well as in the studio, he was always great. He had a real sensibility for what they meant in the songs. Vinny is remarkable, very original, very inventive. He's got great feel and he's a great guy. My style is more straightforward, I would say. So, I try to incorporate more straightforwardness, but a bit of flash as well. Live, I try to be respectful of what other drummers have played, and still incorporate those things that drummers have played into the songs, because I think they're a very integral part of some of the songs, really. I love playing those songs, especially 'I Speed at Night,' and 'Egypt' is always a good one. They're all good once you get going. It's kind of boring playing them in rehearsal, but once you get playing them live, that's the way to do it. I like a challenge, and there's quite a few of them that are a challenge. You do get familiar with them. Obviously, I've been playing them for about fourteen years now. But they're always a challenge. You have to be on your game."

Back to the record, Simon recalls that "Rowan Robertson was very, very young. Smart kid and obviously a brilliant guitar player. But Rowan was listening to and hanging on to everything that Ronnie said, because he was obviously so young and hadn't really been on the road before or recorded very much before that. I'm sure he learned a hell of a lot from Ronnie. And Tony Platt was really good. It was a total collaboration between him and Ronnie. Ronnie is really the producer, but Tony did some things . . . I was coming out of AC/DC and I wanted to get a really big drum sound, so he put me up on a riser and we tried some acoustic panels and things like that; he got for me a really huge sound."

But Ronnie was the boss. "Yeah, and he would have to come down on all of us, sometimes, because he really worked hard and he led by example. What I learned from him the most was how grateful you have to be to your fans. He taught me a lot about that, and it's something that really stuck with me. I always had that anyway, but with Ronnie it was really reinforced. He had a great memory, fantastic memory, could remember all the fans' names, their mothers' names, and just really always let them know how much they were appreciated. One of my best memories working on *Lock Up the Wolves* . . . in Reno there was this bar around the corner and there was a young band in there, and we kind of took over the bar, and that was the first time I played 'Holy Diver' live."

Which begs the question, what was Ronnie's drink of choice? "He liked a Guinness, or any of the British beers, really, Tetley, or Newcastle Brown Ale. But yeah, being on the road with him was great. The thing about Ronnie was, he was all about the music and he was a workaholic. He would just work so much. He would go the distance. It was just an inspiration all the time, being around him. Just to watch how he controls such a huge crowd, those big crowds we played in front of—just fantastic."

Lock Up the Wolves, released on May 15, 1990, opens with a quick-picked rocker called "Wild One," a cryptic paean to outsider status, a familiar theme in the Dio canon.

"I remember when that riff came about," recalls Robertson, who turns in a shredding, circular solo. "I remember I was happy with it, showed it to Ronnie, and he was also liking it. I really didn't know what he would like or not, most of the time. I gave him whatever I had, and if he liked it, he liked it. 'Wild One' was special to me because I was looking for a special guitar riff and it just popped out one day in rehearsal and I thought, oh, this is cool, and I knew it was good. So that was special. I thought that I could put my mark on it, somehow, my stamp. And that one I thought was a success."

But it's Simon who gets to open the song (and album), captured high fidelity, perhaps a little overhot. But soon we're into the dancing riff, in creation of a fast song necessary to announce the new band. At the lyric end, Ronnie quite impressively sums up all his themes with a series of rapid-fire, often-abstract phrases—opening salvo "You say you've never seen the light before" is the perfect setup, as we go in search of the sacred heart.

"Jimmy, as I recall, came up with the riff for 'Born on the Sun,'" continues Rowan, on one of the album's characteristically slow, anticlimactic songs. Ronnie expands upon the theme of the intro track, addressing achievement, even name-checking the "wild one." On the subject of where "wild one" Jimmy was at with his well-publicized heroin addiction at the time, Rowan says that "I didn't know; I was so young. I wouldn't have been able to tell if he was having a bad period. I found him to be just normal. I wouldn't have said, 'Oh, this guy is having bad troubles or whatever.'" "There's a crack in the rainbow," muses Ronnie, as an opening observation, and really, there's a crack in Dio, with this song not exactly propelling the band forward in any way.

"Hey Angel" ("Nothing is a reason for suicide," comments Ronnie on the lyric. "Life is too important.") follows in similar plodding, stomping style, before giving way to "Between Two Hearts," an even slower, Sabbatherian number that verges upon the concept of dirgy power ballad.

"That one was actually written in the recording studio," says Rowan. "I remember that I was sitting in the vocal booth playing with an acoustic, and sort of plinking this little thing, and Ronnie looked through the control window, like, 'Yeah!' [laughs]. He liked it, and then I remember him hashing it out with me a bit and then he asked me for a bit of a change, and then he put in a couple changes. And then actually we recorded it with Teddy, the bass player, on drums, just to demo the music up. Ronnie wrote a melody and some words, and then we recorded it properly with Simon. Because I don't think Simon had come in to cut the drums. He was away or something. But 'Hey Angel' was another one where I thought I could put my stamp on it as a riff, because I was really happy with that riff. I thought it was quite sort of unique, like 'Lock Up the Wolves.'"

Robertson figures that "Night Music" was generated from a keyboard riff, either from Claude Schnell or Ronnie. In any event, it is another frustratingly deflated, stodgy, and boxy rocker, frankly perhaps one of the worst and most grooveless bits of music in the Dio catalog, despite a nice meandering solo from Robertson. "I don't know if he actually came up with any riffs," says Rowan of Claude, "because Ronnie is a guitar-based writer, you know what I mean? But yeah, he was definitely there contributing, which we all did, chord changes, where to go next in the song." Lyrically, there was the night thing again, aligning the song with previous Dio tracks from the darkness including "Shame on the Night," "I Speed at Night," "One Night in the City," and "Night People."

The title track of the album is next, with Robertson indicating that Ronnie brought that one in on guitar. "Ronnie plays enough to be able to write. But don't forget, he was a musician first, playing bass with Elf, and in the '50s, starting out on trumpet. That one captures that really dark Dio/Sabbath magic. The alarm clock at the beginning of that track actually was keeping Jens up all night. Jens came downstairs and said, 'I can't sleep. Take that alarm clock out of the room.' So, we ended up recording the alarm clock for the beginning." As Robertson has alluded to, Ronnie also brought in the title for the song and, by proxy, the title for the record. Once again, Dio is found plodding through a sparse concrete block of a riff, with Simon Wright's simple drumming and Tony's and Ronnie's unforgiving production not helping matters.

"'Evil on Queen Street' . . . Ronnie actually wrote about a sandwich from your home country," laughs Robertson, about yet another lethargic "locked-up" gut stomper. "Apparently, just down the street from MuchMusic in Toronto, is a café with a sandwich called Evil on Queen Street [laughs]. That's where he got the title. Because they were at MuchMusic, I guess. Queen Street . . . the Horseshoe is there; I played in a band called Vast a few years back, a couple of times. And more recently I played there with a guy called Teddy Thompson, who is the son of Richard Thompson, the guitar player. But that song is written about a haunted house, not so much haunted, but evil, I guess. And that was written right at the very end of the writing session, and it started out as just this kind of slow, ponderous blues thing."

"Walk on Water," generated from a Robertson riff, is a fast one quite similar in structure to "Wild One," but still a welcome break from the smothering heft of the balance of the album. "Twisted," however, yanks us back into the mire. "I remember I had something to do with that," recalls Rowan, "because I wanted it to have a kind of AC/DC feel; I loved AC/DC, that kind of boogie, up-tempo blues-stomping kind of feel." With respect to the song's theme, Ronnie had remarked that he took it as a badge of honor when people referred to him as twisted. However, there's a narrative about someone accused of a crime he didn't commit, but with an aggressive personality that made him an easy suspect.

"The next one, 'Why Are They Watching Me,' I remember Ronnie had the title," continues Rowan. "He said, 'Oh, I've got a great idea for title! 'Why Are They Watching Me!'" [laughs]. And I remember the idea for the rhythm was kind of that Judas Priest style, that chugging rhythm." In fact, the song does pump along nicely, with a muscular Priest or Accept feel, notwithstanding the unfathomable "Children of the Grave"-like break halfway through.

Opined Ronnie, back on the press trail, concerning the lyrical direction of this one and others on the record: "My music has always been directed at the lost souls of the world, the people who tend to get kicked around and blamed for the world's sins. There are thousands of those people out there, the long-haired kids who are shunned by society because they don't fit in. I've always been one of those people, so I can relate to them. On this album, we have a number of tunes directed to those souls, like 'Why Are They Watching Me,' 'Wild

One,' and 'Between Two Hearts.' I'm very proud of the lyrics as well as the music on this record because they delve deeply into the hearts and minds of everyone. I must say that this album is like a rebirth for me. I was very displeased by *Dream Evil*, and it pains me to even think about that record. We had obviously come to the end of the line with that version of the band. Everyone thought they were a star, and working in that environment had become just impossible. This one is like the first Dio album in that it's full of power, life, and positive energy."

Finally, there's "My Eyes," a nearly Renaissance-type ballad that revs up into a slow to midpaced thumper before switch-backing into a number of movements, most of them quite impressive and even, in totality, proggy. Says Rowan: "I remember Ronnie had actually asked me if I had any acoustic bits, because that was the kind of song that was needed. That's the way he writes. 'Oh, we should write this type of song, or that type of song.' I came up with the acoustic part in rehearsal, actually, and he just started singing over it right then, just off the cuff. That's basically all I ever remember about the songs, just the initial manner in which they came about. Then they all followed that same pattern, just day in, day out, working them through and getting them right." Lyrically, the song is loose and disjointed but struggling toward the enigmatic, Ronnie sort of name-checking his career highlights, looking back, and marveling at what his eyes have seen, even if the end result of such a long road of rock 'n' roll madness is something akin to the proverbial 1,000-yard stare.

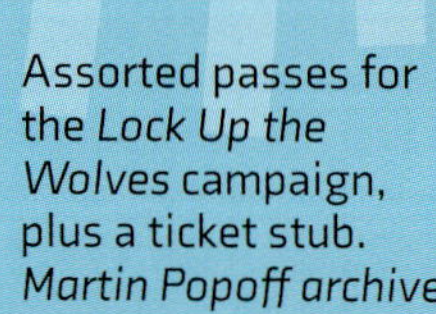

Assorted passes for the *Lock Up the Wolves* campaign, plus a ticket stub. *Martin Popoff archive*

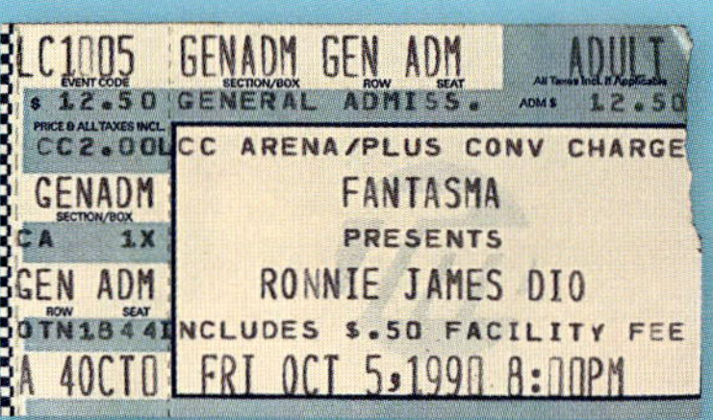

"To me, it's probably not one of the best albums, unfortunately," notes Johansson, looking back on this dour and frumpy dark horse of the Dio catalog. "It sort of straddles styles, I think, in Ronnie's mind. There's like one style before that album and one style after that album. After that, he got more into the dissonant type of thing, with *Angry Machines*. It's sort of like sublimating the grunge era a little bit into the music, but still sounding like himself. *Lock Up the Wolves* was drifting in that direction, but he just didn't know it yet, or something like that. And I think that's maybe also why he fired the guys in the band: because he was frustrated because he wasn't really hearing what he wanted to hear, and he hadn't quite figured out how to do it yet. I still like the album. The singing of course is fucking great.

"But it's a much more basic album than the previous one," continues Jens, looking specifically at the keyboard role. "I think what he did on *Dream Evil* was what he wanted to get away from. There were lots of keyboards, and it was like an '80s album. To me, I think when I started working with him, I could tell that he was refreshed when he didn't have to struggle. Because I'm sort of a little bit of a minimalist. I sometimes preferred not to put things in. And I think for him, that was a relief working with someone who didn't always want to put as much keyboards as possible into every fucking possible spot everywhere. He was like, 'Oh, that's great, maybe a little bit here and a little bit there.' You could tell that he was relieved, because maybe for five or six years, he was struggling with that other guy. I heard horror stories, like the guy had bribed the mixing guy to put the keyboards louder in the mix and things like that. It was like, 'Yeah, I found out later that the guy had been giving money to him!' That type of stupidity. I think he was a bit relieved, but maybe he hadn't found exactly what was in his head in terms of direction. So, I think it's a little bit of a mongrel album because it has a lot of the '80s elements and the '90s elements as well."

It's an interesting perspective. To these ears, *Lock Up the Wolves* isn't grungy; it's just plodding. And *Dream Evil* isn't keyboardy, but rather it's a lot more like the first two albums than people are willing to admit. But to be sure, Ronnie wasn't a fan of it, as indicated above. But from what I know, his memory of *Dream Evil* has been clouded by the problems he was having with personnel. Bottom line, there are a pile of cracking songs on there. It's this writer's favorite Dio album.

Kerrang!'s Jon Hotten wasn't on board with what Ronnie was selling, writing in his review that "*Lock Up the Wolves* will fool no-one. Dio is caught up in a hammy generic trap. Thus 'Born on the Sun' is 'Heaven and Hell,' 'Wild One' is 'Stand Up and Shout' or 'We Rock' and hey, it starts the album! Lyrically, Dio trots out the dragons, angels, and, yes, rainbows, without shame or mercy, and beyond joking. Don't bother calling them a barely digestible pap of sadly clichéd, dementedly mixed, and clumpy metaphors. They may be a huge joke at our expense. You wanna bet on it? *Lock Up the Wolves* scuffs around for a good idea. 'Evil on Queen Street' and the title cut explore the extremes of plod metal. That's boring. Dio is big enough to know competence is no excuse. Living Colour, King's X, and Metallica exist, and Dio won't catch up. That's sad, but time and life move on."

Out on tour, Dio was unfortunately experiencing the waning light of the heavy metal decade, as well as indifference and worse to what people saw rightly as a complete change of blood for his backing band. "It was a year of writing, ending in recording, and then a year touring, or maybe a little less than a year," says Rowan, summing up the *Lock Up the Wolves* era. "Hitting the road, I remember they suspended the wardrobe lady from the lighting rig and doused the support band in flour and water, your usual sort of pranks. Support came from Love/Hate, plus Cold Sweat, whom Wendy managed along with Dio. At one point, Yngwie Malmsteen was supporting, which was great, because I loved his playing growing up, but later on, when I was getting into my shred period [laughs].

Off the album, we played 'Wild One,' 'Lock Up the Wolves,' and 'Born on the Sun.' I think we tried out 'My Eyes' a couple of times. It was mostly theaters, plus arenas, cordoned off. So yes, that was definitely not the height of fame for the band. But we still had the stage set and everything, which was great. I loved playing all of it. I mean, the Rainbow stuff was killer. 'Long Live Rock 'n' Roll,' 'Tarot Woman,' 'Stargazer'—we did a medley of all that stuff. And we did 'Children of the Sea,' which was great, plus 'Neon Knights,' plus, of course, 'Holy Diver' and 'Rainbow in the Dark.' We tried 'Egypt,' I think a couple times, and that didn't stick. Not that I had any favorites, really, but of course, 'Long Live Rock 'n' Roll' and 'We Rock' were great fun, just a blast to play."

Touring for the album actually begun in Europe, with Dio and Bonham backing up Metallica to crowds in the five figures in Germany, France, and the Netherlands, in mid-May 1990. Chicago's mighty doom band Trouble supported the band for five dates in the UK later that month and into June, the two legends playing to crowds of 2,000 to a high of 4,300 at the Hammersmith Odeon, where Iron Maiden's Nicko McBrain guested on drums. Back in America on August 1, as Rowan has indicated, support came quite intensively from Yngwie Malmsteen through the end of the month, a highlight being Geezer Butler standing in for 'Neon Knights' at a date in Minneapolis. Next up was a one-off flight to Germany for the Super Rock festival, featuring Aerosmith, Poison, Dio, Whitesnake, Vixen, the Front, and Cold Sweat. Back in America, support fell to Cold Sweat and Love/Hate for solidly booked dates through September 1990, ending on October 7 in Dallas, Texas.

As we all know, Ronnie was about to embark upon a career change even bigger in magnitude than, say, the jettisoning of a whole Dio lineup. Explains Robertson, "What happened was, at the end of the process, when we came off the last tour, Ronnie went back to do an album with Black Sabbath, *Dehumanizer*. I don't really recall, you know, a lot of warning about it, but I don't know how long he knew about it either. I don't how long it had been on the cards. But these things happen very quickly anyway. And I was sort of free to look for my own avenue, and I did the Violet's Demise thing, which took me too long and too much effort [laughs]."

So yes, the next turn in Ronnie's tale is toward *Dehumanizer*, but before we go, Rowan offers a little more detail on what course his life took. "In the following years, '91 to '95, I was involved with this guy Oni Logan, who used to sing in Lynch Mob [solo vehicle for Dokken's George Lynch]. We formed Violet's Demise, which, start to stop, took us three or four years. We started from scratch, wrote the material and put the band together, got a deal, recorded the album, on Atlantic, with Dave Jerden, who was quite a big producer at the time. And unfortunately, that took me up to '94, and the album got shelved [laughs]. So, it was like four years of work down the drain, and it was a good album, which no one got to hear. It was pretty heavy; a little bit more experimental than anything. It was heavy, in the sense of heavy drums and guitars, but it was a little bit on the Zeppelin side, quite creative. But yeah, by that time, Ronnie was putting Dio back together, and I'd just got the deal with Atlantic, and we were just making the record, so that was it. I mean I was obviously excited about that, and then Ronnie never asked me back anyway.

"Right now, I'm teaching," continued Rowan, speaking in 2004. "I've got a few students, and I'm actually playing in two bands at the moment, Radford, which is a band on Universal, who have had one single out that did somewhat okay, and we're putting another one out. I'm also playing in this band called AM Radio, which I have been playing with for about three years. We've had an album out a little over a year ago, going on two years now, out on Elektra. So, I earn my living through both means, by playing in bands and teaching as well. AM Radio is basically pop rock, really. It's using distorted guitars and heavy drums and all that stuff but more in a pop sense, as far as the melodies and the singer goes."

"I was certainly a little disappointed that *Lock Up the Wolves* didn't amount to a whole lot in its first days of selling," reflects Rowan, now years later speaking with Jimmy Kay. "Though I think it still sold something like 400,000 worldwide. Yeah, it was the old big industry. But as far as what Dio was getting back from the record company, it was pretty much nonexistent. You had Soundgarden and all of these other bands. They just weren't interested anymore. Even at that time. I think touring for him was quite hard, although we had great fun; we had a great time. But what was behind the scenes . . . yeah, they weren't getting any support."

As for the Sabbath thing . . . "You know, I wasn't pissed at all—not in the slightest. Geezer came out to see us on the road, to see Ronnie on the road, and I got to play 'Neon Knights' with him one night, which was incredible. And then when the tour ended, and Wendy told me that Ronnie decided that it was right for him to do Sabbath again, I was a little surprised, I guess, but I wasn't at all upset about it. As for any new music, the only thing that happened is I went to his house a couple of times, knocked out a couple of riffs. That was probably right when he was trying to decide what he was going to do. And that's all—there is nothing recorded. There are two songs I've got, just boom box recordings, that didn't make the record. And I played them for Wendy, and she said that the quality isn't good enough to release them. One was called 'Hell Wouldn't Take Her' and one was called 'River between Us,' and neither of them made the album. And I know that Craig, for instance, has personal stuff that wouldn't have made the albums that he made with Ronnie. But out of respect, he's not going to be just putting them out there. I wouldn't want to tread on anyone's toes and release what I have either.

"In terms of live performances, there are two high-quality ones. One of them was done for radio in Florida—I've got that—and one was done for TV in Germany. I don't know if the whole set was recorded, but there was high-quality TV of it; it's on the internet. I don't think Florida is on the net. It was really good quality, recorded for radio, a proper recording.

"Looking back, more and more, I think it's a great album," laughs Robertson with respect to *Lock Up the Wolves*, adding that the whole thing was quite a learning experience for a guy scarcely seventeen years of age. "I mean, Ronnie and Wendy looked after me. Because I was a kid, you know? I was out to L.A., dangerous place or whatever. It wasn't their responsibility to, but it kind of was their responsibility at the same time. They met both my parents, who came out at different times to see me. We used to hang out at his house a lot, popping out for Indian food around the corner [laughs]."

Jimmy Bain, playing with WWIII, Irvine, California, March 17, 1991. © *Tom Wallace*

Vinny Appice, from the same WWIII show.
© *Tom Wallace*

And did he succumb to L.A.'s temptations? "I think in some ways, but not in others. I wasn't about to be an angel, but I wasn't too destructive or crazy either."

"Rowan was a hundred years old when I met him, even though he was only sixteen," said Ronnie a few years later, looking back. "I never taught him to play guitar, as he was already a stupendous musician. He's like Jeff Pilson; he could play a chair! The most important thing he learned from me was how to write a song, working it through from beginning to end. He never had to learn how to be a good person, because he is, and will always be, one of the sweetest people on this earth. I think my proudest moment will be when Rowan has a hit record, because I know that I've been able to take someone so young and put him through what I've been through without him actually having to experience it. He's such a special kid."

As alluded to, original Dio band members Jimmy Bain and Vinny Appice were to emerge on their own 1990 album, a self-titled from a band called WWIII. Leader of the growly, grinding cabal was vocalist Mandy Lion, and on guitar was none other than Tracy G., soon to become six-stringer in a reconstituted Dio. And what did the Mike

Slamer–produced *WWIII* record sound like? *Lock Up the Wolves*, basically, but with rougher, more histrionic vocals and a hint of hair metal.

Besides the Dio connection, WWIII is remembered for Mandy Lion's visual image, specifically the hat and the long coat. "Well, there was a time when I was doing the hair-teasing thing," Mandy told me in 2004, "but when everybody was doing the pretty thing, I teased it up so high I couldn't walk through doorways. But I'd say since about 1987, I just started dressing the way I dress offstage. I was just tired of it. Actually, I remember when Ian Astbury from the Cult used to come see me play; we were just getting a name around town. We were playing clubs, and I was a big Cult fan at the time. If you remember, at the time, he was wearing like ruffled shirts; he had a pirate look happening. And he used to come and see us play like four and five times in a row, and people were pointing him out to me. And I walked up to him one night and said, 'Thanks, man; I love your music and I'm honored that you're here,' blah blah blah. And to make a long story short, a month later my girlfriend calls me up at rehearsal and she's crying. 'You've got to come and see this!' She had taped the 'Firewoman' video, and when I played that video without sound for my mother, my own mother thought it was me. I'm serious. My own mother thought it was me. That was kind of fucked up."

Future Dio band member Tracy G, with WWIII, at the same Irvine, California, show. © Tom Wallace

Left: Jimmy and Mandy at the same California show. © Tom Wallace

On bringing Tracy G into the band, Mandy explains that "basically, when I found Tracy, he was thirty-six years old, had never done anything. I saw him on a little home video that was shot on a Tuesday night at some club somewhere in the valley, where he played in front of his family and the staff. He'd auditioned for everybody, hadn't done anything, and we kinda became friends, and I wanted him in the band. And my management didn't want him. They were actually, at the time, trying to steal Zakk Wylde from Ozzy. They just wanted a main player, like Vinny and Jimmy. And I said, 'Look, this is my friend,' so I went to bat for him with my label, with my management, everybody, and eventually got him the gig."

Front cover of the *WWIII* album, signed by Vinny Appice. *Martin Popoff archive*

As for Vinny and Jimmy, "Oh, I love them. Everyone I ever played with, I still get along with, except for Tracy these days. I mean Vinny, he's the real deal. He's just so New York, it's not even funny. He's fun to be around, loves kids more than anything. And I think he's one of the best metal drummers ever. Jimmy is [laughs] . . . I mean, every cliché you ever heard about a rock star, Jimmy is it. He loves to party. He bangs everything that doesn't climb up the tree fast enough [laughs]. He's everything you think a rock star should be. The thing is, as far as drugs is concerned with Jimmy, you see, I've never done any kind of drug. So, it's hard for me to understand. But when somebody has done it so much, you're not going to really be able to talk him out of it. The thing with Jimmy is that no matter what he does, he's able to deliver. That's why I was able to put up with it. No matter what he would do, as soon as he would hang the bass around his neck and you put him on the stage, he would deliver. It's sad, because you see somebody hurting themselves that you love, but they're not going to stop until they're ready to."

Constructing the *WWIII* record was not without its own dramas. "Oh my God, yes," continues Mandy. "Mike and I had a big problem. The original mix he wanted to put out was absolutely horrible. See, Mike is the type of guy . . . I think he gets great guitar sounds, and I think that's why Tracy loved him. That he does, but since he's a guitar player, I've got to tell you honestly: I don't think he makes for a great producer. You know, you let that part of yourself go, and you have to understand that a song is not made by guitars alone. I don't think you're the producer. And we had to remix the whole album in two days, because we were out of budget. You know, it was horrible. You couldn't understand a single word. It basically sounded like the music was up front, and there was a construction worker yelling in the background, you know, angry. It was bad.

"But not as bad as what that Steve Jones guy did to us. Do you want to hear about that? Okay [laughs], at the label we had a guy named Steve Jones, who was a complete nut case. He had a band called the Unforgiven; I don't know if you remember them. And he became our A&R guy. He wanted us to use his jousting footage in videos, and he was writing songs for us. I mean, he was an A&R guy, and he's writing songs for us, which sucked ass, and he was pissed off that we didn't use them. It was just a combination of many things, and I finally understand now.

"But I remember having a meeting with the label where they wanted me to—believe it or not, this big meeting—and they're all looking at me and going, 'Hey, Mandy, we have an idea for something controversial. How about you write a song that says Hitler was right?' And I'm like, 'Look, I'm half Italian, half German; my guitar player is Hispanic; my manager is Jewish; my drummer is Italian; my bass player is Scottish. How is that going to work?! Besides, I don't believe in that shit. So, you know, I can't stand behind that.'

"And they go, 'Okay, okay, how about then you write a song about that the gangs are right, because the guitar player is Hispanic?' Like, then I'm going to have shootings, right? So, it went on and on and on. They wanted to have a picture of me blowing the pope's head off with a machine gun, on the album cover. I'm not making this up. So anyway, I turned it all down, and everybody got kind of pissed. But then the day came when it was time to okay the artwork on the CD, and they wouldn't give it to me. So, I ended up not having a CD until I actually had to go to the store and buy one myself. I opened the thing up, and here it is. It says, if you look at it, there is like a thing written over the inside cover, and it says, in German, 'one German race,' which was Hitler's

The four-panel poster image used in the *WWIII* booklet. ***Left to right:*** Tracy, Mandy, and Jimmy. *Martin Popoff archive*

Lock Up the Wolves LP inner sleeve

slogan. But not only that. Not only did they make us look like Nazis, which, obviously, they're going to think I'm the Nazi, because I'm the one who grew up in Germany, but they spelt it wrong! So not only do I look like a Nazi, I look like an illiterate Nazi. I was pissed. You cannot imagine! That was not okay by me. And if you're going to make a statement like that, at least spell it right. Idiots, you know? That's Steve Jones for you."

But it's a solid record that, at least on paper, like *Lock Up the Wolves*, was far enough away from the glam metal forged on the Sunset Strip to have a fighting chance in the emerging grunge era. "I used to get a lot of shit for the first record, because people were saying, you know, that sounds like a teenager wrote it. Well, that's because a teenager wrote it [laughs]. I think it was an honest record then. And I think that's what's important. To this day, everybody wants to hear 'Time for Terror' and 'Love You to Death' from that album. We've got to do those live, all the time."

The quick end to WWIII wasn't all on account of the Third Reich. "No, there were a few things happening," laughs Mandy. "Tracy flipped out because I did that George Lynch thing [a proposed collaborative project for Elektra Records], which was silliness, because I looked at it like it was a running commercial for what we were doing. So, he was mad about that. And then we started writing, and I thought we were coming up with some really unique songs that he didn't like. He wanted to do a more traditional metal thing. And we were coming up with some really unique stuff that you would hear ten years later doing really well. So, we were disagreeing on that. Anyway, as a band we did the whole club thing. You know, first smaller clubs, then larger clubs, twice. Then we did some touring with Maiden and then we split up. We were basically bouncing on and off the Maiden tour whenever they could accommodate us. We were kind of like following along on the same route, and then whenever we could, we would jump on and off."

As for fond memories of those days, Mandy says that "one of the most amazing people I got to make friends with was Stevie Ray Vaughan. I met him at a Sam Kinison party, and Sam was one of the first people who believed in me. He used to have these outrageous parties. He would rent out an old rehearsal studio, with all the rooms, and he would throw these parties where he would invite everybody, from movie stars to pop stars to rock stars to porn stars—just amazing parties—and that's where I met Stevie. He was just an amazing person, especially after he had cleaned up. I actually saw him just a little while before he died, at the Rainbow, and he was all happy. He was always afraid that if he was stopped doing what he was doing, if he would stop doing drugs, stop drinking, he thought that he might not be able to play the way he played. And of course that wasn't true. Once he stopped, he was even better. And yeah, last time I saw him, he was all happy, like, 'Man, I feel great, I feel blessed, I have a great new girl,' and then he died. Same thing happened with Sam. He cleaned

The *Time Machine* VHS video from 1990

Lock Up the Wolves on cassette

up and then he gets killed by these idiots drunk driving. It's cruel."

But then there was the falling out with Tracy. "Yes, well, for someone like that to turn around and tell people you're evil and you're Satan and you're this and that, it just blew my mind. Because I had only done good for him. He's a different kind of guy. He just cuts me out of every picture; he doesn't mention my name; he doesn't say anything. And I'll tell people how I feel. If I don't like you, I'll say it."

Asked why Tracy thinks he's evil, Mandy says that "Tracy fancies himself to be a Christian, and I like to question everything. Even though I have great respect for the Bible, I like to question things. I have questions as far as how God handles things. Of course, it's not like I know better. It's just sometimes I don't understand when little children die or when animals die cruelly. And I'd like to know what he was thinking when he made this place. And I think also that Tracy is the kind of guy, when we were touring, usually radio stations would ask for me because I'm the singer, or one of the other guys like Jimmy or Vinny, to come down to the station and talk to them. Jimmy and Vinny were because of who they were, and like I said, with me, it's because I'm the vocalist. And Tracy resented that with a vengeance. I mean, you can't even imagine how mad he would get."

CHAPTER 8

"This album is a real extension of the Dehumanizer *album."*

STRANGE HIGHWAYS

"I was very disappointed when Sabbath busted up this last time," said Ronnie, talking to the press for the back-to-Dio album *Strange Highways*, after a bad run with his old band for the difficult and opaque *Dehumanizer* record.

"We went through so much to get from the beginning to doing anything, and suddenly it was over. After giving up the careers we had for ourselves—whether it be Dio for me or WWIII for Vinny—it was real disappointing. I feel that we needed more than one album to make a statement. I was happy with *Dehumanizer*, but we needed more output. *Dehumanizer* wasn't my proudest moment, due to the way it was made and the lack of care it afforded individually, but it was still a good record. It was a good beginning, and I was let down when Sabbath fell apart for what seemed to be greed to me. It was like, 'We can get back together with Ozzy for another reunion and make a lot of money and all retire to Hawaii,' or something. When I rejoined Sabbath, I didn't view it as a short-term venture.

Ronnie with Black Sabbath, Newcastle City Hall, UK, September 1, 1992. © *Steve Olley*

For me it was forever! Myself and Vinny possibly wanted to finish our careers with that band; twenty years down the line, we could have all been sitting in wheelchairs, going, 'Remember the *Dehumanizer* album?' while they wheeled us onstage! I wanted it to last; I really did!

"There was this big mud-throwing contest when Sabbath broke up after *Live Evil*," continues Ronnie. "No one wants to see people chuck mud at each other, so I was determined for that not to happen again. I knew a month and a half in advance that the reunion was planned, and that we would be playing with Ozzy. I said, 'Thanks but no thanks,' but for the remaining six weeks, I played and enjoyed myself every night. I never let anyone down and was never angry with anyone in the band. I was happy to be onstage with Tony and Geezer and especially Vinny. Vinny and I talked about it, but the rest of us never communicated. During that time, no one ever asked why I didn't want to do the gig, and never focused on the issue of whether it was more important to keep our band together. The subject was never approached, and I'd be damned if I was going to bring it up!"

To provide a little background, Ronnie was talking about a reunion gig planned between the Sabbath guys and Ozzy in Costa Mesa, California, which was to follow a set of the current Ronnie-fronted Sabbath. Ronnie refused to perform at the show, and one could understand why, since it was likely a trial balloon sent up for a reunion of the guys with Ozzy for permanent, for real. But on paper, it wasn't any sort of display of one-upmanship, or, more accurately, it didn't have to be viewed that way.

Ronnie on the *Dehumanizer* tour at the Mayflower in Southampton, UK, September 6, 1992. © *Steve Olley*

"I broke up with Sabbath that second time because of the shows I was told we were going to do," said Ronnie in 1996. "We had all our shows booked in L.A., and now we were going to change that to become the opening act for Ozzy—which I refused to do! I didn't do it out of a personal thing with Ozzy; I couldn't care less about him. But it was . . . here we were trying to get this band back on the road together, trying to re-form this band and make it special again, and now, suddenly, we were going to be the opening act for the ex-lead singer.

"And I also knew that when that show came, that they were going to announce the reunion between the four of them—which did happen," continues Dio. "So, what was the sense of my doing the show to bolster their careers? They obviously didn't care less about mine. So that was the end of that. The thing is that everybody continually believes the things they hear about me—that I'm some kind of 'Hitler' figure. People who know me will tell you absolutely different. You know, I don't need to defend myself. Was I misunderstood? Yes, I think so, because of the perception people have that of course it's my fault, that two unassuming gentlemen, Geezer and Tony, couldn't possibly make any kind of wrong decision. In that matter, it had to be Dio who was wrong. Those are my beliefs. My beliefs were that I gave up the Dio band and they gave up nothing! They had Black Sabbath and were lucky enough to get Vinny and I to come back and do it. And at the end of the day, our preferences weren't given any credibility. When that happens, you have no communication, which is what we didn't have, and that spelled the breakup. I can only tell my version of the truth, and I believe what I know is correct. Others will hear other things. I think a lot of it was the Ronnie-versus-Ozzy thing that cropped up for some reason or another. I don't know why, because it's never really bothered me what Ozzy does—I'm happy for his success. But it was that more than anything else; you know, 'Oh, I disrespected Ozzy' or something. Like I really care!"

"The Costa Mesa gig was done purely out of greed," echoed Vinny, continuing Ronnie's thought in the same interview (of note, Appice played the gig). "We had a show booked at the L.A. Sports Arena, which is a big place, paying the same amount of money, so why not do that? We could've done our gig there and then driven down and played with Ozzy on the last night. But they chose to do Ozzy's show instead."

"Ozzy called us up," said Geezer Butler, offering his version of the dance card debacle that would help scotch the Dio-era Mk. II. "Well, his wife called my wife and said that Ozzy would really love it if we'd do his last gig with him; sort of put the seal on the end of his whole career. He thought the way he wanted to do his last thing onstage was to do an encore with the original lineup. So, we said we'd do it. We weren't sure if we'd be in L.A., but if we were, we'd do the encore. Then it came to doing the gig with him; we said fine, we'll do a set before he goes on, and then we'll finish off with an encore of the original lineup. We thought it was a great idea. We didn't think of it as a supporting gig for Ozzy; we thought of it as a one-off event. It wasn't as if it was going to be a tour. We thought it would be great for the fans to see both versions of Sabbath.

"Ronnie just saw it as him supporting Ozzy, and Ronnie's exact words were 'I'm just as big if not bigger than Ozzy; then why should I support him?' And that was the way he looked at it. So we just said, 'Well, that's your opinion. We've got our opinion about it and we're going to do it with or without you.' He said, 'Well, you can do it without me then.' That's when Rob Halford came in. Working with Rob, it was so great and so relaxed. We rehearsed three hours with Rob, played his favorite stuff. To us it was a fine afternoon. Although the other gigs with Dio had been going well, we weren't having any fun whatsoever. It seemed to be strained. We had forgotten what fun was like. When we got together and rehearsed with Rob Halford, it was great. We did all the old stuff, and then we did the actual gig. I think it brought back what it was like to have fun in the music. We realized then that the only way we could carry on was to have a good atmosphere."

"I would have liked to see them do a reunion tour," says Ronnie, perhaps a bit incredulously, elaborating on the debacle. "A lot of kids out there would've liked to have seen Ozzy and Sabbath together again. But look what happened: like a cheap pair of tights, it just fell down again! You can't blame that one on me. You have to go to Mr. Ozzy for

Rob Halford, subbing for a protesting Ronnie, with Black Sabbath in Costa Mesa, November 15, 1992. © *Tom Wallace*

that one. He didn't ask me to play at the reunion, but then again, I didn't realize that he asked the others individually, either. Their answers were 'Give me the money, and I don't care about you!' It was a very hurtful thing to do, but I don't have any problems with them. If I saw Tony and Geez, I would give them both big hugs and be very happy to see them. We made great music together, and I like them very much as people.

"Ozzy, though, says he doesn't even know me! I don't want a reconciliation with him, as I felt I never had a conciliation! I don't wish him any ill will. My refusal to do the show had nothing to do with him as a person, but apparently in their eyes it did. If he didn't care if I was asked, then why does he keep going on about it? Shut the fuck up! It isn't important. What is important is that our band broke up, and there was our disappointment at busting our balls for a year and a half to make *Dehumanizer* and suddenly having it all taken away. I enjoyed every single minute of playing with Sabbath, and I enjoyed every single minute of it being over! How would you feel, knowing for a month and a half that someone else was going to take your place? Nobody ever puts themselves in my position. For that time, I had to go out every night and be Mr. Happy. I wasn't able to say anything or talk to anyone about how I felt, because that would make me look like a fool. I just didn't understand it. I felt happy when I did it and more happy and relieved when it was over!

"The sad thing is, I wish we could've made this record and had this lineup ten years ago," said Ronnie, back on message and plumping for his return-to-Dio album *Strange Highways*. "There just doesn't seem to be a vehicle for it to be heard right now, particularly in Europe. During this tour of Europe, we played to two dogs and a cat! We played in some really strange places. We did the same show though. It doesn't matter. That, again, is part of the joy of being what we are: a good band that has pride in itself. No matter how many people we played in front of, we give every minute. I've played to 100,000 people before, so it doesn't really matter. I'm not out to prove anything. The only thing that matters to me is how good the music I'm making is. If it's shit, I don't want to be there in front of 100,000 people or 100 people! When we did the Monsters of Rock tour with Sabbath, we had Pantera's Phil Anselmo sitting at the back of the stage each night watching our every move. He came up and said, 'The first song I ever sung was "Neon Knights," man,' and he sang it for me! That's what young musicians are all about. They go to see their heroes, just like when I used to go see the Who. We're a new band, and that's how we want to be treated, not like some retreads. Forget that you've heard Dio before. If this band had no past, people would be completely blown out! And the next record will be even better!"

The new lineup of which Dio spoke included longtime back belter Vinny Appice on drums, Dokken's amiable and talented Jeff Pilson on bass (Jimmy Bain was actually included early on in the process), and the soon-to-be-controversial Tracy G (Grijalva, to his mom) on guitar. As discussed, Tracy had been part of the notorious WWIII, which also featured Vinny, Jimmy, and the colorful Mandy Lion on lead vocals. The band put out that one self-titled record, which acted as a blueprint to where the Dio sound was doomed to go for the next couple of records—thick, monolithic, heavy, and brutal. Tracy and, to some extent, Vinny would be the guilty parties in the loud and proud stomp of it all, creating a headache-inducing din heavy on rhythm guitars and heavy on very rhythmic drums.

In interviews, Ronnie was prone to say that he didn't re-call Rowan Robertson to the ranks (remember all that praise Ronnie had for his child prodigy) for two reasons: (1) Rowan seemed happy with, and hopeful about, the new band he had been forming with Oni Logan, and (2) Rowan wouldn't be quite right stylewise for the direction Ronnie wanted to take Dio (er, similarities between *Lock Up the Wolves* and *Strange Highways* notwithstanding, especially in the riff department).

With the hiccups in the bass department, Ronnie had himself picked up the fat strings again, having played bass in the early days of Elf. "Yes, when we did *Strange Highways*, I played for about two or three months as we were writing the project because at different points, Jeff Pilson, our bass player, was not available. So, I kept my hand in it a little bit, but it makes me realize, as I did when I chose singing instead of bass playing—because I did both—that you have to be pretty damned good at one or the other. You just can't kind of coast through being good at one and not the other. I decided my joy was in singing, so that's why I stopped playing bass. But every time I do play, it brings me back to the realization of why I did that. Boy, the old wrist hurts, I'll tell you!"

"My prior band to that was WWIII, with Vinny Appice and Jimmy Bain as the rhythm section," explains Tracy G, on the tangled web of cables. "So, when Dio started his new lineup, he had Jimmy Bain and Vinny Appice. They, I guess, liked what I was about in WWIII, my guitar sound and my style, so they told Dio about me. So, I was one of the many guys who went to audition. And I guess, out of all the people who came down, he liked the chemistry between the rhythm section, which he already had, and then this

Tracy G and Vinny playing with WWIII, Irvine, California, March 17, 1991. © Tom Wallace

new guy coming in, which was me. You see, as WWIII, we had already made an album and done a tour. So, when I went to audition for them, it was kind of obvious that it sounded like a band already. And so, it was just up to Ronnie: Was that the direction he wanted? Or did he want to stick to more of his traditional thing? And I think at that time, he was ready for a change, an experiment; he wanted to try something a little different. And when I came in, he was going to take it . . . I can't play like any of those guys, Vivian Campbell, or those past guitar players he had. I can't mimic anybody. I just do what I do, and they either like it or they don't. But he was ready for a change, so he tried for that."

Tracy explains that putting the record together was a pleasant creative experience, with everyone contributing communally. "It was pretty evened out. In this situation, you know, Ronnie is obviously the vocalist and the guy who's been there longer than anybody, kind of the leader, the coach of the ship. So, he oversees all the sounds and everything. But a lot of people asked me, 'How does it start?' When I came into *Strange Highways*, Vinny was the drummer and Jimmy Bain was there for about a week, and then they got into it, so Jeff Pilson came in. So, you've got a guy like Jeff Pilson in the room, and Vinny, who are great natural musicians in their own right; they know their instruments really well. And then me, not knowing what the heck he's doing anyway. I just come in and . . . if I'm playing with people like that, I plug in and basically start to jam.

"And if you're adequate on your instruments, the ideas and the riffs start to flow, off of either Vinny's drumbeat, or I might have a riff and it inspires them, or they might have a riff and it inspires me. And we start to jam on something that feels cool, right?

You just go, and you're recording, and Ronnie walks in the room and says, 'Hey, man, that's pretty good.' We'd just jam like when you were fifteen years old and started your first band and you're jamming in a garage. And that's how that album basically came about. More than half of those riffs, guitarwise, came from even before I was in Dio. They had been floating around my other projects before Dio. Of course, when I got the gig with Dio, with a singer like that and a band like that, I thought, 'I wonder what Ronnie would do if I played this riff?' 'I wonder what Ronnie would sing like if I played this riff?' So, I played these riffs, and then of course the band would join in, and there you go. And sometimes you would get stuck, and you'd need to go someplace else. And then Jeff Pilson would go, 'Well, how about this?' So, it bounced around pretty good, but it's obviously guitar driven and guitar oriented because that kind of music is—it comes from a riff. It's got to come from a riff, because otherwise, what have you got?

"I really don't know," says Tracy, when asked what had happened to Jimmy. "It's a personal thing between Ronnie and Jimmy, the business stuff . . . whatever. One day he just came to practice and said, 'Jimmy's out; we need to find a new bass player,' and they called Jeff, actually just to see if he knows anybody, because Jeff was doing the Dokken thing at the time. So, they basically called him to see if he knew anybody else, and Jeff said, 'What about me?!' And they were like, 'Well, yeah, okay,' so Jeff came, and he had time to do an album and a tour with us. Besides, the Dokken thing wasn't totally busy. Eventually, he went back and did the Dokken thing. You know, Jeff is all over the place; he does all kinds of stuff. He's a really talented guy."

"Absolutely wonderful," says Jeff, looking back at his Dio experience, versus his Dokken gig. "It's a different situation, because in Dokken we were a band and we really worked like a band. Although Don, I think, would have liked to have been Ronnie in that situation, he really wasn't. He had leadership qualities but not on his own, strictly. And we were a band, so we did make democratic decisions. And then you turn to Dio, which really, honestly, wasn't a band. It was Ronnie's band, but he treated it like a band! And it felt like a band. Even though he was very much in charge, always, creatively, he liked everyone to have input, and he pushed for it. Which is a much-better situation as far as getting things done."

As to how involved Ronnie was in the music . . . "Ronnie? Very!" answers Jeff. "You know what it is? A lot of the music we did on the records that we did together came from jamming, improvising. And what he would do oftentimes is sit in the room, and Vinny and Tracy and I would just start playing, and when he liked something, he would just kind of point or whatever, and we would jam on it and take it and sit and talk about it. Even if he didn't play the ideas, a lot of times he would kind of guide us to where he wanted to go with it, but he would let us go with it first; just come up with things. And it was very creative. I mean, he can play. He knows how to play, so he can talk the language. But he liked the way we played and the way we improvised together, so it made it comfortable for him. He just had to sit back and say, 'No, let's try going here and here.' It was wonderful."

Tracy echoes Pilson's good tidings with the situation. "You know, the whole *Strange Highways* album, from beginning to end for me, the writing of the album, making the album, recording the album, and doing the tour, it was the way it's supposed to be; all on ten, all good. I don't know if that's because it was my first album and tour for them, but I think the album is just a reflection of the time. It's a reflection of the moment that happened when it happened. If you listen to that album with any kind of ears and put the headphones on and give it a chance, you'll hear that it's a real album. And it can stand up to anything else, the early Dio stuff, *Dehumanizer* with Black Sabbath. It's a real album that doesn't have too much tightening of the bolts, if you know what I mean. We just kind of let it flow. It was fresh and we were excited, and I think you hear that. It was real, the way I played, and the way all those other guys played too. Productionwise too—Ronnie didn't produce that one. He let someone else come in, and the other guy who came in, Mike Fraser, was really cool. Fraser came in and he didn't jack up our sound or my sound. He just said, 'You guys are heavy. This is like a heavier direction for Ronnie Dio.' And he basically let us do what we do, and he captured the sound. We had already had the songs written. The producer didn't chop anything up. They were already there, ready to go; we had already done the work. And Ronnie is guiding everything. It was a natural album, the way I thought albums were supposed to be written. But then it all changed."

"Those guys were great," laughs Mike Fraser, who has worked for the likes of Aerosmith, Metallica, the Cult, Van Halen, and AC/DC, mostly in a mixing or engineering capacity. "Ronnie is such an awesome guy. I seem to think we got it all done in about four weeks—you know, pretty quick. He usually takes six to eight to do a record. So yes, pretty prepared. Vinny, awesome drummer. I like working with loud guys like him and his brother, Carmine, because the drum sounds always start with the drummer and the tuning of his drums. You can put all the best microphones in the best room, but if the drums aren't tuned or hit properly, they're not going to sound good."

But the album has a huge guitar sound as well . . . "Yup, that's what we were going for. That was Tracy's first album with Ronnie, so that's why we kinda leaned it that way, kinda showcased Tracy a bit on that, tried to fit him over top of the big drum sound [laughs]. We did it all as a band, to get the feel going. And from what I remember, we'd usually go back and fix things up from the live performance or go and do a whole new take and really zone in on getting it in tune and in time. You've got to get that band feel. If you've just got a drummer playing along to a click track, it's not really an inspiration. But if the guitar player is kind of giving it to him, that pushing and pulling, it gets a little more energy underneath him. For good rock bands, I like to have pretty bombastic drums. I like to try to get everything in your face as much as possible, so that it's right there and you can try and hear everything, without something just kind of taking over. So, if there's a Mike Fraser sound, that would be it."

Adds Fraser on nonbusiness fun with the band, "I remember Ronnie telling us some stories when he was in England doing a record and how he could, what was it, get the crystal glass talking? Kind of like a Ouija board [laughs]. He's like, 'Oh, we've got to do that one night, have a séance, get the crystal glass going.' But we never did, and I still regret that [laughs]. I thought that would have been good fun, especially with Ronnie."

I asked Tracy if he could recall which of the songs on *Strange Highways* might have been older songs or indeed shelved WWIII songs.

"'Hollywood Black' was a WWIII riff, as was 'Pain.' 'Bring Down the Rain' was a WWIII riff, and when I say WWIII riff, it's my riff, but back in the day, it was the same thing. I had brought those riffs to that singer and said here, and he wrote words. And I have those songs demoed, the same songs, but with different singing and different words. 'Evilution,' I made there. I made that out at the Dio thing. 'Jesus, Mary' just came there, as did 'Firehead.' There were about three or four actual WWIII riffs that ended up being there. And I played a lot of other ones that didn't end up making the mix."

Essentially, *Strange Highways* wasn't that different in tone from *WWIII* or, for that matter, *Lock Up the Wolves*. That Dio record, as we lamented last chapter, was a startlingly slow and lethargic album. *Strange Highways* is also slow, but the songs are so much better. In fact, it is an album rising quickly in the estimation of throngs of Dio fans. Perhaps it is the thick but unique style of Tracy, or perhaps the pounding nature of Vinny Appice on drums, or indeed, the philosophical similarity between both of their styles, but there's a sweet, sweet aura of high quality about this album that can't be denied.

The record opens with "Jesus, Mary & the Holy Ghost," a terrific midpaced pounder that starkly stops for a crazy verse arrangement that borrows from King Crimson's "21st Century Schizoid Man," with Ronnie spitting out vocals to jagged chords before the band rumbles and tumbles once again. Its many parts are legion, the band creating the sound of a stealthy, stomping monster that ambles off real spooky-like come the closing sequence of the track. The lyric seems to be an ingenious treatise, in clipped, elliptical language, on the violence and supernatural nature of select Bible tales, and how the Good Book breeds fear into the sleeping and waking dreams of those who are perhaps too young to encounter such concepts.

Explained Ronnie at the time, "I think that song, right away, when you listen to the album, tells you how much different this album is going to be than the other Dio product that one might have heard. 'Jesus, Mary,' it's the most unusual of the tracks, but it makes a statement right away. It says, 'Look, we're not what you expected. You expected dragons, witches, and wizards, probably some chintzy Dio product. It's not. It's a real band album.' This album is a real extension of the *Dehumanizer* album. Without me going back to Sabbath again, that wouldn't have allowed me the chance to—or even a reason to—want

Ronnie, 1992. © *Steve Olley*

to do this again. The *Dehumanizer* album was really satisfying. It was really different for me because I changed my attitude lyrically. The band was so huge, and the songs were a lot more modern. And then when there wasn't that band anymore, the choices were 'What do you do? Go back to do *Holy Diver* again?' That's not something a good musician that cares wants to do with his life. He wants to carry on and go forward."

Expanding on this idea of making *Strange Highways* a bit more "real world," Ronnie explains that "the records before were pretty much more fantasy oriented, with magic and wizards and witches. It was pretty feathery images where this one is pretty much black and white. It's much more involved with the world that we see around us when we look out the window today, as opposed to what we wanted ten centuries ago. This album is a very angry, frustrated, black-and-white album, because what I see in the world around me doesn't make me a very happy person. I think four years ago, I could write an album like *Lock Up the Wolves* and still believe that dreams could come true and that there's a lot of hope out there. Today I can't in my heart write about things that are fancy and free when the world is such a horrible, black-and-white place. I think that someone needs to shout out about it. But I'm not trying to make sociological changes. I'm just screaming for people who don't have a stage to scream from. Maybe what I scream, they can scream along to and feel better."

In the same interview, Ronnie characterized "Jesus, Mary & the Holy Ghost" as "a very abstract piece of music. That's what we were trying to accomplish. It strikes an abstract chord in your mind. It just affects you some way; I don't know how, but it does. We wanted that song to be where it is on the album because it set the whole album up for being weird. If you're a Dio fan—and even if you're not—when you put the CD on for the first time and you hear that, you're gonna say, 'What the hell is that?!'"

"Firehead" follows at the same sort of menacing clip, not too fast, not too slow, with Vinny providing propulsion. Ronnie somewhat humorously tackles the concept of the angry young man and what makes him that way, with Dio musing that he won't likely make it to old age, given the heat he emits. Tracy turns in a gorgeous melodic solo before exploding into howling tangents and even a bit of a nod to Viv Campbell.

Next, the title track slows things down considerably, with "Strange Highways" sounding like something off *Lock Up the Wolves* or even *Dehumanizer*. But again, the song is saved by the performance, with Ronnie spitting and growling, enunciating strongly through a lyric that chillingly charts the protagonist's descent into the corners of his own mind.

Tracy explains that the lyric indeed has some connection with the record's uneasy, gruesome, yet tasteful cover art, arguably the best of the Dio catalog. "You know, the guy who did *Strange Highways*, I think he's actually done a couple of Ronnie's new ones now, and I'm not sure of this, *Dehumanizer*. It was some artist they've used before. As far as the meaning, I think they threw the title at the kid, you know, *Strange Highways*, and then it was supposed to be the strange highways of the mind. If you listen to the words of the song, it's about strange places you go in your mind, the brain thing. So, the cover has this weird vibe; I think it's kind of cool, actually, pretty crazy." Tracy is right: the illustrator of the cover is Wil Rees, who also did both *Lock Up the Wolves* and *Dehumanizer*.

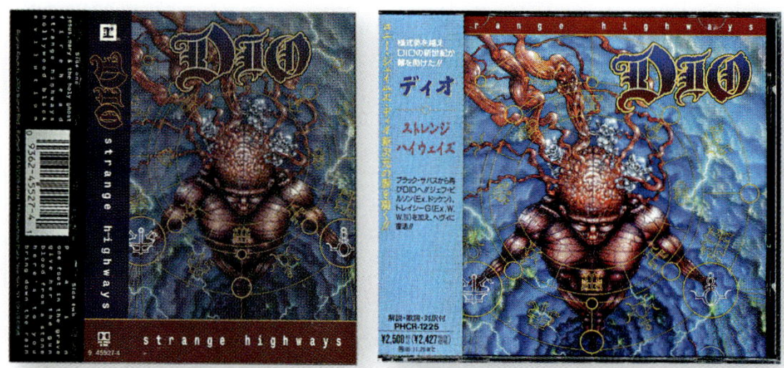

Cassette and Japanese CD of *Strange Highways*

"Hollywood Black" brings the album back to a slow boiling stomp, Ronnie turning in a memorable chorus hook and a harrowing melody for the verse. The lyric captures, with Ronnie's keen ear for metaphor, the pitfalls of looking for fame on the strip, against the enormous odds of having the dream come even remotely or approximately true, versus the very real chance of a nightmare instead. Tracy turns in a nice set of licks for the transition phase, and the song comes out the other end as enjoyable, despite beating the listener black and blue.

"Evilution" follows, with the successful execution of a verse that has no beat—picture Vinny doing a heavy metal version of Stewart Copeland—breaking into an enormous storm of chugging chords as the lead-up to the climactic resolution of the lyric. All told, what you get is an innovative and atmospheric track, with Tracy providing noisy, lurching, dive-bombing sounds amid stacks of sheet metal tumbling to the ground. In effect, it builds upon the promise of the architecturally interesting album opener.

"Pain" is next, once again the band choosing a measured stomp exquisitely recorded, pure Sabbatherian metal (of a *Dehumanizer* disposition) being the order of the day, with Ronnie turning in a graphic yet poetic portrayal of pure, acid-etched exasperation. "Pain" gives way to "One Foot in the Grave," which possesses an oddly funky Led Zeppelin–like riff that soon falls away, exposing a rule-breaking profusion of cool groovy parts. At the lyric end, Ronnie comes up with amusing lines seemingly about various violences simmering just below the surface.

"Give Her the Gun" is a slow, dark, nightmarish ballad with a malevolent "diabolus in musica" heavy chorus, a fitting sound for the tale of sexual abuse and untold other abuses and vengeful retribution to come. Next up is "Blood from a Stone," an explosive heavy track among many strong competitors, Tracy's riff plowing along while Ronnie stacks up images of pathetic human deceit and skullduggery.

"Here's to You" inexplicably opens with what sounds like Def Leppard doing one of their odious hair band chants. But the song quickly recovers, taking off like a dragster, living and breathing fire as the record's one fast track. Ronnie occasionally stops the mayhem for a somewhat questionable "Here's to me" or a "Here's to you," with those

Def Leppard choirs coming back to haunt us near the close of what turns out to be the shortest track on the album.

Closing this record, an album this writer considers to be the very finest of Ronnie's five "slow" albums, is a triumphant, "Holy Diver"-like barnstormer called "Bring Down the Rain," which features a solid marching groove topped with words from Ronnie that provide a hurricane of weather images, as is often the case, applied to emotional situations that are hard to decipher yet unquestionably intense. From a musical standpoint, it's a fitting statement to end the record, set to a tempo just to the right side of attention grabbing and then performed with intention and recorded with heft and clarity. "Bring Down the Rain" is both metaphor and microcosm for the concept of the *Strange Highways* album as a whole, a summary of its psychic and sonic force.

Again, no Dio fan with an open mind to the doomier side of the band should have come away disappointed. Unless you're Geezer Butler. "I just thought he lost total direction on that album," commented Geezer, fresh enough off the debacle of the *Dehumanizer* situation to throw a few barbs. "He tried to be modern and completely missed the point. He said he was doing an industrial metal album, whatever that is. I thought he did it too quick; it seems like a very rushed job to me. I was surprised he failed to live up to his standards."

"I like *Strange Highways*," reflects Vinny. "The sound is like a whole different sound, and the guitar was a bit darker, with Tracy G. I like the album, but the only thing I regret is I didn't play a lot of stuff on it. That was because the drums were so damn big. They were huge-sounding drums, so when the drums sound that huge, it's hard to make fast fills and make them work. So, it was a little bit of a different mindset; I played a lot more straight, as normal people do. And Tracy had a darker guitar sound. I love the way Tracy plays. So, the album was good, but the Dio fans, I think, weren't expecting it to be that dark and really doomy and heavy like that. I think it shocked some of the fans."

Satin backstage passes for the *Strange Highways* campaign. *Martin Popoff archive*

Wrote journalist Andy Martin, in the review of the album for *RIP*, "*Strange Highways* is an all-knobs-to-11 barnstormer of a record that proves that the dejected and diminutive singer has lost none of his grasp—or gasp—of richly malevolent metal. The rest of the band comes with the pedigree to match the front man: drummer Vinny Appice is back and is joined by former Dokken bass player Jeff Pilson and the formidable six-string prowess of ex-WWIII guitarist Tracy G, whose monster riff-mongering adds weight and attack to songs like 'Hollywood Black' and 'Bring Down the Rain.' Elsewhere, 'Firehead' recalls the Sabs' 'Iron Man,' while the opening fury of 'Jesus, Mary & the Holy Ghost' clearly has King Crimson's '21st Century Schizoid Man' as its template. Dio's voice is as powerful as a force nine gale, while the vocalist is clearly venting his spleen; the man is in a rage, and he wants the world to know it! Dio fans will treasure *Strange Highways* like a vampire covets a virgin."

Although *Strange Highways* still possessed the aura of money, or more accurately of expense (it was Ronnie's last major-label album, on Reprise/Warner; plus, it was recorded at the Record Plant), the band eventually found themselves having to curb their ambitions out on the road, as Ronnie's previous comment about playing to dogs and cats might attest.

"The first thing we did was a couple months in Europe," explains Pilson, on the tour for the record, "which was really nice because I had never really been on a long headlining tour, especially in Europe. And it was really fun to watch the whole production. I mean, we were playing huge places. Theaters, that kind of thing, plus some fairly large places. So, I got to watch a fairly sophisticated production from a close angle, and it was healthy to watch, because Ronnie does it better than anybody. I mean, he knows how to run a show first class, absolutely first class. So that was really interesting. So, we did a couple of months in Europe, ended up; last show was Hammersmith Odeon. The band I remember most in Europe was Freak of Nature, Mike Tramp's band. Then we came over and started in the States in the spring of '94. We started off playing fairly large theaters, and we even did a couple of arenas. And it was way overextended, way beyond what we were capable of doing at the time, which we quickly learned. It was fun for me to get to watch the production, but it was also sad, because we had to scale down [laughs], which is never fun. But it was a great experience. I got to watch the whole kit and kaboodle, and it was cool."

Joining the band on keyboards was Scott Warren, who would remain the band's keyboardist to the end, even playing with Heaven & Hell.

"The role of the keyboard player is pretty much mapped out in the music," answers Scott, asked about his role in this famously not very keyboardy band. "That's the role Ronnie wanted. He didn't let anything slip by that he didn't want. So, my role is just . . . I mean, it was one of the few really heavy-rock bands that used at least a substantial amount of keyboards. But they definitely were a supportive role, yeah. I never knew, that I heard of, a statement that ever summed up what he felt about keyboards. But they were obviously important to him. Because, for one thing, as long as I've been in Dio, there have always been some. He took an interest in making sure that I was doing the best that I could do, for the band, and also the fact that it also seemed to be important for him to have me with him again in Heaven & Hell.

"I wouldn't say he played keyboards," answers Warren, asked to what extent Ronnie himself played. "He experimented on the computer, when he was writing songs, with keyboards. And when he got something close to what he was hearing . . . I didn't ever see him play keyboards, but he knew what he wanted to hear. So, when it came to there being something that he couldn't perform, that's when he would involve me a little more. And then also when it came to really getting the sounds, he definitely wanted a strong collaboration. But even the legacy of what he did in Rainbow and in early Dio, I felt proud to play. I mean, some of the parts now, you might say they sound a little old, but in a way, that's cool. What I'm trying to say is I'm honored to play all the keyboard stuff that is involved in Dio. And they definitely played a strong role."

Asked about his predecessors, Scott says, "I never really met Tony Carey. I know Claude fairly well. I think we all have the same background and the same influences growing up, and reasons for deciding to play keyboards as an instrument—talking to Claude, I get that feeling. And I really loved a lot of the keyboard parts that Tony Carey did. I was more influenced by Keith Emerson and definitely Jon Lord, so I kind of rediscovered Tony Carey as I came to play a lot of the Rainbow songs that we'd be doing in Dio. But I don't know how to verbally express how my style is different. I would say that I'm thinking a little more modern, because technology has advanced to the point where I can maybe achieve things that weren't easily achieved in the days of Tony Carey. More, you know, angry sounds, things like that.

"Well, he's human, you know?" reflects Scott, on the subject of Ronnie as a boss. "But when it came to working on the music, he was really focused and creative. It was always fun to watch things develop from his point of view. Of course it was his baby, his band, but it was a team effort too. I really enjoyed working with him, and I learned a lot from working with him. But when it came to the writing, Craig Goldy did a lot of the writing, but keyboards didn't . . . as far as the songs being written, there wasn't a lot of input we needed from the keyboard player, I don't think, because a lot of the songs were based on guitar riffs. So, I wasn't particularly part of that element, no."

"Freak of Nature," recalls Tracy, back to the subject of touring. "That's where the guy Jerry Best, who ended up playing bass for us, came from. He was in that band too. Jerry Best was also in a band called Lion in the '80s, a pretty known band around here. All kinds of smaller bands opened for us. We did a lot of Motörhead stuff, plus some bigger bands. There wasn't like one set band with us the whole time. Through Europe, it moves around a lot. Sometimes you'd get a local band from town, or a band stays with you."

Indeed, Freak of Nature opened for Dio at close to thirty dates all over Europe, the tour commencing in Athens, Greece, on November 4, 1993. After three shows in Athens, the band went to Spain for three shows and then very extensively covered Germany, with single dates in Austria, Italy, and the Netherlands interspersed. Back in the USA, support came mostly from the King's X-adjacent Atomic Opera, with bands such as Godspeed and Love/Hate filling in as well. These shows were almost all club dates. Finally, the tour closed off with a run of five performances in Brazil.

Tracy G, 1991. © *Tom Wallace*

With respect to the set list, Ronnie stayed true to his ethic of presenting the latest album deeply and sincerely, playing around half of *Strange Highways*, including "Jesus, Mary & the Holy Ghost," "Strange Highways," "Hollywood Black," "Evilution," "Pain," and "Here's to You" (some shows dropped "Evilution" and substituted "Here's to You" with "Give Her the Gun"; "Firehead" was apparently played only once). Unfortunately, this meant that the previous four Dio albums were ignored, with the rest of the set visiting Ronnie's three classic eras, Rainbow ("Man on the Silver Mountain," "Long Live Rock 'n' Roll"), Black Sabbath ("The Mob Rules," "Heaven and Hell," and "Children of the Sea," with the latter only on the first leg), and Vivian Campbell–era Dio ("Stand Up and Shout," "Rainbow in the Dark," "Don't Talk to Strangers," "Holy Diver," "We Rock," and "The Last in Line"). The set also included a truncated or broken-up "Heaven and Hell," a drum solo, a guitar solo, and a bass solo, plus *Mob Rules*'s "E5150" as an intro.

In closing, Ronnie looks back on the *Strange Highways* record, ten years down the line, with a sense of fondness.

"I thought it was a hell of a good album. I think it was an album that we had luckily rehearsed enough, with the right people, where we didn't leave too many spaces for Tracy to have to come up with a lot. Because I think that sometimes the things that

Tracy G. © Tom Wallace, plus assorted *Strange Highways* bits and pieces

Tracy came up with were a little bit un-Dio-ish. Later on, though, not on *Strange Highways*. On *Strange Highways* we were very focused, and we had, as I say, a good combination of writing. Jeff Pilson was with us at the time as well, a really good writer, good player. I think it's a very underrated album. It's just got tons of great songs on it. I think it sounds good, maybe a bit overreverbed, but I think it's a great album. When we did that album, the record company just went, 'Whoa, we don't know what to do with this one, so we'll throw it against the wall, and if it does something, we'll support it. If not, the hell with it!' They really did nothing. We were at the back end of getting ready to leave that label anyway; it just wasn't the place for us. But I must say I can't lay the blame on everybody else. That album perhaps sounded too dated—that might have been one of its problems too. The sad part is that you have to make it available for the people to make that judgment, as opposed to having to mail away for it."

CHAPTER 9

"Oh, I guess I suck now."

ANGRY MACHINES

These were the nadir years for metal, and appropriate of that, Ronnie found himself for the first time since the Electric Elves' "Hey, Look Me Over" / "It Pays to Advertise" MGM Records single from October 26, 1967, outside the major label system and onto a feisty, prolific large indie called Mayhem/Futurist. The fruit of this marriage made in metal was to be called *Angry Machines*, and indicative of the band's newly acquired underdog status, the album was combative, abrasive, grungy, and pretty damn good.

Ronnie recaps the acrimonious split with Warner Bros. after so many years, most of them profitable for all parties involved. "No one cared. I think that was the problem. One of the reasons that we're not there anymore is because at the end of the day, we either wore out our welcome or no one cared. This is a real corporate society. The structure now cares only about how many records are sold and not how good it is. So anyway, those people just really didn't have a clue what they were doing with us. It had just come to the end of the road. We'd been there for a long, long time, like twenty years or so. The corporate structure changed, they swept people away, they swept musicians away, and it just happened. Within Mayhem, we saw people who are like they used to be at Warner Bros. in the early days. They were fans. The people who were heads of all the departments, the president, the vice president . . . they were all fans of the music that they were releasing, packaging, and distributing. Now, as I said, it's become a more suit-and-tie structure, where it's 'How much money do you make?' and not 'How good was that record?' So, for all those reasons, we had an opportunity to get involved with Mayhem Records, who have all the same kind of people in the

Open Air Amphitheatre, San Diego, California, August 3, 1998.
Dio were opening for Iron Maiden. © *Tom Wallace*

head positions. They're young, they care, they believe in what they're doing, they're fans. They seemed to me to be the most interested in what we had to offer."

True to his stated intentions and true to his recent career arc, Ronnie was writing real-life dramas. *Dehumanizer, Strange Highways, Angry Machines* . . . this was Ronnie right there shaking his head sadly at the plight of the children of the night. Also indicative of a certain circle-the-wagons aspect to Dio in the alternative-rock mid-'90s, the band was pictured (badly) on the back cover as a three-piece, sad, because of course they could never actually operate that way.

"Well," noted Ronnie, "we always considered Jeff [Pilson] a member of the band, but Jeff's been doing the Dokken project for a while. They did one album a couple of years ago and now they're doing another. That was a commitment that he had that we knew about, so we didn't have any other choice but to wait around for Jeff until he was able to write and record with us, which he did. When it came time to do a photo for the album, management said that they thought it would be confusing if Jeff was included on the album picture. So, it was nothing to do with us. We wanted Jeff's picture there, and I still think it's stupid that he wasn't there; after all, he contributed, so why should that have anything to do with Dokken? But that's the reason there's only three of us, because management wanted it that way."

"Ronnie wanted the four guys, like the band or whatever," confirms Tracy. "But Jeff was doing the Dokken thing again. They told him he couldn't do any photos with us! Some kind of cheesy things like that. Yeah. He was told, and I remember Ronnie was pissed off about it. That's why it's just us three. If you ever look at the WWIII album, it's just three guys too. It's just me, Jimmy, and the singer guy. And there is no Vinny yet."

"I think it is and I think it should be," responds Ronnie, to reaction that the album, Dio's seventh, is combative and very modern sounding. "We've taken steps to understand what's out there. If you don't listen to what you're competing with, you're a fool. And if you don't listen to what the people who are making music like you do, you're a fool as well. I've produced all the records, with the exception of the last one, *Strange Highways*, and I thought many of the songs on it were very dated sounding. It was almost a 'back to the '80s' kind of sound, and that was very disturbing to me, so I decided I would then again step in as producer. Not only I, but everyone in this band knew exactly what we wanted to sound like. We knew that it needed to be more up front, that the guitars shouldn't be doubled, that there shouldn't be a lot of effects on the voice, that the vocals should be straight up, and that the drums be alive.

"It's really more of a harkening back to what we did on *Holy Div*er and *Last in Line*, especially *Holy Diver*, which is a very 'live'-sounding album. It's a very hard edged, in-front-of-your-face album—we wanted to recapture that. To move on to what I hear today, I hear a lot of alternative bands doing things that are interesting, not just from a sound perspective, but also from a musical perspective. In the old days if you wanted to do something that was a little off-kilter timewise, say in 7/4, you wouldn't do it because you were afraid people would break their legs trying to move around to it. In this case, you just listen to the way the younger bands go where they want to go, and I go, 'That's great! That makes so much sense.' You should be able to go where you want to instead of having to go around the corner first and come back again. From listening to all these things and being smart enough to know where modernness lays . . . we just did it this way.

"What happened with *Strange Highways* is water under the bridge," continues Dio, "and that led us to this point, which is important. We started writing in a different manner on that album, and it's carried on in the writing style to this one. We've just taken it a few steps closer to the year 2000 rather than looking back and trying to be a reunion band and thinking, 'Gee, I think they're going to like this one—it sounds like *Holy Diver*!' That's something I never wanted to do."

Hitting the press trail for the record, Ronnie plumped for his guitarist of choice. "Tracy's a monster. He can be both experimental and do the traditional thing well too; he's real special. We write together as a band. Jeff recorded with us, but he's back doing the Dokken thing. Tracy will have a riff he's worked on, or something will pop into his head, because he's like Tony Iommi, a real riff master. So, we write around what Tracy plays and what Vinny plays. Because rock music should be all about feel. This one, what you hear is what you get. There were no effects—it's live, more modern sounding."

"If you just listen to *Angry Machines*, you can hear that something is really different," reflects Tracy, the man at the center of all the abuse hurled at this record, almost instantly upon its release. "I mean, all the fans say is 'Oh, it sucks' and 'Tracy sucks.' People that don't know what's going on, that's how they talk. Because they don't know. They hear it and they just have to blame it on somebody. That's just the way a typical fan would hear it, and that's the feedback you would get. So, I got all the flak for that. I'm shit and I suck, and I can't play like Vivian Campbell. I suck now. Well, who knows? You know, pleasing fans is . . . whatever [laughs].

Tracy G, soon to be on the hot seat. Brick by Brick, San Diego, February 8, 1997. © *Tom Wallace*

"Remember before, when I said I would come in with a riff and we were all playing in the same room? The vibe was better. We would play a riff, and Ronnie would come in and say, 'That's cool.' Well, for *Angry Machines*, when we would start to play a riff, it would take like a month later until he liked something we did. So, you say, either everything we played was shit, or he wasn't in the mood, you know? Something was different. And I tend to want to believe that not everything we play is great, but not everything we play is garbage. Man, we played and played and played and played and played some more, and there was nothing else to play! You can only jam so much, and then there are no more ideas. Once you try, and then you have to go away and come back, then go away and come back.

"Anyway, so, check this out. On the average, it felt like every song on *Angry Machines* took almost a month, to come to the conclusion that that was a finished song. A month! And that's not rock 'n' roll to me. I hate to use that term, because it's stupid, but you know what I mean. Are we, like, curing cancer?! I mean, what's the problem? Oh, I guess I suck now. Tracy sucks, because he can't . . . what?! You know what I mean?! So, the vibe . . . something was different, and we did things that I had never seen that band do. Things like 'Well, we'll use a cover song. We'll use one of Jeff Pilson's songs—lyrics and music! And that will help us get closer to being finished with this album. I'm like, 'What?!' There is one song on there, that Ronnie didn't even write the words! When did that happen? Never, in the years that I had been a Dio fan, had he done a song . . . I mean, he has done a couple cover songs, I think with Blackmore, when they redid 'Mistreated' and stuff like that. But you do a studio album, and he don't need nobody's lyrics! You know what I mean? He's his own guy.

"The vibe was so much like, let's get this over with. Because we're struggling. And nothing against Jeff, and nothing against the song, because I think it's a fucking cool song, but something . . . I just looked at the ground and went, 'Huh?!' That was weird to me. So, I'm trying to answer your question. It was a different time. We didn't have a set bass player. Jeff was in and he was out. We had another guy come in, and then he was out. We went through three bass players in the process of making that album."

As to who these bass players were, Tracy says, "Let's see, first we replaced him with a guy named Jerry Best; Jerry came in. And then we wrote like one song while Jerry was there. Something about 'God hates heavy metal' or something; that one ended up on the Japanese version. Then we stopped, in the middle of trying to write that album. We went to South America and played some gigs, with Jerry. And then we came back, and Jerry was out, and Jeff Pilson came back in and helped finish writing the stuff with us and brought in one of his songs, so we would be closer. Jeff recorded the album with us but then didn't do the tour. A guy named Larry Dennison came in and did the tour. And Larry is the guy who's in my Driven band now too, see? Okay, so we went through a In couple different guys, whatever. It was just a big fat struggle; it was like pulling teeth. And when you hear that album, that's what I hear. I hear stiffness and I don't hear a vibe. Of course, I was there, and I know what happened. But I guess when the rock police fan hears it, he just goes, 'Oh well, somebody sucks here; it must be him' [laughs]."

The amiable Mr. Pilson compares the two records at hand this way. "I had more writing on *Strange Highways*, only because they had only two songs written when I started up with them, and then we did all the rest over a period of several weeks of playing and working it out. That was one of the best working environments I can ever remember, actually, the writing and recording of that record. And then I toured that record. But then I went back to Dokken. And then when I did the *Angry Machines* record, there were already a few songs written on that; probably four or five of those were written before I came on board. Then we wrote the rest. But there was already a kind of precedent there. I still had quite a bit of input on *Angry Machines*. And actually, one song, I wrote, kind of all by myself. *Strange Highways* was more magical for me, but *Angry Machines* was cool too.

"Both records probably should have been called something other than Dio," opines Pilson. "That probably would have given people a better first impression. Because calling them Dio makes them expect one thing, and it wasn't that. I still think there are some great songs on *Strange Highways*, especially the title track and 'Give Her the Gun.' I think it's a very inspired record. There's something very, very cool about that record. But again, it's not really Dio. *Angry Machines*, there are a lot of good qualities to it, but I don't think it's as strong. And I think it almost sounds grungy at moments, which I think was a little out of place for Dio. And that's probably where people really had a hard time with Tracy G."

December 12, 1996, Sporthalle Augsburg, Germany. © *Wolfgang Gürster*

"So, the *Strange Highways* album came out," says Vinny, also taking a stab at comparing the two situations, "and I guess it didn't sell the way he needed it to or wanted it to, and didn't get that many great reviews. Then he tried to maybe go back towards what he originally was, with *Angry Machines*. He started to tighten up the bolts: 'Don't do this, don't do that.' It wasn't as freelance. *Strange Highways* was just like 'Tracy, do what you do.' And that's what I did too, and that's that album. But because it wasn't a huge, big commercial success and all the above, people tried to change things and fix things. And then it just started getting more tightened up."

Still, we mustn't exaggerate this so-called Tracy G factor. Dio had crafted and issued two dark, slow, sludgy albums before *Angry Machines* (three if you count *Dehumanizer*), and it's not that the quality of the present songs is, as a whole, lesser than the works on those. Certainly, *Lock Up the Wolves* is an inferior album, and that was back in the major-label days. And let's not forget that after Tracy left the band, two of Ronnie's next three albums would be similarly sludgy and dour. More on that later, but yes, one might say that Ronnie ended up with fully six "Tracy G" studio albums, except for the fact that four of them were made with Rowan Robertson, Tony Iommi, and then Craig Goldy, who coughed up two of the four, along with *Dream Evil*, which is pretty much a Viv Campbell album.

In any event, yes, *Angry Machines* opener "Institutional Man" is malevolent in grays, browns, and blacks, ill sequenced here at pole position with its disorienting melody and lurching tempo. It's a song that could easily have fit within the flowing folds of *Dehumanizer*'s funeral shroud, and had it been there, we might have been praising Iommi's riff-writing prowess therein enclosed. The band snorts like a bull, particularly Vinny, who's playing proudly Sabbatherian and arch-rhythmic, dropping a beat here and there, an effect that further disorients any listener craving a warm handshake for the starting song.

"It's about people who are institutionalized," explains Ronnie. "It's my point of view of the prison population. There are some who've said to me, 'Oh, I understand you wrote one about people in mental institutions.' Well, I guess you could look at it that way if you wanted to, but that's not what I meant. It was the prison population, because a lot of fans, especially a lot of young kids who are inside, they don't have a lot to listen to other than music and other people snoring, screaming, and yelling in the night. I've been getting a lot of correspondence from these people. I'm not saying that they're all not there because they're supposed to be. I don't get into that; I'm not the judge. But I know the things that they've written to me, how difficult it is inside and how music helps them get over it and how they hope that when they do get out, if they do get out, that they'll be able to do this or do that. Or some want to play guitar or do something else, whatever it may be. These are people who I think feel like a forgotten segment of our population. Because I do have some contact with them through a fan-to-artist relationship, I wanted to write a song for them."

"Don't Tell the Kids" follows at an increased clip, but the riffs are still grinding and low-down, even though much of the track approaches speed metal, given the regular-time and double-time construct. The song is about divorce, with a bonus verse that extrapolates toward the universal. Sprinkled throughout are further universal sentiments in construction of a song that comes out the other end describing, in a general sense, lack of communication. Next up, "Black" is framed upon a funky and yet exotic, atonal riff. Vinny gets to play around it nicely, while Ronnie works in freaky vocal melodies and lyrics that follow nicely on the previous track, addressing this idea of lost innocence at the hands of a cruel world. There's a thespian effect here that recalls Alice Cooper in his prime. "Hunter of the Heart" is a worthy slow track, trundling but just fast enough to portray weight, critical mass. Ronnie is singing strongly like a banshee while his band cooks. The effect is heightened by the album's damnably fortified production, Vinny's drum sound in particular rendered pounding and earthly. At the lyric end, once more Ronnie laments the inevitable corruption that flows from too-enthusiastic participation with this wicked world.

"'Stay Out of My Mind' was Jeff's entirely," says Tracy. 'He brought that in, and Ronnie just copied the way he sang it. How about that? Those melodies and those words . . . it's like we did a cover song of Jeff's. Which is cool, but as I said, we just never did that. And Ronnie even said that to me. He said, 'We'll be that much closer to being done,' and I thought, 'Oh oh.' It

Ronnie and Tracy, Open Air Amphitheatre, San Diego, August 3, 1998. © *Tom Wallace*

Angry Machines CD and cassette

was already weird from then." Plus, the song is slow and atonal, proggy and awkward, as if the band is trying to work on a collective income tax form. It certainly doesn't sound anything like Jeff Pilson's personality. In other words, I guess on the bright side, it's a good fit to this era of Dio, but on the less happy side, it's at the extreme and hard-to-love end of the spectrum.

I asked Tracy if keyboardist of record Scott Warren had much to do with the writing (the liner notes to the album, in fact, offer no clues as to writing credits). "Nothing. He wasn't in the writing process. He wasn't even in the room. Also, most of the keyboard ideas were either Ronnie's or Jeff's. And then, of course, in the studio, Scott would play because he's a better player than anybody else. He would do basically whatever they wanted him to do. Play this, play that. Any keyboard parts you hear are him being guided around. Scott is a good, adequate player, and he could do anything. But when I was in the band, he wasn't part of the writing thing, no.

"A lot of work went into those songs," continues Tracy. "And even though it's not the most happening album, as far as the flow goes, the vibe on it and the sound on it maybe, I still think there are some really cool parts on that album. But I'm looking between all the lines because I was involved in all the little musical parts. It's too bad it didn't just come out better, because, God, there was tons of time and work that went into it. And it just came out like a big turd. And the thing is, it isn't! But it's perceived like that. But between me and you, all the time put into it and all the work, it's like, 'Oh, man, too bad.' I think it was just overly thought out and overly worked.

"Ronnie's . . . how can I say this? He's a perfectionist, very professional, I think, for my opinion, for the status of guy he is. By that I mean, he'll go down in the books as one of the legendary singers of all time, as far as his genre goes. This is my opinion, for holding that label over his head, being one of the guys. I think he's pretty awesome, and he's pretty professional to work with, considering. Because at that level, you can be a pretty big ass, if you know what I'm saying. Some of those guys even close to that level . . . and let's face it, not many people can sing like that guy. Everybody has got their own thing, but you've got to give credit where credit is due. That guy, no matter how old he gets or how long he's been doing it, when he opens his mouth, you've got to call it what it is. The guy can sing; he's very gifted, that dude. Everybody has their moments and their personality, but he's a very professional, dead-on singer, and to work with him, I felt like I was finally in a real situation with a real guy. Yeah, sure, there are moments, like any other relationship. There are moments when it gets tight and weird because personalities rub and whatever. Again, I know other guys who've played with big-time guys, and they tell me crazy stories about someone's personality that is just way over the top, the rock star bullshit crap. Come on, man . . .

"He talked a little bit about his time with Ritchie Blackmore," continues Tracy, on the subject of Ronnie's "mystical" side. "Playing with the Ouija board and the spookiness and ghosts and all that shit. But he never, like . . . how can I say, talked about anything he worships, or Satan is his friend and he's killing goats, you know what I mean? It was just all about making the music, to me. I mean, I don't even smoke, dude. I barely drink, and I do no drugs myself. I'm there because of the music. The music that comes out of my guitar is why I've always wanted to play. That's my interest. The whole thing with the Satan thing and the dark or the drugs, I mean, I don't know what any of that is. I know it's there, and if someone is trying to push it on me, I can tell. And I can tell him to go fuck himself.

Tour notices, pass, and picks

"But no, we laughed about it sometimes, because I would tell him . . . sometimes people ask me the same question you're asking me right now. I would tell Ronnie, 'A lot of people ask me that: "What is Ronnie into?"" Because he seems to come off like, 'Ooh, I'm scary!' And to be honest with you, and I think that's a typical stupid selling marketing ploy, which you've heard since way back in the Black Sabbath days. 'Oh, these guys are into the devil.' That was the record company's thing. And the band, I think they're kind of like me—they just want to play. They're like, 'Whatever, okay.' Some people take it to another level and dream about it and they read about and they worship it. I don't know Ronnie to be like that. But that's just my opinion. I think he's just a guy who's really gifted. And yeah, he likes heavy music, and people perceive him as being kinda scary. When he was younger, his voice was heavy, and then he was hanging out with Ritchie Blackmore because he's a fruitcake too, probably. He's into whatever. I don't know Ritchie Blackmore, but you read all this different stuff. Ritchie is probably a regular guy too. But they want the public, the fans, to think they're not regular, don't you see? Because regular doesn't sell. 'We've got to wear this and we've got to say this, stand like this, make this sign.' It's all so people will start gossiping and go, 'Oh, man, I think he's into . . .' And maybe he is. You know, I don't spend time with him alone. The time when I was in the band . . . if he would've gotten weird with me, I would've told him, 'Get lost.' But he didn't. He's totally normal.

"They're just regular guys too," adds Tracy, on the subject of Vinny Appice and Jimmy Bain. "Jimmy is wild and wacky. I haven't really hung out with Jimmy since, when, '93? Regular guy, good dude, party maniac. Vinny is a little more domesticated, and his wife is really cool. They were one of my favorite rhythm sections to hook up with and play with. Because I was fans of both of them from earlier, when I was younger. Jimmy writes, kind of like a Jeff Pilson. And Jimmy even sings a little bit. He can bring both those things to the table."

And I would think that Vinny as a drummer and Tracy represent an excellent match of styles. Both are heavy, dark, rhythmic, hard hitting, if that can be said of a guitarist.

"Yeah, I got to do four albums with him, from WWIII to three Dio albums. My opinion is that when me and him set up in a room and start to jam, it's just supposed to be. Last time I saw Vinny, he came over here and we were just jamming, working on some new riffs and ideas for some little project he wanted to do. So, we hadn't seen each other for a long time. And he set up on a little drum set in my studio, and it's supposed to be like that. When we play, there is no effort; you don't even have to try with a drummer like that. Because of the way I play and the way he plays, I just shake my head going, 'It's just a shame. We should be in a band together.' Because the music is calling for it from us. Does that make sense?

"Unfortunately, there are all sorts of other things in life that play a part. But you would think the most important thing is you should just play with who is the most natural to play with. I don't know, he might not say that or think that—this is just my opinion now. He's just a natural drummer for me to play with on that level. There are a lot of other great phenomenal drummers. But there is a natural good chemistry between us, between his heavy John Bonham–influenced backbeat, kind of on the slower side, and then my style—it really gels. There's not a lot of work you have to do; you just do it. It's just a matter of us guiding the riffs around. But we've each got projects. We're all just on this planet trying to survive."

Track #6 on *Angry Machines* is called "Big Sister," and like "Black," the song is rife with arcane pregnant pauses. One might even call it Zeppelinesque of melody, especially with that Egypto keyboard lick. The chorus is huge and groovy, and, ultimately, the song is pretty damn successful. "'Big Sister' is another politically motivated track," notes Ronnie. "It's kind of a takeoff of the Big Brother situation from Orwell's *Nineteen Eighty-Four*, but in this case, I substituted the feminine attitude for government. But hey, if you change it and put politics inside of it, it's the same thing."

Next up is "Double Monday," and again, Vinny gets to demonstrate his largesse, jazzing up a proggy yet still very heavy metal number. The lyric isn't much: it's succinct, plain, and essentially about having a bad day—"the worst day of your life times two." At the music end, though, you really hear what Tracy is talking about with respect to how his riffs and Vinny's enveloping of them make glorious musical sense. Plus, we're reminded again how strong a recording Ronnie locks in here. It's hard to shake the fact that the

December 12, 1996, Sporthalle Augsburg, Germany. © *Wolfgang Gürster*

album is on a small label, and that the band picture isn't really portraying a band as such. But put that aside, and *Angry Machines* sounds expensive—not layered or elaborately arranged, but nonetheless making use of the finest gear.

Next, "Golden Rules" is another dark rocker with forward thrust and delectably evil melodies. As with many of the tracks thus far, the band gets to juggle time signatures while Ronnie harrowingly admonishes up top, getting in a few digs at religion. Once more his vocal melodies evoke images of a straitjacketed Alice Cooper, while Tracy, in tandem, solos like a violent inmate at the asylum.

"I don't dote on religion," says Ronnie, who, indeed, usually parachutes in a few snipes and then leaves—and leaves you wondering. "Religion, I think, is something that you can never argue, and you can certainly never convince the other person. Because even though there's a Bible, how concrete is it? It depends on the point of view. So religion is not something I'm involved in, other than the fact that having been in Black Sabbath, it seems like there's a connection. I just think there's a lot of similes and metaphors and things that have gotten me to that point. Religion, much like fantasy, much like the tales of King Arthur, is, again, something that is so difficult to put a hand on and say, 'This actually happened.' It's such a matter of belief that you're really dealing in the same kind of properties. My fantasy writing is coupled with some religious overtones as well because they are part and parcel to . . . again, they're not the same thing, but you see what I mean.

"As for politics, I've not gotten involved because my time is taken doing what I do as a performer. I do deal with charities, though; there are some that are very close to my heart. But politically I just feel that we're in a mess. Bureaucracy has continually eaten itself by the tail, and it's a problem that never ends. It's gotten too big, and it's a horrible place we live in! A lot of that has to go down to the government. It's our government, and it's up to us to change it. We can throw all the barbs we want at the people we elect, but we're the ones who elected them, so it's our choice. But again, the two subjects are pretty unarguable, so I stay away from them."

Ronnie delves further into the vitality and unfortunate resonance and relevance of his current lyrical direction. "I tend to have my finger on the pulse of the world and what's going on around me. It's one of the reasons I changed my attitude for the last three albums about writing more social commentary, because before, it was all about 'If you have dreams, work hard at them to make them come true' and 'The world is full of magic.' Those are wonderful thoughts because they're good escapist thoughts from a bad world. But if you look at the world today, the same person I'm telling to dream is flipping burgers because he can't get a job. So that social commentary is more necessary than me lying from my heart and saying, 'Oh yes, your dreams will come true' because it's what I wrote about before and everybody wants it, and that's crap. You gotta live in the world.

"I read the newspaper religiously, front to back. I used to begin only with the sports pages, but now I'm into the front pages as well. I'm a sports fanatic, so that's why I buy the newspaper, but I've become more worldly. That begins my day. I read a lot of science fiction and like very much to read biographies and autobiographies. I like to see how people have succeeded and how they've failed. That's very important for people to learn: what can make you successful. I'm not saying that by reading that book, you're going to be that person, but there are some insights if you have the brains enough to find out what's for you in this world. I just finished a book about John Paul Getty, so I could become the richest man in the world. It was very interesting to see how a man could accumulate so much wealth and how he did it and how he abused it and his family, which is absolutely amazing to me. So those are the things I like to read because I learn from them. Science fiction writers are ten, twenty years ahead of the world. From Arthur Clarke to Asimov, they've always been the ones who've been the prognosticators of what has become. I mean, they had men on the moon when H. G. Wells was writing in the 1800s. They were talking about putting man on the moon. So, science fiction writers have an imagination that leads me to places more real than science fiction."

Next up on *Angry Machines* is "Dying in America," which grooves deliciously as well, this track being yet another underrated anthem on this much-maligned album. The speed is nice, Vinny is well into his pocket, and Ronnie is rich with melody, something missing from too many *Angry Machines* songs.

"'Dying in America' springs from the dissatisfaction I see from people who appear never to be able to have anything. We want education for our children. Of course we should have education for our children, but to what end? We try to prepare them to be viable citizens, who are going to be able to get a job, and that's impossible right off the

start. So that's a problem. From drive-by shootings to serial murders, all of the things we experience—cataclysmic extremes with the weather, what we've done to the ecology, AIDS; the list goes on and on—it's a pretty miserable place! And I just needed to make a statement, as an American, that this is not the rosy little garden path that everyone thinks it is in the rest of the world. We have as many problems with homeless and the undereducated etc. as anyone does! In fact, we're a first-rate nation with a lot of third-world attitudes inside of it."

Then the album closes . . . with a ballad! Not a dirge, not "Rainbow Eyes" or "Catch the Rainbow," but a true-blue ballad, with piano and strings. "I've always tried to stay away from anything that smacks of being a love song," says Ronnie in defense of "This Is Your Life." "And this is not a love song! Of all ten tracks on this album, nine of them are pretty vicious as far as their content goes. Lyrically, by that I mean they're reality based, like 'Dying in America.' And then on the last song, 'This Is Your Life,' I wanted to show that I had some optimism left for humanity and this world. So, if there is any message, it's that an individual can make a great change not only for themselves, but for humanity. You know, 'This is your chance, it's your life, make something of it!' That's the reason I wanted to include that one and tie it down. I did it with a piano, and I've never done a song with just a piano. But because it was a bit more personal . . . I tried it with a guitar, but it didn't have the personalness that the piano version had.

"The vehicle which you have is what makes the difference," says Ronnie, on how the song allows him a new dimension vocally. "Obviously if you have a good vehicle to sing, and you can sing, that's going to show you off in that light. I've always been pretty

This page and the previous three, additional shots from the performance on December 12, 1996, Augsburg, Sporthalle, Germany. © *Wolfgang Gürster*

single-minded to the kind of music I want to make. I like things that are very, very hard and hard edged. And I thought that, in this case, by putting something so gentle against all that came before, it also had some credibility. I think I've done enough ballads throughout my career so that I've kept 'respect' from other people. Because when they think it's all going to be a matter of shouting this and shouting that, suddenly they get something nice. So, I think I've done enough."

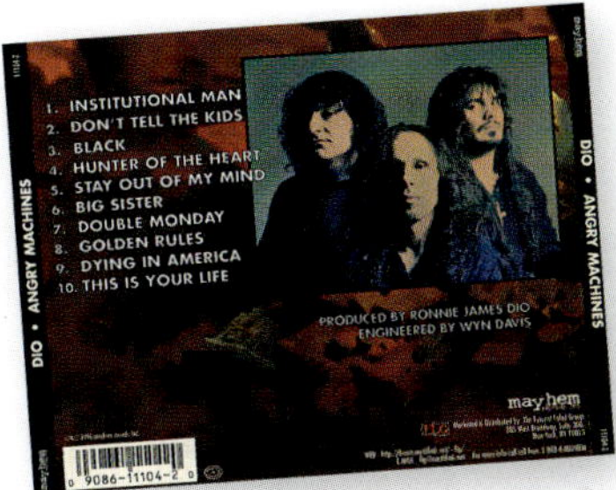

Front and back of the US-issue *Angry Machines* CD. *Martin Popoff archive*

CHAPTER 10

"I'm playing that messed up that it's still affecting you to even email me?"

INFERNO: LAST IN LIVE

With Jeff Pilson unavailable due to Dokken commitments, Dio hit the road in support of *Angry Machines* with Larry "Bones" Dennison on bass, although Bob Daisley jumped on board for Scandinavian dates. Scott Warren augmented the band's sound on keyboards. After touring Europe, Vinny Appice came down with pneumonia, and dates had to be rescheduled. He wasn't on the mend in time for these dates, and James Kottak, of Kingdom Come and Scorpions fame, filled in for seven shows. Pilson did indeed get to play with the band, on a South American swing in late November 1997.

The *Angry Machines* tour was a monster of a trek, even if stateside; Dio was now playing to, on average, fewer than a thousand people a show. November and December 1996 saw the band in the US, with Motörhead supporting most of the later dates, with Lemmy and the crew joining the band in Germany as well, at which time US biker rockers Speedball also supported. Back in America for February 1997, this is where James Kottak filled in for an ailing Appice. Then just like that, in late February, it was back to Europe, with Original Sin supporting. Back in America for April, hot UK doomsters My Dying Bride were the main support, with a third act often picked up from the hosting city. May was spent in Japan and western Canada, with a rare Alaskan gig also logged. June 1997 was booked solid throughout the States, after which the band broke for the summer, then made the aforementioned South American trip, joined by Scorpions, Bruce Dickinson, and the Jason Bonham Band.

The author's copy of Inferno: Last in Live. Martin Popoff archive

Five of the shows (including one in Tokyo) were used as source material for the band's two-CD *Inferno: Last in Live* opus. "Once you've had a dragon and all those kind of things around you, it's very difficult to do anything on a lesser manner," said Ronnie, just before the commencement of the *Angry Machines* tour. "So, we'll bring nothing that moves around and shouts at you, but we'll bring somebody to dress up onstage, obviously to make it look a little more usual, and a backdrop. These days I don't think people are as concerned about that as they used to be. I think it's a matter of they prefer to see you in a small place where they can get a feel for it instead of getting lost in an arena situation. And let's face it—arenas don't sell out anymore anyway, so economically that's not going to happen. What we bring will be perfect for the size of venues we play."

And it was all systems go, healthwise. "I've never really had much problem with my voice, and I think a lot of that has to do with technique—you know how to do it. It's like having good tools, and with good tools you build a good house. If you've got a bad saw, you're going to cut crooked. I've never had a problem; I've never had to cancel a show. I hope that continues. It's just a real tough vocal performance for me every year, and every year I say I'm going to write songs in a lower key, so I don't have to kill myself. But every

Open Air Amphitheatre, San Diego, California, August 3, 1998. © *Tom Wallace*

time I write them higher and higher. The show is very bruising for a singer, not a lot of rest, continuous music. So again, touch wood, I've been pretty lucky with that."

Inferno: Last in Live found Ronnie really seizing the opportunity to demonstrate the spectacular heavy metal career he's had. The only recent tracks served were a surprising show-opening "Jesus, Mary & the Holy Ghost" along with "Double Monday" and "Hunter of the Heart," both from the most recent *Angry Machines*. The rest of the set list was all Sabbath and Rainbow, along with all the big anthems from the first two Dio albums. Only four Dio albums out of a possible seven were represented in the running order.

Performancewise, Vinny really stretched the length of his fills, something that increasingly annoyed Ronnie as time living with Vin would drag on. He's Vin, and he's all over this album, putting on a rhythmic clinic of pure Vin-ness. Tracy, on the other hand, attracted the most derision, for a number of reasons, most that would have to fall within the realm of nitpicking. As discussed, his soloing style was very much of his own archetype, but he was also prone to fills based on dissonance. As well, some of the riffs were played without the staccato precision one expects from a cast-in-stone 1980s metal classic. And Ronnie could riff and augment and fill at fill time as well, so you had three

Larry "Bones" Dennison and the boss, Open Air Amphitheatre, San Diego, California, August 3, 1998.
© *Tom Wallace*

guys that were "chatty" at their jobs. And when there's only one guitar and guitarist in operation, oftentimes chatter can get scattery and clattery, distracting from the root melody and the tradition of these songs steeped in lusty dollops of tradition.

I asked Tracy whether he had felt any pressure in the live situation to duplicate the classic, singable solos laid down by Viv Campbell on those first two Dio records, given how thoroughly they were plundered for use onstage.

"No. That's a good question you've asked me, because we haven't touched on that. Never, since I joined the band in '93, did Ronnie ever say, 'Tracy, you can only be in this band if you do the solos exactly.' He never told me that, and so you never heard that [laughs]. And you can't hear that from me anyway, because, like I say, I mimic, I steal from everybody, the way everybody steals from everybody, sort of, whether they admit it or not. They just do. You go, 'Hey, that's cool, that's cool,' and you make it your own, hopefully. But I'm not one of those guys that can just mimic a solo. And most of the reason why is because I don't want to. I want to play what's coming out of my own gut. I don't want to play what came out of his. It's like, that's not what I was feeling.

"So, he never . . . but he's the boss, right? And I got the gig. If the boss would have said, 'Hey, you're going to have to do that solo as close as you can, note for note,' I would've attempted it, probably. But he never said that. Until the day that they called me and said, 'We need a guitar player who's playing a little bit more like the Ritchie Blackmore days and the Vivian Campbell days.' When they told me that is when I left. That's when I said, 'Well, maybe you need someone else, because what do you want me to do? I've been with you for six years, and what do you want me to do? Start to try to play like someone else now?!' Nah. So, on the live album, that's how I play. That's how I choose to play. And if I had to do it again, I would do the same thing. I would just try to play better. But I wouldn't try to play like anybody. I'd try to twist it up more. It's not even like I try to twist it up on purpose. I'm just going on the instinct of my playing in the moment. I don't know what I'm doing. I just close my eyes and try to go for it. I just try to feel it, you know? It's not a planned thing."

But there were signature passages from old solos that Tracy liked so much that he did indeed pay homage to them.

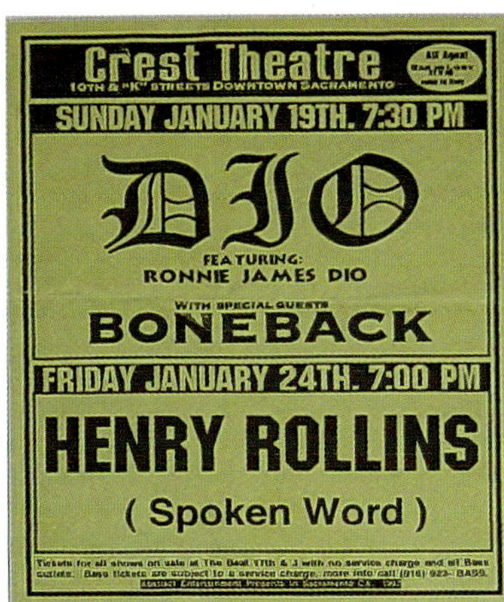

A couple of show notices

"Yeah, some of them, like from great songs like 'The Last in Line.' There will be moments where a solo really sticks out for me. I would call it the skeleton part of the solo. I would take my favorite stick-out parts and try to redo those, and in between all those, work of my own phrases. Yeah, that's a good point, that I tried to do that. Most of them in fact; definitely 'Don't Talk to Strangers.' At one time, we even used to do 'Man on the Silver Mountain,' but almost the whole thing. And I really loved his guitar solo in that. The parts that would touch me, I would try to mimic those. And the other parts, I would try to do something new and give it some fresh life. So yes, 'Man on the Silver Mountain,' because I'm a Ritchie Blackmore fan from way, way back, when he did 'Lazy' and all that shit. I grew up on *Machine Head*.

"I noticed it in every environment," sighs Tracy, when asked if he had detected any hostility toward his playing in the live environment. "But I cannot cut myself too short; I get more positive mail than I do negative from that. I just like to call a spade a spade. I'm not one of these guys to say, 'Yeah, I'm great; I did this.' I'm not that way. There are a lot of people that just didn't like what I do. Because he's already got a huge fan base, so I was up against that. But I get email still, all the time, from people who are totally contrary. I'm looking at an email right now. He doesn't want to interview me, but he just wanted to say that he's really disgusted about the reviews he reads about my playing with Dio, because, of all of the above, every positive thing you can say. He was the total opposite. He thought I took the band in a heavy direction, and I was fresh, I was new, I was my own thing. He said keep doing your own thing. It was totally positive.

"So what people don't know is that I get more of those kinds of emails and comments, personally, than these people who write reviews in magazines for whatever. That's what most of the world reads, so that's what most of the world thinks. Because what you read, it goes into your body, and you believe it. Or these days on the internet, how everybody has an opinion, and everybody has a forum now to speak their mind. So, everybody says blah blah blah and they speak their gossip. I might not have a bunch of people making websites about positive things about me. I have more negative things because that's the world. People want to talk shit. They don't want to praise anybody; they want to say they suck. That's just the way it is. So, I'm cool with it. I kind of like that I offend a lot of people. It makes me laugh, in a funny, quirky way, because I'm like, wow. I mean, I'm playing that messed up that it's still affecting you to even email me? [laughs]. It's kinda funny."

"I think the problem boils down to this," offers Pilson on the contentious Tracy G situation. "Dio in the public eye was very much one kind of thing. And I think Ronnie, understandably, wanted to break from that, make that box a little bigger; he wanted to try some new things. And I think for the most part, people just never embraced what Tracy brought in, that Ronnie wanted to give Tracy a chance with. Tracy is a really great player. There were a lot of really great qualities about Tracy. But he just wasn't of the mold of what the public perceived a Dio guitar player to be. And sooner or later, that's just going to affect the whole thing; you can't keep fighting it. That's what happened. I think Ronnie still loves what Tracy does. He just realizes that Dio is something a little different from what Tracy brought to the picture. I commend Ronnie for trying to break out of the box a little bit. He did some pretty far-out experimenting on a couple of the things we did that I know a lot of people didn't understand. But I still think as an artist, it's a very healthy thing he did. And you know, his Dio music is a little more traditional now again, and I know that the public likes that better. And I'm sure Ronnie enjoys that. But the fact is, you can't be the same artist year after year

Ronnie and Simon Wright. Open Air Amphitheatre, San Diego, California, August 3, 1998. © *Tom Wallace*

after year without going some places. And I think it's a good thing he did. I think Tracy brought some wonderful things to the picture, but just maybe he wasn't the long-term Dio guitar player."

"The last one was the live album," says Tracy, defiant to the end, "which was just a live album, where there wasn't a lot of changing of it, because we were basically playing live, and it is what it is. And that was about it. It was time for him to make another change and, I guess, go back to more of what he came from. I was just stepping outside quite a bit. And to get back to your question, when I left the band, I still kept stepping

outside on my own as far as just trying stuff, guitar sounds, the way I solo, the whole thing. I'm still experimenting. Even though I've been playing for a hundred years or whatever, I still feel like I'm a beginner. Music is like that for me. I'm still experimenting with all these different sounds and expressions, trying to find those tones and those notes that come out of me that express the way I'm feeling at the moment; that's all I'm really trying to do. It can take me into different styles. How has my guitar style changed? I think if anything, it's even more outside now than [it] was back in the Dio days. Which some people might be interested in, and others can't stand it."

"You see, we didn't really plan on doing a live album when we first started the tour, which lasted about a year and a half," notes Ronnie, doing press for *Inferno*. "Our first thought was to put a set together that pleased the people we play for, which is always my first consideration. So this set was put together really for the audience. So, when the time came for us to do a live album, the set was already in place and already rehearsed. Again, it wasn't with any forethought—the tour was planned and then the live album came after.

"Well, you know, it's really sad to me," lamented Ronnie, on the stripped-down nature of the stage show at this stage in the band's career trajectory. "I was always very much influenced by what Alice Cooper did. He was always the master of stage shows; he did things that would knock us all out, from hanging himself to having his head chopped off. Absolutely unbelievable. So, I wanted to follow in that line for a couple of reasons: for one, I liked the theatrical; secondly, I always felt that ticket prices were way too high. We always try to give something back to the people who put us where we were, so we would bring up these huge stage shows. The first stage show we did cost us $150,000, and that was *Holy Diver*. The *Last in Line* set graduated to $250,000. The *Sacred Heart* show with the dragon was $500,000—our money.

"So, we weren't sitting around collecting money. It was $1 million or at least $750,000 stuck back into it. That's an awful lot of money to give back, and I think nobody really understood that we were doing that. We didn't care about it. We didn't try to publicize it. We just wanted to give them a great show. But I think the media put the kibosh to it. They were like, 'Oh, what's this dragon crap? We don't want to see that. Why doesn't the band just go up and play?' Well, we've always been able to do that; that was never a problem for us. But to give something more without raising ticket prices and make the fans appreciate what bands could give them was my attitude. But again, I felt a lot of it was the media slagging it off; starting with the British press, who were very notorious for ripping you down. I would love to do it again, but people take the piss out of you for doing it, so we don't. It's like going to Disneyland and not having Space Mountain there."

Ronnie comments on the paperwork behind performing Rainbow and Sabbath tracks. "The legality is that once something has been recorded, you have the right to record it yourself. Of course, you do have to make payment. It's the same thing with if somebody would cover one of your songs, you would get writing and publishing. You would have to file everything with the proper people, so that the writers and publishers get their money. But no, there's no real permission needed.

"I think *Last in Live* came out really well," continues Ronnie, asked specifically about vocal performances on the album. 'Mistreated' came out really well. I think generally I was pretty pleased with everything. Perhaps 'Holy Diver' is something I remember most from the show. There's a guitar solo and a drum solo on the record, but the guitar solo is a little bit shorter than what occurs live. It tends to get a little bit boring. If you're doing a video, and the guitar solo lasts twenty minutes, it's kind of okay because there's a connection between the sound and video. But when you're just getting the audio, it can get a bit boring. You know, not that vocals don't get boring either—I don't want to be out of the game here. So we cut it down quite a bit. But Tracy is just very consistent. Truthfully, everything is the same with us. We get just as excited as the audience for every song. It's a joy to play, and it's really a luxury to be able to do what you love all of your life. So, if you don't approach it that way and get that pleasure out of it, you shouldn't be in this business. So, everything we do is approached and attacked in a very fierce way. We just go for it."

Asked about the most strenuous vocal performance in the set, Ronnie figures, "As we get towards the end, it's more difficult, only because we've been playing for the last ninety minutes, and the last song ends up being some vicious piece that we did with Sabbath or something. So, it gets to be a reach. I've done the set so many times that I know all the tricks and notes that it's pretty easy. And that's something that we planned, because the physical abuse that the singer takes is a hell of a lot more than the other players take, just from the standpoint of the vocal cords being such a delicate instrument.

"So we do plan the set that I get a rest here and there. The drum solo and the guitar solo of course is something the singer loves the most, because it allows him to go hide behind the amps and take a big breath. I just seem to get stronger as we go, except for those two months where I had the flu in Europe, which was a trying time for me. And then Vinny came down with pneumonia. The keyboard player is the same person we've used on *Strange Highways* and *Angry Machines*, Scott Warren. The bass player has changed between Jeff Pilson and our bass player now, Larry Dennison. Jeff of course has his Dokken commitment that he's quite adamant about; that makes it fairly difficult for us. We love to play with Jeff; we love to write with Jeff. But he has this other commitment, which sometimes gets a bit sticky. You want to say, 'Make up your mind!' But we try to deal with it as best we can. But Larry is pretty firmly in there; he's played with us for the last year and a half on our tour.

"We always started with the mobile unit being brought in," explains Ronnie, on the construction of the live album—which, of note, is the band's first, given that 1986's *Intermission* was an EP. "Hopefully you've got a good engineer back there. If you don't have your own, you hope the guy back there is cognizant of the music that you play, because you know, that's a special thing to be able to catch different kinds of music. Hard rock music, especially aggressive hard rock music, can be very difficult. So, once you have that in place, what the mobile does is hook up to the desk and just takes the feed from there, which is easy for us, because now we have all the good sounds going into the mobile.

"So once that's done, they usually give us the tape to play on the bus. And someone will say how good it sounds, and knowing me, I'll say how awful it sounds: 'Oh my God, what was that? How did I make that mistake?' But from then, we take it into the studio. And in our case, we take it into a studio that has a digital machine, and transfer everything from the analog. I don't like to do a lot of fixing; I like to keep it as natural as possible, because that's the honest way. But we did a couple of fixes on this album; it has to be done. If there's a blatant mistake, it has to be fixed. So, you can just pick the guitar on another track and fix that, same with the bass. You can't really fix anything with the drums. You don't want to go mess with them. And luckily, Vinny is so consistent, you don't really have a problem. Then we just do what we always do with a regular record, mix it down and hope somebody likes it [laughs].

"The mobile—you plan that a few weeks in advance. If we know we're going to be playing a really good hall, and there's a good mobile in the area, maybe you'll call him up a day before. Like I say, if you have a good working crew, especially a good monitor and soundman, it makes life so much easier. All we have to do is go up and play. Our soundman has checked all the levels. He works very closely with the man in the mobile."

"It's a culmination of a lot of things," reflected Tracy, upon his leaving the ranks of Dio after *Last in Live*. "I can only speak for myself. The other members, I don't know. It was never a money thing with me. It's really tough to make money doing it, and if you're ever to make any money doing it, I always thought it was a real blessing. You're just lucky to make money doing something you love to do. I made a little bit of money and got by, so to speak. But there's not much room to complain. Other people might feel different. It was never really a money thing with me. It got to the point where the music was wanting to go that way, and musically I was going another way. It was never that I don't like the

Tracy G brings the noise, Open Air Amphitheatre, San Diego, California, August 3, 1998. © *Tom Wallace*

guy, or he doesn't like me, I don't think. And I notice, he'll get guys, and then they'll be out, and then he'll get them back in the band again. There's a lot of that going on too. Relate it to a relationship with a chick. You know how that goes. Sometimes you can go with her and then break up, but then you're back with her. Which is kinda funky, you know? But it does happen, huh? It's different, but the same. And I've even done it, not in Dio, but other bands before Dio. I've worked with people, then it's over, and then you try again. Because there was something good about the relationship for you to try to rekindle. So, you do it again, but then the same shit comes up.

"I mean, how many times has he gone back and forth with Jimmy Bain? Sure, Jimmy is back with Mandy Lion in WWIII now. Maybe they feel, well, at one time me and you had something happening, but we don't now. But maybe if we regroup, it'll happen again. Because basically, all they are thinking about is their career and their business. It's not really like, I'm your buddy now, all of a sudden. Even though I can pretend to be. Follow me? That's all it is. I mean, we all love everybody, right? Everybody loves everybody. Yeah, right. The truth of the matter is, I'll get back together with you if there is something happening. If not, don't call me. I mean, you know?! Unless someone is a true buddy and a friend and they hang out with you, then it's a little bit different and it goes further than the business. But most of the time, it's based on business. And if Jimmy Bain is sitting in a room with the singer from WWIII or Vinny, trust me, all it has to do with is that they think they can get something off the old name of WWIII when I was in the band. Because that was the only time that band did what little it did, and that was fourteen years ago. And if they're sitting in a room today, it's not because they're bros, it's not because they even give a shit about each other. And I'm just being really honest; that's just the way it is."

If you haven't figured it out, I was having this chat with Tracy back in 2004. WWIII had put out an album in 2003 called *When God Turned Away*, featuring only Mandy Lion from the classic lineup. But in 2004, both Jimmy and Vinny rejoined the band for a spell. And guess what? In 2008, Tracy rejoined, although there's only ever been the two albums to date. And back to Dio: after *Last in Live*, it wasn't only Tracy that would be gone, but there'd be no Vinny Appice steamrolling through rolls at the back either.

"Well, I left the band once before, to go do something with Jeff Pilson, like in 1990," explains Vinny. "I'm the only person who has actually ever left the band [laughs]. No less than left *twice*—everyone else has gotten fired. So, I left to go do something with Pilson, and then we wound up back together with the Black Sabbath *Dehumanizer* album. I did something with Pilson which led to doing an album with WWIII, and then we did a little tour and an album. Then Sabbath was getting back together with Cozy Powell playing drums at that point, with Ronnie singing. And Cozy fell off a horse and broke his pelvis. Plus, it wasn't going very well; it was going really slow, and people weren't getting along with those ingredients there. So, I got a call saying, 'Hey, do you want to come down and play?,' and I said, 'Yeah, man, absolutely!' So, I went to England, and we started writing for the *Dehumanizer* album, and everything was really smooth. And we did that; we did the tour, and that's when I reunited with Ronnie and we started doing Dio after that, because Sabbath, as usual, didn't last.

"And then when we were on tour with the last Dio tour, '98—I don't even know what album that was, *Angry Machines*—the first show, I got a call from Sharon Osbourne saying Bill Ward's had a heart attack [laughs]. Actually, I got a message from Tony Iommi in my hotel room saying call him, blah blah blah, and then Sharon called and explained that Bill Ward had a heart attack, and the boys want you to come and play, and we want you to leave tomorrow [laughs]. So, I went okay, fine, frick, great, great opportunity, I want to do it; I want to play with them.

"But I didn't leave tomorrow because I didn't want to leave Ronnie hanging. So, I told Ronnie and Wendy, his manager, and we immediately got on the phone and got Simon in. It was a long rehearsal, and I was telling him all the stuff to make it a little easier. It was pretty funny hearing all the songs without me playing them. Then the next night I played the last show, on Friday night, and I left on a Saturday to go play with Sabbath. So, Ronnie got kinda peeved off with that. That's the kind of person he is. You have to understand, great opportunity to do it, and it was only for six weeks anyway. So, I could come back and finish the tour blah blah blah, plus I went from playing clubs to playing 70,000-seater places, and ten times the money. But he doesn't understand that."

More shots from the band's show at the Open Air Amphitheatre, San Diego, California, August 3, 1998.
© *Tom Wallace*

CHAPTER 11

"It's a concept album because I needed a reason to do this again."

MAGICA

As we've seen, change was afoot again in the Dio camp. At long last, all the criticism of guitarist Tracy G avalanched in on Ronnie, and it was decided that new blood was needed. Back comes Craig Goldy, axman for the vastly underrated *Dream Evil* album. As well, as discussed, Vinny Appice leaves under messy circumstances, basically to serve as backup quarterback to Bill Ward on the year's Black Sabbath reunion.

At the end of June 1999, Ronnie indicated that he had about "twenty-eight to thirty minutes more of music" to go on what was to become the man's first concept album, adding that, with respect to the lineup, "there might be some changes, so perhaps we'd better not go there. I can tell you a few of the people. Craig Goldy, who was our guitar player before, is our guitar player again. Simon Wright, and me [laughs]. The rest I'm not quite positive about yet. A bass player, keyboard player, and possibly another guitar player.

"It was a decision which had to be made," elaborated Ronnie on switching guitar players. "By that, I mean I loved the way Tracy played, and I liked writing with Tracy. But I'm not a stupid person, and I realized that fans were not very happy with Tracy. We got nothing but negative comments about him. I think it was because I was trying to do something else, and Tracy really fit that need. But you have to look at your audience, for God's sake, and if they don't like what you do, you have to make a change. So, after five years, I decided to make the change. But it wasn't a change to push Tracy out; it was supposed to be adding Craig Goldy, with Tracy. Again, because I'm a pretty loyal person, I didn't want to do that, and I like Tracy, and I like the emotion we had going."

Wendy Dio was feeling much the same way. "On *Lock Up the Wolves*, we had the young new Rowan Robertson, who was seventeen years old, and that was an experience, but those were good times. My least favorite album was *Angry Machines* because I felt that Ronnie had taken a turn that he was being pushed into, to become more industrial. His fans didn't like it that much, and I'm glad he decided to change and go back to the usual way of writing."

Continues Ronnie, "Tracy said, rightfully so, 'Look, I just can't play with another guitar player.' Some can and some can't, and he just didn't want to do that, and so it was a very, very amicable parting of the ways. I just realized that I had to either add another guitar player or have a different guitar player, to take us where we needed to go. So, Tracy was gone. Craig was the guitarist we called first, of course, to say, 'Would you like to do this with Tracy?' And he said, 'I'd love to.' And then Tracy left, and that just left Craig. And it works great; we just had gotten back from Europe with the same lineup we had before, which was the same bass player, Larry Dennison, who may play on this, Scott Warren, our keyboard player, who will probably play on this, and everyone but Tracy. And it worked out really, really well. The difference is that Craig is the classic guitar player in a band like ours, and Tracy was going in a different direction.

"I think the complaints had more to do with the solos," adds Ronnie, getting deep into the Tracy G controversy, "that Tracy didn't follow them very well, although 'well' isn't the word I'm looking for. I guess he played of his own design; he touched on the original feel here and there. But that is one of the things I've learned: when people come to see the music they remember and want to hear it again, they want to hear it pretty true to the way it was originally done. That's what they grew up with and that's what they heard on the radio, and as soon as they hear some strange thing that they don't recognize, that completely rubs them the wrong way. So that's where the complaints were coming from. And again, the solos that we had him play . . . it was a very Tracyesque solo, not nearly the solos that a Craig would play, or a Vivian Campbell would play, or a Tony Iommi or Ritchie Blackmore would play.

"It was more that, as you suggested, that bottom-end, sludge stuff was there a lot. His solos were very effect driven, a lot of screams and noises and whistles, burps and gulps and whatnot. And that again was very disconcerting to people. Again, once you play with Ritchie Blackmore, I think that is the standard that everybody expects that Ronnie Dio is going to come up with. And all the way down the line, I think I did that pretty well, with Craig, Vivian, and of course Tony, who is an icon on his own, which also makes it one step harder. You play with these two great guys . . . and they all considered Vivian to be a great player as well—he may still be. I just haven't heard anything that he has done that is different from what he's doing with Def Leppard. But it was very difficult for Tracy.

"I don't know how he dealt with it, myself," continues Ronnie, on Tracy's state of mind as part of Dio. "I know it just used to murder me. It was really destructive. I tried to keep it together. We went to Russia and we played in Moscow, and I mean the review was absolutely just scathing for Tracy. They were very kind to me, and very kind to Simon. In fact, they loved us; they thought we were great [laughs]. In fact, the comment

The different faces of *Magica*

was 'The only person who deserved to be on the same stage with Ronnie Dio was Simon Wright.' And the rest were just nonentities and blobs, the solos were horrible, and there it was again. And I saw this, and I thought, you know, some change has got to be made. And that was the point where we had already committed to go to Europe and do the festival thing. It had been advertised, it was three weeks before we were going to do it, and Tracy wasn't going to go. So, the choices were to keep it the way it was, go and do the shows with Tracy, and make the change when we came back.

"Craig was just dissatisfied with his life and with what was going on, I guess, and the people he was playing with," answers Ronnie when asked, years later, why Craig had left Dio after the *Dream Evil* album. "I was very surprised that he left and called and said, 'I'm going.' Now, since he's been back, obviously the first thing he said was 'All I can tell you is that that was the biggest mistake I ever made.' You do what you have to do in life, I understand. If you are not happy doing something, then good, I don't want to be around you anyway, not if I have to make music with you. So, Craig left for his own personal reasons, and to have him back again is wonderful. He's matured so much, he's such a calmer person, and he knows what he's doing and what he wants. He's a great musician and a great guitar player, a great friend. I couldn't have been luckier to get Craig back again."

As Goldy told me in 2011, "*Magica* was my favorite period because I felt I had matured. Things had changed in a way that I could feel I could really contribute even greater than before. I learned a lot more about songwriting, things like that, and me and Ronnie had always stayed friends from *Dream Evil* on. During my second marriage, he and Wendy came to the wedding and to the reception, and we would go for beers and stuff like that, him and I, when we could find the time. And I mentioned to him, 'You know, I really regret leaving at *Dream Evil*, and I've changed, and I would really like to come back.' And he says, 'Oh, okay; I'll keep that in mind. Because right now I'm happy, but I'll keep that in mind.' Little did I know a few years later that I would get the phone call: 'I want you back.' Wow, here we go. Now we can do what we should've done a long time ago."

Ronnie elaborates on the idea that it was, in fact, supposed to be both Tracy and Craig on the record and in the band, not just Goldy alone. "That's right, that's very true. So many people had criticized Tracy for the kind of guitar player that he was, that he didn't fit inside of this band. They criticized him for such a long period of time that we just had to have a look around. Obviously, we were not pleasing the people who are certainly our fan base anymore; they still come, but they didn't seem as happy as they used to be. Maybe some of them stayed home. So, I wanted to stay loyal to Tracy. In fact, I love Tracy; I think Tracy is a great guitar player. But he was just the wrong style of guitar player for the typical Dio sound, I guess. So, I wanted to bring another guitar player into it so we'd have two—we'd have the best of both worlds, Tracy and Craig. Tracy could have stayed in the band. I didn't want to lose him, but when I brought it up, Craig said yes but Tracy said, 'Look, it's not Craig; it could be anybody. I can't play with another guitar player.' I understand that. Some people can and some people can't. Some people can sing with others, and some can't—it's not a problem. So Tracy was gone and that left us with Craig, so everything really worked out for us really well. I really wanted one guitar player anyway, but I was willing, for Tracy's sake, just as a friend and fellow musician, to not do that to him. But he chose to do it himself."

Ronnie then delves into the Vinny Appice situation. "Well of course, when Black Sabbath got back together, the first time they had gone out, they had brought Vinny along for . . . yes, that's a good word for it: insurance. So, Vinny insured through the whole tour and didn't play at all. And then when they went out again, they said to Vinny, 'Nah, we don't need you; everything is going to be okay. I guess everything is going to be all right now.' So, when Vinny left, he left at a very inopportune time. It was like just after the first show of the tour we had just started in America, so that was very difficult.

Ronnie James Dio
"Magica"
SPITCD 020

1. Discovery
2. Magica Theme
3. Lord Of The Last Day
4. Fever Dreams
5. Turn To Stone
6. Feed My Head
7. Ariel
8. Challis (Marry The Devil's Daughter)
9. As Long As Its Not About Love
10. Losing My Insanity
11. Otherworld
12. Magica - Reprise
13. Lord Of The Last Day
14. Magica - The Story

Reference & Approval CDR 5/6/99
Hatch Farm Studios
01932 828715
Unit 16, Hatch Farm, Chertsey Road, Addlestone ,Surrey, KT15 2EH

Magica advance promo.
Martin Popoff archive

"Luckily, Simon had played with us before, and he was free, and after two or three gigs we got it really together. Well, it seems to me that if someone does that to you, I don't think you're going to have your arms open to them. It's not going to be like, 'Thanks for filling in, Simon. Okay Vinny, you're back in here.' It goes so much deeper than a musician. I mean, Vinny is a great player, he was like my dear friend, and I still consider Vinny to be a dear friend, but that really hurt. That was too hurtful for me, so I thought, hey, you made your choice; you'd rather go stand around on the side and do nothing with Sabbath than to play in a band that you helped create, and a band that you helped perpetuate. So, at that point I said, what's the sense? And truthfully, I'm very happy with Simon, very, very happy. Because, somewhat like Tracy, Vinny was starting to get full of himself, as a player. I don't mean as an ego—wrong word again. He just started to overplay everything. Whenever Vinny started to get dissatisfied or edgy, he just . . . it didn't really matter, it was just the Vinny show.

"And when Simon came in, as you said, live, we heard everything. I heard all these parts that I had never heard before, because Vinny was always busy filling all the holes. And then when Craig came in, the same thing happened. I suddenly heard all the parts. Because as you had suggested, all that low-end bottom sound was just not us. That's the reason Vinny is not back. I have no idea what he is doing. I wish him well, but I just couldn't take the chance of it happening again. What happens if Sabbath calls again and says, 'Hey, we're going to do a tour.' And in reality, some of the people in that camp would like nothing better than that anyway. I'm sure it was a real point of pride to have wrestled Vinny away. But that's water under the bridge, and everything has worked out well. I don't have any grudges against anyone."

But significantly, back from the wilderness comes . . . Jimmy Bain!

"If it's your band, and people are doing this, I'm sure it's very depressing or stressful," offered Jimmy Bain, probably surprised as anybody to be back in the Dio fold. "Because

The author's copy of *Magica* along with the band photo insert. *Martin Popoff archive*

you really need to know that these people, day in and day out, are going to be on your team. I think Ronnie has felt a lot more secure since I've been back in the band. He knows that at least he's got one person there that he can rely on. And Simon Wright as well; he's exactly the same way. He's a team player, and that makes your decisions a lot easier. You can look ahead and say, you know, I know I'm still going to have a band in six months."

Noted Simon about being back, "Ronnie just always worked really hard—and worked us really hard. He was always going over stuff and was one for changing things and trying new things right through the recording process. Whereas with other bands it might have been 'Oh, that's good enough,' he'd be looking at every little detail and trying parts out a few different ways. But yeah, Ronnie had to come down hard on all of us every once in a while—on Craig, on Doug Aldrich later, on myself, everybody—because he wanted and he expected people to work just as hard as he did."

"Jimmy came into the picture after we'd written it," explains Ronnie. "He called me to tell me that he'd been completely rehabbed now. And step 10 of the rehab was to call people and apologize for the bad things you've done to them. He called Wendy and apologized and asked if I would speak to him after some of the horrible things he said about me when he was drugged out. He called me and said, 'I'm sorry for whatever happened.' And I said, 'Jimmy, I'm just glad you sorted yourself out. I'm not gonna have a go at you now; I'm gonna be on your side.' So, we got the best of everything. Jimmy came back, the best bass player I ever worked with. And also, I got a chance to support him, to help him. Because it's an ongoing struggle and will be for the rest of his life. He's exactly the same person, except he doesn't remember things. He said one time he woke up and he was married [laughs]. Then they both went to rehab, got out, looked at each other, and said, 'What the hell are we doing together?' Well, they were together for one reason. Drug people congregate together. He's doing great now."

Interestingly, with all the turmoil in the Dio camp, it made at least a modicum of sense that there were rumblings of a Rainbow reunion in the wings. Recalls Rainbow bassist Bob Daisley, "In '97 or '98, I was in America, and I was talking to Cozy on the phone to see if he was interested in this, and he said he was. I know Ritchie wanted to work with Ronnie again, and Ronnie said he would only work with Ritchie if we got back that lineup again. Whether it was going to include David Stone, I don't know, but there were definite plans, and some things had been passed across the tables at record companies about a reunion. We were all getting quite excited about it, actually, and then what happened to Cozy was just the end of it all. That was a thing that just came out of the blue and just blew everybody away, and I just think the ball stopped rolling and nothing more was said about it then."

What Bob is referring to is the untimely death of Cozy Powell at age fifty, on April 5, 1998. Powell, ever the fast car and motorcycle enthusiast, crashed his Saab 9000 on Britain's M4 highway, near Bristol. Cozy died at the hospital, of his injuries. At the time, concerning Cozy, there was talk of the above reunion, of sessions with Glenn Tipton and with Brian May and of touring with Yngwie Malmsteen, suspended due to a foot injury. Cozy was also to work with Yngwie on his next album. It is thought that Cozy's final work was for a record by Colin Blunstone of the Zombies.

Here's how Ronnie, in 1999, characterized discussions about that aborted Rainbow reunion. "Well, there's been some talk about it, and there's been some murmurings in the press from Ritchie and probably from me as well. By that I mean, when we were in Europe last—I think I told you this before—Ritchie sent me a telegram, and I sent him one back, and the same question you just asked always comes up over there in Germany. Because that's their dream, I guess, for Ritchie and I to get back together and do something. But as I told you before, he's really happy with doing his Blackmore's Night thing. And of course, now that I've found again something that makes me happy, makes me really want to do this again, there's just no sense wanting to go back to that nightmare. Maybe all of this hasn't happened, because I'm sitting here thinking, 'I don't really want to go through that again.' And maybe Ritchie is sitting there thinking, you know, 'I really don't want to go through all that again!' Because you always think, well, he was the asshole, not me; it's not my fault. But you know, that probably isn't true. I don't think he's feeling that at all. I just think he's happy with what he's doing;

he likes being in control of what he's got to deal with, and he's obviously very enamored with Candice, and so who knows what will happen? I never say no, but at this point, it certainly looks like it will be awhile."

"It came pretty close at one point, but that went away," said Ronnie also around that time, in a separate discussion. "There were just a lot of problems involved in it. There has been contact made between Ritchie's faction and my faction and Ritchie and I . . . but not for those purposes. I mean, I haven't initiated that contact because I just left that up to Ritchie. It was his band in the first place, so it was up to him to make a move, and obviously it wouldn't be that way anymore—it's a different world out there now. I think the crux of that band was always, aside from Cozy, who is not with us anymore, myself and Ritchie, from the way we just wrote and played together.

"But there is still an outside chance. As far as ever touring or doing anything like that, I would think that that would be an absolute impossibility. It's really hard; it's like doing the Sabbath reunion, and you think that everything is going to change, but nothing ever does; nothing ever changes. I don't know if at this point in my life I want to put myself through that. I'm so happy doing what I'm doing now. I'd have to really think about it. Let's face it, money is a big enticer, and I'm sure they are going to chuck some big bucks at us because they already did once. But you've got to be a bit more true to yourself than that. I would do it if I wanted to do it, if it was important. Because I think it is important to a lot of people out there. That band has become . . . I don't know what happened with it, but it became this template for music for a while, and it just seems like such an important thing to so many musicians that I think it would be a shame for them, for the ones who have never seen it, not to see it one more time. I think it would be great, but who knows? There is always a chance.

"Especially in Europe, Rainbow had an incredible effect on so many people," continues Ronnie. "I've spoken to a lot of people in my life who were stunned by the first time when they saw Rainbow and went on to become what they became, not because of Rainbow but because they wanted to be like that. I know Lars Ulrich is one of them, and Yngwie Malmsteen is another. I just know so many people who I've spoken to over there who are in bands and even bands you'd know very well, who go, 'Oh, I saw Rainbow, and for me that was ooh.' It's just amazing how that band was. We were always huge in Europe, but we weren't that massive in America, at least the Rainbow I was in at the beginning of the band. I think we were more of an underground band at that time; I don't know why.

"I remember playing in, I think it was Toronto, at Maple Leaf Gardens. They had to cut the place back pretty drastically; I think we only drew like 1,500 people or so. I thought, 'Well, this isn't going to work.' Then we started to do a little better here and there, but we were smart enough not to play massive places like that. Then twenty-five years later it has become this band that everyone saw at Maple Leaf Gardens. There must have been 150,000 people there, and I didn't see them. That's what happens. But it's been a very important thing especially from the 'duo' combination, which works so well all the time. From Mick Jagger and Keith Richards to Perry and Tyler, there are many more of them. I don't say we were on that level, Ritchie and I, but we created something very unique just as Tony and I did in Sabbath as well. You connect as two musicians who are necessary to make it happen, and it's a magical thing. Rainbow just had impact on everyone because they hadn't heard anything like that before."

On the subject of reunions in general, Ronnie was dismissive, with qualification. "The only one that makes any sense to me is Kiss because so many young people have heard from their parents, brothers, or sisters what a great show it was, and now they'll get a chance to see it. The rest of them . . . there's so many bands reuniting because they failed after the breakup of the band that they were successful with. 'Well, what's the easy way to do it? Let's not go out and find other musicians to create something new. Let's go back and do what we did before!' It's being done because it can be done. I think if you're going to do a reunion, you have to make a good album and step into the future. With Sabbath we did exactly that. I think that the album we made was certainly a lot more timely than a lot of the product I'm sure I'm going to hear these days. But one never knows; I guess they deserve a chance. My feeling is that these bands reunite because they couldn't make it in another direction."

So, with Cozy tragically gone and the Rainbow reunion put on ice once again, Dio continues, as do Ronnie's suppositions on what would become his first album for the new millennium. "I wanted this to be a concept album. It's going to be called *Magica*, and the concept is a fantasy one, which again leads me back to what I did with the first Dio albums and some of the Rainbow things I did, and certainly *Heaven and Hell* and *Mob Rules*. *Magica* is a book of spells, and whoever controls *Magica*, the book, whether good or evil, controls all the people in that world. So, it's about the fight between good and evil. At this point I haven't really gotten prepared to give the whole synopsis of the thing, because it's not all together yet. So, it's in the direction we used to be in before. Again, I mention *Holy Diver* as the point of reference. Craig writes more that way as well, but I've written most of the material until this point. Craig and I have collaborated on two pieces, and the part of the song he did on his own is absolutely magnificent, I think. Again, because I've written everything to this point, it's taken on my character. I always write the lyrics and all the melodies to what I'm singing, of course. But yes, I wrote everything, just as I wrote 'Holy Diver,' and 'Don't Talk to Strangers.' I've written four of the songs. And some orchestral parts as well."

But Ronnie was quick to suggest that *Magica* wasn't going to become too fanciful, at least on the music end of things. "I think it depends on how you view a concept album," he replies, when asked whether we would see wild swings in, for example, the lengths of the songs. "Again, not ever having done this before, and wanting to take some time with it, I don't want to be foolish with it. These things can turn out pretty strange. It will have peaks and valleys, of course: if it has to tell a story, you can't do it all in verse. So, it will tell the story in music as well. There will be a lot of shade and light made up in the music as well. So, it will be much more involved than the things we've done before, but again, retaining the character of Dio music. It will have songs as well that can be removed from the whole process and stand on their own. And it will be connected as well through narration, but not the narration you would expect. It will have narration, and it will be accompanied by a booklet as well that will tell the story. I think that's important because it's really difficult to tell the whole story just with music and very slight narration. So, I wanted to have something that people can read along to, with the idea I had for this, and then just follow along with the music. I'm trying to tell as much as I can in the music, but I want something extra."

True to word, *Magica*, when it did eventually emerge on March 21, 2000, did include an extra "booklet" that indeed offered a very detailed four panels of plot and background, filling out the *Magica* tale amply, in much the same manner that Savatage and King Diamond have been wont to do with their involved concepts, or even Genesis, back at *The Lamb Lies Down on Broadway*. Recall as well that Neil Peart augmented the lyrics on *Clockwork Angels*, Rush's final album and their only concept album.

Still, at partway through the record, Ronnie was noncommittal on song length issues. "I think we'll let them go as long as they need to go; that's the beauty of a concept album. You don't have to be thinking in terms of 'Well, here are thirteen songs; we've got to keep them concise so they can be played and listened to.' It's a concept—the whole journey is, from beginning to end."

As for radical instrumentation, "I don't think so," says Ronnie (metalhead to the end!). "I mean, I wish someone would invent a new instrument, and I'd be more than happy to use it. But we're stuck with what we are stuck with, aside from the fact that we'll use orchestration, which isn't really radical at all. But nothing new. If I hear any new toys, though, certainly I'll use them. Productionwise, I've always known the kind of band I wanted to be in, and what I wanted it to sound like.

"But having said that, I think this will be much, much different from *Angry Machines*. That one had a much more live kind of sound, right in your face; you heard everything, not a lot of guitars being doubled. But again, that's not the way the bands I've been in had been done, from Sabbath to Rainbow to Dio. And that's what I want to go back to. I think it will be a little more plush than last time. But I don't want to go over the top. I don't want it to sound like something that was done in an airplane hangar. It will be very reminiscent of earlier Dio. I've been thinking about this for a couple of years now. It's all new, but of course, there are some riffs I have, because I simply go down to the studio and blaze away on riffs all day, so I have tons of them. And then one day I went down and played an orchestral part on the keyboard and came up with some chords that I really, really loved; it was 'Magica Theme.' I mean, there it was right in front of me. So, I had to carry on from there."

When asked if, as occurs in some concept albums, melodies or themes such as this one would recur through the record, Ronnie replied that "well, that theme will recur, yes. It will begin the entire piece in a really unusual way, all instrumental. What I probably will do is write a song for it as well, perhaps. The narration is recurring; not an awful lot, but it's also very different. It's not Orson Welles or CNN. I mean I'd love to have a voice like that to do that, but it's just been done so much before. This can almost be called a concept lite or something like that. But because in order for it to be a truly masterful piece of work, I think you just need so much time to do that. And I just don't have that kind of time. With recording commitments, these things have to be done at a certain time. That's why I'm thinking concept lite; it just feels like this is something I should have written over the space of two years, but I couldn't because we're a playing band, and that's where I get my joy anyway. And of course, the rest of the time we have to record. So, it's like, here's six months to write, and in that time, there's always other things that come up. So, I'd like this to be thought of as concept lite, although I don't want that to sound dietary or something [laughs]."

Ronnie offers a glimpse into his recording methodology, circa the late 1990s. "I would never actually make the albums in my home studio. I might if I had a studio here, but I would never put a permanent studio in my home. You'd never get out of the house if you do that. I'm not getting out of the house as it is now! I mean, I have to be dragged out of the house in order to get away from it, because Craig comes over every day and we work for about twelve hours every day. At the end of the night, like 1:30 in the morning, I remember what I have to do the next day, which is take my dog out for a walk. If he doesn't have a walk, he'll kill me. He's always awake at 7:00 a.m. looking at me, going, 'Hey, time for that walk.' So, we're off. And then once I'm up, I'm up; I can't go back to sleep again.

"And by that time, Craig is back over and we do it again. So, I don't have much chance to get out of here, and therefore I wouldn't have a studio at home. Plus, there's the fact that I like to go to other places to demo things, because you create a completely different atmosphere in another place. So that's why when you choose a recording studio, you pick something that you look forward to going to. And that's not my home. So we'll do the record, I'm sure, where we did the last one, with the same engineer, a guy named Wyn Davis, at a place called Total Access, which is in Redondo Beach, A great engineer, great musician, great guy, great studio, and, like I say, the studio is in Redondo Beach, to give you a hint of how nice it is down there."

I asked Ronnie how layered or finished he makes his demos. "That's what we're doing right now. Although Simon is here, we haven't gone into proper rehearsals yet. So yes, the riff will be there, but rather than record a full kit, we'll put a drum machine on it for now. I've got a great drum machine with a good rock sound, so it fits the bill. And when we go to do it live, of course we'll have rehearsed it for a month or so, so we'll be very able to go into the studio and not have to waste a lot of time, and we'll just feel free with the material and not have to worry about what's coming next."

About a month and a half after this interview, Jimmy spoke further of his tentative steps back into the Dio band. "I'm working with Ronnie, but I've done another project in the meantime called The Key, and that's just me singing and playing and writing and sort of producing. But I haven't had that released, and I'm still hoping I can get it out; I've worked on that for the last eighteen months, and the guitar on some of it is by Tracy G. With Ronnie, I haven't actually started. We're just getting together and feeling each other out, because we haven't seen each other in quite a long time. But it sounds really good."

Answering whether writing for *Magica* would be part of his duties, Jimmy replied, "Hopefully it will, yeah. I mean, I think I was pretty successful with what I did with Ronnie in the past. I'd like to be involved with the writing, but right now, because I'm just getting back into playing full time, I'm quite happy to do whatever." Quite happy indeed, since the last we saw of Jimmy was the WWIII album with Tracy G and Mandy Lion. "Yes, and after that I kind of fell foul to the demon drugs, and that was kind of like a full-time lifestyle situation. Things weren't going very good for me, so I kind of slipped and slipped and slipped and about a year ago I kind of decided that if I was going to do anything with myself, I'd better change my direction. So, I checked myself into a rehab and cleaned up. So, I've kind of come back from the dead almost. I was basically into almost everything, but my drug of choice was heroin."

Jimmy elaborates on his sidling movements back into the Dio camp, adding a few reminiscences of his early pre-Rainbow days. "I've talked with him. I met with Wendy before they went to Europe. They actually wanted me to do that, the seven or eight shows they did in Europe, the live thing. But unfortunately, I'm kind of applying for a green card here at the moment. I'm from Scotland originally, and I lived in Canada for a while too. My parents still live in Canada; they're from Vernon, British Columbia. When I lived in Canada for a while, I started playing. That's where I actually got my feet wet, and I packed up all my gear in the back of my truck, my bass and my amp, and headed to Vancouver and put a band together and started playing professionally. It didn't work out too well there because Bruce Allen was there, and he didn't like my band too much, so I went back to England after that. This was in the early '70s. I actually immigrated to Canada." Then, of course, came Rainbow, with the whole relationship with Ronnie beginning on the *Rising* album.

Back to the modern day, Dio's *Magica* album, when finally completed, was indeed quite different from the albums of the Tracy G era, although in one large respect it wasn't—the brunt of the album was still quite slow, dark, and huge of bottom end. Still, the record is cleaner, as Ronnie says, more plush, tighter, layered. From the elegant "Magica Theme" and into the first song proper, "Lord of the Last Day," keyboard washes support huge chords and tasteful, bluesy soloing from Goldy. At the time, and still years later, the album's most celebrated track is "Fever Dreams," a sort of "Man on the Silver Mountain" for the new millennium. Its riffs are classic, trundling, rhythmic, signature Dio all the way.

"Turn to Stone" picks up the pace a bit, but the sparse, angular, grayish mood of the album persists, in large part due to Simon Wright's disciplined, straightforward drumming. "Feed My Head" is another track with huge spaces and pregnant pauses, with "Eriel" addressing a trademark Dio gallop, similar to that of "Fever Dreams." "Challis" is a rock 'n' rollsy respite from the sustained gloom, a gloom that returns in spades for the heartfelt, emotional ballad "As Long as It's Not about Love."

Next up is "Losing My Insanity," which again finds the band at a levelheaded heavy metal lope, Goldy throwing in some of his best licks of the record. "Otherworld" again reinforces the slow, Sabbatherian *Lock Up the Wolves* vibe of the record. Closing out the album are reprises of the *Magica* theme and indeed the "Lord of the Last Day" theme, followed, surprisingly, by Ronnie reading, over the course of nearly twenty minutes, the entire narrative portion of the *Magica* tale, with eerie keyboards as backdrop.

"There is a planet called Blessing," begins Ronnie, offering a synopsis of the Magica concept. "And this planet died eons ago and is now just an ice-covered ball. An alien spacecraft comes into their sector and discovers a beacon coming from inside the planet. They follow it, and they discover the story of the *Book of Magica*. The aliens are connected to the entire album. Occasionally they'll talk. There's a song on the album called 'As Long as It's Not about Love,' which they're on, but the song is between the two protagonists, Eriel, who has a song, and Annica. Early on in their lives, she was betrothed to him, and he turned away because he had to deal with the *Book of Magica*. There's a high executioner; his name is Shadowcast. His job throughout the whole thing is to try to defeat the people who hold the *Book of Magica*; Eriel is the high priest of the *Book of Magica*. Shadowcast eventually conquers Eriel and all the people of Blessing and destroys the *Book of Magica*.

"It's then that the aliens realize, after reading the story, that they feel this is a story that could change their way of life. This thing is not a thing; it's a collective, and they don't want the collective to be infected. At the end of it, they say 'Infection, infection. Delete, delete,' and it gets really slow. At the end of the story, back comes the song 'Lord of the Last Day.' Because at the end of the story, evil is defeated, except for Shadowcast, who comes in at the end with a little reprieve, to show you that evil is still happening."

Moving to the music and the assembly of the album, Ronnie figures that "since those songs were written, I'd like to think that myself and Craig Goldy, who wrote this entire album with me, have progressed to a point where we can do that, where the song won't be 'Strange Highways' and won't be 'Man on the Silver Mountain,' but it may suggest that to them, and it'll go to places where those songs have never gone before. So that wasn't a problem for me. I did want this album to be the kind of music that Dio fans come to expect. We've always been known, especially myself, for writing in fantasy matters, and for writing big stories within stories. I felt that *Angry Machines* was a little confusing to the people who had followed us. Although they stuck by us, it was confusing to them. It had just gone into a totally different direction. I wanted to get back to what I fell was important to this band. After all, you have to come to the realization that at some point you are wrong, and I was. I just think I went a little bit over the top with that, in a direction that wasn't really compatible with what I've done before. *Magica* is what I wanted it to be—remembrance of music that I played for such a long period of time, and that people have liked a lot."

At the Forum in London, UK, May 7, 2000. That's Larry "Bones" Dennison, briefly the band's bassist, along with Ronnie. © *Steve Olley*

"Since Ronnie's the visionary of the band, I know that he wanted to do this for a long time," begins Craig Goldy, looking at the *Magica* project in totality. "I remember after *Dream Evil*, we were having dinner and we talked about doing a concept album back then. I guess he waited until he thought the timing was right. Being the way that the shift of the tide in the music industry is so volatile, it's hard for some people to accept anybody from the '70s or '80s, let alone when they do something that's somewhat outside the norm of what they're used to hearing from that artist. And then he had experimented and done some things he hadn't done before, and it didn't seem like it was that well accepted. The concept idea was so close to his heart, he wanted to wait until he thought the timing was right."

"This is an album about people who are good and evil," said Ronnie, summarizing. "The same story that everybody tells, but different characters and a different slant. I wrote the story first with the idea of *Magica* and what it would be, and how it would revolve around the book. As I wrote the first four songs, it led me to where I wanted to go, and Craig came in and we started writing together, and things started to meld. Each day I would write another paragraph or two to the story with each song that came along. A song would be done about a character in the story. I finished the story just before the last song. This way the music led the story. I thought it was going to be a two-CD set, but it didn't end up that long; there was no need for it. It finished properly as one. I think it can be broken up into the individual things that people like. The way that this album is constructed was not timely. It's like a *Reader's Digest* album. I didn't have the luxury of having two years to play with it. It's not a full-blown operatic sort of thing, and I don't want people to treat it that way. It's a concept album because I needed a reason to do this again. Without it being a concept album, I would have just written nine or ten songs that would have been just that—songs. I enjoy creating a story; this really works for me. But they can still be taken out as a single song and still be good; there's just more to it."

Ronnie stated his motivations for the record this way in conversation with Dmitry Epstein: "I felt that a few albums we did before *Magica* were confusing musically, and wanted to restate our objective by doing a complete fantasy project to reconnect with that portion of our appeal, to ourselves and Dio fans. Fantasy has they always been a great part of Dio music and allows me as a story writer to reflect on this world, by creating another with most of the same problems."

"It's something I've been wanting to do for a long time but nothing that I ever thought about doing" is the way Ronnie framed it, speaking with *MetalRules*. "None of the bits of this particular piece had been inherited from any past thoughts that I've had at all, because the way I write is I write for the moment, I write for the project. Now I'm writing a concept piece and I have to start at the beginning, and it started with the title *Magica*, and it went from there. I just started to write a fantasy story about *Magica*. What was *Magica* going to be? Well, I made it a book and so on and so forth, and away it goes. Then I wrote the songs and musically wrote it around the story. It's really easy to do. It's the easiest album that I've ever written because it led me. Every time I had to turn around and write something musically or lyrically, it was exactly where I needed to go. It was something I've wanted to do, but again, a new process and one I couldn't have done without Craig."

Mused Ronnie on the future, "I know what I'll do next time: a lot more straightforward album. Just more song oriented, not a concept of any kind. I think that's probably what's expected, but we're going to do something more straightforward. Then after that, probably the next two albums will be parts 2 and 3 of *Magica*, because I want to make it a trilogy."

"When we started out, he had most of four songs already written," confirms Craig, on Ronnie's description of the record's origins. "'Magica Theme,' 'Lord of the Last Day,' 'Fever Dreams,' and portions of 'Feed My Head' were already done on tape. I had a few ideas on tape as well. When I heard what he had done, I was like, 'Wow!' I really liked them, so we pretty much left them alone rather than mess with them too much. It's easy to change things too much, usually with good intent, but it's not always what's best for the song. In that spirit, there wasn't any inherent publishing struggle. A lot of bands do that. They don't say it, but it happens. Everyone wants their input to get their name on the songs so they can get that royalty check. So many people will keep pouring out ideas to try and convince everyone else that their idea is better, so can ultimately get that check. We've never had that kind of relationship. We just wrote the music according to what we liked and what worked best for the album.

Ronnie and Craig at the Rock City in Nottingham, UK, May 8, 2000. © *Steve Olley*

"Ronnie had a sort of synopsis of the story when we started," continues Craig, "but most of it was written as we went, while we created the album. We'd spend all day writing the music, and as we developed lyrics and melody lines and chord progressions, the music gave way to more of the story. Sometimes we'd have trouble with a song we were working on, so Ronnie would sit down and work on the story for a while, and eventually it would inspire something that he'd bring back to the songs, so they really grew from each other, the songs and the story helping to create the other. It was so cool when I'd come into the studio in the morning, and Ronnie would be there at his computer and have some more of the story done. After a while I had all this paper! Pieces of paper with a few paragraphs here, half a page there, and eventually I had this huge pile of fragments of the story. We really did write it as we worked, because he had an idea and portions of songs, but he didn't know exactly what ultimate twists and turns he wanted, so we just dove in and did it as we went.

Rock City in Nottingham, UK, May 8, 2000. © *Steve Olley*

"Ronnie's musical qualities complement his singing qualities," adds Craig, further with respect to the writing process. "It's really an asset because as a musician he writes songs that are vocal friendly. When you work with a guy like that, you also learn to write songs that are vocal friendly. A lot of guitar players write songs that are guitar friendly so they can showcase what they do. But they're not always vocal friendly. As a musician, he can play guitar, bass, and keys and he programs a drum machine. So, there's a lot of things he does, and we can understand each other on that level. He knows music theory and chord progressions, so he can tell me, 'No, why don't you do a B flat inside that D? I know it's gonna make it sound weird, but let's try it that way.' And more often than not, it works. Unlike a singer who goes like, 'We need a new chord here!' That's the trouble. A lot of people don't understand the concept of melody first, then lyrics. You'll find these singers who come in with pages of lyrics and then try to cram those words into the structure of a chord progression and try to use the melody to fit their lyrics, and a lot of times that doesn't work well at all. With Ronnie, that's never the case because he understands the importance of melody first, lyrics second. He's writing with at least an idea of the melody and chords that are intended for those lyrics. It's a harder job, but that's what it takes to write a great song.

"So many times when we're in the studio, one of us is running the boards while the other is playing, and we learn a lot from each other that way. It helps me a lot because

I can take what I learn and apply it to other projects and other people I work with. On the album, Ronnie and I play all the keys, mainly for the sake of expediency. Keyboard players have a tendency to be constantly tweaking and fine-tuning and changing the sounds, and they can eat up a lot of studio time! Not to say that guitar players don't have their quirks too! [laughs]. Ronnie and I just play what we think is right, and if it sounds good, we keep it. We've never felt the need to bring in a specialist to do what we've always been able to accomplish ourselves."

All told, *Magica* turned out to be a polarizing album in the Dio camp, with many appreciative of the ambitious concept and its similarly mystical and foreboding backing track, and many finding the record stiff, too slow, even a bit too eager to embrace the fantasy themes with which Dio himself has always had a bit of a love/hate relationship. The addition of the narration somewhat cloys as well, detracting from the experience, even though one should be able to safely shunt it aside as a bonus track. Whether the sci-fi tale Ronnie is sitting there reading is up to the man's highly allegorical and poetic standards is debatable as well. Still, for this writer, it is the album's laborious and blocky critical mass at the music end that causes fatigue. Coupled with the dark nature of the tale, I find listening to *Magica*, well . . . depressing.

Ronnie pins part of the album's opacity and heft on Craig Goldy's guitar style. "I think so; I think you'd have to definitely say that. Craig's sound has thickened and broadened out a lot since the *Dream Evil* days; he plays slightly differently, I find. I think he knows what it's supposed to sound like for Dio. I think he knew that when he came into the band the first time, and he knew what I wanted this time; it was just there. We've never had a problem. It was just one of these magical things where we just sat down and wrote and played like twelve hours a day and didn't know what time it was. I really haven't experienced that for a really long, long, long time. In fact, maybe never. It's a just a special relationship that we've built up musically and personally too, because we're good friends and we've known each other for so long. But without him, I could have never written *Magica*—no way."

Out on the press trail for the album, Ronnie reiterated some of the intentions from the above "work in progress" interview with the writer, illustrating a contrast, or at least the tweakings, between the planned charting of *Magica* and the final outcome.

"I wanted to do it because we needed to get back to the space we were in before, and that is writing more fantasy-oriented material. I think that is one of the things we are known for. We could do bigger and more-important-sounding songs; that is another thing that we have been known for. This was an opportunity to do so because there was a story. I'd written a story that was a fantasy, so therefore this album had to be a fantasy piece. I didn't want it to seem that we had to go back and do this type of music again because the other stuff wasn't making it and all that crap. I wanted there to be a reason. I didn't want it to seem like we had to go back to our roots, so to speak. There was a reason to it because there was a story. I wanted to write a fantasy-based piece because for the last five years or so, everyone said, 'I wish you would write some stuff like you did before.'

"But I wanted there to be a reason, so I wrote the story of *Magica* first and then wrote the songs around the story itself. That gave me a reason to do it without thinking that I gave up and had to go back and be what I was before. I also narrated the story at the very end of all the music. It took us about five weeks to write it. Goldy and I wrote it all. It took us about five weeks to record it; we were very prepared. We took some pains to be ready. We wrote it at my home and then recorded it in the studio. It is the first concept thing that we have ever done, and hopefully it will lead to two more. It won't be the next album, but it will be the one after that. I won't even think about doing anything with *Magica* until after another album."

"*Magica* indeed was a highlight for both Ronnie, me, and the band Dio," Craig explained to Jeb Wright, looking back after the end of the band and Ronnie's death. "Ronnie had always wanted to do a concept album, clear back to right after the *Dream Evil* album. So, when I got the call to rejoin Dio, it came shortly after another vision I had of me being back in the band. That too was very special. I had just finished an album where each song was connected to each other like the Pink Floyd album *Dark Side of the Moon* [this was probably 13th Floor; no material ever emerged]. The album began with sound effects, and then each song faded out and into what I called 'sound effect scenarios' that then faded into the next song.

"Meanwhile, Ronnie was already working on the first couple of songs for *Magica* and had been writing the story that went along with what was to be a trilogy. Since Ronnie and I had remained friends ever since 1983, we were able to just pick up where we left off as a team. But this time, I had learned so much leading up to that point. Ronnie actually missed working with me. He and I had the very same work ethic and were also quite willing to use unorthodox methods to get the sounds that we wanted, regardless if it was 'the right way' to do things by the book. We often challenged each other not even knowing it really, 'cause the final outcome was the boss this time and not just one person.

"He was such a hard worker," reflects Craig. "He could play guitar, keyboards, and bass; program the drum machine; and run the recording software on the computer by this time. I was much quicker than he was at programming the drum machine and running the computer, so I told him, 'Why don't you let me do all the grunt work? That way you can use that amazing mind of yours to its fullest extent by not being lumbered with drum machines and computers. You be more of the executive producer, so while we work, your mind has a chance to flow unencumbered. When you hear something that might otherwise have gone unnoticed while you were busy programming the drum machine and running the computer, you can stop me right as the inspiration hits you.' He said, 'Okay Goldy, let's give that a try.' And it worked out quite nicely.

"He and I would always record the entire album at his home studio before we ever stepped foot into those expensive recording studios to record the album for real. This gave us a chance to know what we wanted long before we started in the actual recording studio. After we recorded the entire album, we would sit together and make extensive notes for when we would enter the professional studio. When I say 'extensive,' I mean extensive! As we recorded, he and I would often trade places doing the keyboards and bass. As we did the keyboards, we would write down which sound, from which patch, from which bank that particular sound came from, so that we could just go straight to it when it came time to record for real.

"We did the same thing for his vocals. We would write down if he doubled the lead vocal in certain sections, added a harmony above or below, if he doubled that harmony and what type of harmony/harmonies they were—a third above, a third below, and so forth. Once we got into the actual recording studio, my notebook was quite full. I was the only one invited into the console room while he did his vocals. Usually no one was ever allowed to be present while he did his vocals. Ronnie would ask me, 'Okay, Goldy, what did we do here?' I would look at my notes and tell him. He would often ask, 'Are you sure about this, Goldy?' I would confirm our notations. That is when he gave me the newest nickname, 'the Great Goldini,' which later became 'Goldini'! So, then it was 'Goldini, what did we do here?'

"He and I did all of the keyboards for that album. We did the 'sound effect scenarios,' the aliens and the music beneath the story. It was quite an undertaking to have this album all run together like *The Dark Side of the Moon*, but we did it! Ronnie was very proud of this album, and I don't blame him. I saw how he labored on his lyrics and the story lyrically and songwritingly speaking. Since the law was 'melody first and lyrics second,' this makes it very difficult to create lyrics that will pierce your soul like his did.

"As I mentioned before, a song is either a story you are telling or a conversation you are having with the listener within a musical environment. Since the melody dictates how many syllables you have for your lyrics, this can be quite challenging.

"But I saw how he labored hour after hour, day by day, to get his lyrics the way he wanted them. And let's not forget, you still have to rhyme, which makes the task just that more challenging. He was the master of this. I got to see and hear his method, and I've gotta tell you, it's a difficult one. I have been able to utilize what I have learned from just that alone. The internet has changed things drastically, but the method that is involved in writing music that reaches people's hearts in such a way, that's due to the impact that music has upon them, that they are unwilling to go without that music. Well, that process is still the same, and it always will be until the day that we become cyborgs! Ronnie was gracious enough to show me his method.

"Also, he and Wendy would often pull back the curtain and show me what was really behind there," continues Craig. "They often brought me along with them as they met with record company executives. No one else was invited to come along but me. Back when I was in Rough Cutt, Wendy was a paralegal, so she showed me how to read contracts. Now I can negotiate my own contracts because of her. So, this time, for me, being back in the band was just so amazing and another dream come true. As Ronnie and Wendy put it, '*Magica* put Dio back on the map after previous failing album sales.' That too was a very special part of music history for me to be a part of it. In one interview Ronnie gave about this album, the interviewer went on and on about how much he loved this album called *Magica*, and Ronnie was, once again, so gracious as to say, 'Well, I couldn't have done this album without Craig Goldy!' That was very special when I saw and heard that interview. I love that song 'Lord of the Last Day.' There are some very cool elements in that song that, to this day, I still get chills when I hear it. I just don't listen to that stuff as much as I did before because it's just too damn emotional and sad for me, even after nearly seven years, to listen to. I still listen to Rainbow and his days

Above and opposite: Dio on the *Magica* tour at the House of Blues in Chicago, Illinois, November 29, 2000. Support on the night came from Doro Pesch and Yngwie Malmsteen, who did many US dates with Ronnie and the boys. © *Greg Olma*

with Sabbath, but often the albums he and I did together are the most difficult to listen to right now—still."

As for what Simon Wright thought of the experience . . . "All the albums have their moments, but *Magica* really sticks out for me. It was a really well-thought-out album, and it was a real pleasure to do. It had a lot of depth to it; a lot of thought went behind it. It was quite gratifying to finish it and listen to this epic. Songs ran into other songs, long songs are in there, and I think it turned out fine, and that was something I was quite proud of. But *Master of the Moon* was a cool album too, and so was *Killing the Dragon* [laughs], which was a bit more straight ahead and not quite as dark as, say, *Master of the Moon* was, a little bit more rock 'n' rollsy, yeah. It's funny how albums turn out. For one reason or another, it's what you're feeling at the time or writing at the time.

"But *Magica*, well, since I've been in the band, we've used Wyn Davis, and a studio down in Redondo Beach, California, called Total Access. We would talk first when we first met up, and we would tweak little things, but they were all done basically the same way, with backing tracks first. He had a really cool drum room in the back there, and we always seemed to get a really . . . what's the word, true live sound, which I always thought was the best way to go, really. Nothing too sampled. But yeah, with *Magica*, Ronnie would present it in written form, tell us the story, and there was just always surprise after surprise. There was a lot more to the story than we got to deal with, and that's why there were plans for *Magica II* and *Magica III*. You mention the slow tempos, but I never really saw that. There were a lot of slow songs, but Ronnie always tried to get the fast ones on there too."

Once the band hit the road, Ronnie really let the crowd have a huge taste of the new album. "We play almost all of *Magica* live; it's been great. We do a piece that is fifty-five minutes long. That's not all we do, of course. We start the first half hour of the show with things that people have grown up with and that they want to hear from *Holy Diver* etc. Then, we do all of *Magica*. After fifty-five minutes, people are going, 'What was that?!' It's such a good album. We have done it song by song. There are connector pieces in it, of course. I think you get more enjoyment listening to it off the CD. Each song does stand up by itself; that makes it acceptable. When it's all over, I think most people are stunned. They go, 'What was that?!' Then they go, 'Yeah!' Then we do another forty minutes of things that people want to hear from us. We drop in 'Heaven and Hell' or 'Man on the Silver Mountain'; it's a great show. It's almost two hours long, and there are twenty-three songs that we do. It has been accepted very well, and I could not be happier. All the people who have the record and come up with it to be signed all say it's a great record. So, I think that we did the right thing."

Above and opposite: more shots from Chicago. © *Greg Olma*

"We did *Magica* live for a long time after it came out, because it was such an epic," recalls touring keyboardist Scott Warren. "When I first joined Dio, Ronnie had mentioned to me that he wanted to do something like that. He didn't call it *Magica* because it wasn't written, but probably the first day we ever sat down and talked, he was encouraging me to stick around in Dio because he had this epic that he wanted to write that involved a lot of keyboards. So, when we took *Magica* on the road, it was a lot of very creative and very demanding parts, demanding in the sense that there were a lot of layers of keyboards going on, more than just one part at a time. There were a lot of different sound effects and things, and I was doing all of that live, not using tape or anything else—none of it was to tape. That's one thing—if you wanted to ask me what I prided myself on—was managing to accomplish a lot of different parts at one time, for live, whereas a lot of other bands or artists might use tape, or ADH or something like that. So, when it came to *Magica*, it was a lot of fun, because there was a lot more involvement of wall-to-wall keyboards and orchestrations and things like that. So that one sticks out to me a lot more than the others. But I really enjoyed revisiting a lot of the Rainbow stuff. Whenever we've been able to incorporate any of that stuff into the set, it's always been a pleasure for me."

Touring just before the release of *Magica*, specifically in November 1999, saw bassist Chuck Garric helping out (even if Jimmy was essentially "in the band" at this point). Chuck also filled in for the early non-US dates in place of Bain after the album's issue as well, in May and June 2000, with Jimmy taking over all subsequent dates. The November dates were dubbed the Monsters of the Millennium tour, with Dio, Motörhead, Lion's Share, and then Manowar as headliner, playing extensively through Scandinavia to crowds averaging in the four thousand range. Of note, Dio were also a mainstay of Europe's celebrated festival season, in June 1999, playing Austria, the Netherlands, Sweden, and Germany, highlights being Bang Your Head and Sweden Rock.

For the *Magica* tour proper, Dio picked up the Unband for March and April 2000 dates throughout America. May and June saw the band in Europe with a variety of

support acts, after which America was assaulted again, with Doro Pesch and Yngwie Malmsteen supporting through the end of the year. February and March 2001 saw Dio teamed with Armored Saint and Lynch Mob, after which a six-date South America sojourn was completed. In late April, Dio stormed Scandinavia with Alice Cooper and Ratt, after which it was Alice, Dio, and stoner rockers Orange Goblin in the UK to close out a long, long batch of shows for this quintessential working band.

Peripheral but quite commendable to Dio during the *Magica* era was Ronnie's work with the Children of the Night charity. "It's about twenty years old," said Ronnie at the time, "and we've been involved for about ten years. We've been able to build a shelter for them in Los Angeles, a wonderful facility, with a lot of wonderful people contributing too. Among them are Ozzy Osbourne, Richard Marx—just a lot of people who care. It's run by the woman who founded it, named Dr. Lois Lee, who is now a psychiatrist or psychologist.

"She is one of the most incredible people I know," continues Dio. "She is one of my heroes. She began this because she was concerned about all the young runaway kids who would come to Los Angeles and be picked up at the bus stop by the pimp and shucked into prostitution, AIDS, or drugs and drug sales and die by the time they were fourteen or fifteen years old. She physically went out to take some of these kids off the street. She has been put in the hospital before with a broken nose, broken arms, and broken legs from taking these kids away from pimps. She started the organization, and ten years later I got involved in it. At the beginning, she took these kids into her own home. A lot of these kids are sexually abused and run away. They are twelve to fourteen years old. We've been able to build a shelter for them already with twenty-four beds and a school; they have a lot of support. The difference between this organization and the government organizations is that if the government finds a runaway child, then by law the child has to be sent back to where they came from. This is where it all began anyway—they were sent back to the exact same dysfunctional attitude he or she came from. That's real clever! Because Children of the Night is a private organization and privately funded, the kids can stay at the shelter until they are eighteen years of age. While they live there, they are prepared for the type of jobs that they want to do. They are put in the right direction. Unfortunately, a lot them have AIDS, so it's to help them ease the remaining part of their lives."

While doing press for *Magica*, Ronnie spoke of future plans for Children of the Night. "We are going to do a song that we have already written—Craig and I—that will have about six singers and six guitar players on it. I don't want all of the same people this time. Yngwie wants to do it and he did on the last one, so there's that possibility. As far as other guitar players go, I think Vivian will contribute, so that would be great. Bruce Dickinson is going to sing on it. We haven't really finalized all the people yet because it's a matter of time and when we can do it. With all the touring and other albums arriving, it will probably happen when we come back from doing this album. I'm sure that's when we're going to have to fit everything in. We are also going to do an album with unreleased tracks that have been given to us by other bands from around the world. We are also going to rerelease the *Hear 'n Aid* thing on CD at the same time, because it's only ever been available on CD in Japan."

On October 3, 2000, Warner/Rhino issued a compilation called *The Very Beast of Dio*, which quite impressively managed to go gold in the US (up into March 2009), demonstrating the strength of catalog. The author was commissioned to write the liner notes for the album, with Wendy Dio very graciously sending a deluxe RIAA gold award out here to Toronto, as a thank-you for providing the liner essay.

Although Ronnie's death put an end to the imagined *Magica* trilogy, the original album lived on to see a couple of reissues. The 2013 version moved "Magica Story" (now called "The Magica Story") to a second disc, with instrumental Japanese bonus track "Annica" and new song "Electra" added. There were also five live performances of *Magica* songs. A 2019 reissue included "Electra" but omitted "Annica," while featuring on the second disc nine *Magica* songs performed live on March 31, 2001, in Buenos Aires, Argentina.

Signed *Magica* and *The Very Beast of Dio*. *Martin Popoff archive*

PRESENTED TO
MARTIN POPOFF
TO COMMEMORATE RIAA CERTIFIED
SALES OF MORE THAN
500,000 COPIES OF THE
WARNER BROS. / RHINO
COMPACT DISC
"THE VERY BEAST OF DIO"

Martin Popoff archive

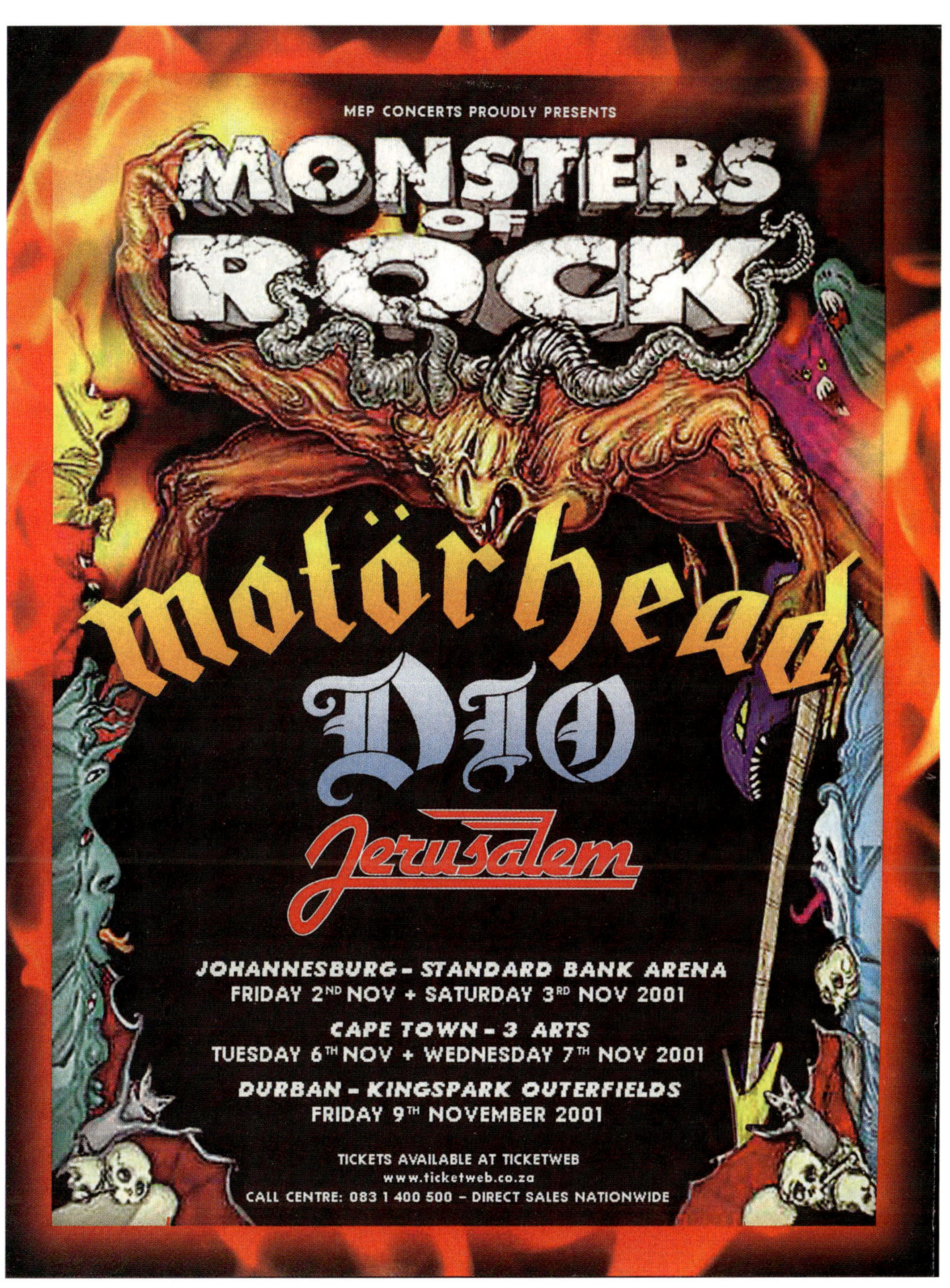

Dio and Motörhead together in South Africa!

CHAPTER 12

"There was a word that he used sometimes, called jolly. If something was too jolly, it was not good."

KILLING THE DRAGON

Whether it was the response from the fans, who had now endured summarily fifteen years of huge, thick, Black Sabbath *Tyr*-like albums from Ronnie, or whether it was some internal drive within Ronnie to rock swiftly once again, there was no question that *Killing the Dragon* was a different, livelier Dio than the grumpy band from records recently previous. And looking back, it is indeed testimony at least to the man's unswerving vision that no fewer than five records—four with Dio and one with Sabbath—had this boxy, blocky, doom-laden vibe in common. And all of this with wildly different lineups, including three different guitarists among them.

Killing the Dragon, as we shall see, brings into focus yet another guitarist, one Doug Aldrich—formerly with Lion, Bad Moon Rising, and Burning Rain—who would last but one album as part of the fold before moving on to Whitesnake and then the Dead Daisies. But in reality, *Killing the Dragon* turned out to be a record that is a mix of Doug and Craig Goldy, with Craig only writing for the project. Indeed, Craig's writing on *Killing the Dragon* graphically underscores the man's chameleonlike qualities, with "Goldini" at this point in the saga having been part of three very different records with Ronnie: *Dream Evil*, *Magica*, and the current barnstormer.

Ronnie sets the table, with a treatise on the album's cheeky title; cheeky because he knows he's going to get pasted to the wall with more simplistic accusations with respect to his dungeons-and-dragons milieu. "*Killing the Dragon* is really a metaphor for the dragon being government, an evil government leader or dictator, etc., all the negative things people have to go through as far as dealing with their leadership. So, there are references in this song, for instance, i.e., a dragon taking a child—that's what dragons always do. But again, it's just a metaphor for an evil tyrant of some kind. There are parts about a lord that is so mean that he gives ice to the cold people. And the last reference touches upon technology, small gods with electrical hearts, things like that. So, it's about what happens when evil rears its ugly head—eventually, people revolt and say we've had enough of this. Eventually, people will rebel against things that are unjust to them.

"I think most notably it's just song, song, song, song," continues Ronnie, on the album's buoyant joie de vivre. "It's not connected in any way. That of course is what made *Magica* what it was, the connection of the story. There is no story on this album; it's just songs we wanted to write. I think the other difference is that the songs are a lot faster, not nearly so many dark and doomy pieces. That's the main difference, that it's an album, straight out—have a listen."

Summing up the recent career trajectory, Ronnie figured that "*Angry Machines* was an album that did not make me happy. I felt it was necessary to attack my career from the standpoint of what we were and what people expected from us. *Magica* was a complete fantasy piece, and *Killing the Dragon* is a lot like *Holy Diver* and *Last in Line*. I planned it that way. With those two albums we could portray both sides of what the band is supposed to be.

"Eight of the songs we attempted to write with Craig," notes Ronnie, with respect to the behind-the-scenes personnel shuffles. "Craig's writing credit is, I think, on three of the eight that we wrote first. The two we wrote last are 'Along Comes a Spider' and 'Scream.' So, of the other eight, three of those songs—'Throw Away Children,' 'Push,' and 'Rock and Roll' [irritatingly, spelled this way in the lyrics and 'Rock & Roll' on the back of the CD, with neither being the most usual; i.e.; rock 'n' roll!] are the ones that Craig was involved in. So, the other five were Jimmy and myself, and the other three were Jimmy, myself, and our new guitar player, Doug."

Ah yes, Jimmy Bain. Even though the celebrated and capable songwriter was credited as part of *Magica*, writing credits on that album went half to Ronnie and Craig, half to Ronnie alone—not much coming in from Jimmy. Was it nice to have Jimmy back in the fold writing? Was Bain being prolific this time around?

"Well, I think with us doing five of those tracks together, he must be pretty damn prolific," notes Ronnie. "Yeah, he's been great. We were forced to do this. We wanted to write the way we wrote last time and the way we've always written, and that's with a guitar player as well. I mean, you really need that connection. Neither Jimmy nor I are very good guitar players, but we're good enough to write riffs, and we've written songs obviously. But it makes it so much easier when you've got a guy who really has his chops together. 'Oh no, play this chord, how about an F minor? G minor 7th?' You know, it's harder for us, but we've been doing this so long, we have good musical ability anyway. But Jimmy has been great. It's just like we'd done when we were together before. Nothing's changed at all. He has the same methods and so do I. It's been really easy.

"And he's been clean and sober for four years now," adds Ronnie, clearly proud of the recovery of a dear friend, when asked about Jimmy's chosen work in the real world while away from music—life as a courier. "Oh, no [laughs]; that's over with. That's something Jimmy was doing before he got into this band. He was trying to deal with his life, and that meant feeding himself, and he wasn't doing a lot musically. But once he got back into the band, he did what Jimmy always does, and that's music. And that was very important to Jimmy and important to me as well, that Jimmy had a family now again to deal with. But you need support. Jimmy is a strong person, and he's dealt with it when he dealt with it. You know, 'I'm coming this close to dying; nah, I don't think I want to do that.' It took him some time to brighten up and be the smart man that he is, and that's why he's been clean and sober for so long and that's why he'll remain that way. He's just got a great attitude on life, and he thanks God every day, or thanks someone every day—I wouldn't propose to tell his religious pronunciations—but he certainly thanks someone every day to be lucky enough to beat this. But Jimmy's great. He's the best.

"Craig was going through his blue period," sighs Ronnie, delving into the painful subject of Craig's ouster from the band. "He's working for a limousine company, I believe. I don't know what his involvement is with it. I just know his involvement wasn't with us. He got married, and his wife had two kids already and then she became pregnant, and they've had another one. His responsibilities meant—and we could see it in the writing process—that his mind was in a lot of different places. And most of the time, it wasn't where we were at. We could see it was going to be difficult. But because *Magica* was fun to write and because it worked so well, I thought, let's keep this together. Unfortunately, the circumstances weren't the same. Before, he was totally immersed in it, and now his little toe was just testing the water. So, it made it horribly difficult for us. The easiest thing for me to say is that Craig didn't play very much or very well on what we were doing, and Doug sure as hell did.

"But I want to preface it with that," qualifies Ronnie. "I don't want to demean Craig's talent. He's a very talented guy. He's a really, really excellent guitar player. Now, in comparing the two, I would say that Doug is a real guitar player. I mean, this guy lives and breathes guitar—this is what he's always done—coupled with a really mature attitude about what he's doing. No incredibly huge opinions of himself and just so capable. I mean, just the most capable guitar player I think I've ever played with. The guy is really something special. And you know, again, it's one of those things you say in an interview, but I think the proof is in the pudding. Anyone who listens to the guy playing any of the solos on the album will definitely hear how good this kid is. I mean he's just fabulous. He knows so many different forms of music, but he's really more blues based than anything else. That's where Doug comes from, a really blues-based kind of thing. Doug jokes that he stopped listening to music after the end of the '70s because he just didn't like what he heard. It was all the things he heard before that made him work hard, from Hendrix to Stevie Ray Vaughan to Page to Ritchie to Tony. And mentioning all those people was really nice, because those are people I've played with or certainly admired throughout my history. So Doug brought to the table so much ability.

"The backing tracks came alive. When we did them with Craig, we honestly just went, 'Okay, that's good enough.' Because he just didn't want to be there anymore. There was no vibe; he didn't care. We got to the point where it was just such hard work. We went, 'That's good enough.' But when Doug came in, it just came alive, and happiness started again. He just made all the difference in the world to us. And that was just due to Doug's playing, which, as far as I'm concerned, is above reproach. And because of his attitude . . . he wanted it to be a Dio album. He didn't want it to be a vehicle for him to be something else. He wanted to be part of this band, and he just succeeded so marvelously. We just marveled at him every night. Sitting there listening to him do a solo, we would go, 'Oh my God, did you just hear that?!' And he'd say, 'Let me try this now.' And we'd go, 'What?! You're going to try something else?!' This is what used to happen with Ritchie. Ritchie would play that way. He would do a solo, and he would go, 'How's that?' And we'd go, 'Great!' And then he'd do another one completely different and then do another one completely different—just amazing. I can't say enough about Doug; he's the business, and boy, I'm just so thankful that we got him."

Dragonslayer Doug Aldrich. © *Steve Olley*

Asked if he had considered any other guitarists, Ronnie says that "because we had played with him before, and we knew what a good guitar player he was, one that we thought of was Rowan Robertson. But Rowan has changed a lot musically. He doesn't really come from the same space we come from anymore. He's the same great person and the same great guitar player, but I just had a feeling this wasn't quite what we were looking for. That was it; there wasn't anybody else, really.

"Luckily, Doug came along at absolutely the right time. I think Jimmy had seen Doug and said, 'Look, I don't think we're going to be very happy with what's going on here; maybe you should think about whether you would be interested.' And he said, 'Oh yeah, that would be great.' Because he's always had his own band. He's always had to do his own things, and as he told us, what he wanted to do at this point was to not have to be the one who made all the decisions. He wanted to be someone who came in and would be part of the band and not have to worry about that burden on his shoulders. Well, that's always been my burden, so that made it a little bit easier for him. But he came in with that approach, and it was wonderful, because not only that, he found out that we are very open people as well, that we wanted his contribution. We didn't want him to sound like Vivian or Craig now or Rowan now. We allowed him to do what he had to do, and gave him the time to do it. Not that he was slow, because he certainly

Ronnie and his new sidekick, Doug Aldrich.
© *Steve Olley*

wasn't. We tried to embed in him that this was a band, not something where you're coming in to fill a hole in the dike until we get it repaired. So I think for all those reasons, it really, really worked to its ultimate."

The brightness and snappiness of *Killing the Dragon* certainly derives from Ronnie's stated philosophy this time around, and from the energy and enthusiasm brought to the band by Doug. But it also might be a byproduct of the band availing itself of new recording technologies.

"Truthfully, the only difference is that with this one, we did all of it on ProTools," says Ronnie, in reference to the widely popular system for easily cutting, pasting, tightening, and otherwise facilitating the recording of albums. "None of this was analog at all. That was a great difference, but the trap of course is that ProTools has so many things it can do for you that unless you're prepared with your songs and your arrangements, once you go into the studio, you can fall into this false trap: 'Oh well, we don't really need to do that; we can take this part and stick it over here.' With digital editing these days, you can do absolutely anything. So that's a trap you can fall into, and it's one we didn't fall into because we were prepared.

"And we wouldn't fall into it anyway because it's phony; it's a fake thing, and you don't want to do that. So, we just used ProTools as the tool that it is, and were very, very surprised with the difference in sound. Not with the difference in sound, but that there wasn't much difference in the sound. A real aficionado will hear a little bit of it here and there, but I think it was mastered—and mixed, certainly—so well by our engineer, Wyn Davis. He just has a real grip on what ProTools is and how it translates back to analog, and how it relates to analog. He just really, really got it together. And when we mastered it . . . as a matter of fact, the guy who masters all of our product, Eddy Schreyer, Eddy said, 'Wow, this is unbelievable! You did this on ProTools?!' And that was really the pat on the back we all needed.

"But production values, no, nothing different," continues Ronnie. "We did it the same way. We did the backing tracks. It was a lot more difficult this time because we went in with Craig and did the eight backing tracks, because we thought this was still going to work. We took a break over the holidays, Christmastime, and found out absolutely that it wasn't going to work. So, I dismissed Craig and we were lucky enough to find another guitar player right away, and we went in and scrubbed all of Craig's tracks, and then Doug went in and did his. So that was the only difference in production, in that we had to do the backing tracks twice. And thankfully, we did do them twice because they came out better this way anyway."

"It was kind of a weird situation, because I had come in after most of that stuff had been written," affirms Aldrich on wading into the Dio fray. "So, I remember getting down to the studio, and I was looking at the . . . you know, when you're at a studio, they always put a board on the wall with the song that you're working on, and progress that's being made on each song. And I noticed there were only eight songs, and I was thinking, 'What's up with that?' And they said, 'Well, we need a couple more songs.' So, Jimmy and I got together at my house, basically, and within a couple hours, we had six or seven ideas we had put down on CD for Ronnie, where I would just program a drum machine and we would work out these things. They were basically just an intro, main riff, the first part, maybe a B section, and then a chorus, and we would leave it at that. That would give Ronnie a taste of what we were representing. And we played him that stuff, and he didn't really like focus in on it. I don't know, maybe he had some other stuff he wanted to pursue.

"So, we kind of put it on the back burner, and we started banging around some stuff that he had, which was kind of more heavy, dark and slow stuff. And I kind of felt like we already had that covered on the record a little bit, with songs like 'Rock and Roll' and 'Throw Away Children.' And so, I thought, well, maybe something kind of in the vein of 'Holy Diver,' that really heavy . . . I don't know; you don't really call it a shuffle, that [sings it]. Yeah, it's like a slow trot, 'Heaven and Hell' / 'Holy Diver.' I thought something like that would be cool, so that's where 'Scream' came from. And then Jimmy had this riff for 'Along Comes a Spider.' Jimmy plays guitar, but he plays it just very simply, so I kind of took his idea and tried to soup up the parts a little bit, and then we just finished the arrangements with Ronnie, and that's how they came together.

Spitfire tour poster for the *Killing the Dragon* campaign

"But really, it was a thing where, I don't know if Ronnie was really wanting to go in that direction just yet, but we kind of felt that the record needed that stuff for balance. And at the end, the thirteenth hour, right before we really had to get the record finished, we just kind of forced those songs on Ronnie a little bit. He liked them, but he didn't like them enough until he actually got some vocal stuff on them that made sense for him. When he first played me 'Scream,' I thought, that is kick-ass; I love that. So, we went in and recorded those two with Simon and then finished them all off. But I like that record a lot. It's fun for me to listen to, and it was really stressful for Ronnie, because making a change right in the middle of the whole thing was probably rough on him. And he ended up having to spend a little more money having to bring me in, when he did, but the record was cool, and the only regret I have is that I wasn't there from the beginning to write all that stuff."

"The thing about Ronnie is he's a real, real perfectionist," reflects Doug. "He wants it the way he wants it. And with me, I felt like he gave me a little more free rein, because in recording, he wasn't there sitting watching the whole time. In the beginning he would sit there, and he'd be doing his crossword puzzles and I'd be playing, and I'd say, 'Hey, Ronnie, what do you think of that?' And he'd go, 'That's cool, I like that, this part here; I'd like to work on that some more.' And I would just carry on. But when it came to doing solos, he just let me do my thing and gave me free rein."

Japanese ad announcing the upcoming album

Years later with Doug we covered similar terrain, only by this point he was able to contrast working with Ronnie versus David Coverdale. "Ronnie was very, very focused and set in what he wanted—he knew exactly what he wanted it to sound like. And it started with writing. I actually only wrote two songs with Ronnie, just because of the situation, but he knew exactly what he wanted. If something wasn't how he'd want to do it, he would be positive and say, 'That's really cool, but I think, you know, it's got to be more grand; we've got to take it further. Think of it in this way.' He inspired me to push deeper. And with David, David was very open to any kind of . . . if I said to him, 'I think it sounds really good if I play the part on the banjo,' he'd go, 'Great, go for it!' And that's definitely not something that Dio would do. He really wanted the sound a certain way. He really didn't want you to fluctuate on that. Which . . . I respect both ways."

"Onstage, Ronnie totally gave me the stage for five minutes every night, to do a guitar solo," says Aldrich, with respect to this top-notch version of the band on the road. "So, I think he really felt comfortable. The bottom line is, if somebody made a mistake, he would let you know. Not after the show, but right there; he would tell you. And then he would go back to singing the song. And it was interesting. But at least you knew where Ronnie stood, and you knew how he felt. There was no secret about that. And then at the end of the day, he would say, 'We're cool, right? You understand what I was talking about?' And mostly with me, there was never a problem, but I respected that he told people how he felt, and they would make the adjustments from there. But he's a great guy, man. He's an amazing singer and he delivers every night. And he's really dedicated to his fans, which is another thing I really respect. So that's cool."

If it wasn't so much Doug getting the evil eye from the boss onstage, I wondered if perchance it was Jimmy. "Periodically, you know," ventures Aldrich. "I think there was a different dynamic between Jimmy and Ronnie because they had so much history. Periodically, he might say something that he was a little concerned about with Jimmy, but I'm not sure that Jimmy . . . you know, if there was one person that Ronnie maybe didn't talk to and could have talked to more directly, it's Jimmy, maybe out of respect. He didn't want to get in Jimmy's face about anything. But he had some concerns with Jimmy on certain things, and sometimes . . . Jimmy just does his thing. He doesn't really want to know about any details; he just wants to get a bass on and rock."

"So there ended up being maybe a little bit of personal separation, or a disconnection between those two," reveals Doug. "And then after I split and Craig came back, I think Jimmy was just 'Nah, I'm not into it.' And I did see them play with Maiden, and I thought they sound really good. Jimmy looked happy, and him and Ronnie were playing off each other onstage really well. But then after that tour was over, I think Jimmy just kind of faded away. I sensed that a couple times. I actually ran into Jimmy and said, 'You need to . . . whatever this situation, you need to work it out with Ronnie.' And obviously they never worked it out, and they parted company."

Rumors were afoot of Jimmy falling off the wagon again. "I don't know; we all have things that are vices," reflects Doug, diplomatically and respectfully. "I'm not sure which wagon. There's probably a lot of wagons that we can all fall off of. You know, Jimmy is a real . . . he's one of the old-school great bass players, and Jimmy has been through everything in his career, and maybe for him, he was hanging out with some people that I don't know if they were the best influence on him or whatever. Bottom line is, when I worked with Jimmy, Jimmy was sober and played great. So that's all I can really say.

"But I noticed sometimes he would hang out with people that, you could tell, just wanted to hang out with him because he was Jimmy Bain. There was a time actually in Quebec that he went out with some people, and I was like, 'All right, Jimmy, we've got to get out of here. It's late; we have a gig tomorrow; we have to travel before the gig.' And I remember I was in a taxi, holding Jimmy's hand, and there was some guy that he had met, and all of a sudden, they were best friends, and he was pulling Jimmy out of the cab from the other side, wanting to continue partying. It was like four in the morning already. So that's the kind of thing, you know? Jimmy is a real rock star. People want to be with him, you know? I'm talking about people that aren't musicians. And you know the kind of people I'm talking about, because they probably do the same with you. They just want to hang with a rock star or a writer or a record company guy and be a part of it. And it's all good for a little while, but the real reality is, these people think it's party 24/7, and we gotta sleep. So, Jimmy was hanging with some people like that. But I have nothing but the greatest respect for Jimmy, as does Ronnie, I'm sure. He's a bad ass. He lays it down."

Keyboardist Scott Warren was also on the road with the guys. "He's a very funny, interesting, unique person," chuckles Doug. "I can't really . . . you know, without really speaking about it, I can't put it into words. He's a very simple guy, I guess, in terms of what makes him happy. He loves to create things on his keyboards, and he loves to perform live. He's got a unique live performance style that is kind of his own. And when I say simple, you know, give him a nice glass of red wine and a little snack at the end of the night and he's happier than anybody. I don't remember him ever being in a bad mood; he's always pretty happy. He did play on the records too, but it was a little bit here and there, a few intros. Ronnie wasn't keen on keyboards throughout the song. But live, Scott would find a way to sneak in there, and he was really good at doubling guitar riffs during guitar solos. You know, for the title track, 'Killing the Dragon,' he might accentuate the stabs of the chords, periodically. But he didn't have a whole lot to do. It wasn't like it was Hammond B3 going on all over the place or anything."

Killing the Dragon, issued on May 20, 2002, opened boldly and briskly with its sharp title track, a ripsnorter of a galloping metal anthem that was arguably Ronnie's most impressive riff rocker in years. Explained Ronnie with respect to the lyric, "The dragon symbolizes those who perpetrate injustices against us. In fantasy tales, dragons were notorious for stealing children and feeding them to their babies. During the first part of the song, I sing, 'Someone has taken a child.' The second part is about a cruel feudal lord. The third part is about 'electronic serfdom.'"

This is one of those songs where you gotta listen to the fade and slowly turn it up. Why? Well, the band does some of the most interesting jamming on the record, switching up the gallop mathematically in demonstration of prog rock chops we rarely get to hear from Dio. Says Doug, "We were just kind of twisting the riff around. That was something that was, I think, decided on before I got there. I could be wrong. But if it was a band figure, it would've been done before I got there, because the drums were already cut, and I just put the guitars on it. But maybe if it was a guitar thing that was changing it up, it might be something that Ronnie and I did in the studio. I can't remember, actually. But I heard that, and I thought it was a really kick-ass song. I felt like I dug in deep on that song—it was good."

And following the impressive title track, things didn't let up in the least, with "Along Comes a Spider" also grooving up-tempo and hummable, fiery licks everywhere, all business at the upper end of the midpaced spectrum.

"Spiders eat their young and their mates," said Ronnie, when asked about the lyric. "The song is about guys who believe that they've gotten over a relationship but are inevitably dragged back into it. I don't want to write mere love songs. I want to write something that lets the listener use his or her imagination. I often get painted into a corner, however, and someone will complain that I've used the word 'rainbow' again. I finally decided that this is what I had in me, and this is what you're going to get. I try not to get into the intricacies of it all. The word 'love' presents a broad canvas. I don't like to point directly at it. Relationships are personal things. How am I going to make someone understand relationships by singing about Rosie and Bob or Jack and Diane? I'd rather work with a broad landscape in dealing with the subject. I usually write with a lot of innuendo so that the listener can make up his or her own mind about what is being said. If I point too directly at the subject, it becomes my song, and I don't want that to happen. I want it to be our song."

As a songwriter, Doug is credited only on "Along Comes a Spider" and the track directly after it, "Scream." "Yeah, Jimmy, Craig, and Ronnie wrote the majority of stuff," concedes Aldrich. "I think Jimmy and Ronnie did write everything together, including the stuff that I worked on with them. And Jimmy, he was great, man. I mean, you're making me kind of think back in my memory, that he was a strong melody guy, and I think he just had good, simple ideas that were not too . . . you know, sometimes us guitar players, we can overthink things and try too hard sometimes. Jimmy would just be very simple and kind of get right to the point of what the song needed. But when I was there, Ronnie was definitely involved in every aspect of the music, from the drums to everything. It was just awesome to see how he was so into it. I would show up there at ten in the morning or something. We would all show up, and he would be in his kitchen listening on like a little old-school transistor radio to sports radio. And he would be like, 'Right, let's go.' And we would go down into the studio, and we would be there from 11:00 a.m. till 7:00 or 8:00 p.m., whatever, and it was just really cool. And like I said, Ronnie was very particular about what he wanted. There was a word that he used sometimes, called jolly. If something was too jolly, it was not good. That was not good. It was like, 'You know, it's a bit jolly, don't you think?' And I'm like, 'Okay, I got you.'"

As for the relationship between Ronnie and Jimmy . . . "It was good. I mean, they loved each other. I think that a couple a times on the road, maybe Ronnie was a little concerned about Jimmy. Maybe he wasn't fully aware of what Jimmy was up to. But it turns out, now in hindsight, there were a couple times when Jimmy would fall off or whatever. And I think Ronnie was maybe concerned about that a little bit here and there. And when I left the band fully, to join Whitesnake, I think things deteriorated somehow between them a little bit. Because Ronnie wanted to get Craig back, and maybe Jimmy wasn't as keen on that. From what I understand."

Next is "Scream," one of Ronnie's faves on the record. It's panoramic and even chivalrous, fully immersed in a lumbering "Heaven and Hell" or "Dream Evil" psychic space, driven by a throbbing bass line and slashing accents. "We put movie stars, athletes, and rock stars on pedestals," explains Ronnie. "When we look at these celebrities, we see only the good, only their happiness. When they go home, however, they are exactly as we are. Behind their smiles, they scream. The moral is, don't let someone else be your guide. Direct yourself. Sure, there are always guidelines, good people who we can emulate. At the end of the day, however, even Gandhi screamed."

"Better in the Dark" is the record's fastest track yet, recalling the Viv Campbell days with all sorts of fireworks from Doug. Ronnie says this one "is actually about a woman who is so ugly that the only time she can get laid is during the night, so she tends to run around with other monsters. She always leaves before the sun rises because you might not want to ever come back if you see her during the day. I was thinking about some of the ugly women I have known. They all looked good in the dark, but when I saw them in the morning, I wished they were pizzas. I think most things are better in the dark. Heavy metal is better in the dark."

Doug uses this song to answer the question we've been asking this whole book: Why is the second half of the Dio catalog so slow? "If you've got a fast riff like 'Better in the Dark,' I believe—and it was a cool song and everything; it was great, actually, I loved it—but I could see where, you know, he's singing in more of a fast Rainbow type of thing, or the early Dio stuff. When you've got a slower song, with some dark chords to it, he could really dig deep about the subject, I feel like. I think it opened up for him. He just loved dark and heavy. I think that kind of music opened something up for him. The things he could write about and visualize were more-moody things, deeper subjects."

US and Japanese *Killing the Dragon* CDs

"Rock and Roll," musically, is closest to the black 'n' bluesers on *Magica* (or even *Angry Machines*), but lyrically it's one step beyond. Ronnie touches on this tale earlier in the book when we talk about "Holy Diver," but it's extra salient here as well.

"That one really has a theme more than anything else on the record," begins Ronnie, "because there was a conscious effort to do that. This happened at the time of the World Trade Center incident. I'd spoken to a DJ I know in New York, a guy named Eddie Trunk, who is on WNEW there, and he's my real lifeline to what's going on in the city. So, I gave Eddie a call to find out if everybody was okay in New York and pass on my condolences and support. It was just my way of getting a message out to the people of New York—after all, I'm a New Yorker anyway.

"So, in speaking to Eddie, he said, 'They banned some of your songs.' And I'm like, 'I'm sorry, what?! They've banned them? For what reason?' 'Well, they tried to take everything out that had any sort of connection whatsoever.' And I have no idea why. I didn't think any of that mattered. And it really annoyed me. It annoyed me to the point where I wrote a song about that. And the gist of the song is, when anything happens in a negative way, we all scream out for the warrior. Where are the soldiers? They'll take care of it! But at the same time, they're taking the soldiers and they're saying, 'Okay, go over there and die now, but you can't listen to this song.' I mean, that seems so inconsistent to me, with respect to democracy for a start, and with freedom of thought and acceptance. It just really annoyed me. And 'Holy Diver' was one of the songs they banned, and I just thought, this makes absolutely no sense to me whatsoever."

"Push" is next up on the record, and given its melodic, upbeat nature, it's a natural for first single, which it became, accompanied by a classy, upmarket video. The full-on production clip for the track included a cameo by hit comedy duo Tenacious D. They open the video busking an acoustic version of "Heaven and Hell," which includes new lyrics like "The devil is never a maker / I think that he's coaching the Lakers." Ronnie sidles up and pays them to play some Tenacious D instead, and then the song kicks in. This led to a friendship between Ronnie and Jack Black and then ultimately Ronnie featuring in the *Tenacious D in the Pick of Destiny* movie. The song failed to chart, but perhaps the presence of a proper video had something to do with the record finding the #199 on the Billboard 200, a small victory for this band long past its wider pop culture relevance.

"Guilty" is yet another grooving, big-beated midpacer, which drops out for a moody, mystical vocal melody over big blocky chords before the chorus returns to the infectious opening theme.

"I like 'Throw Away Children' a lot," offers Ronnie, on the album's third-to-last track. "I think that's a really excellent song and a great song to sing, probably my favorite in that respect." Given that it's a subject near and dear to Ronnie's heart, the world of runaways and the logical though sad choices they often make between the lesser of two evils, one would think it would be a natural for Children of the Night.

"In fact, it was going to be," continues Ronnie. "It was going to be the Children of the Night song, but they wanted something in a different way. They said it was too depressing. I didn't understand that, because I thought you couldn't find a much more

The stunning Marc Sasso album cover. *Martin Popoff archive*

depressing subject or theme than running away or being thrown away by their parents. But they wanted something a little more anthemy, so we're going to have to try to write something else. But the song was so good, there was no way I was going to let it go. I was very happy that we could do it ourselves and that I was going to sing it alone without having to share the song with other people. It's a very personal song to me. I mean, it would've been fine to have other people sing it as well, but this way I got to do the whole thing, so I was very happy about it.

"I wanted kids to be part of this song because it is about children," says Ronnie, on the subject of the song and its use of the King's Harbour Church Children's Choir. "The title was suggested by one of the Children of the Night, who has since passed on. He said, 'No one wanted us, so they threw us away.' The choir was a great bunch of kids. The funniest part was that their parents came to the recording, and they were saying things like 'I saw you with Sabbath and Rainbow' and 'I saw Dio at the L.A. Forum.' The

kids were so talented. When they began singing, the hair stood up on the back of my neck, and our drummer, Simon Wright, had a tear in his eye."

"Before the Fall" is another aggressive rocker, featuring Simon in a rock 'n' roll pocket and Aldrich riffing with bravado, hitting a succession of eccentric but thoroughly workable melodies. Then we get a weird one, "Cold Feet," closing the album on an uncommonly bright note. Ronnie quickly cops to this one being the odd one out on the album: "I keep getting asked, 'Do some Elf; do Elf, Elf, Elf! Do an Elf song!' And I keep going, 'You know, we're not that—Elf is Elf.' So at one point I just sat down, after somebody said that to me, and started cranking out this more basic rock 'n' roll kind of stuff. And Jimmy said, 'I love that!' And I'm like, 'You do?!' So Jimmy and I continued on with that one, and we wrote 'Cold Feet.' And I just think, because what it is—its feel—I just think it's the farthest away from us, and strangely to me, it seems to be one of the songs people like."

And that was it—Dio had most deftly turned in a record that thrilled and spilled fans of the classic Dio albums to no end. *Killing the Dragon* rocked proudly with spring in its step. Ten tracks were on offer, and ten tracks took their places well paced and sequenced for the ebb and flow and shift of life. This was a band on fire once again. As an incredible adjunct to the story, *Killing the Dragon* was reissued with some enticing bonus tracks. Along with a screensaver and the amusing "Push" video, included are two tracks of Ronnie with none other than Deep Purple. "Fever Dreams" gets a quick kick and rhythmic smarting from Ian Paice, with the presence of Purple turning this *Magica* highlight into something approaching a classic. However, their treatment of "Rainbow in the Dark" is played too bouncy, lacking in power—I think this one needs Viv and Vinny. The strange collision of forces that had, for years, nodded at each other from passing trains took place due to the bands touring together, along with Scorpions, in a power package for the ages. On May 31, 2002, the three bands took the stage in Las Vegas, with Scorpions as headliners, after which Scorpions and Deep Purple alternated into and out of the headlining slot. The bands toured hard together through June 2002, after which Dio hit Quebec with Voivod as support, with the Toronto show warmed up by locals Scratching Post.

"The problem with what we're doing is we're only playing for an hour," said Ronnie at the time, citing one of the key byproducts of playing backup. "Playing for an hour

Ronnie James Dio, thespian. © *Greg Olma*

really limits what you're going to do. You start thinking, well, what are we going to play? Should we do something that they haven't heard for a long time, a lot of those, or do you play the way you've got to play the game, which is you may as well go out there and obviously kick them up the ass with the things they obviously want to hear? How can you get away without doing 'Holy Diver' or without doing 'Don't Talk to Strangers' perhaps? The things people really know you for, 'Rainbow in the Dark.' So right away you're kind of covered. We haven't done 'Egypt' for a long time so we're going to do that, even in the short set, the one-hour set. And we'll also do 'Children of the Sea,' which we haven't done in a long, long time.

"And when we do the headlining tour, we'll have to draw back into other things, of course, from 'Invisible' to 'We Rock,' 'The Mob Rules,' 'Neon Knights.' There are a lot of choices. It's going to be hard to deal with, because we'll be doing a one-hour set for a month and then for four shows we'll be doing an hour and forty-five minutes, so we'll have to kind of keep up on it. You do tend to forget the things you're doing sometimes. But the one-hour set will be mainly the staples, with three songs from *Killing the Dragon*. We'll begin the set with 'Killing the Dragon' and at the moment do that, 'Rock and Roll,' and 'Scream.' But we're thinking of adding 'Push' to it as well; I'm not sure. We won't add to it; we'll replace something with 'Push.' An hour doesn't give you the latitude to do the things you've got to do. Because we want to do parts of 'Heaven and Hell' as well. With one hour, you're really dealing with compressing things. But we've always been good at that, so it won't be a problem. But the beauty of it is, you know, it's just one slammer after another.

Poster and pass. *Martin Popoff archive*

"Well, not between us there wasn't," says Ronnie, about the potentially thorny issue of headline status. "We would certainly always defer to Purple, a legendary band and obviously they've been friends for a long time too. There's certainly no animosity between us and them or Scorpions. I mean, we've all been friends for thirty years. That's something that has to be beaten out between the Scorps and Purple. It is what it is. There are times when you think, you know, I think we've had as many hits in this country, or even anyplace, as others have, lately, or in the last twelve or thirteen years or whatever. But if you get into that kind of mindset, you get into a battle-of-the-bands mindset, and that's not what this is. We're just going to go out and be what we are, entertaining hopefully. We'll be a good prelude to whoever goes on next. And I'm assuming that is Purple. I think Scorpions is headlining. So again, I think if there's any kind of bitching and moaning going on, it would be by either of those two. But certainly not by us, no."

Ronnie takes in stride that his band, and metal generally, isn't attracting the same crowd they did back in the day. Like many historians on the subject, Ronnie ascribes the downturn to the profusion of major-label hair metal bands in the early 1990s.

"I think all of us suffered greatly from it. We weren't playing arenas anymore. A lot of bands didn't play anymore at all. Most of them got there without having a hell of a lot of talent. Once that went away, they had to prove where their metal was. They couldn't survive unless it was in the era where even bad bands could be pushed to the top of the heap. When it went away, we just played smaller places. That is what we've always done. We play. Luckily, we have a European audience as well. We have a South American audience and a Japanese audience. We had a lot of places to go. I think the most important thing is that every time we play, people see just how good the band is. There has always been a good band with Dio, and this one is the best. I think that consistency is the idea here. All of the records we've done have been very consistent. I might not have liked them all, and some other people may not have liked them all, but they were consistently good. They were well played and well produced. They were thought out. I think being kicked in the balls the way some bands have been from the '80s helped."

Ronnie and Doug, the Fillmore, San Francisco, California, November 12, 2002. © *Dion DeTora*

The three tremors—Klaus, Ian, and Ronnie—continued on after Dio's short Canadian visit, into Cleveland in early July, intensively toward August 4 in Ronnie's hometown of Los Angeles. In late August, Dio began its requisite European swing, first supporting Deep Purple and then with a variety of backup acts through early September 2002, with Oliver/Dawson Saxon supporting in the UK, all this happening as Biff Byford of the real Saxon was readying himself to lower the boom on his ex-bandmates and end the confusion that Graham Oliver and Steve Dawson had been causing in the marketplace.

CHAPTER 13

*"You can read between the lines—
that's sort of where I'm coming from."*

EVIL OR DIVINE: LIVE IN NEW YORK CITY

Back in America on November 8, 2002, Dio embarked on an extensive second leg in support of *Killing the Dragon*, with Hammerfall and King's X in tow. Two nights before the end of the tour, Dio would film a show at the Roseland Ballroom in New York (on a Friday the thirteenth) for DVD release in 2003 as *Evil or Divine: Live in New York City*, with the set emerging as a live CD as well, but not until February 22, 2005.

Festival season was again nailed prolifically and efficiently in 2003, after which the band traversed America for a third time, with the like-minded Motörhead and Iron Maiden as part of another strong bill, through July and August of that year. Like night and day, this jaunt affirmed the popularity of Iron Maiden. Attendance for this package was often into the five figures, whereas the Scorpions/Purple/Dio bill was woefully underattended, with huge venues often coming up a quarter or a third full.

"He's got one of those all-time great voices," says Lemmy, about his ersatz tour mate. "Especially considering where it comes from. He's not a big barrel-chested geezer like me, you know? He really whacks it out; he's great. We've toured three or four times with Dio. Ronnie is great, man; I like Ronnie. He's a good laugh. He has an English sense of humor, which is pretty rare [laughs]." And Jimmy? "Oh, I've seen Jimmy Bain face down in his food in the Rainbow a lot of times, before he got with Dio. But I've known Jimmy since he started playing when he first came around to London. I met Jimmy when he was in Wild Horses. So, I've known Jimmy longer than most people I know. Jimmy's fine; he's a good bass player too. The interesting part about Wild Horses is that they fired Brian Robertson, and it was his band [laughs]. How bad is that, you know? Were they trying to tell me something?"

Continuing to make up for the lack of a live album in the 1980s. *Martin Popoff archive*

A week before the Roseland DVD shoot, Ronnie had this assessment of how the protracted *Killing the Dragon* tour had gone. "Well, Jimmy has been with us for *Magica*, the album and the tour, and Jimmy fit in right away. I mean, there was barely a breath there between when he was there in 1990 until now. And Doug is such a great guitar player, just very fluid. The band kicked in right away right from the gates. There was just never a problem, and I never expected there to be one. You choose the right people and you get the best results. No hitches at all.

"We've added to the show we did with Scorpions and Purple. Now we're doing between an hour and thirty and an hour and forty. We added two songs from *Magica* that we hadn't been doing on the summer shows, 'Lord of the Last Day' and 'Fever

Ronnie always treated his fans like family. Grand Ballroom, San Francisco, California, October 29, 2004. © *Dion DeTora*

Scott Warren and Dio fan and collector Dion DeTora at the Grand Ballroom, San Francisco, California, October 29, 2004. *Dion DeTora archive*

Dreams.' And we're doing a couple more encore songs: 'We Rock,' which we did not do during the shows, and sometimes, due to time restrictions, we weren't able to do 'The Last in Line' or 'Rainbow in the Dark,' depending on which one we decided to take out for that day—we kind of switched them around. It's a longer set, and it's the set that has more breadth to the guitar solo. When you have a nonspecific amount of time to do whatever you want to do, you just tend to make things a bit longer, with more audience interaction, and, like I say, a longer guitar solo."

Added Ronnie, with respect to Manhattan's Roseland Ballroom, "We've played it before; it's a good-sized gig, very conducive to filming. The company we're using is a New York–based company, which makes it a lot easier. Our affiliation with the lighting and sound people is a very strong one in New York as well. So, it's a good choice, more for the supplies that we need and secondary to the fact that it's a good gig and that New York crowds are great for us. There probably will be some family, a few people who turn up from upstate New York. But I don't expect a lot. The consideration is the show this time; there's not a lot of chance for schmoozing to go on because we want to get it right. I think the less outside things we have to be concerned with, the easier it's going to be for everybody, just from a purely mental-clearing state.

"We wanted to use pyro. We've always been known for that, but, of course, pyro is impossible to use at that particular venue. We're using some things that are much like that but in a lighting-design fashion. We're using a lighting designer who designed like *Holy Diver*, *Sacred Heart*, *Last in Line*, all of the big shows that we did, Paul Dexter. So, he's bringing in a lot of special things, and he's the best as far as I'm concerned. So, it will be a wonderful visual show. Once again, it's not something that really concerns me until I see it, because my concern is for the musical part of it. I'll let someone else deal with that, and hopefully at the end of the day, I'll look at it and say, 'Whoa, that was good.' But you know, 'Did we sound good, and did we perform well?' is what I'm always concerned about most."

Ronnie's concern resulted in a punchy DVD and single-CD live set. The band efficiently rocks its way through a standard collection of Dio anthems, along with recent tracks a such as "Killing the Dragon," "Push," "Rock and Roll," and "Fever Dreams." Rainbow is touched upon twice, Sabbath twice as well, with "Children of the Sea" being a bit of a welcome wild card.

Ronnie states that there weren't any touch-ups done to the Roseland recordings. "We never really had a problem with having to go in and do that. Because the band has always been so good, not only good players, but we've always been so well rehearsed with a real high ethic, so it didn't matter if it was being recorded or not. You got the same show all the time, which is one of the reasons why when we did this DVD, we only filmed it once. I mean, most bands film five or six shows and intersperse it with this or that because it makes life easier for them. But I've never had a problem. Right from the very first live album I ever did, which was Rainbow's *On Stage*, which was also . . . we went into the studio, Martin Birch and I, and we mixed. Ritchie came in once, in the ten days we were mixing it, and said, 'How's it going?' 'Good.' 'Okay, bye.' And he left. So obviously, we had done the right thing when we played it. So that's always been my ethic. 'We know it's going to be a DVD; that's okay, we can go back and fix it in the studio.' Well, that's not reality. That's not what people come to see. They come to see it done right the first time. You should be able to capture that.

"I think the only differences between the DVD and the CD is that there are some omissions for the CD, for time consideration. I think the drum solo got axed, and I think they took a lot of the repartee out. So, you get song, song, song, rather than me waffling on. None of the songs have been taken out, I don't think. I'm really not sure. I hate to plead such ignorance on this one, but it wasn't my project." In fact, 'Lord of the Last Day' had been deleted for the CD issue.

Asked for a remembrance of the Roseland show, Jimmy relates that "somebody threw a condom onstage and had cream cheese on it or something, and it's right about foot from where Ronnie stands. And I'm thinking, we're shooting a movie here and some smart-ass throws up a condom, and I'm looking at it and thinking, I'm not picking that up, goddamn it. But I knew that he would, you know, if the cameras didn't see it [laughs]. But we had to get rid of it. It was like Spinal Tap. I'm looking over to try get the attention of a roadie, trying to signal him. He's scared to come on because we're filming. So, I ended up just grabbing one of the towels on the drum riser and grabbing this thing at arm's length and throwing it off the stage. But it was just that; the one night somebody throws up something disgusting onstage, it's the one day you're filming. I'm not sure if you see that on the DVD. I think you see me with the towel as far away from my nose as possible."

"Writing for me doesn't happen until the project begins," added Ronnie, mapping out future plans for the band at this juncture. "I don't do things on the road. When we finish this, we'll take some time away from it, and we'll need some time away from each other, I'm sure. We've been on the road for about eight months now, and it's been pretty grueling. We need to spend the holidays . . . obviously we'll see each other over the holidays, but away from this situation, being thrown together so closely. Following that,

I'm going to go back home for a while. By home, I mean New York, to see my folks, just for a week or ten days or so. Then when I get back to L.A., I'm sure I'm going to just be chomping at the bit to do something anyway. So, I'll begin writing for the album then, which should be *Magica II* and *III*. So at least there's a plan for that. And Doug Aldrich is just like I am; he can't stand to sit around and do nothing, so that will be interesting. But most important is to just take a bit of time away from this and generally gather our lives around us again.

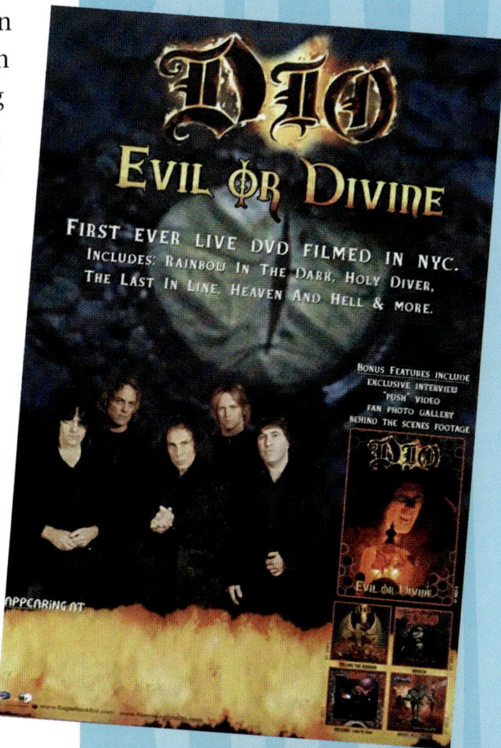

A couple of posters printed up by the band's label, Spitfire. *Martin Popoff archive*

"There's so much more music to do," says Ronnie, dismissing any thought of writing his autobiography, something he would be asked about regularly. "We have another album to do, and that's going to be long process, and it's going to be a very involved album for me because it's going to be *Magica* again. When that stops, you know, I may have some time this year, because we plan on only going to South America for a very brief period of time, probably in February, and then only doing festivals this year. I've had enough of touring constantly. I think it's important that we take steps backward and not be quite so available for a time. For the next proper tour, I'd like to put together a wonderful package or be part of a package like we did with Scorpions and Purple, without being the opening act, quote unquote.

"And Jimmy, I'm sure he's writing," continues Dio. "He has his guitar out here and he's doing some things. And as far as doing things in his life, it's the same as mine: play the gig, get on the bus, and go to next gig, ad nauseam at times. It's Doug's writing I'm looking forward to because he has so much to offer; he's such a great musician. Jimmy has a tendency to write little things and we'll sometimes use them, whereas Doug and I, we have a tendency to write big things and use them all the time."

Months later, up into April '03, Jimmy indeed offered that "we're writing right now. Ronnie and I got together . . . it must be a month and a half ago. We've got about four songs done for the new record. We've had a few problems with the guitar player situation the last couple of albums. But we just get together, and if there's a guitar player there, there's a guitar player there. If there's no guitar player, we just write anyway. And as you know from the last album, we did pretty good, him and me, on our own. So, if we have a guitar player there, it's great. If we don't, we just carry on anyway. We've gotten that kind of attitude after having major, major problems with Craig Goldy when he was in the band. He just kind of lost interest. He wouldn't show up, and when he did show up, it was better if he wouldn't show up. We sort of ended up having to tell him not to show up [laughs] because he had nothing to say musically. When it's like that, it's better to have somebody not there. It's sort of like a black cloud hanging over.

"There are a couple of things that sound a little different, different rhythm pattern here and there. We have a very high standard about our albums. We don't want to just do another album kind of thing. We're very picky. When we get together, we have fifty or sixty riffs, and we kind of weed through them and find something we both like and then build on that. I'll take it to a certain point and say, well, this is crap, and we'll start on something else. It's just a weeding-out process. I don't think there's anything particularly incredibly different."

Already the seeds seemed to have been sown to turn the record into another "songs" album, and not anything to do with *Magica*. "I'm not sure yet," cautioned Bain. "I don't think we've really decided as yet. Ronnie would like to do that, and we're kind of leaning toward that. And I'm kind of, I don't want to appear diverse and having a different direction than Ronnie, but I think likely you can go and say it's the next *Magica*. I don't think it's going to be as contextual as the last one. I think he has a story; I don't know. Maybe it might be easy for him, but that was my objection. That was my point. We don't want to spend a year working on a record. Well, maybe we do; I don't know. But I certainly think that with the band and the climate the way it is, you want to do the album and get it out quickly. You don't want to be hanging around for a year and a half. You can read between the lines—that's sort of where I'm coming from [laughs]. The last one we did really quickly, and it was really productive and it felt good, and I think the fans loved it. It was more of a back-to-basics album. I'd like to keep things a little simpler. Not that I don't have broad musical horizons, but with this band, you just want to put something together and get it out. Because there's a time frame we have to deal with."

CHAPTER 14

"He used to say I feel silly out there singing this song if it's too bouncy."

MASTER OF THE MOON

In September 2004, Ronnie was ready with a new record. And it wasn't called *Magica II*, but *Master of the Moon*. Surprising to all (although perhaps somewhat in the tea leaves), Jimmy Bain was gone, off to rejoin forces with Vinny Appice and Mandy Lion in WWIII. In his stead was returning Dokken disciple Jeff Pilson; although on tour, venerable bassist journeyman Rudy Sarzo took over, with Rudy having plied the fat strings most notably for Quiet Riot, Ozzy Osbourne, and Whitesnake.

Said Jimmy to the Dio message board: "My heart wasn't into it; when your heart isn't in it, you can't really do it anymore. I want to do something where maybe I can get rich, as opposed to other people getting rich and I didn't. That is unfortunate, but such is life. When you join a band, you think that everything is going to be great, and it doesn't end up like that so you have to leave after such a long time."

Back on guitar was Craig Goldy, guitarist of choice for *Dream Evil* and *Magica*, although we mustn't forget that he was involved in most of the writing for *Killing the Dragon*, before quitting to be replaced by Doug Aldrich, for completion of the record and much touring. In any event, a North American tour was immediately drawn up to commence virtually upon release of the record.

"He's kind of the perennial guitarist," chuckles Simon. "First, there was Rowan Robertson, a really young guy but just really enthusiastic, more of a bluesy guy, and Ronnie really knew how to get the best out of him. Tracy G, he was more of a heavy metal guy, bit of a different guitarist, and Doug Aldrich, again, kind of bluesy. Craig

Goldy has been there for a lot, has done a lot of work with Ronnie, and just understands Ronnie and really got to know him well."

"Unfortunately, we didn't get to pursue this chemistry Ronnie and I had," explains Doug Aldrich, on his departing from Dio. "But maybe in the future we'll get the chance to write some more stuff. There is actually some stuff we wrote in 2003 that was going to be maybe for whatever new record Ronnie was going to do. And one of the things is an amazing song, and I actually thought that Ronnie might record it. But I never heard about it, and it's not on *Master of the Moon*, but maybe one day I'll get Ronnie and say, 'Ronnie, can we finish that tune and record it?' And maybe I'll put it on a solo record or something. Who knows?

"Ronnie's a great guy," continues Aldrich, "and I guess it was a little bit weird in the beginning when I left, you know, the way the whole thing worked out. I was under the impression—and Ronnie had said that—that he was going to make a new record, after *Killing the Dragon*. And he said it was going to be a thing called *Magica II* and *III*, a kind of a continuation of his *Magica* record. And I knew that the *Magica* record took a long, long time.

"So I said to him, 'David asked me to tour with a reunited Whitesnake.' And he said, 'Yeah, cool.' It was originally going to be two months, and I knew that he was starting to write. But then he also needed some time off. He had had a long year. The *Killing the Dragon* tour was a hundred shows or something, maybe more. And I thought maybe he had needed some time off, and I hadn't really heard from him, and David said, 'Well, we're going to carry on.' So, I said, 'Cool, let's rock.' And then right around that time, Ronnie had gotten some offers, which were a really cool thing, for the band to open up on some Iron Maiden shows, in the summer of 2003. And I had already committed to David, and it got to be a conflict of time. Anyway, the psychological profile of it . . . I love Ronnie. We're all cool now and tight again. And I saw him several times this year already, got on great, had really good conversations, and potentially I'd love to write with Ronnie down the road, when schedules work out."

"I think it's an awful lot more realistic," said Ronnie, comparing *Master of the Moon* to *Killing the Dragon*. "I think the answer to all that's because of the time period in which we were writing this particular album. Not like anything has changed today, but it was a time of extreme terrorism, hundreds of thousands of people dying in Africa, rape in Sudan, global warming, the war in Iraq, the list goes on and on and on. And at that particular point, it was kind of difficult to be happy. I think *Killing the Dragon* was a lot more cheerful a rock album than this one is. And I think it just wasn't as bad a time, in my mind. But because I wasn't being bombarded with it all around me, and because I am a person of the world, I think that this album is a lot more realistic, and there are things that touch upon the paranoid attitude

Author's copy of *Master of the Moon*, signed by Simon Wright. *Martin Popoff archive*

DIO
MASTER OF THE MOON

that we all have to have now, because who knows where the next bomb is going to go off? So, I think once again, it's a product of the times in which it was written."

"*Master of the Moon* is one of those albums that the fans are either going to like or dislike," said Ronnie to *Brave Words & Bloody Knuckles*'s Carl Begai. "It's just that kind of an album. I don't know why there's such a difference between it and *Killing the Dragon*, because it was the same people that wrote both. Craig Goldy and I wrote the bulk of the last album, so I don't see what the difference is, but I guess it's the way you feel at the time. I think *Master of the Moon* is a little bit doomier, a little deeper, so it's going to appeal to some fans. And those people who only want songs like 'One More for the Road,' well, you've lost out. For this album, this is what I felt like writing, what affected me at the time. The status of the world—the Iraq war, 9/11, mistakes being

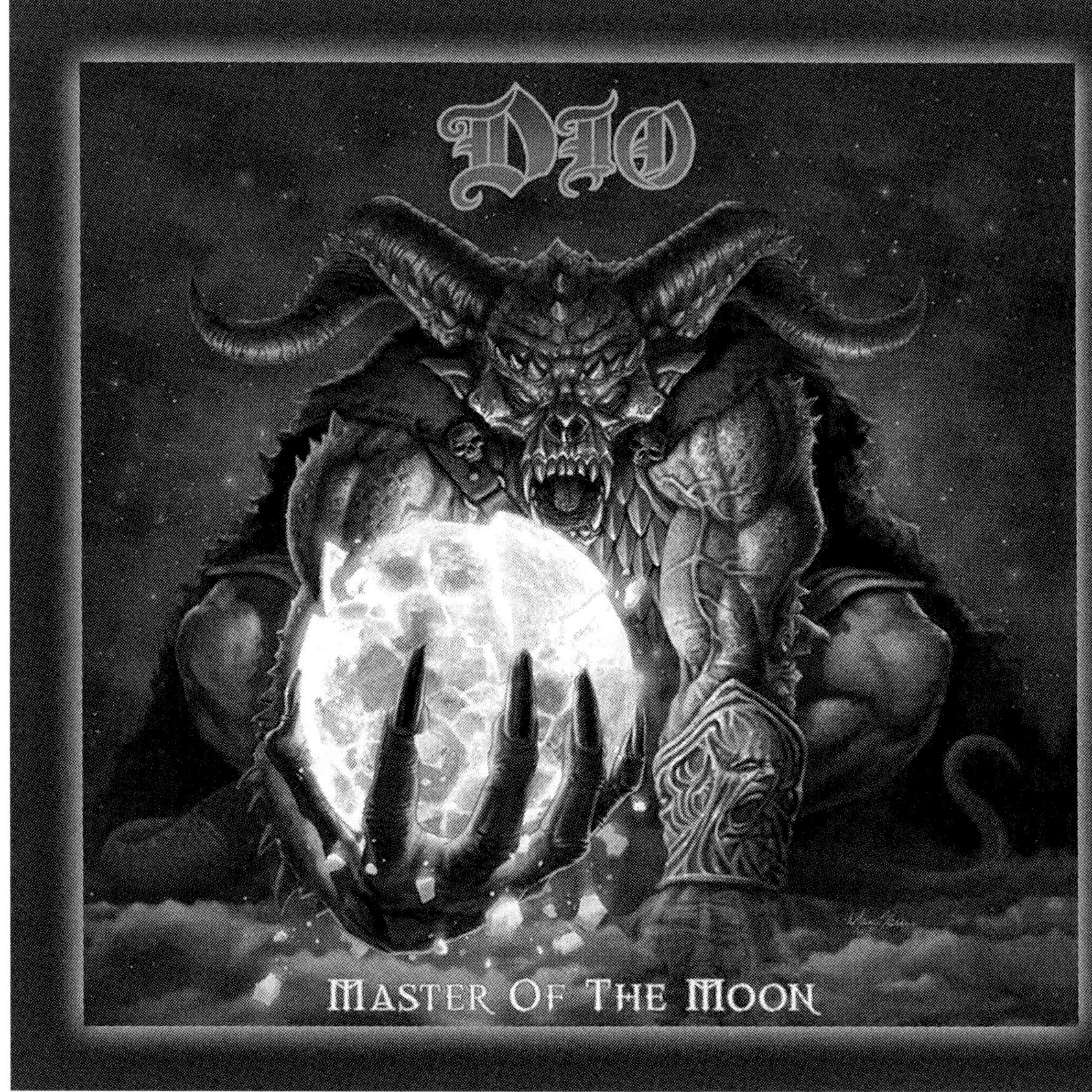

made—had a great impact on me. If you're not affected by that, I think you're a robot. The way these things touched my life came out in the writing.

"I was actually going to do *Magica II* and *III* together," continues Ronnie, "but things happened—like Jimmy leaving—and the time needed to do those albums wasn't there. I felt it was better to just do an album and not waste our time and be unhappy with the end result. It's going to happen eventually. I'm not even sure if the next album will be *Magica II* and *III*, though, because there are components on this new album that could have been used for the story. It'll depend on how I feel when it's time to get down to work."

Ad from *Burrn!* magazine, announcing the new album. *Martin Popoff archive*

In a separate interview, Ronnie expanded on the album's themes of real-world relevance, this idea that "being around so much paranoia of terrorism and watching all the people dying in Africa and what just happened in Russia are good examples of what inspired these lyrics. Basically, they are about the things that make us paranoid. Where is it going to come from next? I could not write any fantasy lyrics with what is going on around me. This is not a fantasy world; this is the real world. I was living in that real world, and I wrote more-realistic lyrics. I don't think there is any question the world is absolutely truly worse. People being killed senselessly every day is not something that happened before. Of course, there were six million Jews killed in World War II, and they were innocent, but it was a different situation. It was organized with Hitler, and it was a world thing. It was good vs. evil. What are the motivations now? Surely it can't just be about Palestine. It can't just be about Saddam Hussein. You have to lock your car door, don't you? You have to lock your house door, don't you? I didn't have murders going on in my hometown. I didn't have child abuse going on in my hometown. Was it because it didn't happen, or was it just that we didn't know about it? I am sure some of it went on, but it was a different world. Rules were different then. Because of the rules changing so drastically, we are in a bad, bad time of our existence. I think it is worse than any time that I have been in, ever.

"You can't stop something that involves people who don't care if they are not alive anymore," continues Ronnie. "Terrorism is like that. There is a promise of something better for them, so they don't care. If someone is coming to attack me and I have a gun and I point it at them, then they are like, 'Go ahead and shoot.' If the situation were reversed and someone was coming at me with a gun and told me to get out of there, then I am out of there and I am running the entire way. When you are dealing with those kinds of attitudes, then there is no winning situation at all. People find out what they can do by taking others hostage and by beheading them, and they gain power. That really smells like the end of the world to me."

One thing the listener will notice right away is the album's beefy production. For this writer, the album is a bit on the slow and lumbering side, hearkening back to *Lock Up the Wolves* and *Magica*, two most definitely on the starchy side of the catalog. Ronnie agreed that *Master of the Moon* deals body blows. "Well, I think it's the heaviest of the Dio albums, in terms of production, so far. I'm really very pleased with the sound of the album. It's just what I wanted to accomplish, and so much of that is due to the interpretation of our engineer Wyn Davis, who can interpret what I want and get it for me. But I think it's a much, much heavier album than anything we've done before. It's been likened in some ways, probably because of the tempos of the songs, to the *Dehumanizer* album I did with Sabbath. So, I think, if there is any kind of descriptive word, it would probably be a bit more like *Dehumanizer* than anything else."

More on the pointed difference in velocities, Ronnie aims to stress that *Master of the Moon* is not the rock 'n' rollsy record *Killing the Dragon* was. "The closest we've come to that *Holy Diver* vibe was *Killing the Dragon*, which is one of the reasons why there was instant acceptance. Everyone was saying, 'Yeah, this is what we were looking for.' But you know what? I don't write for you, sorry. It's your right to criticize, but I'm

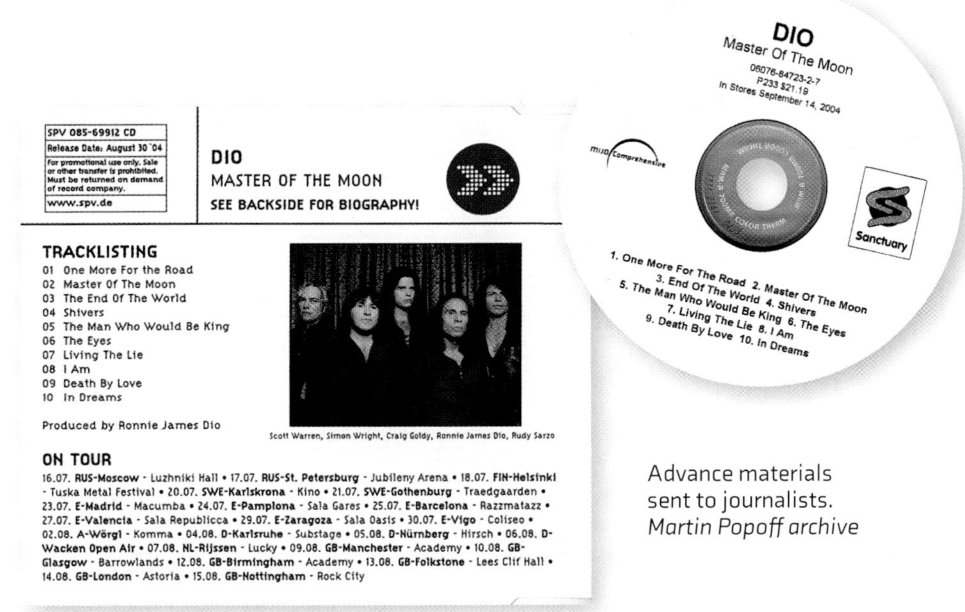

Advance materials sent to journalists. *Martin Popoff archive*

not going to write an album for other people. I'm writing it for how I feel, because I have to wring it out of myself, which becomes difficult year after year after year. Especially when people have high expectations. The thing is, the people who have supported me and the bands I've been in feel the same way I do, so they'll accept the fact that *Master of the Moon* is the album I wanted to make right now."

"I did do, yes," begins Craig, on whether he noticed Ronnie's predilection for doom over the more up-tempo stuff this time around. "I can't really speak for him, but knowing him as well as I do—and people have asked me this before, in an interview—but the only thing I can think of is based on a conversation him and I had in the past. Being the front man, there were certain songs that we would play, maybe from Rainbow or Black Sabbath, and on the feel of the song, he would go, 'That's too bouncy' or it's too this or it's too that. And it's because it would influence the way he would walk onstage. He doesn't dance onstage, but as a front man, the feel of the drumbeat of the song dictates how he would walk onstage and his presence onstage. He's a really intense, deep man, and so if the music is slow and intense and deep and dark and creeps a little bit, he feels this physical power. It doesn't make him feel like he's hopping around and prancing. He used to say, 'I feel silly out there singing this song if it's too bouncy.'

"Having said that, I think there are some really good songs on there," continues Goldy. "I think that one, for some reason like *Dream Evil*, is underrated as well. That was the first album that I really didn't play a lot of fast stuff on. It's mainly just melodies. Actually, that's the first time we actually sat together, and he would sing me ideas and I would learn

these melodies and we would incorporate it into the solos, instead of me ripping through stuff. Instead of 'See, look at what I can do,' it was 'Let's see if we could come up with stuff we could hum through.' And I thought okay, that's a good idea; let's try that. That was an interesting slant on solos, with that particular album."

"After a while, criticism doesn't even bother me," muses Ronnie. "I already did *Holy Diver*, I already did *The Last in Line*, I already did *Heaven and Hell*; so, doing them again wouldn't give me any satisfaction. *Dehumanizer* is a great example; we got back together, and everybody thought, 'Here we go, *Heaven and Hell* ten years later.' But that was the farthest thing from our minds. We labored extensively to make sure it wasn't a rerun, and that again disappointed a lot of people. It was a great album, but it was misunderstood, as this new one probably will be.

"But I'm living for the moment. We live in a time when trying to compete with what is new and young out there is impossible. I'm not trying to do that. You'd have to be an idiot to be this old and try to compete with people who are that young, so I don't think of it that way. I just want to be sure that every time I do a new album that it isn't resting on the laurels of *Holy Diver*. I can compete with these younger guys from a talent perspective. I'll gobble up anybody who thinks they can sing better than I can in any way, shape, or form, but that's not the point. It's a competitive market, but I'm not geared for that anymore. And I won't be doing this forever [laughs]. The support we have is beyond belief. People are so adamant about what I've done because I've been fortunate enough to be in three bands that have made classic albums, from *Rising* to *Heaven and Hell* to *Holy Diver*. And there were other great albums in between. Most careers last five years, if that, but mine has lasted so much longer than that because of the people I've played with

Grand Ballroom, San Francisco, California, October 29, 2004. © *Dion DeTora* and because of the fans who have always been there for me."

Summing up in conversation with Dmitry Epstein, Ronnie said that "as far as my interpretation of heavy goes, *Master of the Moon* is the heaviest production for me since *Dehumanizer*. Everything can be heard so well yet blends together when listened to as a whole sound. The vocal sound was not recorded to be far in front, but like the other instruments, its richness of sound in recording makes it very hearable."

Postcard promoting shows in Russia and Ukraine. *Martin Popoff archive*

Asked about his cast, Ronnie remarks that "Simon Wright is like a small locomotive, like a small freight train. He's great! He's just so steady and plays with so much strength. That comes probably from his days with AC/DC, but I'd like to think it's from his days with us. He's just a great friend of mine, which is very important to me as well. Our keyboard player, Scott Warren, has been with me for almost ten years now. He's also so capable in doing anything that I ask him to do. It's hard to be a keyboard player in this band because we don't feature keyboards, but he's just one of those keyboard players that I can rely on. And again, a great person. You can see how important that is, to have good people! And Craig interprets the songs that we have done from Rainbow and Sabbath better than anybody I've ever heard, and these are not even his own songs! He does a magnificent job in them. Plus, he's great to write with, and again, a good person and a friend."

"Yes and no!" was Craig's answer when he was asked by Jeb Wright if he had been difficult to deal with when it came to the Dio band. "Yes, because I was still a fan, and I used to drive him crazy when I would get into that moment where I couldn't believe I was working with Ronnie James Dio. That is when he wanted me to move quickly!

"When you are sitting right smack in the middle of a dream come true, for me anyways, I can't help but be overwhelmed at times. He had to get me into 're-entry' of the earth's atmosphere if he was going to get me to do what he wanted me to do at that exact moment. No, because we really had so much in common with our

A couple of passes related to the *Master of the Moon* campaign. *Martin Popoff archive*

Left to right: Simon Wright, Scott Warren, Rudy Sarzo, Ronnie James Dio, Craig Goldy. Grand Ballroom, San Francisco, California, October 29, 2004. © *Dion DeTora*

work ethics and how we treated the fans. And to the music industry professionals on our guest list, he'd often say, 'It's *soooo* good to have Craig back in the band!' Sometimes there were family issues where I just couldn't leave them stranded while I was doing band stuff. Another time my hand started to make a 'crunching' sound whenever I would try and make a fist—that was the scariest time in my life! The doctors did everything—x-rays etc.—and nothing showed up as a possible reason for this problem. Then one day Rudy Sarzo looked at me and said, 'You should take better care of yourself. You might be experiencing a potassium deficiency. Eat more bananas, drink Gatorade, and take potassium supplements. I thought, it couldn't be that simple, could it?! And Wendy would often call me and say, 'We're not giving up on you kid; hang in there. Something will happen and make things better.' It turned out that Rudy was right! And I was back in the band."

Delving into the goods on offer, I asked Ronnie to explain the significance of calling the record *Master of the Moon*.

"It's the title of one of the songs, and it was a title that sounded best for a title of an album. We didn't want to call it *One More for the Road* or *The Eyes* or *In Dreams* or *Living the Lie*. *Master of the Moon* has the best lyrical flow to it as an album title. And it certainly brought more things to mind—to my mind anyway—for an album cover. And then obviously, hey, what looks good on a T-shirt? That's another important thing you have to go through. So yes, the song was bigger and darker, and it matched the artwork.

"But the song itself was just a song I wrote about a friend of mine who has a son who is fourteen, going through all the things fourteen-year-old kids go through, being screamed at, yelled at, told you must do it this way and you must do it that way. He's trying to grow into his own skin and find his own way, but he's always being told what to do. And the people in the song say to this boy, you know, if you turn around, you can face the sun and we can make you be like everyone. Obviously meaning that, hey, stay in the light here where we can see you, where you can't do anything on your own. Because the sun is so powerful, you must be 'master of the moon.' So, in their eyes, it's a deriding term, 'master of the moon.'"

"He doesn't want to be just like everyone," said Ronnie, offering a slightly different explanation in a separate chat. "The operative line is 'face the sun.' People think the sun is everything, so the moon must suck. I called him 'master of the moon' because he is not doing what people think he should be doing. He is a master of crap, I guess."

Musically, even though the title track is slow to the point of minimalist, it's anything but crap. There's a sophistication of arrangement to this one, or if not arrangement, measured pacing. The highly melodic chorus is a pleasant surprise—however brief in execution—before an interesting instrumental passage leads back into the blocky and despondent verse.

As Ronnie mentioned, the title also translated into incredible cover art. "It's the same guy who did the cover for *Killing the Dragon*, a guy named Marc Sasso. I spoke to Marc, and I told him what I wanted and what my vision of it was, and he sent me back a rendering of it. It needed a change here and there, but he got the attitude right. You need interpreters for your ideas, and Marc is a good interpreter of what I want to see. He is a liaison for me, and it has worked well. It is important to me. We are not dealing with album covers anymore, which is a shame because you could really see the art then. Even in the shrunken environment we have now, it is important that someone sees the CD and goes, 'That must be a Dio album.' I think you have to make that connection right away. I think if you have a pansyish-type album cover, then you must have pansyish-type music.

"I actually quite like most of the things I've written this time," replied Ronnie, when asked about another lyric he particularly finds key on the album. "I'm not always so up on myself. I think there are some clever ideas on this one. 'One More for the Road,' just because of its content, and just because it's going to be such a misunderstood song, from its meaning perspective, anyway. I think 'One More for the Road' is one of those. Most people think, oh, one more for the road means going on tour again, go have another beer for the road, or whatever. But the song's actually about executions. It begins with the witch hunts, where a child could say, 'That person's a witch!' 'Oh, we should burn that person,' and that's what happened collectively. You know, 400,000 people died in Europe during the witch hunts, only from the word of someone who really had no right to say it. And obviously, we know now that none of that was true. At the end of the verse, it's 'Let's burn one more for the road,' as we do with witches.

"And there's a verse about a guy who was accused of a crime he didn't commit and is found guilty and is just about to be executed. And I guess, sarcastically, he's saying to them at the end of all this, 'There's a cross that you can't carry because it's heavier than hell. And if you should meet your maker, just pray that he won't yell, 'One more for the

Newcastle University, Newcastle, UK, October 13, 2005.
© *Steve Olley*

road!' Again, it's really meant to explain an observation of mine, and that is, life has seemed to become a whole lot less meaningful than it used to be before. And I mean 'a' life. And sometimes a group hysterically tends to say, 'Okay, let's kill a whole bunch of people.' It doesn't seem to matter; it doesn't seem to be important. So, the final statement for me was, no matter what god you believe in, just hope that if you are at that god's doorstep, he doesn't have the same attitude that you had as human beings: 'Hey, let's burn another one.'"

"Ronnie felt we needed a fast song on *Master of the Moon*, so we came up with that one," recalls Simon. "It has some elements of 'Stand Up and Shout' in there. There are a lot of Dioisms about it. We used to open up with that song for a little bit—killer song. There's a lot of great stuff on this album, and I really think it will give the fans an inkling to the other albums from that time. Even though I played on the bloody thing, I really am a fan of the music. There are some great songs on there. It's worth taking a look at."

"One More for the Road" is in fact the album's opener, and what a killer way to announce this well-balanced album. Ronnie's right when he talks about the heaviness of this record's production. Barring the fact that this is one of Ronnie's very best songs ever, and a fast, riffy one at that, the combination of the molten guitar tones and cannon-proud drum sounds makes this a heavy, heady headbang indicative of all that is very fine about the Dio franchise.

"I always try to get a little bit of optimism in my music!" laughs Ronnie with respect to "The End of the World." "It seems to me that fools own the world. If I happen to watch television, it seems all that is on is a bunch of reality shows with a bunch of fools making fools of themselves. They are making millions and millions of dollars while there are people starving somewhere else. We watch these people stumbling about eating worms. It just seems to me that fools have got the sunshine. It must be the end of the world." This one's another plodder, but like the title track, it's sort of charming despite its Notes slouching pace. The verse is starkly melodic, with Ronnie right up front and refreshingly conversational. The chorus pulsates with a little more metal, but oddly enough, it's not hard to picture Simon Wright's old band playing some of these simple chords.

"'Shivers' . . . that is more of a relationship-type thing," continues Ronnie, on a track that sounds very much obtuse and daring like an *Angry Machines* highlight of sorts. "This is about a person who has never been afraid of anything in their life until they got involved with this other person. It could be anyone. It could be the devil or the guy's girlfriend, or it could be God. This person who has never been afraid is suddenly very afraid of what he or she sees."

Ronnie continues with commentary on "The Man Who Would Be King," another slow yet regal and malevolent number buttressed by strong vocal harmonies. "That song could have been on *Magica*. When I started writing this album, I wanted to do *Magica II* and *III*. Due to time restraints, I didn't think I could do a proper job, so I decided to do a normal album. I was in *Magica* mode, and this song came out. It started out to be a song about Richard the Lionhearted, who led the first Crusades back in the ninth century. He sends soldiers down to Jerusalem to take the city back from the infidels, who were the Islamic people. As I wrote the song, it began to sound like George Bush to me. We have soldiers dying in the Middle East for what I think is no apparent reason. The song evolved into a correlation between the Crusades and what is going on now. I guess that kind of shows that the world really doesn't change now, does it? In those days they had bows, arrows, and knives, and now we have nuclear weapons that could destroy the earth. This song is my little political statement, but I am not a political person. I don't think musicians should be that. I am not going to stop a war. The only thing that will stop a war is the number of body bags lined up on the pier and the amount of mothers and fathers crying for them.

"That's about paranoia," says Ronnie with respect to "The Eyes," a song almost too similar in heft and tone to its immediate predecessor. "We are paranoid over when the next terrorist attack will take place; we don't have any control over it. Having no control over something like that causes extreme paranoia. I used the example of the eyes in the sense of people spying on us all the time. Secrecy is invaded."

Ronnie calls strident, fiery rocker "Living the Lie" "more of a personal statement about people I have seen abuse themselves, especially with drugs. If you believe the lies that people are telling you who don't really care about you, then that is evil. The song is really just about people who don't care about others and lead them down a garden path that they should not be led down. In the end, you have a lie that you start living and believing. I am too smart to fall into that trap. I have seen people around me, and I have seen what they become and how their lives fall apart. I never wanted to be that. I wasn't brought up that way. My folks told me that there is a certain way that I should live my life. They showed me some examples and said I could live it that way, but they preferred I didn't. I really care for my folks, and they have always given me great support in all the things that I have tried to do. I figured that they were telling me the truth, and they were. I believe in the reality that bad things are going to make you worse and that good things are the things that you should gravitate to."

Simon, "I got two song credits on *Master of the Moon*, 'Death by Love' and 'Living the Lie,' which I was very, very proud of. We spent a lot of time on those, the demos and stuff, and we were getting a bit stuck with how to approach 'Living the Lie,' and I came up with this drum riff. It wasn't that complicated, but it did get the ball rolling, and it just seemed right at the time. And Ronnie thought that I deserved getting some songwriting credit on that one, and the other one too, which was great. On *Master of the Moon*, there's some pretty good stuff that I did okay on. There's a track, 'The Eyes,' which is pretty good. But it's always difficult to talk about yourself."

"Sometimes I write things that are more personal," continues Ronnie, addressing "I Am," the record's best slower-paced track, a song that could have held its own on *The Last in Line* or *Dream Evil*. "Maybe I felt at the time that I was being taken advantage of. The same things that happen to me happen to everyone. I might start with something that happened to me, but I will write it for someone else. A message that I preach a lot is that nothing can stop you. It doesn't matter what your physical stature is or what people tell you what you can be or can't be. You must try. Trying is the best part of it all. Screaming out 'I am' means that you are a person and that you are not a number. You can survive.

"I have always lived my life like that. I do what is best for me. Musically, what is best for me are the things that I have done. I am lucky enough now to control my own destiny. Being in some of the other bands was just as good for me. I didn't have total control, but I didn't care. I had enough input to make it be good work, and that is fine. Having control is a wonderful thing. I have enough control to be able to say yes or no. A lot of ideas are bantered around in a band, and someone has to say no or yes. If you don't, then you are just going to keep talking about them. People are going to have different opinions, and nothing will get done. I am able to say, 'This is what is going to be done.' I stick to my guns, and it is the way that I have always been."

Closing the ten-track record are "Death by Love" and "In Dreams." "'Death by Love' is about people I see who are so affected by a broken relationship that it seems to kill them. There are a lot of ways to die. You can be shot or stabbed, but death by love is worse. You don't die. It doesn't end for a long while, and it seems to be so devastating to people. I never have understood that. You just have to move on and get over it. Human emotions are pretty strong. The song is really just about that. With respect to 'In Dreams,' a lot of people think that the dreams they have are going to come true. A lot of times that is just not true. You have to have a vision. Just because you dream, it does not mean it is going to come true—you have to make it come true. Everything seems to happen to people in their dreams, but when they wake up, it's just the same as it was. Dreaming is cool, but it is you who has to make the dream come true."

From a musical standpoint, "Death by Love" is an interestingly middle-of-the-road rocker for Ronnie. Catchy, relaxed in a midpaced pocket, sturdy, and dependable of riff, this one has a few twists and turns, most notable being the rise to its brief chorus. "In Dreams," on the other hand, is another sharp but slow one, similar to "I Am" with respect to the way it adds to the album's complexion; namely, that both songs serve as bridges between the stark and laconic material, on one hand, and the couple of Aldrich-style butt shakers, on the other hand.

Moving on, I asked Ronnie about Goldy's particular strengths on his instrument.

"He, like our engineer, is very, very able to interpret some of the things I'd like him to do. And he also has a real simpatico with the kind of music I've always liked. Because it's the same kind of music he's always liked. And I think we've grown together in that interpretive way. We have the same work ethic. He's tireless, just like I am. We want it always to be done the right way, and never let anything be taken for granted. I think his playing on this album is absolutely excellent. I think this is the best guitar work Craig has done, certainly on a Dio album. And his contribution as a writer—and not only as a writer, but as a comrade—is very, very important to me. He brings this incredible tool to the table. And I don't want to use that word to describe him, absolutely. He's certainly not a tool; he's not a screwdriver or a pair of pliers. But he's got so much expertise that people probably don't even realize. It's just so easy to say, 'Play this for me.' Okay, done. No argument, no 'Why do you want me to play that?' Because he understands what it is I'm looking for, because we have that kind of bond. So those are the things he brings to the table.

"I think a lot of the musical creativity is because Craig and I have been writing together so long," reflects Dio. "We wrote *Magica* and a bit of *Killing the Dragon*, as well as this entire one. When you continually write with the same person, then the signature really comes out. I think that has a lot to do with it. Doug Aldrich was the writer on only two of the *Killing the Dragon* songs. Craig was in the band when we started that album, and he and Jimmy Bain and I wrote a lot of the songs. Craig left the band for his own personal reasons, and then Doug came in. That entire album was done except for two songs, and Doug and I wrote them."

When asked about the mysterious craft of sequencing an album, Ronnie replied that "I think you're so involved in the music, from writing it and recording it for five months, that you get a feel of what should be and what shouldn't be. One thing to consider is the key of the songs. You don't want three songs in the key of A to be one right after another; you need musical contrast. Generally, it's what looks right. An important song should not be stuck on the end of the album. You look for a great opening song that is fast and well paced. Hopefully, they won't be in the same key but if they are, you might just switch song 2 with song 3. It really is just the feel and what looks and sounds best with keys and tempos.

"You know, I don't think there were any songs that were very difficult at all," figured

Newcastle University, Newcastle, UK, October 13, 2005. © *Steve Olley*

Ronnie at the time, when asked about difficult technological or writing conundrums. "I don't remember an awful lot of difficulty. Maybe it's because we've gotten so damn good at it after all these years. But I don't remember anything being that difficult. I think the most adventuresome song was 'The Man Who Would Be King,' adventuresome because it has different textures that were not used before. The intro is a B3 kind of thing, à la Procol Harum a little bit. And the song was bigger in scope, not only from my perspective of attempting to write lyrically, but to put together musically so I had some cohesion. I think that was the most difficult of the lot.

"We are prepared by the time we get into the studio," says Ronnie, deflecting a comment that perhaps he is a bit of a taskmaster in the studio. "I don't get into people's heads. I am not the guitar player, but I make suggestions because I think I know what that person plays sounds best; that is what a producer does. If this is what a person wants to do, then let's hear it. If it works then it works, and if it doesn't, then let's change it. A musician is a musician. They color the product. Otherwise, what do I need them for? I might as well just play bass guitar, use a drum machine, and sing—that is not what a band is all about.

"I am not a taskmaster at all. Anyone who has ever recorded with me—most, anyway—will feel at the end of the day that what we recorded was worth the hard work. It is a job; it is your work; it is your profession. When you have done it this long, it is not a frivolous thing anymore. Rock music has become respected enough to become a profession. It was not that way when I started. Job may be the wrong word. Job makes it sound like it's not fun. It's not like having to work from nine to five. This can be fun. We party a bit in the studio, but after a while it's counterproductive. You don't party at your job, so why should I be partying so heavily at my job? I am not a taskmaster, though; that is just not true. We have had our nights of drunken debauchery as well. It doesn't happen very often, but there are times where you have to lay back and take it easy. 'Do you want a drink?' 'Yeah, let's drink for a while.' Sometimes you get more productivity out of that than you do working all the time.

"You've got to be human," continues Ronnie. "It is a job, but it can't have fences about it. We are talking about musicians who are high-strung people who need to be cared for a lot of times. They also need to have their lead. You are that guy who says yes and no, but if you can't laugh at the same time, then no one is going to respect you. They respect you because you are as good as they are. They will respect you if you are fair. Fairness is not to drive people with a whip all the time. But performing is the best part for me. Making albums gives me a chance to go perform. The live concert is showing people how good you are, have always been, and will always be. It is all about how you connect together. The kind of adulation that you get from doing a good job is the payment at the end of the day. It is nice to get some money for it, but that is never what drove me. I love being in a band. It's like us against the world. That is what keeps me going all the time. Playing in a band is most important. It is the camaraderie of us accomplishing something together."

Ronnie indicated pretour that the band would be playing "The Eyes" and "One More for the Road" from the new record, adding that "if there's a great need to include another one, we will. The problem, of course, is that our job is to go out and please an audience.

And so many of them are going to come to hear songs that we just can't get rid of, that we have to do, from 'Holy Diver' to 'Don't Talk to Strangers' to 'Rainbow in the Dark,' 'Heaven and Hell,' and 'Stargazer.' We're doing 'Gates of Babylon' this year, 'Rock 'n' Roll Children,' as I mentioned before, 'Stand Up and Shout.' 'Hey, you didn't do "Stand Up and Shout?!"' Well, you're kind of lumbered. But I think in a lot of ways, you don't really want to go right off the starting line and say, 'Hey, we're going to bore you with four or five tunes you've never heard before.' So, I think it's good to do the songs that are important. And of course, it's necessary to do them because you've just come out with a new album. For God's sake, you're proud of it. But it's just very difficult when you have as much history as we have, to do those things without disappointing too many people. So, we will be doing those two, and another one perhaps as well.

"We've got one track for Japan," noted Ronnie, on whether anything beyond the tidy ten on the record existed. "So, there were eleven tracks done. Whether or not we release anything in Japan is . . . I'm not sure. It's not really a great market anymore. So, for the first time in our lives, we have an extra track, if that happens. But I'm sure it will surface somewhere. It's called 'The Prisoner of Paradise,' and it's just about somebody who overindulges, so they become a prisoner of the paradise they get from, say, drinking or drugs or too much sex, or whatever your vice may be.

"There are no reunions for me," says Ronnie, closing in fitting fashion with a question that continued to follow the man like an albatross. "There is no reunion with Rainbow and there are certainly no reunions with Black Sabbath. I went there twice, and it didn't happen the second time, either. I don't want to be involved in that anymore. They are doing what they want to do with Ozzy, and that is good for them. I wish them all the best. There is nothing backward at all about what they are doing. We had an opportunity to do Rainbow about five or six years ago. It just didn't quite work from a record company / management standpoint. It's a shame that it didn't happen. It was going to be one show televised and recorded in Tokyo. We could have finally given the people what they wanted. That didn't happen for all these years, and I don't have time for that anymore. I tried to make my window of opportunity open for it, but that window has closed. My career will be Dio, and that will be the end of it. But it is nice that people care enough to want that to happen. They care about us after all these years, and they remember what good things Ritchie and I did, but those

Japanese tour ad. *Martin Popoff archive*

days should be left where they were. They were great days, and we made some really great music, but life goes on. Too many times people who reunite in that classic manner are doing it because they can't carry on in this day and age. I can, so I am going to continue doing it."

Dio kicked off the *Master of the Moon* tour in Russia in July 2004, with these dates featuring *Holy Diver* performed in its entirety. Scandinavian dates followed, and then the rest of Europe, including more of Spain than is usual. Amusingly, hard-hitting power metal band Mob Rules opened some of the stops. Viking Skull opened dates in the UK, after which the band went to South America, in late August 2004. September and October saw the band back on home turf with Anthrax and Fireball Ministry supporting.

A Japanese trek had the band supported by supreme stoner rockers Spiritual Beggars, led by guitar legend Michael Amott of Arch Enemy fame. But before that, Dio played metal fests in Mexico and Puerto Rico.

Said Ronnie just days before Puerto Rico, "I'm working on ideas for the next album, which will be *Magica* based. But right now, we're writing the song for Children of the Night, the charity thing we're going to do, which is the same as the *Hear 'n Aid* one we did. If we ever find the time. Because we have to go to Puerto Rico on Thursday. We're doing a show on Saturday in Puerto Rico, just a one-off. And that's put a crimp in the time, because I like to be prepared for any show we do, whether it's one or fifty. So we're doing ten days of rehearsal to make sure we're on top of it, to make sure I can still sing. And when we get back from Puerto Rico, we'll get right back into dealing with the writing of that song."

"And because I just switched my digital recording system over to ProTools, it's another learning curve for me. So that's taken a little bit of time as well. But the next project will be Children of the Night, and then off we go, on the road. We won't be finished touring yet, until probably October, maybe November. We've got a month to do in Russia, festivals this year, the European tour to do, UK, Japan, Australia, South Korea. So we've got a lot of places we have to go. That's going to preclude writing another album right away, of course. I guess it helps that the live CD is out, which will give us a little bit of a breather. But hopefully the next album will be *Magica II* and *III*; I'm still shooting for that."

Indeed, as it came to pass, festival season in Europe was covered, along with Russia extensively, plus the Ukraine, UK, and finally mainland Europe, where the band performed with Uriah Heep and Asia. Once back from all this, Ronnie and his band were hard at work on a new studio album. Yet another dynamic had been added to the shape-shifting Dio saga: Rudy Sarzo became the bassist of choice for the proposed next record, and it was a bit up in the air with respect to whether Doug Aldrich or Craig Goldy would be part of the team, with Doug returning and filling in at least for the last bit of touring while Craig nursed an injured arm, which had him playing Russia on painkillers.

That was an interesting development, for the course of a Dio album has always had—let's face it—much to do with the fire in the belly of the guy holding the ax. But whatever the direction the next Dio album was going to take, his team would be delivering a work of painstaking quality. *Master of the Moon* was such an album, with the record also striking a nice balance between doomy and Sabbath slow, on the one hand, and up tempo, on the other hand. The songs were strong, as was Ronnie's voice, astoundingly

A signed stub from London, UK, plus another shot from the Grand Ballroom, San Francisco, California, October 29, 2004. © *Dion DeTora*

into its late sixties. Let's ponder that for a minute: no one, but no one, in rock, let alone metal, was singing and pushing it and producing like this man at this age. It's a feat underreported and hard to overestimate. Sure, B.B. King could sit and bend a few notes, but who out there was belting out heavy metal magic night after night, on some of the longest tours in the business, with bus, train, and plane delivering this legend to your town until the next beckons?

"I broached with Ronnie the painful subject of Jimmy Bain, who, like Pete Way with respect to UFO, was at one point the boisterous rock 'n' roll heart of the band. "I haven't personally spoken to Jimmy for a while," sighs Dio. "But he stopped into our office. I just heard from him. You know, it's sad when you do things like this, and someone goes away from the band, and someone takes his place—you normally don't hang out so much anymore. It's not like he's going to stop by and listen to Rudy play. I understand all those things, but it's a shame that it happens that way.

"But I haven't turned my back on Jimmy at all. I think Jimmy's a really special person, but he has a lot of special problems. You know, we've tried. We really, really have tried, throughout all of this, to help him and be supportive. But Jimmy is his own man, makes his own decisions, and he made the decision not to be in this band anymore, I think it's a drastically wrong one, only because where do you go from here, Jimmy? I mean, you can't keep doing this, because after a while, everybody's going to go, 'How many more times are they going to kick him out of the band?' We didn't kick him out; he left. But that's what it looks like. How many more times is he not going to be in that band? And the next thing you'll do is go back and play in WWIII again? Well, you know, good for you, mate. What are you going to do? Are you going to go from the pride of what you accomplished and the things you created inside of this band, the twenty-five-year history that it's had, and you're going to turn your back on it? For what reason, I don't know. I don't understand that. But that's why he's Jimmy. I don't know how he thinks. Maybe his mind was clouded by something; I don't know."

On a business note, let's not forget that *Master of the Moon* was also an album recorded for Sanctuary Records, and with the huge financial losses in that camp and attendant talk of office closures and plummeting stock, there immediately was the prospect that Ronnie would be label shopping once again.

CHAPTER 15

"When you're working with somebody like Ronnie James Dio, there's so much to learn from him."

HOLY DIVER—LIVE

Beginning in Russia, on September 11, 2005, Dio began playing live the entirety of the landmark *Holy Diver* album. The band then did this through eastern Europe and western Europe and into the UK, where an extensive campaign eventually landed them at the Astoria on Charring Cross Road in London, October 22, where the show for about two thousand adoring headbangers was recorded for subsequent DVD and CD release. Next came Ireland and a lone show in Israel (supported by local metal heroes Orphaned Land), followed by a Scandinavian tour with Uriah Heep and Asia to close out the year.

May 2006 found the band back in Europe supporting the release of the DVD and two-CD *Holy Diver—Live*, issued April 17, 2006, on Eagle Vision and Eagle Records, respectively. Shows for the duration of 2006 were scattered, totaling under thirty, but still Dio found themselves taking it to fans all over the world. The year culminated in a free New Year's Eve concert to an audience estimated at seven thousand at the city square in Kavarna, Bulgaria, with Ronnie and the mayor of the town celebrating the new year onstage together. The show was also broadcast live on Bulgarian TV.

There were a couple of wrinkles to the lineup for the *Holy Diver—Live* album. Doug was back on guitar, deputizing for an injured Craig, and storied journeyman Rudy Sarzo was in on bass.

"Yeah, in 2004 I got the phone call," explains Rudy, on how he came to join Dio. "I was on tour with Yngwie Malmsteen, and I got a phone call from Wendy to come down and record what became *Master of the Moon*. And because I was on tour and I was committed to finish the tour with Yngwie, I declined. But I said no, as soon as I'm done with my commitment here, I would love to join the band. She said okay, give me a call. So, I did, and in 2004 I became a member of the Dio band. Jeff Pilson, you know, I believe he was already working with Foreigner. I might be wrong, but I believe he had some of that stuff going on. I'm not aware of what they told him or did not tell him, but I can only tell you what they basically told me [laughs]."

SPV promo photo. *Clockwise from left*, Simon Wright, Scott Warren, Ronnie James Dio, Rudy Sarzo, and Craig Goldy.

Asked about his new work environment, Rudy remarks that the boss didn't have much instruction for him pertaining to what to do onstage, but that "Ronnie was one of those guys that leads by example. I mean, we've all been doing this for long time, so you are either gonna get it or not, you know? Still, when you're working with somebody like Ronnie James Dio, there's so much to learn from him. I was just in awe of his performance, and the way that he communicated with the audience and communicated with all of us. Onstage, just to hear him sing and watch him become one of the characters from his songs right there in front of my eyes was magical. It was a magical experience working with Ronnie James Dio. So many people really love him. I think he's the most beloved—and truly loved, not in his celebrity status, but in a heartfelt status; you know what I mean? I've played with some really super, super well-known people from a celebrity standpoint, but the thing with Ronnie, it was more that it was heartfelt."

I asked Rudy if he recalled Ozzy back in the early '80s saying much about the guy that had taken his Black Sabbath gig. "Well, I mean, let's face it," begins Sarzo, "it's common knowledge about this huge rivalry going on, between the Ozzy and Sabbath camps back then. It's not something that I ever talked to Ronnie about. The last time I played with Ozzy was thirty years ago, so by the time I was playing with Ronnie, it was like twenty-five years, and he'd gone back and forth with the Sabbath guys so many times. Then Ozzy started playing with Sabbath, so it was all water under the bridge. Everybody had matured as musicians and as human beings. So, it wasn't really worth revisiting with him. But back then, there was a lot of competition between those bands."

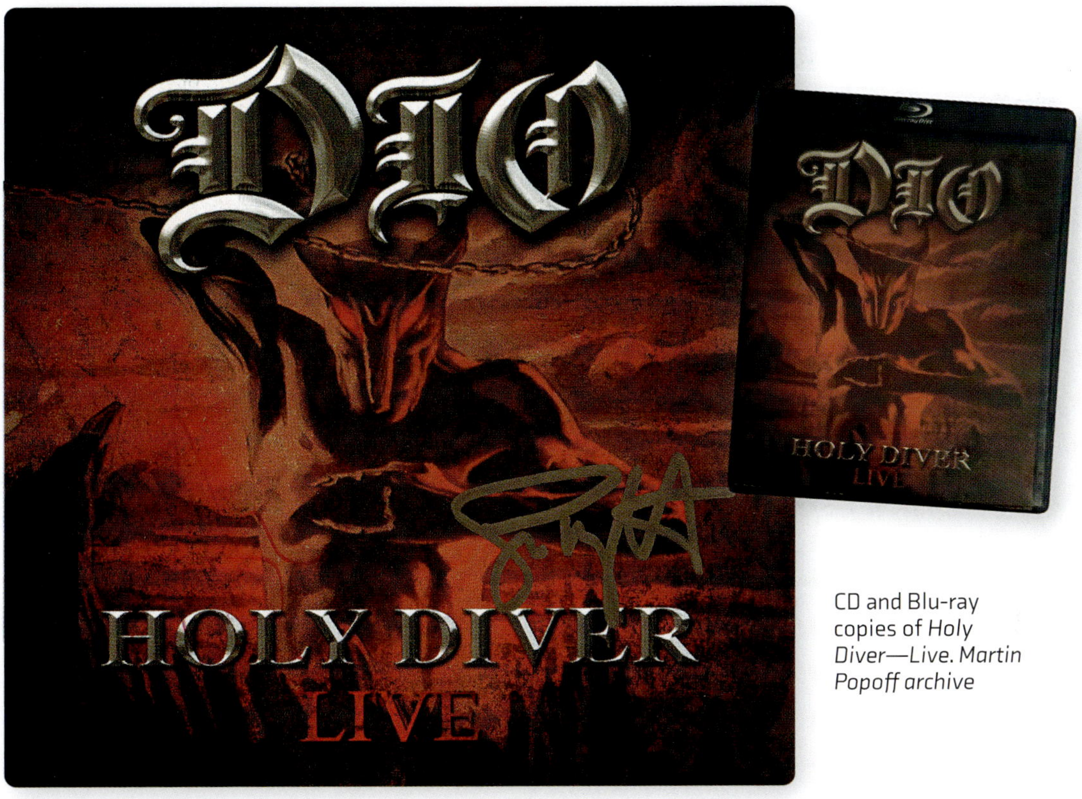

CD and Blu-ray copies of *Holy Diver—Live*. *Martin Popoff archive*

The *Holy Diver—Live* album offers the classic 1983 debut but also so much more. The first disc is dedicated to *Holy Diver*, kicking off with Ronnie's narration, in which he basically name-checks the songs in sentence form. Once his warnings dissolve, along with the spooky music, the band tears into "Stand Up and Shout," with Doug and Simon immediately distinguishing themselves with opening salvos that are on fire. "Gypsy" includes a sprightly, energetic, and chops-mad drum solo, exquisitely recorded, and "Shame on the Night" finds Doug doing a guitar solo, shredding like a maniac, before going into the complete opposite, a slow Hendrix-like blues, and then coming out with an arrangement that includes drums and keyboards from Scott Warren.

The second disc offers two of the very best non–*Holy Diver* Dio selections in "One Night in the City" and "We Rock," but also two Sabbath songs and fully four Rainbow songs, including, most wickedly, "Tarot Woman" and a groovy "Gates of Babylon." Unfortunately, "We Rock" is a bit of a mess at the guitar end, and "Heaven and Hell" is typically vamped up too loosely by Ronnie. But elsewhere the band is firing on all cylinders, Ronnie bravely playing with phrasing and cadence, Doug channeling specifically just enough Ritchie Blackmore to strike a cogent balance, and Simon doing precisely the same when it comes to Vinny Appice.

Of note, Dave Ling, in his excellent liner essay penned for the album, informs us that the show on the night in fact opened with "Tarot Woman," followed by "Sign of the

Southern Cross" and "One Night in the City." As he also divulges, postshow the band went in search of "the finest curry house in Soho."

Again, experiencing this album, we're left with a mountainous "What if?"—namely, what if the classic Dio lineup had issued a double-LP gatefold live album, perhaps from the *Sacred Heart* tour? Done right, we might have another record that is part of the conversation of greatest live albums of all time. Instead, we're left with documents from the CD era, rock solid as they are, given the professionalism of the band, but nonetheless less special as music industry "events."

"I've done some writing myself," said Ronnie in December 2006. "I've probably got five or six things myself, some material for the next Dio project. But unfortunately, all the time that has been taken to be going back and forth to England. Man, I went from England to Japan, Japan back to here, home again, and then, two days later, left back for England again. Went from England and did some more shows, for five days, went back to England. So, I was on this jet-lagged rollercoaster that you just wouldn't believe. And it took a lot of time to do it, because I had commitments in the meantime. Tony had a couple commitments in the meantime. So, it meant that we couldn't just start on, say, January 1 and go until January 30. It had to be kind of in between. But once again we were lucky enough that when we started the project, when we first went over the two things that we put together, we were like, 'Whoa, this is great! I can't wait to get back to these.' So, the anticipation was going to be there anyway. Now we can finish these things, now we can record them, now we can write, now we can mix. So, with that kind of perspective looming up ahead of you, which is a good one, it just made it easy for us to take it along as we did, as much of a pain in the ass as it was for me, travelwise."

The Tony of whom Ronnie speaks is of course Tony Iommi. Into 2007, as a fully fledged member of his old band, now rechristened Heaven & Hell, Ronnie explained of Dio and the prospects of an album: "We haven't talked about that at all. What we've talked about is doing Heaven & Hell, as a project, for a year. I mean, I still owe my record

A couple of passes and a ticket stub for a show in Helsinki

company another Dio album, and I certainly want to do one. I'm not going to lose the deal without any problem. That's not going to happen. So I look at it as this is what we're doing. We'll see what comes after it. Obviously, we could do a full Heaven & Hell album very, very easily. We're getting pretty good at it. But that's something we'll have to talk about down the line, because I've got other commitments myself."

In other news related to both Dio and Heaven & Hell, Vinny Appice had a record out called *Frozen Summer*, put out under the band name 3 Legged Dog, which included in the ranks a certain well-known Dio bassist.

Explains Appice, "Yes, it's Jimmy Bain on bass, Carlos Cavazo from Quiet Riot on guitar, and another guitarist, Brian Young, who played with David Lee Roth, and a vocalist, Chas West, who played with Jason Bonham. And we just released a CD on the internet two months ago that's doing really, really well, so we were going to do a tour this year. But obviously Heaven & Hell is taking precedence on that. So, we're going to release a video. We're going to do a video in February, and this way, while I'm out on the road, we can have a video out, and that can be used as a tool to reach a lot of people. 3 Legged Dog sounds really cool; it's kind of a mixture between Dio and Soundgarden."

On the subject of Jimmy, Vinny says, "He's still alive [laughs]. Yeah, he comes and goes. When he's down here he plays great, on bass, and people love him. He's been around so long; people love to see him play. He still parties, but as long as he's doing everything he's supposed to do onstage, that's cool. And Chas West, who actually sang with George Lynch a little bit, he's a party animal, but he's a good singer. But Jimmy's doing good. He called me about a year and a half ago, to try and put something together. And that's how we hooked back up, and he did all right, cool, and then we went through different guitar players and found Carlos, and then we found Brian. I started writing with this guy, and he came up with some great stuff, and that's what got us a deal. So, Jimmy's doing good, and me and him play fucking as tight as shit together. It's great."

But Heaven & Hell—Ronnie, Tony, Geezer, and Vinny—turned out to be a big deal. On April 3, 2007, Rhino/Warner issued a Black Sabbath compilation called *The Dio Years*. Most of it didn't exactly qualify as news, but front-page worthy was the inclusion of three brand-new songs from Heaven & Hell; namely, "The Devil Cried," "Shadow of the Wind," and "Ear in the Wall." On May 1, we got an archival Dio-era Sabbath live set called *Live at the Hammersmith Odeon*, which was quickly followed by a Heaven & Hell album called *Live from the Radio City Music Hall*. July 22, 2008, brought a box set of the three Dio-era studio albums along with the *Live Evil* live album called *The Rules of Hell*. The crowning jewel of the campaign arrived on April 28, 2009, when Heaven & Hell delivered their one and only studio album, *The Devil You Know*. This was to be Ronnie's fourth record with Sabbath, and the last album of his long and illustrious career.

This is not the place to document the Heaven & Hell experience—all my interviews with the guys take up many pages in my book *Black Sabbath FAQ*—but it was interesting to hear Scott Warren's take on the situation, with the keyboardist telling me that "there were a lot of things being discussed I wasn't privy to. All I know is that I got a call from

Tony, before we began the Heaven & Hell venture, and we just talked a little bit and it was pretty much 'Okay, cool, we seem to be on the same page.' It was kind of interesting because according to Tony, one thing that was of a concern to him was that a lot of the keyboard players . . . well, he hadn't had that many different keyboard players, but for instance, Geoff Nicholls, I guess, played a little guitar, and he wanted that, and I don't play guitar. So, I had to do a little convincing that I could accomplish this with keyboards, with layers of keyboards. And my prowess at duplicating rhythm guitar parts—at least enough to lay down a bit of them—would give him something that he would feel freer to solo over.

"But it was interesting. I haven't really auditioned for bands a lot of times in my career, and that certainly wasn't an audition for me, but I felt like it was in my own self, because I thought, well, this is Black Sabbath, and this is something I always dreamed of doing, being able to play with these guys. And coming in with Ronnie, it was just like I was already there, I was already in, I was already part of the team. I felt like that from day one. It was very comfortable. I mean, those guys were very . . . they are superstars, and so there's always that, but I mean, how can I explain it? It was a really great experience."

Further on the crucial role of mimicking rhythm guitar so Tony could solo, Scott says, "I have a sampling keyboard, and that's a part of the technology that I use, which means, as I said earlier on, that I avoided using as much as I could. I always want to be honest and play things with my fingers live as much as possible. I do incorporate samples into it, but there's always been a fine line for me to where I say, 'Is this justified as far as someone . . . is this actually a performance or not?' That's always been something in my mind that I considered important.

"So, there were a couple times where Tony, on some of the last studio record, had some songs where he had done just layers of guitars. It was something that I thought he would really appreciate having all of that happen live. And Heaven & Hell, or Dio, or the Dio Disciples, they're not about to play to a running tape or a click track. So that means yes, I am to perform it live, but some of that I had to sample a little bit. But I incorporated that into my performance as well. But for the most part, you are playing a grinding organ sound. And you're coloring it a little bit, so it doesn't just sound like Deep Purple. That was one of the conversations I had with Tony early on, that I could do that, but I try to make it sound a little bit more beyond just the distorted organ, which has already been done to its ultimate extreme by Jon Lord. So, I tried to take it a bit further, adding some guitar tones to it and using technology, whatever was available nowadays to make that sound heavier and darker and bigger."

But it wasn't as if Scott was going to be working with just this one monster band moving forward.

"There will be Dio plans, of course," promised Ronnie, on August 13, 2008, right in the middle of the Heaven & Hell Metal Masters tour. In fact, between Heaven & Hell legs, Ronnie took Dio on tour in Scandinavia (adding one Spanish and two UK dates), May 27 through June 21. These would be the last Dio dates ever. "But we're doing this project now," continued Ronnie, "and we've probably got four to five more songs to write, I would think, and they were talking about touring for all of next year. Then we can work on doing the Dio project. Because just before we started this tour, I did a Dio tour in Europe; we did some of the festivals there."

It seemed innocuous at the time, but chatter with Ronnie back in April 2009—the last time I'd ever speak with him—turned to the subject of staying healthy, of keeping fit.

"I ran," begins Dio, "and I was a baseball player. You know, I just walk every morning, 3 or 4 miles, get my lungs in action. And other than that, no, I don't do anything. I don't exercise. My voice . . . I don't warm up, ever. I've just been able to do it at this level, over time. A lot of it is a matter of technique. I've got a strong voice and I know how to use it. Some days . . . I hope it's not going to go soon."

Asked about his diet, Ronnie said, "I only eat once a day; sometimes I don't eat at all. Very bad with that. It's certainly not anything I recommend to anyone. But I get into my routine and I'm just . . . I'm not hungry, I don't want to eat, for no reason, and I just eat a meal in the evening and that's it. You know, I should have a better diet, but I don't. You know, it's silly to stuff yourself. Silly also to not eat all day long, but it's also silly to stuff yourself with a giant meal, especially if you're going to bed in a couple hours. I just make sure I have something, because at that point you get hungry. I just make sure I have something in my stomach because I have work to do."

When I remark that a low-calorie intake has helped him stay thin, he figures, "A lot of it is just my natural metabolism, probably. So, I would think, yeah, that my caloric content is down quite a bit. But I probably make up for the lack of calories by eating a high-calorie meal [laughs]. I'm not a vegetarian, and I don't eat vegetables. I don't believe in vegetables. Fish or meat and that's it. Or potatoes or something like that. So, I get enough of what I need, plus, again, a lot of it is being a little bit cautious about what you put in your body and walking all the time."

"He thought it was indigestion," said Wendy, when I talked to her six months after we would lose Ronnie to gastric cancer on May 16, 2010, at the age of sixty-seven. "He thought it was indigestion. When he came off the road, he said it's indigestion, and Tony had to cancel some tours because of his hand, and he was going in for an operation on that. So Ronnie was going to go out and do a short Dio tour in the meantime, and we had the tour set up and were ready to go, I had shipped the equipment on the Friday, and I think on the Monday before that he was complaining, and I said, 'Let's go to the doctor,' and we went over to the doctors, and they gave him some stuff for indigestion—for acid reflux, actually. And he was still complaining, like a few days later. So, I took him back to the doctor again and they did some blood work, and then on Friday we got the news that he had cancer."

"He was philosophical, and I don't know if he was upbeat, or what beat he was," reflects Simon, after he got the news. "But he didn't emotionally withdraw. He appreciated that we were all around and said we're all there for you. But I think he really took a good, hard look at his life and tried to really take care of himself."

I asked Simon his fondest memories of being part of the Dio band now that it was over. "There were so many. I think one of the fondest times was going to Russia, where we started in the West and went right across the East. We got the feeling we were sort of the trailblazing band, that not a lot of bands had done this. There were some really strange hotels we were in, and strange train rides, or we were in the bar just having a great time. The Russians have a great sense of humor, but they're not really happy people, if you know what I mean. I mean, they would laugh at jokes, and they would joke around, but they don't go around smiling and saying, 'Have a nice day.' I don't mean that as a knock on the Russians, but it's no surprise, really, with all they've been through. But playing live, you just got the feeling they were really appreciative, and they just went crazy."

"He was my friend and my family," explained Craig, reflecting on Ronnie. "He was the first and last of his kind. I try and keep his way alive. He had a totally different kind of work ethic, songwriting method, and his way with the fans. I strive to make sure that this did not die with him as best I can."

As alluded to, Doug Aldrich found himself back in the Dio band when all this happened. "Yes, well Craig was busy doing something, and Ronnie wanted to keep his pipes going and keep his guys working. He always wanted to keep his band working and busy as much as possible—around his Heaven & Hell schedule. It was the end of year, and he said, 'You know, Craig is busy; can you do some dates with us?' And I said, 'Well, when you and Wendy talk and it's all cool, I would love to, man.' So, he said, 'We're going to rerelease the live album that we had done in New York and also the *Killing the Dragon* album, do a double LP for promotion of the tour.' And the tour was going to be called Tour-nado.

"And he said, 'We need a new song to be kind of extra, and I've got a couple things, a couple ideas we can work on.' And he actually gave me a tape of—it was a CD, actually—of a song that he recorded by himself with Simon, where they just put a basic straight beat on it, and Ronnie played bass and put two guitars on it and sang and even doubled his vocals. It was kind of a proper demo that just didn't have a solo on it, really cool, but very haunting. And I think he just changed his mind that he wanted to basically snag one part of that song and write a whole new song. So I just put that on ice; I put a solo on it, but I just put it on ice. And then we got together and said, 'This is the part of the song I really like,' and he worked up a basic arrangement for 'Electra,' with that part from the first song. We recorded it, and Ronnie was really happy with everything.

"But he was in pain while he was singing," continues Aldrich. "And he was even in pain when we got to his house and we were talking about, you know, rewriting the song and doing it how he wanted it. He was having stomach issues. And then we got in the studio and he's singing and wincing, because he was in pain. And so that's the memory I have of that. Wyn Davis mixed it, and it turned out really cool.

"But then we were going to go on and start rehearsing, and Ronnie, he loved to rehearse. He would be the first one there and the last one gone. When I joined the band in the beginning, we rehearsed like six weeks before our first show. That was like six days a week and took Sundays off or whatever. But he loved it. So, when we got in rehearsal a couple weeks after 'Electra' had been mixed, he would get there, but he would be sitting on the couch. Then he would get up and he would sing the set twice, and he would just kind of stand there and sing it. We would do it twice. The whole set. And then he'd go, 'Okay, guys.' And then one day he stopped about halfway through the second time, and he goes, 'Guys, I gotta knock it on the head. I'm just not . . . man, my stomach is killing me.' And that's when we said, 'Ronnie, you really gotta go and get checked out.' 'I know, I know.' But he didn't want to go to the doctor. But he did go, and then he said it was some, like, antacid; he had heartburn and maybe an ulcer or something. That was something that the doctor thought at first, but then after they did blood work, they realized he was sick.

A couple more goodbyes from 2004—Scott, Rudy, Ronnie, Craig, and Simon. Grand Ballroom, San Francisco, California, October 29, 2004. © *Dion DeTora*

"And then one day, the last day, the tour had already been set, to go on this tour, and he didn't show up. And then Wendy told Simon to tell us, 'Look, Ronnie's got to go to the doctor again, and you guys should just run through the set a couple times.' And I was like, this is not right. Ronnie missing rehearsal?! The last rehearsal before we would go?! It just felt . . . I don't even know how we made it through the set. And I can't remember if we did it once or twice, but Wendy walked in, and she gave us the bad news. And it was just like, oh man, still, I can see her walking in knowing that okay, this is not good. Wendy doesn't show . . . she never showed up at rehearsal.

"The next day we all met up at his house, trying to cheer him up. And I'd gone and gotten him a juicer. Because he hated . . . you know, I said, 'Ronnie, okay, everyone knows, when you have stomach cancer, you need to take care of your stomach.' He would basically only eat meat. And he loves curry; he loves hot, spicy curry and the beef, meatballs—that's all he ate. He didn't eat vegetables. So, I got him a juicer and a bunch of carrots and celery, and apples and stuff, and I said, 'Dude, I know you don't like this, but if you juice it, it tastes different. And in that case, you can get a ton of vegetables in one little glass.' And he's like, 'Oh, I'll try it.'

"And we hung out with him all day and we had a drink, and he said, 'I'm gonna have to quit drinking.' And we said, yeah. And that was the last time I saw him. We texted for, you know, off and on a couple times a month. I would check in on him, and he was in pretty good spirits until the last text that I got. I said, 'How it's going?,' and he says, 'Man, I just went through a rough chemo and it's really kicking my ass.' And I was, 'I'm sorry.' We would talk a lot about sports, to keep his mind off of other things. And he was excited because there were dates for Heaven & Hell coming up that summer, the following summer.

"And then I actually happened to be out of the country," continues Doug. "I was with Glenn Hughes and Simon and Yngwie and George Lynch. We were doing this . . . it's like a guitar show in Bologna, Italy. We all did sets by ourselves, but then at the end, Glenn was going to sing, and we all jammed together. And one of the songs we played was 'Long Live Rock 'n' Roll,' which Glenn dedicated to Ronnie. That night we went to dinner, and about one in the morning—everybody was there, Yngwie, George, Derek Sherinian—and we got a call from Wendy saying that Ronnie was not good and that they had taken him off any . . . they were just basically trying to keep him comfortable. And he was going to . . . he's not going to be around much longer. I went and told the guys, and we all said, 'Wendy, I'm going to come straight there when I get off the plane.' I was sitting next to Derek Sherinian flying home. We landed and my phone just took off and it was too late—he was gone."

A final goodbye. Scott Warren, Rudy Sarzo, Ronnie James Dio, and Doug Aldrich (missing is drummer Simon Wright). Newcastle University in the UK, October 13, 2005, on the band's *Holy Diver – Live* campaign. © *Steve Olley*

EPILOGUE

"I was able to stand by the side of the stage, watching night after night—unbelievable."

So that was it: the man on the silver mountain had succumbed to stomach cancer on May 16, 2010, after an immense career comforting and rocking millions. His last show turned out to be a Heaven & Hell performance on August 29, 2009, in Atlantic City, New Jersey. A send-off befitting Ronnie's legend was held two weeks after his passing, at the Hall of Liberty at the Forest Lawn Hollywood Hills cemetery in L.A., attended by many rockers as well as fans.

Forever the elder statesman of metal, the strongest voice, the nicest guy . . . it's indeed a crippling, brutal irony that for the longest time, he was the wise old man of metal, but now, Ronnie does not live to see actual old age. As we've seen, Ronnie would have liked to have created more Dio albums, and he would have liked to have wrapped it all up in an autobiography he'd picked at for years. His wife and manager, Wendy Dio, indeed toiled away and finished what Ronnie had begun, issuing the official autobiography, *Rainbow in the Dark*, in March 2022. The book brings the story up to 1986. The author of the fine first-person volume is Ronnie James Dio, with Mick Wall and Wendy Dio billed as cowriters.

There's one thing we can rejoice in, and that is that the man went out in a blaze of glory, a frenzy of activity, and a level of living tribute few get to see. If time was cruel to Ronnie, it was almost as if he laughed back at it, controlling the timing, putting a punctuation mark on his career that seemed so bold, beautiful, and deliberate, that you'd almost think there was some evil or divine prescience there.

Heaven & Hell, at the Europahalle in Karlsruhe, Germany, June 14, 2009.
© *Mohammed Osama Hassanien*

Of course what I mean by this is that in Ronnie's final two years with us, he and his Sabbath pals saw the issue of two live albums (and an additional one posthumously), a box set, and a compilation with three new songs, plus a weighty, well-regarded album of all new material called *The Devil You Know*, all of it toured with unflagging intensity, grace, and distinction up and down North America and Europe, during one trip into Japan, and then back to Europe for celebrated festival season, goodnight.

I've always found it interesting that Ronnie viewed his bands as projects to knock down within given time frames. And yes, most pertinent among these, given the sad event of Ronnie's passing, is the way in which Ronnie never gave up on his band Dio. Heavy in the midst of Heaven & Hell hoopla, as you can see, if asked he would forthrightly discuss plans for the next Dio tour or Dio album, keeping that little engine that could—it was once a big engine, bigger than Sabbath, frankly, for about five years starting in, say, early 1984—in the public consciousness, all the while unwittingly adding to the charm of that franchise.

Ronnie's triumphant times with Rainbow, with Black Sabbath, and with Heaven & Hell are tales I've told in other books. But there is indeed a wrap-up to the Dio band story we must do that goes beyond *Master of the Moon* and *Holy Diver—Live*. And for most of the upkeep of Ronnie's legacy that we will discuss, we can thank Wendy for her hard work in this regard.

Heaven & Hell, Europahalle, Karlsruhe, Germany, June 14, 2009. © *Mohammed Osama Hassanien*

In the space of a single week in late 2010, we saw two archival live releases demonstrative of Ronnie's prowess. First came *Dio at Donington UK: Live 1983 & 1987*, on November 9, followed by *Heaven & Hell: 30 Years of Heaven & Hell*, on November 16. "This is something that Ronnie and I wanted to do," explains Wendy with respect to the Donington memento. "We wanted to form our own label, and we had started to do this before Ronnie got sick. We had gone through different tapes, and we said, 'Well, this sounds pretty good,' and it was a BBC recording of '83 and '87. So, he took it down to Wyn Davis, his engineer, who does his masters and stuff, and Wyn remastered it. Ronnie was very happy with it. I had called BBC for permission, as you have to. It wasn't bootleg or anything; it was the original tapes from BBC. But then Ronnie got sick, and we put it on hold. But I wanted it to come out because I knew it was something that was dear to Ronnie's heart. He was actually effectively the producer on it, and unfortunately, he didn't see the finished package."

And as of this juncture in November 2010, there was more planned. "Yes, we've got Ronnie's cousin David 'Rock' Feinstein's record coming out on the twenty-second. He was in Elf. Ronnie had written a couple of songs with him, and they were planning on doing another Elf album. And so, it comes out on his solo album as David 'Rock' Feinstein, and there's a song sung by Ronnie called 'Metal Will Never Die' on his record called *Bitten by the Beast*. We have a *Holy Diver* picture disc vinyl coming out on the twenty-

This page and opposite: Record company publicity shots of Heaven & Hell

fifth, and that finishes our releases for this year. Next year we have a lot of releases, and we're just going through them all, looking for what we're going to put out. We have about five *Magica* songs that Ronnie was in the middle of writing. And there's another song that was written by Ronnie's cousin that Ronnie sang on as well. But that hasn't been out yet. We are also putting together a tribute album that we'll put out in October of next year, with the money from that going to the Stand Up and Shout Cancer Fund."

Record company publicity shots of Heaven & Hell

The tribute album did indeed happen, but not until March 2014, issued through Rhino. *Ronnie James Dio—This Is Your Life* featured Anthrax, Tenacious D, Adrenaline Mob, Corey Taylor, Halestorm, Motörhead (performing with Saxon's Biff Byford), Scorpions, Doro, Killswitch Engage, Glenn Hughes, Rob Halford, most of the past Dio band members, and then Metallica, who slam their way through an impressive nine-minute medley. Also included was Ronnie's piano and strings

Vinny Appice, Europahalle, Karlsruhe, Germany, June 14, 2009. © *Mohammed Osama Hassanien*

ballad from *Angry Machines*, which served as the package's title track—"This Is Your Life" is the final song on both records.

One of the two Japanese bonus tracks (the other being Stryper on "Heaven and Hell") is "Stand Up and Shout" performed by Dio Disciples. This was to be a new band of brothers who would go out and spread the gospel of Ronnie in a live setting.

There have been a number of musicians that have cycled through Dio Disciples, but the core of the band consists of Craig Goldy, Tim "Ripper" Owens, Simon Wright, and Scott Warren. On bass we've seen Rudy Sarzo, Toby Jepson, Bjorn Englen, and James Lomenzo. Other singers have included Oni Logan, Mark Boals, Doro Pesch, and John Retta. Vinny Appice and Gonzo Sandoval have drummed for the band, and even Rowan Robertson toured with them, in 2013.

"That's exactly what it is: a bonding experience," Simon told me back in 2011. "When Ronnie died, it hit us all pretty hard, but we got to do these great songs he'd written and talk to the fans, and they just love it. Dio Disciples is just a great way to keep this great music alive. So, when Dio Disciples comes your way, come out and see it; you won't be disappointed. We're just in the basics of the plan of the moment. We're going to start out in Europe. It goes through June to the beginning of July, and then I think we're going to take a bit of a break, and hopefully we're going to start in September in America. Wendy is kind of involved in every aspect—it's a close family. We thought long and hard about doing it, and there was a lot of discussion, but it just became apparent that we've got to do this. We can't just walk away from this. It was a combination of all of that."

"Most people would probably think that I would want to get as many things on there that I cowrote with Ronnie, but that wasn't the case," adds Craig, asked about the set list. "It was mainly just what do we think the fans would want? Simon and I were sitting around thinking wouldn't it be cool to play a lot of the songs that we hadn't played

Craig Goldy and Ripper Owens at a Dio Disciples show at the Rockpile in Toronto, Canada, July 18, 2013. © *Bill Baran*

before? Like, ever. And then when time went on, it kind of morphed, as we talked to the rest of the guys in the band. It's really for the fans, and I would think they probably appreciate more the songs that they really know well and that meant something in their lives. For me, 'Stargazer' was a big song in my life, before I ever even met the man. There are songs you want to play, but there are some you have to play too.

"As the years go on, you see things differently," reflects Craig, asked about how Ronnie changed over the twenty years they worked together on and off. "It just seemed to me that in the days of *Dream Evil* and *Sacred Heart*, where all the stage sets were so elaborate and with so many things going on, I don't think he really had a chance to fully enjoy it, because so many details had to be taken care of. At the end of the day, if something didn't work, in his mind—I know this—people are going to blame him, whether it was his fault or not. So, there was a lot of responsibility. But as time wore on and the stage sets became simpler and simpler, I think he got a chance to enjoy things more. He laughed more and he enjoyed things more, because he didn't have so much responsibility on his shoulders."

"I change my mind every time we start making a set list," laughed Ripper at the time, just as the band was coming into view. "I always enjoy singing 'Stand Up and Shout,' and I think I never sang it until the Hail! project. It's just such a great song to sing live, and one where you can hear the crowd singing along. There were so many to pick from. 'Stargazer,' 'Catch the Rainbow' . . . any of those. My main goal was to try and put all the songs in that every person in the crowd can sing along with. Ronnie was just unbelievable, from start to the finish. With me, I was able to tour with him. I did a solo run with Heaven & Hell there, at the end, so I was able to stand by the side of the stage, watching night after night—unbelievable. So sweet and innocent and beautiful at times, and yet so evil at times, from the start to the finish."

Specifically on singing Ronnie's songs, Tim says that "Ronnie and I had different voices, and I think that's what makes it so great. Singing him, I have to try to figure out the way to attack it. It's not something where I'm just going to start singing. I have to figure out the exact way to sing it. I think he's the most challenging singer that there ever was, and that's what makes it so much fun. He had such a high natural voice that I would have to break into a falsetto at times. I noticed him singing high notes the last two years. If you go back and listen to the beginning of 'The Mob Rules,' all of a sudden, he belts out this high note. It was funny, so he had that. But like you said, he didn't seem to use it, but he actually had high notes as well like that.

"I had started working on the Beyond Fear stuff, and I had just got signed to SPV," explains Tim, on how he became part of the Dio family. "And right before I signed, I'd actually sent Wendy a cassette tape. She was the only manager—to be honest with you—that I sent my cassette tape to, a demo tape of Beyond Fear. And about a month later, out of the blue, she called me, and she said she's very interested. Her exact words were that she wasn't sure she wanted to take on anybody, but she spoke to Ronnie about it, and Ronnie said that she should definitely manage me, and that totally started it."

As for Dio Disciples, "She knows what Ronnie wants—and wanted—and she's the only one, really, who does. She started talking about it and Simon Wright started talking

Geezer Butler and Glenn Hughes at the tribute concert for Ronnie, July 24, 2010, as part of the High Voltage Festival in Victoria Park, London, UK. © *Mohammed Osama Hassanien*

about it and it seemed like a great idea, because of the fact that Ronnie's music is going to live forever. Thinking that nobody was going to sing that stuff again, that's why we wanted to celebrate Ronnie. Right now, it's only Europe. One step at a time. Just take it one step. The thing is, I opened up a whole year to do this. I had planned on touring solo for the summer, and I planned on doing it in August, planned to go to Australia. I had all these tours planned, and I actually canceled everything just so I could start to have this open up. I hope to tour the world with it, because I want to go to Chile and have these kids sing along and shouting 'Ronnie James Dio!' and celebrating. I want to go to Greece, and I wanted go to Canada and go everywhere."

Back at the office, Wendy kept up with archival releases. *The Very Beast of Dio Vol. 2* was issued under the Niji Entertainment banner on October 9, 2012. The album included the semi-non-LP "Electra" and "The Prisoner of Paradise" along with "Metal Will Never Die" from Dave Feinstein's album.

"This compilation is really cool," noted Simon, "with some great stuff from this period that has been overlooked, covering sort of 1996 into the 2000s. And it's also got things like 'Electra,' which was the very last track we worked on, sort of a preview of what *Magica II* and *Magica III* were going to look like. It was recorded as a one-off, because we did a reissue of *Holy Diver—Live*, and we thought we'd have something for that. 'Metal Will Never Die' is the very last thing Ronnie ever recorded, with his cousin Rock Feinstein. 'The Prisoner of Paradise' was a really hard track to get, a Japanese bonus track for *Master of the Moon*. There are still four or five other things, in demo form, that Ronnie sang on that we'll let Wendy decide what to do with."

Speaking with Jeb Wright, Simon added that "this album digs deep. *Killing the Dragon*, *Magica*, and *Master of the Moon* are great albums and would go well in any Dio fan's collection. Scott had been in the band for seventeen years, and I had been there for thirteen. Craig has been in and out for one reason or another, but he has been around a long time, and so it felt like a family. At one point or another we all commented to each other that it was like being in a family. Wendy and Ronnie always looked out for each of us.

"I went through a bad divorce," continues Simon. "I don't know what a good divorce is [laughs]. I was going to leave the band, as I'd just had enough. Ronnie told me not to do that. He told me to come stay at his place. He had five bedrooms, and people were always staying there. I went over there and got settled in. When we weren't playing music, we would build stuff and garden and start drinking around 10:30 in the morning [laughs]. It was a big house, so I could do my thing and he could do his thing. I never left, but it worked out."

Back to the compilation, Simon summarizes that "there are songs that could sit well on a Rainbow album or an early Dio album—*Killing the Dragon* had that kind of feel to it. *Master of the Moon* is classic Dio with a bit of dark Sabbath stuff going on. *Magica* was an adventure; there is incredible singing on that album. This collection will show the fans that have not checked out these albums what they are missing. The cool thing about *Magica* is that it had these segues and it had the same vibe about it with a lot of the songs; it had its own chemistry. But once the songs are taken out of their original album and put on this retrospective, then they kind of take on a whole new perspective. I listened to this whole album a couple of days ago, and they kind of sound different."

One of a spate of Heaven & Hell–related releases. *Martin Popoff archive*

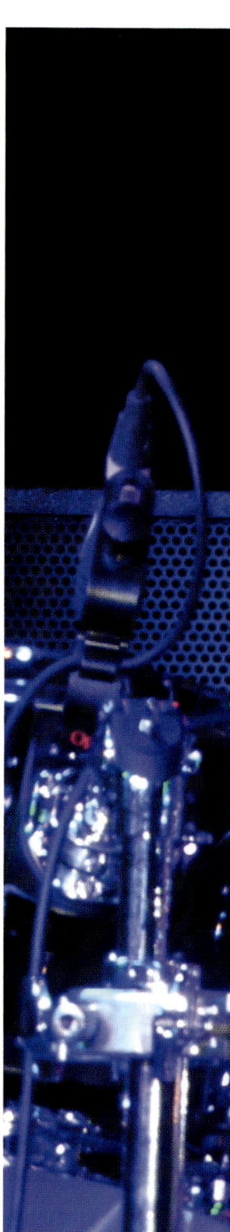

Talk with Jeb then turned to Dio Disciples, who were now about to hit Canada (where the author caught the show, at the Rockpile in Toronto).

"Craig, Scott, and I are on a lot of these songs, and we want to play them. We have to put in 'Heaven and Hell' and 'Rainbow in the Dark' and all the others, but we are trying to put in as many as we can. We are always thinking of the fans, as we are fans as well. Toby [Jepson, who had replaced Ripper] told us midyear that he's got some production commitments, which is fine. It's difficult bringing this band together because we all do other projects. We recruited Oni Logan, and he did a rehearsal with us the other day and he sounded great. He's a good guy and he knew Ronnie. He knows Wendy, and I've known him for quite a few years. Rudy Sarzo is not with us, as he is going out with Geoff Tate. We brought in a guy named Bjorn Englen, and he has a lot of respect for Ronnie and his music. He has played with Yngwie Malmsteen and a few other guys."

"I saw that," replies Wright, when Jeb brings up the fact that Vivian, Vinny, and Jimmy had resurfaced, also as a Dio tribute act of sorts, called Last in Line. "I guess they are entitled to do that. They were in the band, and they played on the albums. I'm just not sure how sincere they are about it. I am pretty sure you see why *we* are doing it. If it's going to happen then it's going to happen. They are entitled to do it, and I am sure it will be good, as they are great players. You could get into a big, big argument about all of this, and I just don't want to do that.

"Ronnie's legacy is everything. I was a fan of his for years," continues Simon. "It wasn't just his singing, which was incredible, but it was his songwriting. Ronnie always surrounded himself with brilliant musicians. His legacy is amazing. He has been in so many bands, and he has helped them create their popularity and *re-created* their popularity in some cases. He has always come up with incredible songs, and he was just an amazing person. He was a tough guy as well, as he was the boss. He could be the boss, and that is what a band needs. You need a leader in a band, and he was the leader.

Vinnie Appice, at the Rock Wars show he did with his brother, Carmine. The venue was the Rockpile in Toronto, Canada, May 10, 2013. © *Bill Baran*

Vivian Campbell with Last in Line, Toronto, March 2017. © *Bill Baran*

He could really push us. He always had an eye on the road ahead. He was a very smart guy. I really miss him.

"This is a job in the sense that we were Ronnie's band. Ronnie was work, work, work, and some more work. We have got accustomed to that. You have to give 110 percent. It is our work to keep his songs alive. When a family member passes away, you don't forget them; you find ways to remember them. Ronnie was a musician, and we are musicians. It is a labor of love because those songs are so brilliant. What spurs us on is that it is our job to do this. I have other projects that I do, but I do choose to do this. We don't make a lot of money doing this. I tend to go elsewhere for that. It is not for the money that I do any of it. I just love playing drums, and if people want to pay me, then that's just great."

As for Wendy and Ronnie . . . "They were friends first, and they really understood one another. She had her job taking care of his business, and he had his job being creative. She looked out for him just like he looked out for her. It was a very special relationship."

Speaking of Wendy, the mother hen of the family kept working, organizing the release of *Finding the Sacred Heart: Live in Philly* on May 29, 2013, and *Live in London: Hammersmith Apollo 1993* on May 12 the following year.

Last in Line, featuring Viv, Vinny, Jimmy, and vocalist Andrew Freeman, issued a debut album of twelve original songs called *Heavy Crown*, on February 19, 2016. Three weeks before the album hit the shops, Jimmy Bain was gone, taken by lung cancer on January 23, 2016. At the time of his death, he and the band had been part of the Def Leppard *Hysteria on the High Seas* package, scheduled to play the next night.

Even though Scott Warren ended up throwing in his lot with Dio Disciples, in the beginning he was part of Last in Line. As he explained to Jimmy Kay from *The Metal Voice*, "When Last in Line started rehearsing, the very, very first rehearsal we did, even before we made the choice of—that's not even the right word—even before Andrew had waltzed into the picture, when it was just Jimmy, Vinny, Viv, and myself . . . when we were all in the room, it fell to me to figure out how long it was since we'd been in the same room together. And I think I calculated that it was like twenty-six years. Which was just mind-boggling. If we'd been born the last time we got together, we'd already be pushing middle age. It's like what the fuck—twenty-six years go by?! It certainly didn't feel like it was that long.

"But regardless, Vinny started 'Stand Up and Shout,' and then we played it like we'd been playing it last week. Which really is a testament to Ronnie's work ethic. Because we never stopped until it was perfect. And to Ronnie's credit, that's why Dio never did a bad show. Because we were rehearsed within an inch of our lives, man, and we could do that shit drunk, blindfolded, throwing up. Well, Jimmy actually was drunk and blindfolded many times. But we always pulled it off. And here it was twenty-six years later, and we just nailed it. So, after about twenty minutes of playing, the door to our rehearsal studio opens up and these kids that are rehearsing down the hall stick their head in and go, 'Don't mean to interrupt you guys, but you're the best Dio cover band ever.' So, here's the thing: the music sounded exactly the way it had sounded in 1983 to 1986, as it should.

"But at first my thought was, when is Ronnie going to walk in? Because it really felt like we were doing sound check, and Ronnie was going to walk in and grab the mic and it was going to be like the old days. But the fact is that Ronnie didn't walk in. And as good a job as you may think that Andrew did or didn't do, it doesn't really matter. Because it was never Dio. I mean, I was happy to do it because it was fun. At least it was supposed to be fun. And maybe it was for a little while. But with Ronnie we were in the presence of greatness, and that made all of us better. Without Ronnie being there, I don't know, man; it just seemed really . . . I don't really want to say pointless, but empty."

Warren wouldn't be part of the first Last in Line album, nor would he be there for *II*, issued February 22, 2019 (both produced by Jeff Pilson), or *Jericho*, issued March 31, 2023, and produced by Chris Collier. Playing bass on *II* and *Jericho* is Phil Soussan, notable for his stint with Ozzy.

Next from the Dio camp, in 2017, came the famed Dio hologram, with Wendy showing her willingness to be innovative. Spending upward of $2 million on the project, its use was limited, and the proposed US tour was aborted. Still, the very attempt put Ronnie in a class with Tupac, and the publicity alone would have been of some value. There was also the 2022 documentary called *Dio: Dreams Never Die*, and the love-in of all things Ronnie was on once again.

"It's very surreal," mused Craig at the time, concerning the hologram. "I find it both heart-wrenching and at home performing to the sound of his voice. The hologram is really more of a grand gesture on the part of Wendy Dio to the fans and the new generation that is getting to know him for the very first time. Watching those young faces see it, basically, in their minds and in their eyes and to hear it with a live rock band, they are just mesmerized! And that can be rewarding at times. Holograms will be for those who are missed so badly by fans around the globe. A hologram is the future for that particular scenario."

Ad for the virtual concert experience

"Yeah, well, hollow is the word I used in the interview I did about Ronnie, what his thoughts would've been about the hologram," adds Scott. "And with that in mind, I won't presume to tell you what I think about what certain people are doing with his memory. But it just seems to me that it isn't about Ronnie anymore. They can say it's about keeping him and his music alive, but nobody ever made holograms of the Beatles, and their music is still alive. I think there are decisions based on more-pragmatic concerns; I'll put it that way. You've got a bunch of guys who can't find gigs. They're managed by the same woman who has contacts all around the world with agencies and promoters. And what can be a more natural thing than taking these out-of-work musicians and putting them on tour and making a little money while you're at it? Again, don't get me wrong. Not to take anything away from these guys. They all do a great job, and if the fans are happy about it, that's all that matters. But you're not asking me about what the fans think. You're asking me what I think."

Wendy Dio, capable keeper of Ronnie's flame at the tribute concert for Ronnie, July 24, 2010, in Victoria Park, London, UK. © *Mohammed Osama Hassanien*

What we all think is that it still feels so recent that we had Ronnie in our lives, even though it's been fourteen years as of this writing.

The reason for that—I'm sure of it—is because the guy was just so personable and available, always around, always supporting the metal, always planning, and then scheduling. And despite the huge attention he was rightfully getting for fronting Heaven & Hell, he never lost his enthusiasm for the band celebrated by this book.

Case in point . . . "I've got about six or seven pieces I wrote after we finished this album," Ronnie told me during my last chat with him on April 13, 2009. "My plan was always to do *Magica II* and *III*. And I can still do *Magica II* and *III*, so I'm embarking on that kind of writing. So, after we finished the Sabbath album, the Heaven & Hell album, I still really need to do that. So, I'm putting them all right towards *Magica*, which is certainly a different kind of situation from Sabbath anyway, so I don't feel like I'm cheating anyone. But should we need an extra song, I've got a couple. But yes, I'm planning on doing that. When that will happen is when I have some time away from what we're doing. Certainly, towards the end of this year, when we finish touring, then we'll sit back and figure out what's going on—Simon, Craig, Rudy, Scott, and me. Tony, Geezer, and Vinny know I want to do this, and I know Geez wants to do something.

Europahalle,
Karlsruhe, Germany,
June 14, 2009.
© *Mohammed Osama Hassanien*

I don't know what Tony wants to do. But we'll need some time away anyway. So, we'll see what happens with Dio at the end of this. I mean, I love that band. I love the band and playing in it, and I have no plans to ever stop, whatsoever. There will always be Dio. Always."

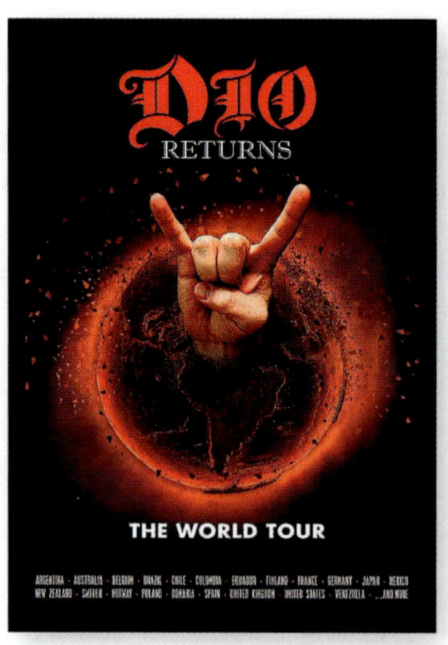

THE DIO DISCOGRAPHY

A few points on format: I've included a notes section for anything I thought was interesting and, er, notable. Quote marks around songs only in the aforementioned notes section. Spelling and punctuation of song titles, plus timings and order of the names in the credits as per actual release, US issue as priority. I've noted side 1 / side 2 designations for releases from the vinyl age, which I've always figured ends in 1990, when the CD age is ushered in for real. I've cut out a few of the formalities you see in the studio section when it comes to live albums. However, I did figure it was important to point out the personnel on the record. Paring back even further, compilations are kept simply to a name-check and year of release. Also in that department, I've left out the few fine Ronnie James Dio career retrospectives, given that this is a book focused on the Dio band.

A. STUDIO ALBUMS

Holy Diver

May 25, 1983, Warner Bros. 1-23836

Produced by Ronnie James Dio

Side 1:

1. Stand Up and Shout (Dio, Bain) 3:15
2. Holy Diver (Dio) 5:54
3. Gypsy (Dio, Campbell) 3:39
4. Caught in the Middle (Dio, Appice, Campbell) 4:15
5. Don't Talk to Strangers (Dio) 4:53

Side 2:

1. Straight Through the Heart (Dio, Bain) 4:32
2. Invisible (Dio, Appice, Campbell) 5:26
3. Rainbow in the Dark (Dio, Appice, Bain, Campbell) 4:15
4. Shame on the Night (Dio, Appice, Bain, Campbell) 5:20

Notes: Initial band lineup is Ronnie James Dio (vocals), Vivian Campbell (guitars), Jimmy Bain (bass), and Vinny Appice (drums). Black-and-white photo collage inner sleeve.

The Last in Line

July 2, 1984, Warner Bros. 1-25100
Produced by Ronnie James Dio

Side 1:

1. We Rock (Dio) 4:35
2. The Last in Line (Dio, Bain, Campbell) 5:48
3. Breathless (Dio, Campbell) 4:09
4. I Speed at Night (Dio, Appice, Bain, Campbell) 3:26
5. One Night in the City (Dio, Appice, Bain, Campbell) 5:14

Side 2:

1. Evil Eyes (Dio) 3:38
2. Mystery (Dio, Bain) 3:55
3. Eat Your Heart Out (Dio, Appice, Bain, Campbell) 4:02
4. Egypt (the Chains Are On) (Dio, Appice, Bain, Campbell) 7:02

Notes: The band lineup now semiofficially includes Claude Schnell on keyboards. Black-and-white inner sleeve, band shots on one side, crowd shot on the other.

Sacred Heart

August 13, 1985, Warner Bros. 1-25292
Produced by Ronnie James Dio

Side 1:

1. King of Rock and Roll (Dio, Appice, Bain, Campbell) 3:49
2. Sacred Heart (Dio, Appice, Bain, Campbell) 6:27
3. Another Lie (Dio) 3:48
4. Rock 'n' Roll Children (Dio) 4:32

Side 2:

1. Hungry for Heaven (Dio, Bain) 4:10
2. Like the Beat of a Heart (Dio, Bain) 4:24
3. Just Another Day (Dio, Campbell) 3:23
4. Fallen Angels (Dio, Appice, Bain, Campbell) 3:57
5. Shoot Shoot (Dio, Appice, Bain, Campbell) 4:20

Notes: Black-and-white inner sleeve, band shots and credits on one side, lyrics to title track on the other.

Dream Evil

July 21, 1987, Warner Bros. 1-25612

Produced by Ronnie James Dio

Side 1:

1. Night People (Dio, Bain, Appice, Goldy, Schnell) 4:06
2. Dream Evil (Dio, Goldy) 4:26
3. Sunset Superman (Dio, Bain, Appice, Goldy, Schnell) 5:45
4. All the Fools Sailed Away (Dio, Goldy) 7:10

Side 2:

1. Naked in the Rain (Dio) 5:09
2. Overlove (Dio, Goldy, Appice) 3:26
3. I Could Have Been a Dreamer (Dio, Goldy) 4:42
4. Faces in the Window (Dio, Bain, Appice, Goldy, Schnell) 3:53
5. When a Woman Cries (Dio, Bain, Appice, Goldy, Schnell) 4:43

Notes: Purple-and-white inner sleeve, band shot and credits on one side, lyrics to "All the Fools Sailed Away" on the other.

Lock Up the Wolves

May 15, 1990, Reprise CD 26212

Produced by Tony Platt and Ronnie James Dio

1. Wild One (Dio, Robertson) 4:05
2. Born on the Sun (Dio, Robertson, Bain, Appice) 5:36
3. Hey Angel (Dio, Robertson) 5:00
4. Between Two Hearts (Dio, Robertson) 6:30
5. Night Music (Dio, Robertson, Bain) 5:05
6. Lock Up the Wolves (Dio, Robertson, Bain) 8:33
7. Evil on Queen Street (Dio, Robertson, Cook) 6:04
8. Walk on Water (Dio, Robertson, Johansson) 3:44
9. Twisted (Dio, Robertson, Bain, Appice) 4:45
10. Why Are They Watching Me (Dio, Robertson) 5:04
11. My Eyes (Dio, Robertson, Johansson) 6:36

Notes: Personnel is Ronnie James Dio (vocals), Rowan Robertson (guitars), Teddy Cook (bass), Simon Wright (drums), and Jens Johansson (keyboards).

Strange Highways

January 26, 1994, Reprise 9 45527-2
Produced by Mike Fraser

1. Jesus, Mary & the Holy Ghost (Dio, Grijalva, Pilson) 4:13
2. Firehead (Dio, Appice, Grijalva, Pilson) 4:06
3. Strange Highways (Dio, Appice, Grijalva, Pilson) 6:54
4. Hollywood Black (Dio, Appice, Grijalva) 5:10
5. Evilution (Dio, Appice, Grijalva, Pilson) 5:37
6. Pain (Appice, Dio, Grijalva) 4:14
7. One Foot in the Grave (Dio, Appice, Grijalva, Pilson) 4:01
8. Give Her the Gun (Dio, Grijalva, Pilson) 5:58
9. Blood from a Stone (Dio, Appice, Grijalva, Pilson) 4:14
10. Here's to You (Dio, Appice, Grijalva, Pilson) 3:24
11. Bring Down the Rain (Dio, Appice, Grijalva, Pilson) 5:45

Notes: Personnel is Ronnie James Dio (vocals), Tracy G (guitars), Jeff Pilson (bass, keyboards), and Vinny Appice (drums).

Angry Machines

October 15, 1996, Mayhem 11104-2
Produced by Ronnie James Dio

1. Institutional Man (Dio, Grijalva, Appice) 5:08
2. Don't Tell the Kids (Dio, Grijalva, Appice) 4:19
3. Black (Dio, Grijalva, Pilson, Appice) 3:10
4. Hunter of the Heart (Dio, Grijalva, Appice) 4:13
5. Stay Out of My Mind (Pilson) 7:11
6. Big Sister (Dio, Grijalva, Pilson, Appice) 5:35
7. Double Monday (Dio, Grijalva, Appice) 2:55
8. Golden Rules (Dio, Grijalva, Appice) 4:54
9. Dying in America (Dio, Grijalva, Pilson, Appice) 4:38
10. This Is Your Life (Dio, Grijalva) 3:25

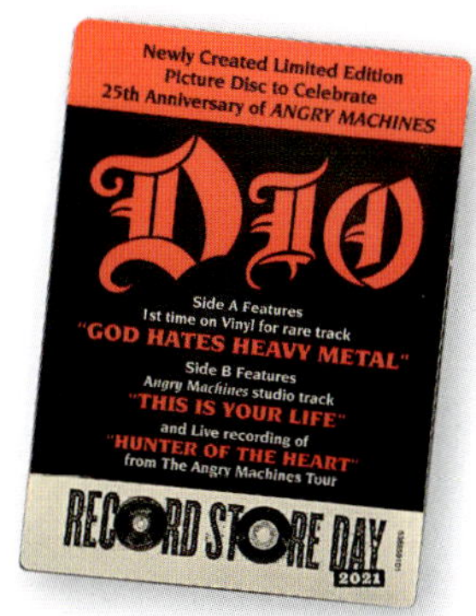

Notes: Personnel is Ronnie James Dio (vocals,) Tracy G (guitars), Jeff Pilson (bass), and Vinny Appice (drums).

Magica

March 21, 2000, Spitfire 6-70211-5020-2

Produced by Ronnie James Dio

1. Discovery (Dio) 0:54
2. Magica Theme (Dio) 1:16
3. Lord of the Last Day (Dio) 4:04
4. Fever Dreams (Dio) 4:37
5. Turn to Stone (Dio, Goldy) 5:19
6. Feed My Head (Dio, Goldy) 5:39
7. Eriel (Dio, Goldy) 7:25
8. Challis (Dio, Goldy) 4:22
9. As Long as It's Not about Love (Dio, Goldy) 6:28
10. Losing My Insanity (Dio, Goldy) 5:04
11. Otherworld (Dio, Goldy) 4:56
12. Magica—Reprise (Dio) 1:53
13. Lord of the Last Day—Reprise (Dio) 1:44
14. Magica Story (Dio) 18:23

Notes: Personnel is Ronnie James Dio (vocals, keyboards), Craig Goldy (guitars), Jimmy Bain (bass), and Simon Wright (drums).

Killing the Dragon

May 21, 2002, Spitfire SPT 15211-2

Produced by Ronnie James Dio

1. Killing the Dragon (Dio, Bain) 4:25
2. Along Comes a Spider (Dio, Aldrich, Bain) 3:32
3. Scream (Dio, Aldrich, Bain) 5:02
4. Better in the Dark (Dio, Bain) 3:43
5. Rock & Roll (Dio, Goldy, Bain) 6:11
6. Push (Dio, Goldy, Bain) 4:08
7. Guilty (Dio, Bain) 4:25
8. Throw Away Children (Dio, Goldy) 5:35
9. Before the Fall (Dio, Bain) 3:48
10. Cold Feet (Dio, Bain) 4:11

Notes: Personnel is Ronnie James Dio (vocals), Doug Aldrich (guitars), Jimmy Bain (bass), and Simon Wright (drums).

Master of the Moon

August 30, 2004, Sanctuary 06076-84723-2

Produced by Ronnie James Dio

1. One More for the Road (Dio, Goldy) 3:18
2. Master of the Moon (Dio, Goldy) 4:19
3. The End of the World (Dio, Goldy) 4:39
4. Shivers (Dio, Goldy) 4:15
5. The Man Who Would Be King (Dio, Goldy) 4:58
6. The Eyes (Dio, Goldy) 6:27
7. Living the Lie (Dio, Goldy, Wright) 4:25
8. I Am (Dio, Goldy) 5:00
9. Death by Love (Dio, Goldy, Garric, Wright) 4:22
10. In Dreams (Dio, Goldy) 4:26

Notes: Personnel is Ronnie James Dio (vocals), Craig Goldy (guitars), Jeff Pilson (bass), Simon Wright (drums), and Scott Warren (keyboards).

B. LIVE ALBUMS

Intermission

June 1986, Warner Bros. W1 25443
Produced by Ronnie James Dio

Side 1:

1. King of Rock and Roll (Dio, Appice, Bain, Campbell) 3:24
2. Rainbow in the Dark (Dio, Appice, Bain, Campbell) 4:34
3. Sacred Heart (Dio, Appice, Bain, Campbell) 6:10

Side 2:

1. Time to Burn (Dio) 4:24
2. Rock 'n' Roll Children (Dio) / Long Live Rock 'n' Roll (Blackmore, Dio) / Man on the Silver Mountain (Blackmore, Dio) 9:38
3. We Rock (Dio) 4:34

Notes: Craig Goldy replaces Vivian Campbell on guitars—but only on the cover art and the new studio track, "Time to Burn." Otherwise, this is a live EP featuring the departing Vivian Campbell on guitars. "Rock 'n' Roll Children" includes a medley of Rainbow songs "Long Live Rock 'n' Roll" and "Man on the Silver Mountain." One month previous, in May 1986, *The Dio EP* was issued in the UK, in 7-inch, 10-inch, and 12-inch formats, featuring four tracks, one being new studio track "Hide in the Rainbow." This is the first non-LP track issued by the band, other than edits and live tracks.

Inferno: Last in Live

February 24, 1998, Mayhem 11115-2

CD1:

Intro
Jesus, Mary & the Holy Ghost
Straight Through the Heart
Don't Talk to Strangers
Holy Diver
Drum Solo
Heaven and Hell
Double Monday
Stand Up and Shout
Hunter of the Heart

CD2:

Mistreated
Guitar Solo
The Last in Line
Rainbow in the Dark
The Mob Rules
Man on the Silver Mountain
Long Live Rock 'n' Roll
We Rock

Notes: Personnel is Ronnie James Dio (vocals), Tracy G (guitars), Larry Dennison (bass), and Vinny Appice (drums).

Evil or Divine: *Live in New York City*

July 1, 2003, Spitfire SPT 15253-2

Killing the Dragon
Egypt (the Chains Are On) / Children of the Sea
Push
Stand Up and Shout
Rock & Roll
Don't Talk to Strangers
Man on the Silver Mountain
Guitar Solo
Love Live Rock 'n' Roll
Fever Dreams
Holy Diver
Heaven and Hell
The Last in Line
Rainbow in the Dark
We Rock

Notes: Personnel is Ronnie James Dio (vocals), Doug Aldrich (guitars), Jimmy Bain (bass), Vinny Appice (drums), and Scott Warren (keyboards). Also issued on DVD.

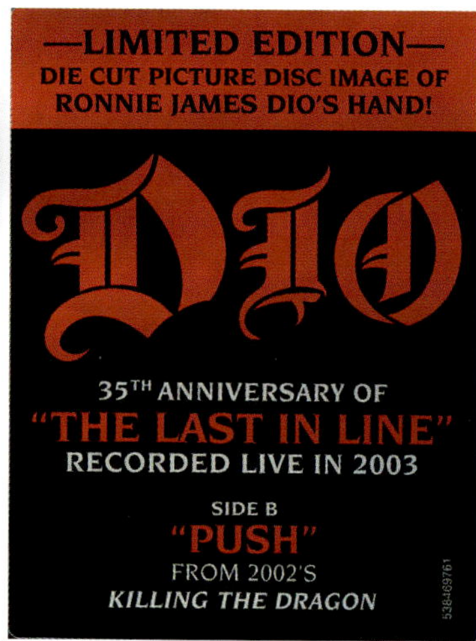

Holy Diver—Live

April 17, 2006, Eagle ER 20088-2

CD1:

Stand Up and Shout
Holy Diver
Gypsy
Caught in the Middle
Don't Talk to Strangers
Straight Through the Heart
Invisible
Rainbow in the Dark
Shame on the Night

CD2:

Tarot Woman
The Sign of the Southern Cross
One Night in the City
Gates of Babylon
Heaven and Hell
Man on the Silver Mountain
Long Live Rock 'n' Roll
We Rock

Notes: Personnel is Ronnie James Dio (vocals), Doug Aldrich (guitars), Rudy Sarzo (bass), Simon Wright (drums), and Scott Warren (keyboards). Also issued on DVD.

[captions]

At Donington UK: Live 1983 & 1987

November 9, 2010, Niji Entertainment Group NEG001

CD1:

Stand Up and Shout
Straight Through the Heart
Children of the Sea
Rainbow in the Dark
Holy Diver
Drum Solo
Stargazer
Guitar Solo
Heaven and Hell
Man on the Silver Mountain
Starstruck
Man on the Silver Mountain (Reprise)

CD2:

Dream Evil
Neon Knights
Naked in the Rain
Rock 'n' Roll Children
Long Live Rock 'n' Roll
The Last in Line
Children of the Sea
Holy Diver
Heaven and Hell
Man on the Silver Mountain
All the Fools Sailed Away
The Last in Line (Reprise)
Rainbow in the Dark

Notes: Archival release. Personnel for the 1983 set is Ronnie James Dio (vocals), Vivian Campbell (guitars), Jimmy Bain (bass), and Vinny Appice (drums). The 1987 set finds Craig Goldy replacing Vivian Campbell while adding Claude Schnell on keyboards.

Finding the Sacred Heart: Live in Philly 1986

May 28, 2013, Eagle ER203222

CD1:

Draco Ignis
King of Rock and Roll
Like the Beat of a Heart
Don't Talk to Strangers
Hungry for Heaven
The Last in Line / Children of the Sea / Holy Diver
Drum Solo
Heaven and Hell
Keyboard Solo
Guitar Solo

CD2:

Sacred Heart
Rock 'n' Roll Children / Long Live Rock 'n' Roll / Man on the Silver Mountain
Time to Burn
Stand Up and Shout
Rainbow in the Dark
We Rock

Notes: Archival release. Personnel is Ronnie James Dio (vocals), Vivian Campbell (guitars), Jimmy Bain (bass), Vinny Appice (drums), and Claude Schnell (keyboards). CD version of 1986 video, which was also issued on DVD in 2004.

Live in London: Hammersmith Apollo 1993

May 13, 2014, Eagle ER203572

CD1:

Stand Up and Shout
Strange Highways
Don't Talk to Strangers
Evilution
Pain
The Mob Rules
Children of the Sea
Holy Diver
Heaven and Hell
Man on the Silver Mountain
Drum Solo
Heaven and Hell (Reprise)

CD2:

Jesus, Mary & the Holy Ghost
Hollywood Black
The Last in Line
Rainbow in the Dark
We Rock
Here's to You

Notes: Archival release. Personnel is Ronnie James Dio (vocals), Tracy G (guitars), Jeff Pilson (bass), and Vinny Appice (drums). Also issued on DVD.

C. COMPILATIONS

Diamonds: The Best of Dio (1992)
Anthology (1997)
The Very Beast of Dio (2000)
Anthology: Volume Two (2001)
Evil Collection: The Very Best (2002)
The Collection (2003)
Metal Hits (2005)
The Very Beast of Dio Vol. 2 (2012)
A Decade of Dio: 1983–1993 (box set of first six albums; 2016)

INTERVIEWS WITH THE AUTHOR

Aldrich, Doug. June 20, 2005.
Aldrich, Doug. December 4, 2020.
Appice, Vinny. May 15, 2002.
Appice, Vinny. December 10, 2005.
Appice, Vinny. December 23, 2006.
Appice, Vinny. December 22, 2007.
Appice, Vinny. May 10, 2013.
Appice, Vinny. January 19, 2019.
Bain, Jimmy. July 27, 1999.
Bain, Jimmy. April 15, 2003.
Bain, Jimmy. 2009.
Campbell, Vivian. April 29, 2003.
Campbell, Vivian. October 28, 2004.
Dio, Ronnie James. 1996.
Dio, Ronnie James. June 30, 1999.
Dio, Ronnie James. April 8, 2002.
Dio, Ronnie James. December 5, 2002.
Dio, Ronnie James. September 15, 2004.
Dio, Ronnie James. February 20, 2005.
Dio, Ronnie James. December 19, 2006.
Dio, Ronnie James. August 13, 2008.
Dio, Ronnie James. April 13, 2009.
Dio, Wendy. November 24, 2010.
Dio, Wendy. February 12, 2021.
Fraser, Mike, May 16, 2005.
French, Jay Jay. August 26, 1999.
G, Tracy. 2004.
Goldy, Craig. June 3, 2011.
Goldy, Craig. April 23, 2013.
Lion, Mandy. January 15, 2004.
Owens, Tim "Ripper." June 3, 2011.
Platt, Tony. July 3, 2020.
Restey, Pete. February 2, 2017.
Robertson, Rowan. September 29, 2004.
Sarzo, Rudy. July 20, 2001.
Sarzo, Rudy. October 15, 2004.
Sarzo, Rudy. July 9, 2012.
Warren, Scott. June 3, 2011.
Wright, Graham. October 29, 2004.
Wright, Simon. June 3, 2011.
Wright, Simon. October 3, 2012.

ADDITIONAL CITATIONS

To give credit where credit is due, here is a list of reference materials respectfully used to flesh out the story. Thanks to all the scribes throughout the years who took it upon themselves to cover Ronnie and his many facets. For tidiness's sake, although sources are italicized throughout the book, I've left everything regular here, save for album titles.

"An Interview with Ronnie James Dio: With a Rainbow on His Shoulders . . ." *Aquarian Arts Weekly* 540 (September 12, 1984).

Andrews, Rob. "The Metal Terminators—Dream Evil Propels Metal Merchants to New Heights of Glory." *Hit Parader*, 1987.

Barton, Geoff. "Dutch Courage." *Kerrang!* 71 (June 28–July 11, 1984).

Bonutto, Dante. "Little Dreamer." *Kerrang!* 100 (August 8–21, 1985).

Cecolini, Vincent N. "Still Slaying Dragons after All These Years." *Metal Maniacs* 19, no. 8 (October 2002).

Dickson, Dave. *Intermission* record review. *Kerrang!* 124 (July 10–23, 1986).

Dickson, Dave. *Sacred Heart* record review. *Kerrang!* 101 (August 22–September 4, 1985).

Doreian, Robyn. "Dio: The Eternal Flame." *Rip*, May 1984.

Dream Evil record review. *Guitar*, December 1987.

Dunn, Sam. Interviews with Jimmy Bain and Ronnie James Dio.

Elliott, Paul. "Little Big Man." *Music Express* 95 (October 1985).

Epstein, Dmitry M. Interviews with Ronnie James Dio. Let It Rock/dmme.net, 2005.

Evans, Rick. "Dio: The Evil Eye." *Hit Parader* 245 (February 1985).

Evil G. Interview. *Maximum Metal.*

Evil G. Interview with Ronnie James Dio. *MetalRules*, 2001.

Fasolino, Greg. "Ronnie James Dio: Indomitable Dreamer." *Faces*, January 1988.

Foglio, Charrie. "Dio Putting 'Stars' in the Eyes of Relief Victims." *Jam*, 1986.

Gett, Steve. "The Last Shall Be First." *Metallion* 1, no. 2 (October–November 1984).

Goh, Sir Thomas E. "You're All Fools, Dio Rules!"

Henderson, Tim. "Spellbound!" *Brave Words & Bloody Knuckles* 37 (January–February 2000).

Hogan, Richard. "Beyond Star Fears with Ronnie James Dio." *Circus* 310 (December 31, 1985).

"Holy Savage: Steve Hammonds talks to Vivian Campbell." *Metal Forces* 2 (Winter 1983–84).

Hotten, Jon. *Lock Up the Wolves* record review. *Kerrang!* 289 (May 12, 1990).

Hotten, Jon. News piece. *Kerrang!* 275 (February 3, 1990).

Julie, Kevin. Interviews with Ronnie James Dio.

Kay, Jimmy. Interview with Rowan Robertson. *The Metal Voice*, July 16, 2015.

Kay, Jimmy. Interview with Vinny Appice. *The Metal Voice*, October 19, 2017.

Kay, Jimmy. Interview with Vivian Campbell. *The Metal Voice*, February 21, 2019.

Kay, Jimmy, and Alan Dixon. Interview with Claude Schnell. *The Metal Voice*, August 19, 2018.

Kay, Jimmy, and Alan Dixon. Interview with Wendy Dio. *The Metal Voice*, August 23, 2021.

Klusener, Edgar. "Rock 'n' Roll Is Just a Game." *Metal Hammer* 4, no. 3 (February 20, 1989).

LaDuke, David. "Dio Unleashes Angry Machines." *Ballbuster* 1, no. 3.

Loud, Lemmy. "Dio: As in Ronnie James." *Crucible* 1.

Martin, Andy. *Strange Highways* record review. *RIP*, 1994.

Mueller, Don. "Dio—the Metal Magician." *Hit Parader*, 1987.

Murray, Jim. "A Trip into the Inferno." *Ironworx* 1, no. 6 (1997).

Newton, Steve. "Interview with Ronnie James Dio." Ear of Newt, December 20, 1985.

Percy, K. K. "Dio." *Northern Metal* 15 (August–September 1986).

Ristic, Alex. "Man on the Magic Mountain." *Brave Words & Bloody Knuckles* 38 (April 2000).

Roemer, Doug. "Long Live the King." *Snap Pop* 1, no. 11 (May 2000).

Rose, Jennifer. "The Last Laugh: Leaving Black Sabbath Behind, Dio Gets Tough and Stands Tall in the 90's." *LiveWire* 4, no. 9 (1994).

Rusk, Bruce. Interview with Craig Goldy. House of Shred, February 26, 2001.

Secher, Andy. "Dio: A New Beginning." *Hit Parader* 313 (October 1990).

Secher, Andy. "Dio—Fighting Mad." *Hit Parader* 265 (October 1986).

Secher, Andy. "The King of Rock 'n' Roll." *Hit Parader* 257 (February 1986).

Secher, Andy. "Swords and Sorcery." *Hit Parader*, 1986.

Shapiro, Marc. "Ronnie James Dio: Never Say Die." *Hit Parader*, 1984.

Smith, Mike. "Metal Health." *LiveWire* 7, no. 3 (February–March 1997).

Sutherland, Jon. "I Have Read Too Many Things That I Must Reply To. Ask Me Whatever You Want, and I'll Tell You the Truth": Ronnie James Dio." *Record Review* 7, no. 4 (August 1983).

Wilshire, Carol. "Heavy Metal Band Dio Puts On Elaborate Show." *San Francisco Times*, December 1985.

Wright, Jeb. *Classic Rock Revisited* (interviews).

ACKNOWLEDGEMENTS

First and foremost, I'd like to thank Wendy Dio for all she's done for Ronnie and his legacy over the years, including getting Ronnie's book out as well as her work on the documentary. As well, special thanks to Agustin Garcia de Paredes, who applied his eagle eye to a copyedit of this lengthy tome.

AUTHOR BIOGRAPHY AND BIBLIOGRAPHY

At approximately 7,900 (with over 7,000 appearing in his books), Martin has unofficially written more record reviews than anybody in the history of music writing across all genres. Additionally, Martin has penned approximately 130 books on hard rock, heavy metal, classic rock, prog, punk, and record collecting. He was editor in chief of the now-retired *Brave Words & Bloody Knuckles*, Canada's foremost heavy metal publication, for fourteen years and has also contributed to *Revolver*, *Guitar World*, *Goldmine*, *Record Collector*, bravewords.com, lollipop.com, and hardradio.com, with many record label band bios and liner notes to his credit as well.

Additionally, Martin has been a regular contractor to Banger Films, having worked for two years as researcher on the award-winning documentary *Rush: Beyond the Lighted Stage*, on the writing and research team for the eleven-episode *Metal Evolution*, and on the ten-episode *Rock Icons*, both for VH1 Classic. Additionally, Martin is the writer of the original metal genre chart used in *Metal: A Headbanger's Journey* and throughout the *Metal Evolution* episodes.

Then there's his audio podcast, *History in Five Songs with Martin Popoff*, and the YouTube channel he runs with Marco D'Auria and Grant Arthur, *The Contrarians*. Martin currently resides in Toronto and can be reached through martinp@inforamp.net or martinpopoff.com.

• • •

2025
Dio: The Unholy Scriptures
A Dangerous Meeting: In the Shadows with Mercyful Fate
A Million Vacations: The Max Webster Story
Guns N' Roses at 40
Hallowed By Their Name: The Unofficial Iron Maiden Bible
Blockbuster! The Sweet Story

2024
Judas Priest: Album by Album
Behind the Lines: Genesis on Record: 1978–1997
Entangled: Genesis on Record 1969–1976
Run with the Wolf: Rainbow on Record
Queen Live!
Led Zeppelin: A Visual Biography
Van Halen at 50
Honesty Is No Excuse: Thin Lizzy on Record
Pictures at Eleven: Robert Plant Album by Album
Perfect Water: The Rebel Imaginos

2023
Kiss at 50
Dominance and Submission: The Blue Öyster Cult Canon
The Who and Quadrophenia
Wild Mood Swings: Disintegrating the Cure Album by Album
AC/DC at 50

2022
Pink Floyd and The Dark Side of the Moon: 50 Years
Killing the Dragon: Dio in the '90s and 2000s
Feed My Frankenstein: Alice Cooper, the Solo Years
Easy Action: The Original Alice Cooper Band
Lively Arts: The Damned Deconstructed
Yes: A Visual Biography II: 1982–2022
Bowie @ 75
Dream Evil: Dio in the '80s
Judas Priest: A Visual Biography
UFO: A Visual Biography

2021

Hawkwind: A Visual Biography
Loud 'n' Proud: Fifty Years of Nazareth
Yes: A Visual Biography
Uriah Heep: A Visual Biography
Driven: Rush in the '90s and "In the End"
Flaming Telepaths: Imaginos Expanded and Specified
Rebel Rouser: A Sweet User Manual

2020

The Fortune: On the Rocks with Angel
Van Halen: A Visual Biography
Limelight: Rush in the '80s
Thin Lizzy: A Visual Biography
Empire of the Clouds: Iron Maiden in the 2000s
Blue Öyster Cult: A Visual Biography
Anthem: Rush in the '70s
Denim and Leather: Saxon's First Ten Years
Black Funeral: Into the Coven with Mercyful Fate

2019

Satisfaction: 10 Albums That Changed My Life
Holy Smoke: Iron Maiden in the '90s
Sensitive to Light: The Rainbow Story
Where Eagles Dare: Iron Maiden in the '80s
Aces High: The Top 250 Heavy Metal Songs of the '80s
Judas Priest: Turbo 'til Now
Born Again! Black Sabbath in the Eighties and Nineties

2018

Riff Raff: The Top 250 Heavy Metal Songs of the '70s
Lettin' Go: UFO in the '80s and '90s
Queen: Album by Album
Unchained: A Van Halen User Manual
Iron Maiden: Album by Album
Sabotage! Black Sabbath in the Seventies
Welcome to My Nightmare: 50 Years of Alice Cooper
Judas Priest: Decade of Domination

Popoff Archive, 6: American Power Metal
Popoff Archive, 5: European Power Metal
The Clash: All the Albums, All the Songs

2017
Led Zeppelin: All the Albums, All the Songs
AC/DC: Album by Album
Lights Out: Surviving the '70s with UFO
Tornado of Souls: Thrash's Titanic Clash
Caught in a Mosh: The Golden Era of Thrash
Rush: Album by Album
Beer Drinkers and Hell Raisers: The Rise of Motörhead
Metal Collector: Gathered Tales from Headbangers
Hit the Lights: The Birth of Thrash
Popoff Archive, 4: Classic Rock
Popoff Archive, 3: Hair Metal

2016
Popoff Archive, 2: Progressive Rock
Popoff Archive, 1: Doom Metal
Rock the Nation: Montrose, Gamma, and Ronnie Redefined
Punk Tees: The Punk Revolution in 125 T-shirts
Metal Heart: Aiming High with Accept
Ramones at 40
Time and a Word: The Yes Story

2015
Kickstart My Heart: A Mötley Crüe Day-by-Day
This Means War: The Sunset Years of the NWOBHM
Wheels of Steel: The Explosive Early Years of the NWOBHM
Swords and Tequila: Riot's Classic First Decade
Who Invented Heavy Metal?
Sail Away: Whitesnake's Fantastic Voyage

2014
Live Magnetic Air: The Unlikely Saga of the Superlative Max Webster
Steal Away the Night: An Ozzy Osbourne Day-by-Day

The Big Book of Hair Metal

Sweating Bullets: The Deth and Rebirth of Megadeth

Smokin' Valves: A Headbanger's Guide to 900 NWOBHM Records

2013

The Art of Metal (coedit with Malcolm Dome)

2 Minutes to Midnight: An Iron Maiden Day-by-Day

Metallica: The Complete Illustrated History

Rush: The Illustrated History

Ye Olde Metal: 1979

Scorpions: Top of the Bill (updated and reissued as *Wind of Change: The Scorpions Story* in 2016)

2012

Epic Ted Nugent

Fade to Black: Hard Rock Cover Art of the Vinyl Age

It's Getting Dangerous: Thin Lizzy, 81–12

We Will Be Strong: Thin Lizzy, 76–81

Fighting My Way Back: Thin Lizzy, 69–76

The Deep Purple Royal Family: Chain of Events, '80s–'11

The Deep Purple Royal Family: Chain of Events through '79 (reissued as *The Deep Purple Family Year by Year*)

2011

Black Sabbath FAQ, The Collector's Guide to Heavy Metal: Volume 4: The 2000s (coauthored with David Perri)

2010

Goldmine Standard Catalog of American Records, 1948–1991, 7th edition

2009

Goldmine Record Album Price Guide, 6th edition

Goldmine 45 RPM Price Guide, 7th edition

A Castle Full of Rascals: Deep Purple, '83–'09

Worlds Away: Voivod and the Art of Michel Langevin

Ye Olde Metal: 1978

2008

Gettin' Tighter: Deep Purple, '68–'76
All Access: The Art of the Backstage Pass
Ye Olde Metal: 1977
Ye Olde Metal: 1976

2007

Judas Priest: Heavy Metal Painkillers
Ye Olde Metal: 1973 to 1975
The Collector's Guide to Heavy Metal: Volume 3; The Nineties
Ye Olde Metal: 1968 to 1972

2006

Run for Cover: The Art of Derek Riggs
Black Sabbath: Doom Let Loose
Dio: Light Beyond the Black

2005

The Collector's Guide to Heavy Metal: Volume 2; The Eighties
Rainbow: English Castle Magic
UFO: Shoot Out the Lights
The New Wave of British Heavy Metal Singles

2004

Blue Öyster Cult: Secrets Revealed! (updated and reissued in 2009 with the same title; updated and reissued as *Agents of Fortune: The Blue Öyster Cult Story in 2016*)
Contents under Pressure: 30 Years of Rush at Home & Away
The Top 500 Heavy Metal Albums of All Time

2003

The Collector's Guide to Heavy Metal: Volume 1; The Seventies
The Top 500 Heavy Metal Songs of All Time

2001

Southern Rock Review

2000

Heavy Metal: 20th Century Rock and Roll
The Goldmine Price Guide to Heavy Metal Records

1997

The Collector's Guide to Heavy Metal

1993

Riff Kills Man! 25 Years of Recorded Hard Rock & Heavy Metal

Ronnie with Geezer and Tony. Ronnie always said that "Heaven and Hell" was the greatest artistic accomplishment of his career.
© *Martin Popoff*

Seen here with Black Sabbath, Vinnie Appice was the backbone of the classic Dio lineup. © *Rudy Childs*

INDEX

In terms of methodology, first, we've exempted the names of Dio band members (at least the major ones), due to the fact that in some cases, sensibly, some of these appear in the book hundreds of times. These have been left in the index, along with the designation "see introductory note." Second, given that the chapters are both structured and titled primarily by album, these also have been left in the index but not indexed. Instead, they've been given the designation "see chapter [#]." Third, there are a few additional miscellaneous entries that have been given the "see introductory note" designation for the same reason as above, namely that the high number of times that they are mentioned renders the indexing of each instance somewhat meaningless. Finally, I've not included the discography section when it comes to building this index.

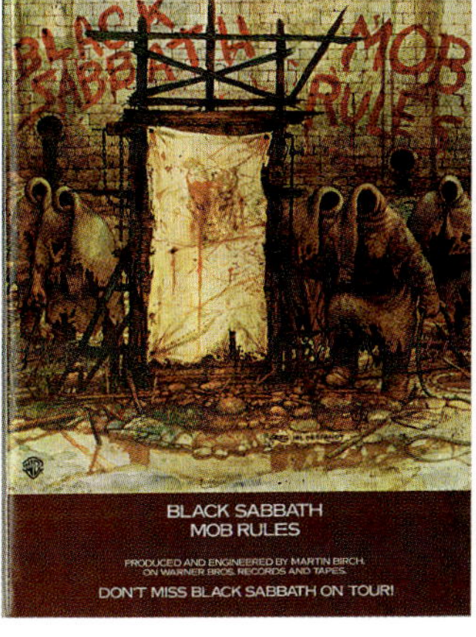

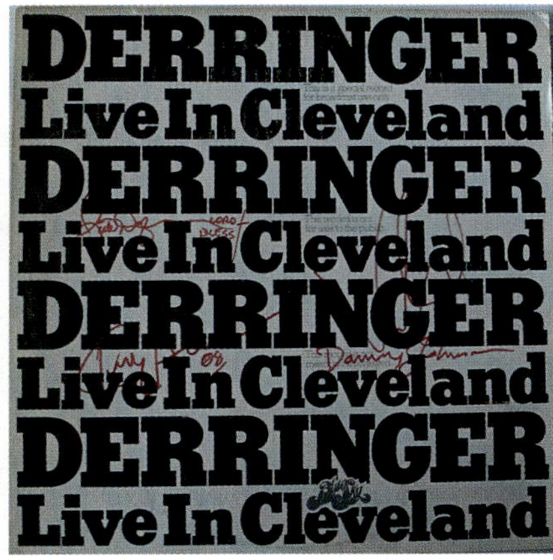

Derringer

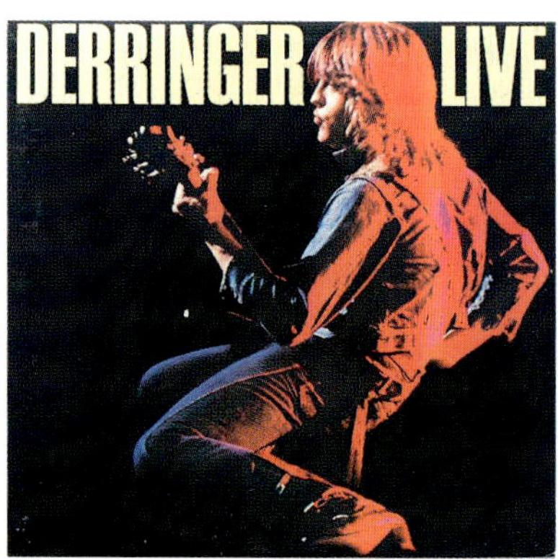
DERRINGER LIVE

Black Sabbath
live evil

Stories and Works of
Ronnie James Dio
Long Live Rock 'N' Roll

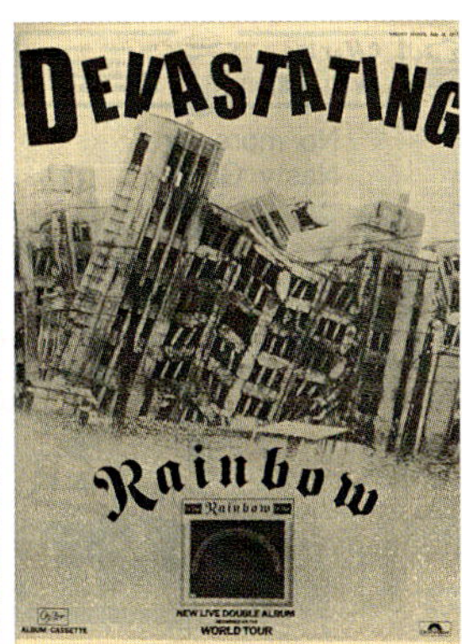
DEVASTATING
Rainbow

GERMANY 2009
Access All Areas

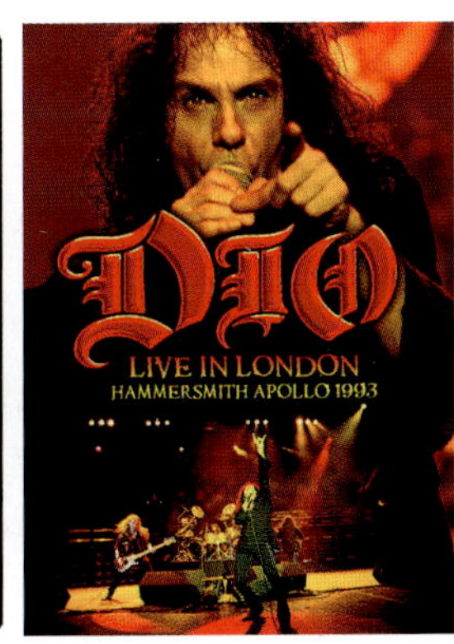
DIO
LIVE IN LONDON
HAMMERSMITH APOLLO 1993

DIO
DIO
RECORD STORE DAY

HEAVEN & HELL
ALL ACCESS

DIO
THE VERY
BEAST OF
VOL. 2

DIO
RETURNS
US TOUR 2019
SPECIAL GUEST: Love/Hate
THE WILTERN • FRIDAY, JUNE 28

DIO
Side A 1. DREAM EVIL (Live At Donington '87) - 4:56
Side B 1. NAKED IN THE RAIN (Live At Donington '87) - 7:29
45 rpm

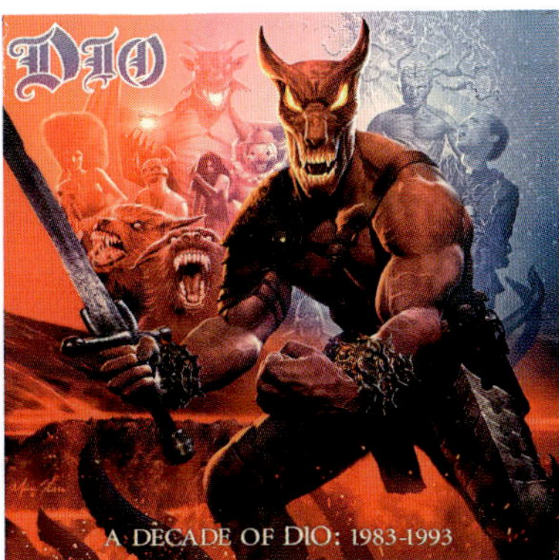
DIO
A DECADE OF DIO: 1983-1993

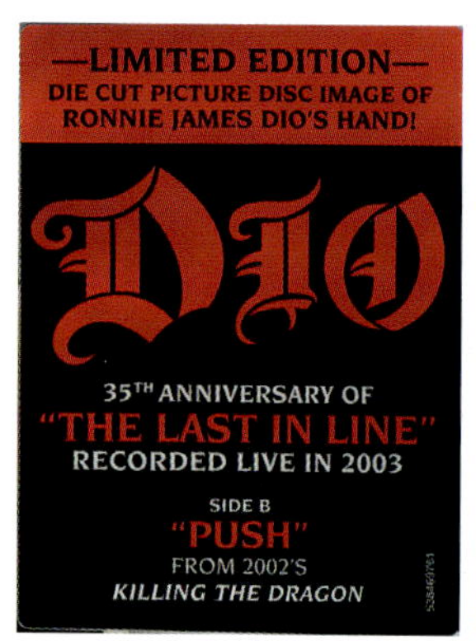
—LIMITED EDITION—
DIE CUT PICTURE DISC IMAGE OF RONNIE JAMES DIO'S HAND!
DIO
35TH ANNIVERSARY OF
"THE LAST IN LINE"
RECORDED LIVE IN 2003
SIDE B
"PUSH"
FROM 2002'S
KILLING THE DRAGON

DIO
DREAM EVIL

RSD BLACK FRIDAY
DIO
1ST TIME ON VINYL!
Recorded Live at Donington in 1987
on the Dream Evil Tour
Newly Designed Art image Based on
original Dream Evil Tour Merch

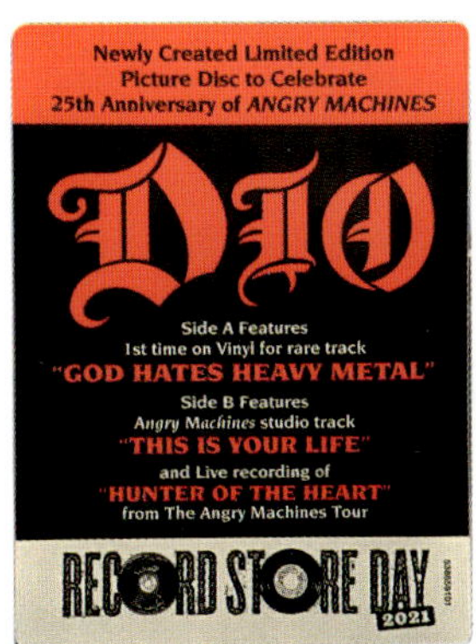
Newly Created Limited Edition
Picture Disc to Celebrate
25th Anniversary of ANGRY MACHINES
DIO
Side A Features
1st time on Vinyl for rare track
"GOD HATES HEAVY METAL"
Side B Features
Angry Machines studio track
"THIS IS YOUR LIFE"
and Live recording of
"HUNTER OF THE HEART"
from The Angry Machines Tour
RECORD STORE DAY
2021

Heaven & Hell
tony iommi
geezer butler
vinny appice
ronnie james dio
tour
radio city live! music hall
2007

DIO
DOUBLE DOSE OF DONINGTON

HEAVEN & HELL
THE DEVIL YOU KNOW

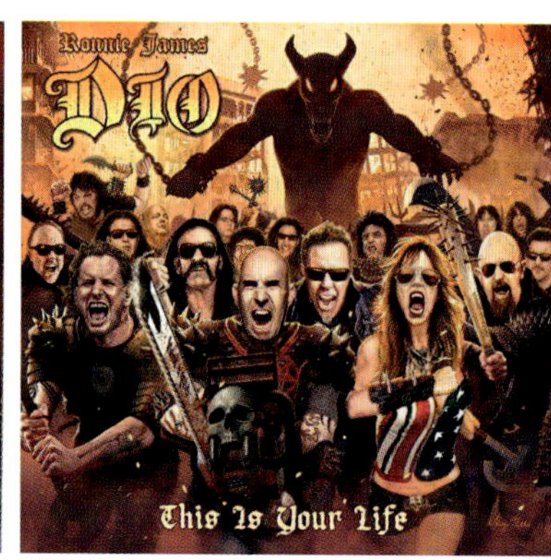
Ronnie James
DIO
This Is Your Life

DIO
DIO

MAMA & Rock
HIGH VOLTAGE
FESTIVAL
SATURDAY 24 JULY 2010
SUNDAY 25 JULY 2010
MAIN STAGE
ZZ TOP
heaven & hell
A Tribute to Ronnie James Dio
FOREIGNER
GARY MOORE
THE ANSWER
THE UNION
ELP
JOE ELLIOTT
IAN HUNTER
DOWN 'N' OUTZ
JOE BONAMASSA
BACHMAN TURNER
UFO • THE QUIREBOYS
HAMMER
Black Label Society
SAXON
CATHEDRAL • HAMMERFALL
ORANGE GOBLIN
BLACK SPIDERS • NEW DEVICE
DOWN
Opeth
CLUTCH
HIGH ON FIRE
AUDREY HORNE • LETHARGY
PROG STAGE
TRANSATLANTIC
ASIA
DWEEZIL ZAPPA
BIGELF • FOCUS
PENDRAGON
TOUCHSTONE
marillion
ARGENT
URIAH HEEP
MAGNUM • STEVE HACKETT
MARTIN TURNER'S WISHBONE ASH
THE REASONING
LONDON VICTORIA PARK
WWW.HIGHVOLTAGEFESTIVAL.COM
Custom built by rock fans, for rock fans